ANTHROPOLOGICAL FILM AND VIDEO

IN THE 1990s

Jack R. Rollwagen
Editor

THE INSTITUTE PRESS
Brockport, New York
1993

DEDICATION: To My Children: Mark, Valerie, Matthew, and Julie.

The Institute, Inc.
56 Centennial Avenue
Brockport, NY   14420   USA
Telephone: (716) 637-6531

Library of Congress Catalog Number: 93-79690

Main Entry Under Title: Anthropological Film and Video in the 1990s
Series: Case Studies in Documentary Filmmaking and Videomaking
The Institute Press.
Includes index.

ISBN 0-9635206-1-X

This book is printed with soy bean based inks on 50% recycled, acid free paper.

Printed in the United States of America. Printed by:
Dual Printing, Inc.
340 Nagel Drive
Cheektowaga, NY   14225
Telephone: (716) 684-3825

First Printing, September, 1993
10   9   8   7   6   5   4   3   2   1

COVER DESIGN: Jack R. Rollwagen

PHOTO CREDIT: The photograph on the front cover is a computer frame-grabbed, digitally enhanced image from the forthcoming video-tape:TZINTZUNTZAN IN THE 1990s: A LAKESIDE VILLAGE IN HIGHLAND MEXICO. TAPE 2: Tzintzuntzeños Talk About Their Lives and Work, Kris Marsala, Director of Photography, Jack R. Rollwagen, Producter.

TABLE OF CONTENTS:

ANTHROPOLOGICAL FILM AND VIDEO IN THE 1990s

I. ANTHROPOLOGICAL FILMMAKING/VIDEOMAKING

II. CONSIDERING THE PRODUCT AND PROCESS: SELF-EVALUATIONS OF ANTHROPOLOGICAL FILMS

III. ANTHROPOLOGISTS EVALUATE ANTHROPOLOGICAL FILM/VIDEO

IV. ANTHROPOLOGICAL "FILMS" AND THE NON-LINEAR FUTURE

V. ANTHROPOLOGICAL FILMS
AND THE UNIVERSITY CLASSROOM

from ANTHROPOLOGICAL FILM AND VIDEO IN THE 1990s
Jack R. Rollwagen (editor). Brockport, NY: The Institute, Inc.

Introduction

Jack R. Rollwagen
Department of Anthropology
SUNY College at Brockport

The beginnings of a documentary cinema coincide almost exactly with the beginnings of anthropology as a discipline. Both came into being during the last decade of the 19th century. Documentaries about peoples and cultures (produced by early filmmakers of many nationalities) were recorded and shown in theaters throughout the world not long after the invention of the motion picture camera in 1885.[1] Louis Lumière's first film "Workers Leaving the Lumière Factory" (1895) preceded Harischandra Sakharam Bhatvadekar's filming of a wrestling match at Bombay's Hanging Gardens by only two years. From the very first, documentary filmmakers turned their attention to peoples and cultures around the world because they knew that there was an audience for such films. There still is.

However, it was apparent that such early and short "novelty" documentary films would not continue to attract the audiences that the filmmakers wanted in order to make filmmaking a financial success. Furthermore, not all filmmakers held financial "success" as the reason for their filmmaking. Filmmakers, in general (and documentarists along with them), began to wrestle with the problem of conceptual frameworks for the integration of larger amounts of filmic material than those in the early films mentioned above.

Out of this struggle to evolve conceptual frameworks for documentary filmmaking, there arose two major choices: gen-

1

eralization and specialization. Some documentary filmmakers continued to produce documentaries without committing themselves to particular disciplinary frameworks, while others perceived their filmmaking as a specialization within a particular discipline. This dichotomy continues today. However, that picture is somewhat more clouded than this explanation seems to suggest. As far as I know, anthropology created the concept of "ethnography" (although other disciplines have subsequently adopted the term). Ethnography was, at least initially, a process by which anthropologists described (in writing) cultural systems according to the tenets of their evolving discipline. Ethnography was clearly understood in early anthropology to be a way of studying cultural systems in order to ultimately arrive at ethnology (that aspect of anthropology in which ethnographic research is integrated into cross-cultural research in order to make generalizations about human beings around the world and over time). "Ethnographic" filmmaking within anthropology was thus understood to be a way of documenting life in cultural systems within the framework of anthropology which was then to be used in a variety of ways to advance anthropology as a discipline.

Unfortunately, "ethnographic" filmmaking has also acquired another meaning. Just as the concept of "photographic" has lead many people to believe that the camera "captures the reality" which is in front of it, so (to many) the concept of "ethnographic filmmaking" conveys the idea that what is important is the camera and its recording of the "reality" toward which the documentary filmmaker points it. Thus, people with little (or no) training in anthropology have become "ethnographic" filmmakers (and have been recognized as "ethnographic filmmakers") as a result of their involvement in capturing "the reality" of cultural systems. The fly in the ointment, of course, is the problem of "the social construction of reality." How do we understand that which we see? And, ultimately, within what conceptual framework do we deal with what we see (and record on film/videotape)? There have been a variety of ways that non-anthropologists have tried to "solve" these important problems.

First, there are those documentary filmmakers who have chosen to proceed in filmmaking in cultural systems as if the discipline of anthropology did not exist. The films of the worst of these are splendid proof of the need for a discipline such as anthropology in which people profit from the mistakes of others. [2] The films of the best of these filmmakers demonstrate their intent to try to re-create the discipline of anthropology anew but by another name.

Secondly, there are documentary filmmakers who have collaborated in some way with anthropologists in the making of their films. The worst of these have employed anthropologists in some manner marginal to the real decisions about the filmmaking, arguing that audiences will not be entertained by what is obviously a boring, academic approach. The best of these have based their films upon anthropological approaches and findings, (a) assuming that some knowledge of the "social construction of the reality of the other" is important in the most basic decisions about the film; and (b) that entertainment does not necessarily require the total de-construction of the ethnography of a cultural system and its remaking so that it conforms to the understandings of our own, but rather that in attempting to understand that other we encourage ourselves to grow.

However, anthropologists have also been struggling to develop an anthropological filmmaking tradition of their own. The films produced by Bateson and Mead about Bali (in what is now Indonesia) were probably the first truly anthropological films (i.e., [a] films produced by anthropologists, [b] films which were conceptualized within the disciplinary frameworks of anthropology, and [c] films which recognized and dealt with the problems of the sociology of knowledge). Asen Balikci's monumental series on the Netsilik Eskimo must also be mentioned as some of the best of anthropological films when measured by the above criteria.[3] The films by André Singer should also be mentioned as major contributions to anthropological filmmaking. (See the "Films Cited" section of Singer's article; 1988: 379-380.) Tim Asch's association with Napoleon Chagnon on the Yanomamo series (Asch 1988), and with Linda Connor on the Bali series (Connor 1988) are important efforts in the area of collaborative filmmaking between a filmmaker and an anthropologist. (Other examples of anthropologists as filmmakers can be found in Rollwagen 1988.)

In anthropology, this conceptual struggle has resulted in at least three major approaches to anthropological filmmaking: (1) filmmaking for research purposes (collecting footage never intended to be shown to general audiences); (2) filmmaking for aesthetic purposes; and (3) filmmaking for educational or instructional purposes. Obviously each of these is stated in terms of the primary conceptual goals of the anthropologist/filmmaker in making the film. I do not intend to imply that filmmakers whose intent is to make an anthropological film for educational purposes or research purposes cannot also be concerned with aesthetic ends as well, for example; nor that those who make films for aesthetic purposes cannot also orient the film toward educational or instructional purposes. However, in discussing anthropological filmmaking it is important to distinguish between the primary and secondary goals of the filmmaker in the filmmaking process since not considering those goals obfuscates the discussion.

Filming for Research Purposes. Many anthropologists who are not necessarily filmmakers collect film photographs, film footage, and video footage on their research so that they, their colleagues, and their students can return to that footage for post-fieldwork research. Every year for the past decade there has been a meeting of anthropologists interested in such research filming during the two days preceding the annual meeting of the American Anthropological Association.[4] Photography (and, by extension, filmmaking/videomaking) as a research tool is the central focus of Collier and Collier's VISUAL ANTHROPOLOGY: PHOTOGRAPHY AS A RE-SEARCH METHOD. This kind of filming is not discussed in this book.

Filmmaking for Aesthetic Purposes. By contrast, film-making for aesthetic purposes is quite common in anthropological filmmaking and videomaking. Story-telling is as old as human history. Filmmakers make films in order to entertain and to amuse (and film audiences come to film screenings in order to be entertained and to be amused). Organizing a film around the life of one individual or another is a quite common way to structure a film. Obviously in such an endeavor, anthropologists (like narrative filmmakers from a variety of back-grounds) select those aspects of an individual's life which they feel best convey those concepts which they want to convey to others.

It is also true that a film oriented to aesthetic ends can utilize "a story" (or "narrative") written by the filmmaker (or others). Anthropological films with written scripts, however, do more than meet the primary goal of entertainment and amusement of an audience. They also (a) convey information about cultural systems (based on some anthropologist's ethnographic investigations and checking procedures in a particular culture [see Rollwagen 1988b]); (b) may convey conclusions that anthropologists have arrived at through comparisons between individual cultural systems (based on ethnological research and checking procedures); and (c) very frequently incorporate other frameworks which may link the discipline of anthropology to the more general frameworks in the sociology of knowledge (e.g., a World System approach to the study of contemporary cultural systems [see Rollwagen 1980a and 1980b] or an approach to the study of contemporary cultural systems based on political economy).

Filmmaking for Educational or Instructional Purposes. The primary goal in educational or instructional filmmaking is to convey conceptual frameworks, to interpret for audiences that which they would otherwise find difficult, to expand consciousness of other peoples, other cultures, and other places, and so forth. Since this is the goal, the approach to filmmaking may differ from the approach of those whose primary purpose is to entertain. Although there is something of instruction in almost every anthropological documentary, in this kind of filmmaking the primary goal of the filmmaker must be clear so that the organization of any particular film may be more clear, and also so that the production of more than one film in a series takes on its own logical structure.

Although it may be true that films "speak for themselves" about the filmmaker's work, it is also true that writing is in some ways more efficient in communicating thoughts. The process of anthropological filmmaking is such that although much of a filmmaker's thoughts and conclusions are embodied in a film, others may not necessarily know why those decisions were made. Thus, writing about anthropological filmmaking fills an important function in advancing anthropological filmmaking.

This book came into being for two reasons: (1) the incredible success of ANTHROPOLOGICAL FILMMAKING: ANTHROPOLOGICAL PERSPECTIVES ON THE PRODUCTION OF FILM AND VIDEO FOR GENERAL PUBLIC AUDIENCES (Rollwagen, 1988) led me to believe that there are a sizeable number of individuals who are interested in anthropological film and filmmaking; and (2) the continued attacks on anthropological filmmaking (by documentary filmmakers and others) and the misunderstandings that they promote require some response.

ANTHROPOLOGICAL FILMMAKING was published in 1988. Between 1988 and 1992 it sold more than 3,000 copies, a phenomenal number for an academic publication with such a specific topic. During this same period of time, the attempts by non-anthropologists to discredit the anthropological filmmaking enterprise continued and, in fact, increased. Voices, from newly created disciplines and perspectives, have raised the same old, tired, and discredited arguments in new words and from new perspectives. "Record reality!" "Let the people speak for themselves!" "Don't interpret!" "Don't impinge upon the event that you are filming!" These criticisms are (to a large extent) written by individuals ignorant of anthropology as a discipline, and (more importantly) are written without any understandings of the sociology of knowledge.

Meanwhile, an increasing number of anthropologists have been producing films themselves (or working on films with others) and thus have been gaining experience and insight into the processes and problems of filmmaking. Secondly, recent advances in technology have changed the nature of future filmmaking, perhaps transforming the "playing field" forever. This book discusses this recent experience in anthropological filmmaking, in evaluating anthropological (and other) films and videos, and in using anthropological (and other) films and videos in the classroom. My hope is that as many people will find it interesting and useful as did those who bought and/or read ANTHROPOLOGICAL FILMMAKING.

NOTES

1   As Armes (1987: 2) indicates, "...the history of film exhibition and to some extent film production is virtually as long in the non-Western world as in the West." According to Barnouw (1974:11): "Starting in February [1895] in London, an avalanche of foreign *cinématographe* premières began. Within six months after the Paris opening the *cinématographe* was launched by the Lumière organization in England, Belgium, Holland, Germany, Austria, Hungary, Switzerland, Spain, Italy, Serbia, Russia, Sweden, the United States — and soon thereafter in Algeria, Tunisia, Egypt, Turkey, India, Australia, Indochina, Japan, Mexico. Within two years Lumière operators were roaming on every continent except Antarctica."

2   Like Berger and Luckman's "man in the street," this kind of documentary filmmaker "...does not ordinarily trouble himself about what is 'real' to him and about what he 'knows' unless he is stopped short by some sort of problem. He takes his 'reality' and his 'knowledge' for granted. The sociologist [and anthropologist] cannot do this, if only because of his systematic awareness of the fact that men in the street take quite different 'realities' for granted as between one society and another. The sociologist is forced by the very logic of his discipline to ask, if nothing else, whether the difference between the two 'realities' may not be understood in relation to various differences between the two societies" (1967: 2).

3   Without providing an exhaustive listing, some of Balikci's major films on the Netsilik Eskimo are: AT THE WINTER SEA ICE CAMP, FISHING AT THE STONE WEIR, AT THE AUTUMN RIVER CAMP. See Balikci's article (1988) in ANTHROPOLOGICAL FILMMAKING. See also his entry in the DIRECTORY OF VISUAL ANTHROPOLOGY.

4   The schedule for these meetings appears in the annual program of the American Anthropological Association. For example, in the 1992 (91st Annual Meeting of the American Anthropological Association in San Francisco) Program, the "Visual Research Conference" meetings were held throughout the day on the Tuesday before the AAA meetings began, and on the Wednesday morning on which the meetings began.

REFERENCES CITED

American Anthropological Association (1992). Program. Washington, DC: American Anthropological Association.

Armes, Roy (1987). Third World Film Making and the West. Berkeley: University of California Press.

Asch, Timothy (1988). Collaboration in Ethnographic Filmmaking: A Personal View. IN Anthropological Filmmaking: Anthropological Perspectives on the Production of Film and Video for General Public Audiences, Jack R. Rollwagen (ed.). Chur, Switzerland: Harwood Academic Publishers, pp. 1- 29.

Balikci, Asen (1988). Anthropologists and Ethnographic Filmmaking IN Anthropological Filmmaking: Anthropological Perspectives on the Production of Film and Video for General Public Audiences, Jack R. Rollwagen (ed.). Chur, Switzerland: Harwood Academic Publishers, pp. 31-45.

Barnouw, Erik (1974). Documentary: A History of the Non-Fiction Film. London: Oxford University Press.

Berger, Peter L., and Thomas Luckmann (1967). The Social Construction of Reality: A Treatise in the Sociology of Knowledge. Garden City, NY: Anchor.

Blakely, Thomas D., and Pamela A.R. Blakely (1989). Directory of Visual Anthropology. Washington, DC: American Anthropological Association.

Collier, John, Jr., and Malcolm Collier (1986). Visual Anthropology: Photography as a Research Method. Albuquerque: University of New Mexico Press.

Connor, Linda (1988). Third Eye: Some Reflections on Collaboration for Ethnographic Film. IN Anthropological Filmmaking: Anthropological Perspectives on the Production of Film and Video for General Public Audiences, Jack R. Rollwagen (ed.). Chur, Switzerland: Harwood Academic Publishers, pp. 97 - 110.

Rollwagen, Jack R. (ed.) (1988a). Anthropological Filmmaking: Anthropological Perspectives on the Production of Film and Video for General Public Audiences. Chur, Switzerland: Harwood Academic Publishers.

Rollwagen, Jack R. (1988b). The Role of Anthropological Theory in "Ethnographic" Filmmaking. IN Anthropological Filmmaking: Anthropological Perspectives on the Production of Film and Video for General Public Audiences, Jack R. Rollwagen (ed.). Chur, Switzerland: Harwood Academic Publishers, pp. 287 - 315.

Rollwagen, Jack R. (1980a). Cities and the World System: Toward an Evolutionary Perspective in the Study of Urban Anthropology. IN Cities in a Larger Context, Thomas Collins (ed.). Southern Anthropological Society Procedings No. 14. Athens: University of Georgia Press, pp. 123 - 140.

Rollwagen, Jack R. (1980b). New Directions in Urban Anthropology: Building an Ethnography and an Ethnology of the World System. IN Urban Life: Readings in Urban Ethnography, George Gmelch and Walter Zenner (eds.). New York: St Martin's Press, pp. 370 - 383.

Singer, André (1988). Choices and Constraints in Filming in Central Asia. IN Anthropological Filmmaking: Anthropological Perspectives on the Production of Film and Video for General Public Audiences, Jack R. Rollwagen (ed.). Chur, Switzerland: Harwood Academic Publishers, pp. 371-380.

FILMS CITED

At the Winter Sea Ice Camp. A film by Asen Balikci. (A film in four parts: Part 1[1968: 30 minutes]; Part 2 [1968; 30 minutes]; Part 3 [33 minutes; 1968-1969]; and Part 4 [1967; 35 minutes]. color.) Distributor: National Film Board of Canada.

At the Autumn River Camp. A film by Asen Balikci. (1968; 60 minutes; color.) Distributor: National Film Board of Canada.

Fishing at the Stone Weir. A film by Asen Balikci. (1967; 55 minutes; color.) Distributor: National Film Board of Canada.

from ANTHROPOLOGICAL FILM AND VIDEO IN THE 1990s
Jack R. Rollwagen (editor). Brockport, NY: The Institute, Inc.
© 1993, The Institute, Inc. All rights reserved. ISBN 0-9635206-1-X

Charting Content, Freezing Structure: A Methodological Base For Visual Ethnography

Fadwa El Guindi
El Nil Research
Los Angeles

ABSTRACT: In this paper a detailed analysis of the film EL SEBOU': EGYPTIAN BIRTH RITUAL is presented and the coherent film theory that informed its making is explicated. It is argued that visual ethnography must have three features: (1) self-sufficiency of the visual document without necessary recourse to extensive written material, (2) interdependence of process linking data-gathering, analysis, and film construction, and (3) contextualization of the domain filmed within the culture as a whole. Eight parameters collectively identify the vision behind the entire process from fieldwork, to film production and ethnography construction. These parameters constitute the basis for a theory of the visual ethnography of *EL SEBOU'*.

Visual Anthropology: Reifying Terms, Confounding Players

The visual anthropological literature is replete with terms at times used interchangeably, at others reified as distinctive

11

forms or approaches. Some examples include: observational cinema, cinéma verité, cinéma direct, reflexive film, research film, sequence film, analytic film, interpretive film, scientific film, footage film, monograph film, ethnographic film. In his 1988 publication Yasuhiro Omori focused his discussion on footage film and ethnographic film. He draws the analogy from print anthropology between footage film and field notes, ethnographic film and monograph. He characterizes the difference as part/whole, analytic/interpretive, scientific/ethnographic, or differential length (1988: 192, 194, 196).[1]

Before developing an interest in the visual, I stated my position on the theoretical basis for fieldwork (1986). Now that I have made visual ethnographies I will restate my position as it applies to the visual construction of ethnography particularly as it developed in the process of making the film EL SEBOU': EGYPTIAN BIRTH RITUAL. Footage film and ethnographic film are two constituent phases in a process of ethnographic film production and construction held together (or should be) by anthropological analysis. Both are ethnographic aspects of the same process, not two different kinds of film.

In the process of ethnographic filmmaking, fact-recording footage or "sequence filming" becomes an essential phase in data-gathering, and is basic for and should be informed by analysis. Film sequence selection itself must be subjected to methodological rigor. If, as Rouch states, we need to "tie cinematic language to scientific rigor" (Rouch 1975: 94), ethnographic filmmaking must become simultaneously analysis and evaluation, an arena for experimentation with techniques to enhance rigor. This does not mean that a visual ethnographer must choose between humanistic quality and scientific rigor. They must be combined. In the field, Rouch's notion of "participant camera" links camera and people, turning filmmaking into a stimulant for mutual understanding and dignity. It is a visual field technique of both humanistic and methodological value for enhancing the quality of field filming.

Cinema direct, as Rouch prefers to call this filming orientation, is direct filming of actions, and direct contact between filmers and filmed. Unlike "cinéma-verité," cinema direct does not make claims for truthfulness, only for the necessity of contact, and the hope that it will play a catalytic role in the film process.[2] The intent is to maximize dignity and respect for the people as quality data are recorded.

The quality of the relationship between filmmaker and people filmed is crucial, but is sometimes over-romanticized as "rapport" often is in anthropology. A phrase such as "style of interacting with people" (Asch and Asch 1988: 172-173), unless placed within the process of building an analytic framework and film construction and unless it is itself subjected to rigor as field technique, tends to assume that establishing rapport and having a "good" relationship with the indigenous population somehow magically translates into anthropological data-gathering, visual or non-visual. If so, any sensitive journalist documentarian renders anthropology dispensable in ethnographic film.

The key lies in methodological and theoretical rigor. Sequence filming or footage film, in addition to its archival value, records facts out of which a data-base[3] is built according to an analytic framework, as the anthropologist constructs a visual ethnography.

Three participants are equally significant in the process of visual ethnography: the anthropologist/filmmaker, the people filmed, and the viewer. Debate in visual anthropology sometimes confounds these participants and their differential role in the process. Culture-bearers are engaged in social and cultural construction, the film ethnographers are engaged in visual ethnographic production, and the viewers are engaged in reflexive reality interpretation. This orientation shifts reflexivity from the ethnographer to the viewer. In agreement with

Omori, reflexivity is a quality of film viewing experience as "one takes on the thoughts and consciousness of a participating member from a different culture," thus gaining a "reflexive experience." The viewer gains reflexive experience by participating, as it were, in the event through "a mental process (by which) the emotionally involved viewer seems to enter the screen, and then experience an identification with the people who appear in the scene, a temporary emotional tie between the viewer and the image called *participation affective* by Edgar Morin . . . a mental process of becoming one with the image on the screen" (Omori 1988: 194).

This is a different notion of reflexivity from Ruby's usage (1982). It is not the filmmaker who is reflexive nor is it productive to classify a film genre as reflexive. Rather reflexivity is a process which occurs during viewing, in which the viewer feeds additional interpretation into the process.[4] Viewing is where the reflexive aspect of ethnographic filmmaking lies. When viewing is non-indigenous the element of unconscious presuppositions about the culture being viewed enters the process. Very relevant in this respect is the systematic study of student responses to films shown in anthropology classes at the University of Southern California, in which Wilton Martinez (1990, 1992) has found that ethnographic films, even those most approved of by anthropologists, are interpreted in ways that reinforce ethnocentric stereotypes of nonwestern cultures. This raises the issue of "reflexive" processing by viewers and the difficulty in shaping or predicting it. Omori's experimentation with systematic measuring of indigenous "feedback" viewing of his two films (1983, 1985) must be pursued. More work needs to be done to shed light on the relation between film construction and this interpretive viewing process, particularly across cultures, since it appears to be the domain that becomes penetrated by subliminal prejudices of racism or domination.

The Case of EL SEBOU': Film Synopsis

In 1986 I directed the filming of a private family ceremony widely held in Egypt in celebration of the birth of newborns and their initiation on their seventh day of life. I made EL SEBOU': EGYPTIAN BIRTH RITUAL riding high on bliss, which I recognize in hindsight as the bliss of ignorance about film, a state that simultaneously carries with it an emancipation from film conventions.

The film is a visual ethnography of the birth ritual in Egypt called *EL SEBOU'* celebrated on the seventh day following the physical birth of a child of either sex by Coptic and Muslim families from all status-groups, rural and urban. Traditionally, this was the occasion for naming newborns, circumcising boys and piercing the ears of girls. Today these practices are deritualized in the urban centers and in most cases take place separately from the *Sebou'* ceremony on the seventh day. Characteristic of the Egyptian ritual depicted in the film is the gender-linked imagery reflected in the ceremonial clay pot and the cosmological symbolism embedded in the numerical value "seven." It continues to function as a key ritual for initiating newborns into the Egyptian social cultural world. The film presents it as a key rite-of-passage with its three universal phases of transition (separation-liminality-incorporation) as newborns cross the threshold out of gender and status neutrality to join his/her gender world and a family that will determine and define his/her identity.

The film also links Egyptian birth to gender symbolism, to traditional crafts, to folk beliefs, to cultural notions of strong womanhood, and to the importance of the family. It takes the viewer along with the ritual leader to the old bazaar in Cairo to purchase *Sebou'*-specific herbs and spices, to the 150-year-old pottery village in Fustat (Old Cairo) to see the *Sebou'* clay pots being crafted, and to al-Ghouriyya (Cairo) to see the *Sebou'* candles being made and *Sebou'* pots decorated.

The particular *Sebou'* ceremony depicted in this film is that of a pair of newborn twins, a boy and a girl, celebrated by an upwardly mobile, lower middle class, Muslim family in urban Egypt. (See Figure 1.)

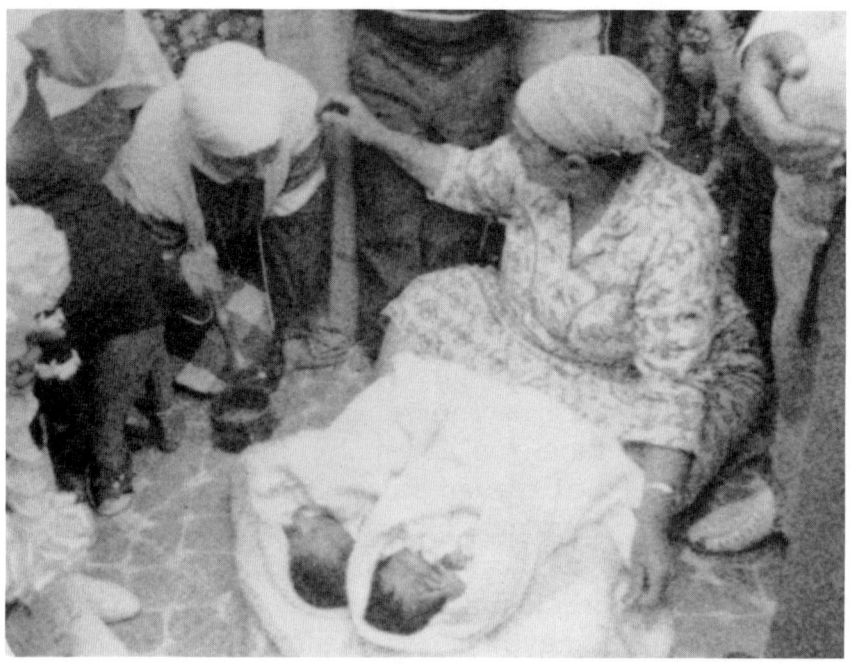

FIGURE 1: Photo from 16mm negative of film *El Sebou'* of newborn twins on top of ceremonial sieve (*al-ghorbal*). Photo courtesy El Nil Research, 1986.

Film Analysis

Much conventional wisdom was broken in the film EL SEBOU'. But, in accordance with this anthropologist's goal, including intended audience, EL SEBOU' meets certain criteria of adequacy. The notion of adequacy in ethnographic film pertains to establishing standards intended to enhance conceptualization and methodological rigor in the production of a visual ethnography. Specifically, it is contended here that adequacy can be achieved by linking data-gathering (traditional and visual), data analysis (grounded in anthropological insights), and film construction into an interdependent process.

Unbound by existing film convention but concerned with ethnographic standards of adequacy (El Guindi 1986: 7-43), I set my goal (vision) to produce a self-sufficient visual ethnography of EL SEBOU' ceremony aimed for a particular audience, rooted in an authentic cultural identity dignified by indigenous voices and concrete spontaneous expressions, interpreted from a non-Orientalist, non-Eurocentric, non-androcentric perspective,[5] given form by the universal processual pattern of rites-of-passage, contextualized by ethnographically relevant images, based on a generalized analysis of the ritual as a specific cultural domain, and informed by the abstract structure underlying Egyptian ceremonial life in general.

These parameters formed the vision for EL SEBOU' behind the entire process from fieldwork, to film production and ethnography construction. It is broken into eight constituent components proposed as parameters collectively constituting the basis for a theory for a film. They are:

1. a self-sufficient visual ethnography
2. intended audience
3. authentic cultural identity dignified by indigenous voices and concrete expressions
4. avert Orientalist, Eurocentric, and androcentric interpretation
5. the universal processual form for rites-of-passage
6. contextualization by ethnographically relevant images
7. a generalized analysis of the specific cultural domain as a ritual

8. the abstract structure underlying Egyptian ceremonial life in general

Methodological Experimentation

With these objectives in mind I began the film project. After
some shooting and prior to the focal ceremony I decided to
share my analysis of the ritual with the cameraman and
soundman, neither of whom had any familiarity with the
ethnographic documentary genre, rather than simply rely on
directing camera moves and framing during the shoot. Sharing
the analysis was intended to ensure comprehensive coverage
of concrete and abstract aspects. These are: the *Sebou'* itself which
consists of two days. (1) the day of the *Sebou'*, the seventh day
after birth, during which a number of ceremonies and activities
that take place in the household of the newborns. (2) Other
related ceremonies and events that take place on the eve of the
Sebou' in the same home. Shooting was planned for both days.
(3) Other components of the ceremonial event constitute: the
various participants, special foods, specific beverages, ceremonial crafts, and folksongs. This was to serve as the contextualizing
material. Shooting the crafting of ceremonial candles and clay
pots and bazaar purchasing took another two full days.

Charting Content

In the field prior to shooting the ceremony, I had made a
chart of all aspects of the ceremony shown in analysis to be key
elements in the ritual, by dividing these elements into three
groups, each in a vertical column: Aspects, Actions, and Objects (see Figures 2 and 3). The category Aspects refers to
abstract observations, that can be indirectly shown through
concrete illustrations. The category Actions referred to con-

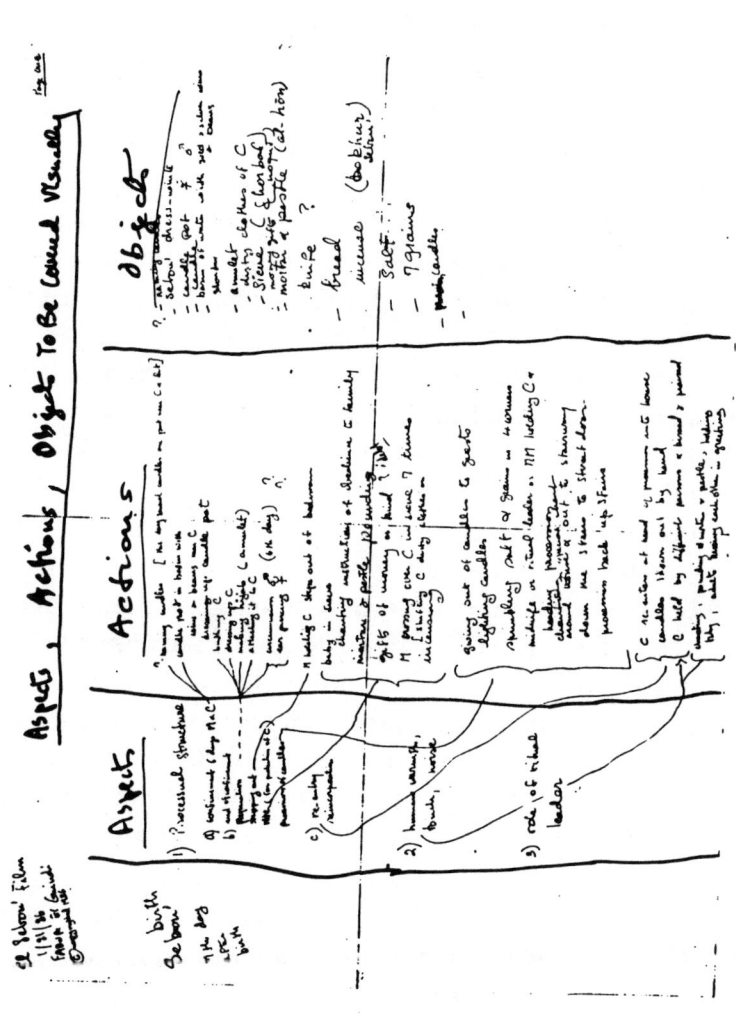

FIGURE 2: Original chart (part one) drawn spontaneously by the anthropologist in the field in January 1986 used to guide film team pre-shooting discussion.

crete movements (lighting candles, the ritual meal, winnowing the babies in a sieve) and the last one Objects was intended to cover ceremonial crafts, and physical objects such as the ceremonial pots, the sieve, the candles, the candy sacks, etc.

The discussion with the filming team comprised of sharing ideas and concerns, familiarizing everybody with ethnographic filming and my objectives for EL SEBOU'. I discussed my charted research results of the event and went over each grouping elaborating on the significance of each element in the ritual and hence the necessity of capturing it on film footage. In the category "Aspects" I discussed the kinds of behaviors that might spontaneously occur which would illustrate each of the abstract qualities, e.g bonding, family warmth, same-sex identification, etc.

Together we considered how all these charted elements, particularly the abstract ones, were to be translated into film footage, and simultaneously capture spontaneity in behavior that is outside the structured analysis.

The exchange was useful in many ways. One area of discussion that resulted was the complex simultaneous activities that I wanted covered and the limitation of using one camera. I was committed to the use of one camera to minimize disruption and distancing from the people. Another interesting facet in the exchange was when the cameraman expressed the attitude that he was already very familiar with the *Sebou'* and knew exactly what to shoot and how to frame. In the discussion it was evident that his knowledge was either that of a native culture-bearer whose intimate familiarity with his own culture without anthropological training was preventing him from "seeing" certain elements in the ritual, or experimental (rather than analytic) in which his vision was concretely (in a non-generalized way) tied to a specific *Sebou'* experience, that he assumed will be emulated in the one to be filmed.

Attesting to the methodological value of the chart in enhancing rigor is the one accidental omission. I inadvertently

```
El Sebou' Film/Analysis Chart
based on chart drawn in
field on 1/21/86                    ASPECTS, ACTIONS, OBJECTS
Fadwa El Guindi                       To Be Covered Visually
@ Copyright 1986
```

ASPECTS	ACTIONS	OBJECTS
1) Processual Structure	? naming candles/ 7 candles lit by head of NB	naming candles
a)confinement of newborn 6 days	Eve of Sebou' (6th day)	incense candlepot
	candle pot in water basin w/ coins & beans near child "dressing up" candle pot filling gift sacks w/ candy & peanuts/chickpeas serving "mughat"	pot candle basin w/ water & beans bowl w/ 7 grains gift sacks, candy peanuts mughat
b) end of confinement 7th day 1- preparation	bathing child dressing up child making "hijab" (amulet) attaching it to child	white sebou' dress dirty diaper amulet scissors
2- stepping out threshold crossing	MM carries NB out of bedroom Candlepot also brought out	
3- candle procession	Candles given out to everyone and lit RL holds dish with 7 grains & and salt MW/RL/MM holds NB & heads procession down bldng Chanting sebou' chants Sprinkling of grains in 4 dir. Proc. down stairs, to street gate and back into flat	procession candles dish of 7 grains incense

```
El Sebou' Film/ Analysis Chart (Continued)
```

ASPECTS	ACTIONS	OBJECTS
4- initiation rite	NB in sieve pounding brass mortar & pestle chanting obedience instructions to NB M stepping over NB 7 times incensing dirty diaper & knife shifting winnowing NB noqut/gifts of money over NB	
	-------------------------------- missing from field chart {rolling sieve across room} --------------------------------	
c) re-entry/ reincorporation	NB held by different persons, touched, kissed Giving out candy sacks to children Dancing Ceremonial meal/fatta	
2) proxemics- human warmth,touch, noise		
3) role of ritual leader		
4) bonding M/Ch Women Family		

FIGURE 3: Retyped chart (parts one and two) from original for clarity.

omitted one constituent element of the content and this one omitted element was subsequently missed during shooting by the cameraman.[6] Furthermore, the value of the chart lies in the comprehensive, yet economical, coverage reflected in the content and amount of film footage. Outside the ceremony day and the pre-ceremony eve, contextualizing was achieved by shooting bazaar purchasing of ceremonial herbs, spices and ritual objects, and the crafts of candle-making and pot-making. By envisioning these contextual scenes as integral to the ceremony, a non-linear approach turned out to be a major strength of the film.[7]

While the study of the *Sebou'* ceremony took two years, total shooting of ceremony days and contextualizing events was accomplished in four full days. Total footage ratio was 3: 1.

Freezing Structure

Editing, like shooting, was informed by the same structure built in analysis of the ceremony and my articulated vision of its construction as a film. As I have argued elsewhere in my work on Zapotec ritual (1986), fundamental to the notion of structure is the point that it derives its properties, as culture-bearers participate in their culture, from the way people act on things and through the operations they perform on them.

During the course of field investigation, whether for the purpose of print or visual ethnography, the data-base (visual, non-visual, or both) is progressively accumulated and, concurrently, a theory gradually builds. The processes of accumulating data and building a theory are interdependent since structure is the underlying reality, and it is in the process of uncovering the structure that a theory is formulated. Therefore, the structure is also the film theory. Since structure is a process which gives rise to formalization it is the formalization, and not the structure, that is the creation of the anthropologist; structure is the creation of the culture-bearers. The formalization informing filming and film construction is based on the eight parameters discussed above and is shaped by three components: (1) the universal form of rites-of-passage, (2) Egyptian ritual structure, and (3) contextualization.

(1) Rite-of-Passage Form

This refers to the linear, processual form shown by Van Gennep to be universal for the class of rituals known as rites-of-passage in which culture participants pass from a marked state of separation to a marked state of incorporation. The period in between is a transitional, liminal period. This sequential form provides a chronological sequencing order to events.

First, it was established in analysis that the *Sebou'* is a rite-of-passage. Then, events and activities in the ceremony that illustrate this sequential form of phases were identified on the basis of field data and research. To ensure their coverage in the filming these were included in the analysis chart prior to shooting. Filming the two days of the ceremony (eve of the *Sebou'* and *Sebou'* day) followed this order in close to real time.

(2) Ritual Structure

The analysis of the ceremony led to the discovery of a dualistic structural theme underlying all private and public life-cycle Egyptian rituals: (1) the individual life-cycle ceremonies of which EL SEBOU' marks the beginning point, and (2) the collective calendrical rituals, of which my second film, EL MOULID: EGYPTIAN RELIGIOUS FESTIVAL, is a good example. This internal theme defining the whole system of Egyptian life-cycle ritual consists of the two cosmologically significant numerical elements of *seven* and *forty*.

As evident from the very name of the ceremony, the *Sebou'*, an Arabic word deriving from the root *sab'a*, meaning seven, occurs on the seventh day of life celebrating the coming out of newborns. *Seven* continues throughout the *Sebou'* to mark the various ceremonies and activities. There are seven grains sprinkled around the house, the mother steps seven times over the newborn lying in a winnowing sieve, etc. The *Sebou'* ceremony on the seventh day also marks the end of separation and liminality and the ceremonial incorporation of the newborn.

While seven days is the period of transition for a newborn child whose confinement ends after the *Sebou'*, the mother remains in confinement for *forty* days after which is her "coming out." The *Sebou'* celebrates the child, not the mother.

Furthermore, a cursory examination of major Egyptian lifecycle rituals shows that *seven* and *forty* mark all life-cycle Egyptian ritual, so that, for example, mourning for a deceased is for the duration of *forty* days, but celebrating the birth of a 12th century holy man by visiting his tomb is for the duration of *seven* days.

In my construction of EL SEBOU' I wanted to mark this duality of *seven* and *forty*, as they are represented temporally and concretely through certain actions. One way would have been to resort to the print medium and print the information to be conveyed. I rejected that approach, hoping that cinema rather than print would creatively inform this aspect of film construction. The idea to use existing film technique[8] evolved at the editing table. It was decided to represent a "threshold point" by stopping action at that point.

Seven is best marked at the point in which the newborn twins were carried out of the bedroom past the threshold and into the more public area of the home. Representing *forty* is at the point at which the mother stands on the side, clearly not joining the procession down the building stairs and back into the flat, marking the end of the liminal period for the newborn. A frame was stopped at each point to mark the complementary opposition, child/mother, seven/forty. In other words, by freezing the frame one is freezing properties of the structure. This way the freeze frame is used not for drama as it is commonly used but rather to visually represent the oppositional property of Egyptian ritual structure, to highlight the structural theme of "seven" and "forty," without having to resort to "print" techniques or drama.

(3) Contextualization

The film opens with a scene of a *Sebou'* shop in the bazaar and a woman, called Um Sayyid, at the counter facing the salesman. Another scene shows a man carrying decorated candles coming out of a candle-decorating shop into the winding alleys of Khan El-Khalili bazaar in Cairo.

These two sequences set the context for the ceremony in a ritually relevant way. The camera then takes us into the intimacy of a family home, usually inaccessible to "foreigners." We see two babies almost completely covered, sleeping in a large bed, surrounded by family members, one of them blowing incense around the room by swinging a long-chained incensor. On each side of the bed is a clay pot concealed by commercial decorations and battery operated lights.

The clay pot is a key ritual object. (See Figure 4.) The very shape of the pots and "dressing them up" emphasize gender. Inception of life is marked by a strong cultural definition of gender and affirmation of gender difference. The pot becomes, in essence, a symbol of creation, and the *sebou'* a transition to a gendered cultural life.

Other than gender symbolism, the pot, a key ceremonial object, links contemporary Egyptian ritual life to its past tradition. In ancient Egypt the creator Khnum "creates" by fashioning the child and "the other" out of clay. Clay is linked with creation. As we see in the film the gendered "dressing up" of the clay pots attributes to them anthropomorphic qualities, as

FIGURE 4: A drawing by graphic artist Daphne Shuttleworth, Office of Folklife, Smithsonian Institution, depicting the ceremonial clay pots: a Girl's Pot is *Ollah*, a Boy's Pot is *Abri'*

if the pot is the child, or "its other." Its shape represents the newborn's gender, it is "dressed up" by the mother and the father, and it is carried out of seclusion along with the newborn. We see the family "dressing up" the pots with jewelry.

In order to show the shape of the pots which is significant, we again move out of ritual space and its linear time to the pottery village where the pots, "undressed" as it were, were being crafted in detail by the potter Hag Saleh. So early on in the film, and before the main ceremony day itself, we have already been visually introduced to the key "participants" in the event: the family, one (of two) ritual leaders, and the newborns to be initiated. Also we have by then been shown many key ceremonial objects: clay pots, incense, seven grains, beans soaking in water, and candles. In addition we have seen several key activities and rites on the eve of the *sebou'*: buying ceremonial objects, lighting the candle in a clay pot, protecting the newborns, "dressing up" the gendered pots, drinking *mughat*, and packing candy in *sebou'* sacks. Folksongs spontaneously sung during the ceremonies were subtitled in verse by verse form (rather than phrase by phrase) to preserve processing continuity for the viewer.

Ritual Space Within Culture Space

Ritual space is structured by the processual linear universal form characterizing rites-of-passage and the thematic duality characterizing Egyptian life-cycle ritual as a whole. That is, the

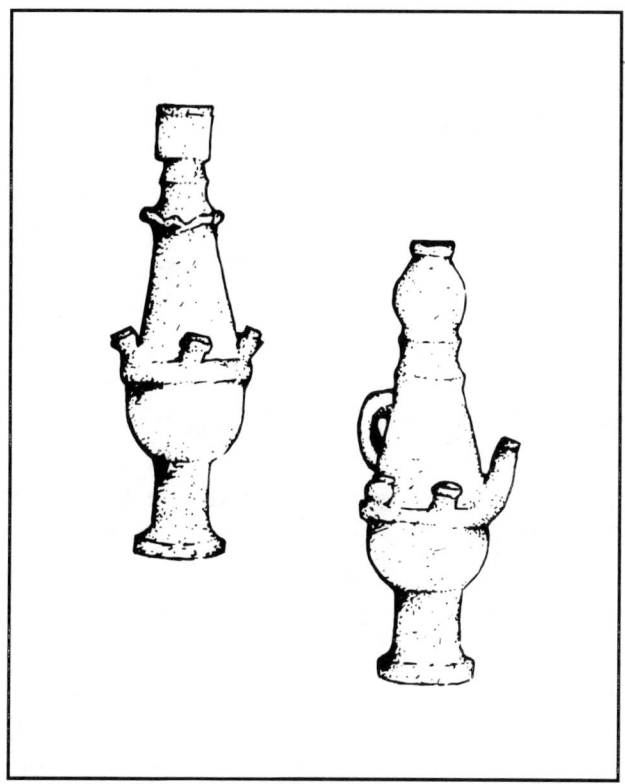

two aspects, the processsusal form and the thematic structure of Egyptian ritual, together constitute the abstract parameters that demarcate the *Sebou'* ritual space.

Throughout the *Sebou'* the ceremony takes place in the privacy of the home, in the privacy of the family. In other words, all the events and activities that occur on the eve and the day of the *Sebou'* remain bounded by ritual space. It would have been possible to limit filming to this space and still have an interesting film. However, if we look back at the parameters discussed earlier, specifically numbers (3), "authentic cultural identity dignified by indigenous voices and concrete expressions," and (6), "contextualized by ethnographically relevant images," we find that the film theory specified contextualization of this specific ritual within the larger culture.

Consistent with the technique of breaking linear chronological time by moving out of ritual space, the viewer is again taken out on the day of the *Sebou'* for the making and commercial decorating of ceremonial candles. Contextualizing was the means selected in the film construction process to provide the events and the people with an authentic cultural identity situated in the larger cultural context. However, contextualization is itself informed by the parameters of the film theory and must use "relevant" images. Relevance is determined by ritual analysis. Consistent with this orientation, the ritual was also contextualized by using three key women in the family whose voices interpret events as they occur.

By intermittently suspending ritual time by means of key ritual personnel, we move out of the linear mode, breaking the chronology as it were, to see ritual relevant activities: clay pot crafting, candle crafting, herbs, incense, spices, candy purchasing, etc. This is contextualizing. It links ceremonial events taking place within ritual space to the wider cultural space without losing the consistency or the momentum of the main event that is the focal subject of the film ethnography. This linkage between ritual space and its wider cultural space is diagrammatically represented in Figure 5.

As the analysis of the film EL SEBOU' illustrates, essentially ethnographic film consists of a research/filming cycle consisting of a body of data, acquired by anthropological methods, structured in accordance with an analytic framework, and documented via the visual mode of shooting film footage ultimately given form as a film. Both shooting and final film are informed by a coherent film theory. It is argued here that visual ethnography is characterized by: (1) self-sufficiency: the aim of a visual ethnography is to be presented to students and scholars of anthropology and culture (in area studies) as a coherent whole without *necessary* recourse to written material; (2) inte-

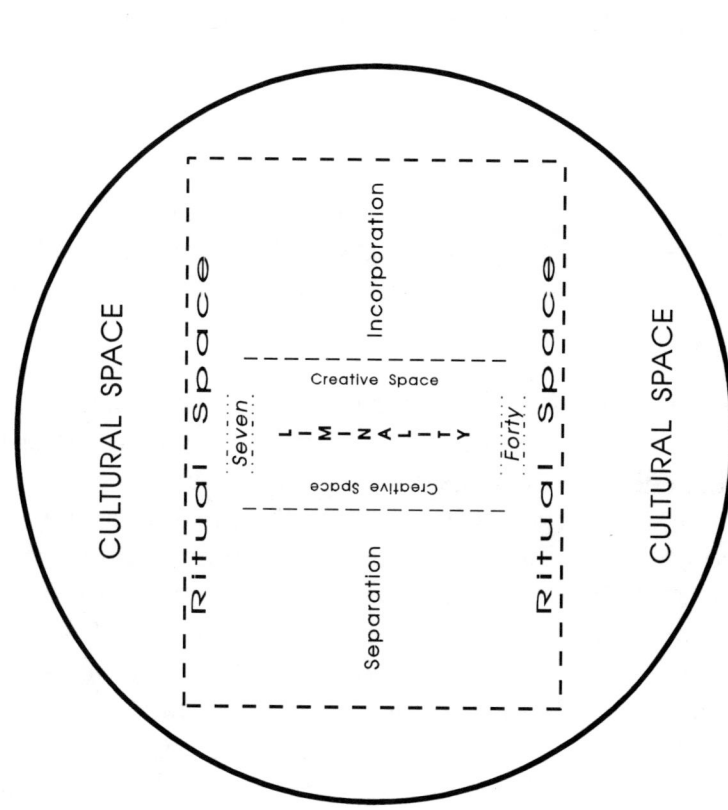

FIGURE 5: A diagrammatic representation of the film theory informing all phases of film production and construction of *El Sebou'*, demonstrating the relation between universal ritual form, Egyptian ritual structure, ritual space, and culture space.

gration of ethnography and film: visual ethnography is generated by an interdependent process linking data-gathering, analysis, and film construction, and (3) the cultural domain being filmed as a visual ethnography is defined and examined in terms of its relevance and meaningfulness within the culture as a whole and according to an underlying structure and its component elements uncovered in analysis.[9]

Conclusion

> *"we must know the culture: to acquire*
> *this knowledge there is no better tool*
> *than ethnographic film"* (Jean Rouch 1974)

In conclusion, I am in agreement with the spirit of Jean Rouch's comment, but would restate it this way: to experience another culture from a distance there is no better tool than film, as it can, as Mark McCarty puts it, "capture the feeling, the sounds, and the speech . . . from the intimate ground of those inside it" (1975: 50). To *know* a culture and visually present it "to others for serious and intelligent evaluation" (McCarty 1975: 50), we need to establish and systematize standards of adequacy that guide the production of ethnographic film.

Current visual anthropology debate tends to fall into two orientations: one that is informed by cinema and implicitly or explicitly finds primacy in cinematic arguments, vocabulary, and analogies over the ethnographic, and the other that apologizes for anthropology, assumes ethnographic primacy, and calls for a theory of culture to inform film equally as any ethnographic work.

What is lacking is a comprehensive body of ideas that aims to systematize techniques built out of an approach that integrates ethnography and film in a unified visual ethnography.

A new integrated form of ethnography and film must develop and be informed by standards of adequacy set by visual anthropology without granting primacy to cinema or to ethnography. My analysis of the process of construction of EL SEBOU': EGYPTIAN BIRTH RITUAL is presented here as a step in this direction.

ACKNOWLEDGEMENTS

Some aspects of the analysis in this paper were presented in "The Making of El Sebou': Methodological Considerations for Ethnographic Film" in the panel "Visual Research Strategies - Visual Anthropology in the '80s," at the 12th International Congress of Anthropological and Ethnological Sciences (IUAES) in Zagreb, Yugoslavia, July 28, 1988. An earlier version of this article was presented at "Film As Ethnography" conference at the 2nd Royal Anthropological Institute Film Festival, Manchester, England, September 24-28, 1990.

Funding for research and filming of El Sebou' was provided by Smithsonian Grant # 9068440000. Additional support was provided by The Office of Folklife Programs, Smithsonian Institution, and the Max-Plank-Institut, Seewiesen, Germany. For assistance and support, I thank Hisham Fathy, Tarik Fathy, William C. Young, Chris Donnan, Patsy Asch, Alicia Gonzalez, Peter Seitel, Richard Kurin, Daphne Shuttleworth, Ursula Koch, Wulf Schiefenhövel, and Dwight W. Read.

I am grateful to El Nil Research for granting me release time for research and writing of this paper.

NOTES

1   Omori (1988: 192) states that "...within visual anthropology there are two main forms that films take. First, there are simple footage films...taken as fieldnotes....Secondly, there is the ethnographic film (like a monograph) which is shot in a comprehensive way and organized around a theme related to the entire culture being studied. Footage films are short films recording a technical process or scenes of human behavior within a group. The monograph film tends to be longer and has a story constructed on a specific theme."

2   That is why Rouch prefers the term to either "observational cinema" which for some embodies a certain distance from the catalytic,
intersubjective stance (MacDougall 1975), or "cinéma-verité," which
immediately raises the spectre of "truth" (Feld 1989: 223-247).

3   There is a difference between a fact and a datum. A fact is a thing
that has actually happened or is declared to have existed, while a datum
is something admitted for use as a basis for making an argument or for
determining an unknown relation. Although all data derive from facts,
not all raw facts are data. The theoretical orientation determines what
facts become data in analysis.

4   On this point of imaging and interpretation of images see my
analysis of the image of the Gulf war as covered by CNN (El Guindi
1991).

5   I was concerned about the deeply entrenched effect of the orientalist,
the colonialist, the sexist, and more recently the western feminist
orientations in shaping, not only images of the Arab East, but worse,
indigenous self-images. Aware of the imaging and distorting consequences of visual documents, my challenge was to visually portray an
ethnographically constructed Arab cultural reality and escape, on the
one hand, the deep influence of these orientations on attitudes of and
scholarship by the West of the East and, on the other, their inevitable
effect on producing a defensive indigenous posture. Does the answer
lie in "going indigenous?" Is correcting imaging accomplished by
"going indigenous," or would this simply turn imaging into self-
imaging, or worse a "cover up?"
        Doing anthropology is at its best when the anthropologist first
succeeds albeit relatively in the shedding of, or at least distancing from,
one's culture. Studying one's own has its problems of which anthropologists are all too aware. McCarty (1975: 48) briefly mentions the
problem of too much familiarity with a culture for filmmaking. It is even
more problematic in visual ethnography than in print ethnography.
Often this is too much emphasized at the expense of the more serious
problem facing anthropologists from colonizing cultures filming the
colonized. There is an arrogant resistance to debating problems inherent in the latter.
        With effort, it is possible in print or visual ethnography to portray
the culturally constructed reality without reducing culture bearers to
invisibility or subordination, without treating them as noble savages or
depicting their culture as exotica. Almost every ethnographic film
depicting Islam, for example, even when an Islamic practice is portrayed briefly, would be considered insulting by Muslims. Many such
films get rewarded in ethnographic film festivals in Europe and the

United States. Another common pattern on films in Africa is projecting purity from Islamic influence in the image. Overcoming such distortions would involve both (1) shedding deep-seated attitudes, and (2) devising methodologies to ensure better portrayal. It is easier to accomplish the latter.

For other aspects of making EL SEBOU', see my earlier article (1988). For reviews published of the film, see Abu-Lughod (1988), Bodman (1990), Lobban (1988), and T.B. Stevenson (1990).

6   Furthermore, this highly structured pre-shooting session worked well in sorting out roles and jobs for different members of the team, hence enhancing coordination. In the field, I established my position as director of the project vis-á-vis the cameraman and his crew. This was further reinforced by having everyone address me as "doctora." The title provided the Egyptian male team members with a familiar authority structure which allowed them to transcend gender in the hierarchy, particularly in light of my evident ignorance, at the time, of the technical aspects of filming.

7   In his review of EL SEBOU', Lobban echoed the response of many when he wrote that "...ventures into the store of herbalist, the craft of candle-making, and the Fustat potters who make gender-specific pots for the ritual" are "positive features" of the film that "give substantial added depth which helps to articulate the birth ritual to the wider society" (1988: 242-243).

8   In response to my question at the editing table "What is usually used in film for emphasis?", the editor working with me, Luis Pérez-Tolón, proposed a few possibilities including the "freeze frame." Together we watched a number of films utilizing the freeze frame technique and it was evident that consistently freeze framing was used to "dramatize," a quality unrelated (as far as I could tell) to any analytic aspect of the subject matter.

9   Fundamental to the notion of structure is the point that it derives its properties, as culture-bearers participate in their culture, from the way people act on things and through the operations they perform on them. During the course of field investigation, the data-base (visual, non-visual, or both) is progressively accumulated and, concurrently, a theory gradually builds.

The processes of accumulating data and building a theory are interdependent, since structure is the underlying reality, and it is in the process of uncovering the structure that a theory is formulated. This theory is what informs filming and film construction.

Therefore, the structure is also the film theory. Since structure is a process which gives rise to formalization it is the formalization, and not the structure, that is the creation of the theoretician; structure is the creation of the culture-bearers.

REFERENCES CITED

Abu-Lughod, L. (1988). Review of the Film, EL SEBOU': THE EGYPTIAN BIRTH RITUAL by Fadwa El Guindi. Visual Anthropology 1(4): 497-499.

Asch, T., and Patsy Asch, (1988). Film in Anthropological Research. IN Cinematographic Theory and New Dimensions in Ethnographic Film. Senri Ethnological Studies No. 24., P. Hockings and Y. Omori (eds.) Osaka: National Museum of Ethnology. pp.165-187.

Bodman, Ellen-Fairbanks (1990). Review of the Film, EL SEBOU': THE EGYPTIAN BIRTH RITUAL by Fadwa El Guindi. Middle East Studies Association Bulletin 24(1): 117-118.

El Guindi, F. (1986). The Myth of Ritual: A Native's Ethnography of Zapotec Life-Crisis Rituals. Arizona: University of Arizona Press.

El Guindi, F. (1988). The Making of El Sebou'. Visual Anthropology 1(4): 499-507.

El Guindi, F. (1990a). On Making An Ethnographic Film On Egypt—El Sebou': Egyptian Birth Ritual. MERA Forum.

El Guindi, F. (1990b). El Sebou' Film Study Guide. Los Angeles: El Nil Research.

El Guindi, F. (1991). Images of Domination, Voices of Control: Covering The Gulf War. International Documentary: Journal of Nonfiction Film and Video. Reprinted in MERA Forum XIV (1): 3, 1991 and CVA Review: Revue de la Commission d'anthropologie visuelle, and as War 'Game' Casts Iraqis as Losers in Media and Values, Fall 1991.

Feld, Steven (1989). Themes in the Cinema of Jean Rouch, Visual Anthropology 2(3-4): 223-247.

Hockings, P. (1975). Principles of Visual Anthropology. The Hague: Mouton Publishers.

Hockings, P. and Y. Omori (eds.) (1988). Cinematographic Theory and New Dimensions in Ethnographic Film. Senri Ethnological Studies No. 24. Osaka: National Museum of Ethnology.

Lobban, Jr., R. A. (1988). Review of EL SEBOU': THE EGYPTIAN BIRTH RITUAL by Fadwa El Guindi. American Anthropologist 90(1): 242-243.

MacDougall, David (1975). Beyond Observational Cinema. IN Principles of Visual Anthropology, Paul Hockings (ed.). The Hague: Mouton Publishers, pp. 133-145.

Martínez, Wilton (1990). Critical Studies and Visual Anthropology: Aberrant Versus Anticipated Readings of Ethnographic Film. CVA

Review, pp. 34-47.

Martínez, Wilton (1992). Who Constructs Anthropological Knowledge: Toward A Theory of Ethnographic Film Spectatorship. IN Film As Ethnograph, Peter Crawford and D. Turton (eds.) Manchester: Manchester University Press, pp. 130-161.

McCarty, Mark (1975). McCarty's Law and How to Break It. IN Principles of Visual Anthropology, Paul Hockings (ed.), The Hague: Mouton Publishers, pp. 45-51.

Morin, Edgar (1956). Le Cinéma, ou l'Homme Imaginaire. Paris: Les Editions de Minuit.

Omori, Yasuhiro (1988). Basic Problems in Developing Film Ethnography. IN Cinematographic Theory and New Dimensions in Ethnographic Film, P. Hockings and Y. Omori (eds.) Senri Ethnological Studies No.24, Osaka: National Museum of Ethnology, pp. 191-204.

Preloran, J. (1975). Documenting the Human Condition. IN Principles of Visual Anthropology. P. Hockings (ed.). The Hague: Mouton, pp.103- 108.

Rouch, Jean (1974). The Camera and Man. Studies in the Anthropology of Visual Communication 1(1): 37-44

Rouch, Jean (1975). The Camera and Man. IN Principles of Visual Anthropology. P. Hockings (ed.). The Hague: Mouton, pp. 83-102.

Ruby, Jay (1982). A Crack in the Mirror: Reflexive Perspectives in Anthropology. Philadelphia: University of Pennsylvania Press.

Ruby, Jay (1989). The Cinema of Jean Rouch, Special Issue. Visual Anthropology 2(3-4).

Stevenson, T. B. (1990). Review of EL SEBOU': EGYPTIAN BIRTH RITUAL by Fadwa El Guindi. MERA Forum 18(1): 9-10.

FILMS CITED

El Sebou': Egyptian Birth Ritual. 1986. A film by Fadwa El Guindi. 27 minutes, color. Purchase 16mm $670, VHS $270, rental $70 from El Nil Research, 1147 Beverwil Dr., Los Angeles, CA 90035 (310/553-5645, Fax 310/556-0703).

El Moulid: Egyptian Religious Festival. 1990. A film by Fadwa El Guindi. 38 minutes, color. Purchase 16mm $840, VHS $340, rental $85 from El Nil Research, 1147 Beverwil Dr., Los Angeles, CA 90035 (310/553-5645, Fax 310/556-0703).

Seven Young Gods of Fortune: Fertility Rite of Dosojin. 1983. A film by Yasuhiro Omori. 68 minutes, color.

Festive Housewives. 1985. A film by Yasuhiro Omori. 35 minutes, color.

SUGGESTED READINGS

Callender, C. and F. El Guindi (1971). Life-Crisis Rituals Among The Kenuz. Cleveland: Case Western Reserve University Press.

El Guindi, F. (1990). El Sebou' Film Study Guide. Los Angeles: El Nil Research.

El Guindi, F. (1991). Aspects of Gulf Arab Culture and Society. Los Angeles: El Nil Research.

Fernea, Elizabeth W. (ed.) (1985). Women and the Family in the Middle East: New Voices of Change. Austin: University of Texas Press.

Gilsenan, Michael (1982). Recognizing Islam. New York: Pantheon Books.

Shaheen, Jack G. (1984). The TV Arab. Bowling Green, Ohio: Bowling Green State University Popular Press.

from ANTHROPOLOGICAL FILM AND VIDEO IN THE 1990s
Jack R. Rollwagen (editor). Brockport, NY: The Institute, Inc.
© 1993, The Institute, Inc. All rights reserved. ISBN 0-9635206-1-X

Presenting Dr. Fritz: The Making Of An Anthropological Monograph On Video About A Brazilian Spiritist Healer-Medium

Sidney M. Greenfield
Department of Anthropology
University of Wisconsin-Milwaukee

ABSTRACT: Brazilian Spiritist healer-mediums, through whom the spirits of deceased physicians and surgeons are said to work, have been reported to perform surgeries without the use of anesthesia and antisepsis. Patients operated on generally claim to experience little or no pain, bleed only slightly, if at all, and few, if any, cases of infections or other complications have been recorded.

In 1982 I began what has developed into a long term study of the subject. In 1988 I co-produced with John B. Gray a video documentary about one healer-medium.

This essay examines the addition of visual techniques to the range of methods I had employed previously in doing anthropological research. First, however, I explain how I came to undertake the study of Spiritist healing and surgery. In doing so the relationship between Spiritist healing, anthropological theory and my previous studies in Brazil are explored. This is followed by an examination of why I came to use video technology in the research and to make THE RETURN OF DR. FRITZ: HEALING BY THE SPIRITS IN BRAZIL

The anthropological monograph is the standard means of presenting the results of anthropological research. Unlike the written monograph, few anthropological films and videos include in depth analysis of the meaning systems that inform exotic behaviors described. The viewer is assigned written materials that provide the analysis and explanation.

In making THE RETURN OF DR. FRITZ, I tried to include the analysis and explanation within the presentation. I argue, therefore, that it should be thought of as a visual monograph, a category that does not exist, but which should.

Introduction

Since the middle of the twentieth century, if not before, often uneducated and untrained Spiritist healer-mediums in Brazil have been reported performing surgeries and other therapeutic procedures under the guidance of deceased physicians and surgeons said to come from the spirit world who take over their bodies in the tradition of spirit possession. The often spectacular operations they perform, in which patient's bodies are opened with anything from a rusty knife to a scalpel, or even an electrical saw, to remove tumors and/or other growths, are done with apparent disregard to the presence of germs or other sources of infection. Furthermore, the patients are given no anesthesia. Still, most patients report experiencing little if any pain, bleeding is usually slight and few if any cases of post surgical infections or other complications have been recorded.

While these events are difficult both to comprehend and explain, the subject, which has been covered in the Brazilian press, has been the theme of several popular books, and has been reported extensively by the Brazilian electronic media, had not been studied by anthropologists. In 1982 I began what has developed into a long term study of the subject. In 1988 I co-produced with John B. Gray a video documentary about one of the healers I had studied. In a career that goes back to the mid-1950s, I had never before used either film or video as part of my research and had never considered seriously the making of films and documentaries. I was neither trained as, nor do I consider myself today, to be a "visual" anthropologist, although I have now made four documentaries and am working on a fifth. Instead, I see myself as a general anthropologist who has come to use video, and to make documentaries as the result of working on a particular problem whose investigation and reporting was facilitated by the use of visual techniques. My goal is not to make films and documentaries as such, but instead to enable me to collect additional data that will add a dimension to the analysis that then will expand the ways the results of the research can be presented.

Writing ethnography requires, among other things, that an author translate the meanings of events described from the cultural context in which they were produced into the culture of the audience to whom they are being described. The anthropological monograph has developed over the years as the primary vehicle for describing events in one culture that are to be explained (i.e., translated) in ways that convey their meanings to an audience. There has developed thus far no analog to the anthropological monograph in the field of film and videomaking. In making THE RETURN OF DR. FRITZ: HEALING BY THE SPIRITS IN BRAZIL, I found myself grappling repeatedly with the question of just how much the viewer has to know and understand of the world of meaning that for Brazilian Spiritists informs the events depicted on video tape to appreciate and comprehend what is being shown to them. As I found myself adding background and explanation to the script, I soon realized that I was actually producing a monograph that would be shown on video.

Studying Spiritist Healing

Although I had known about Spiritist healer-mediums and the reputedly extraordinary surgeries they performed since my first visit to Brazil in 1959, I had never had the opportunity to meet any healers and observe their work until 1982, and then it was by coincidence. I was living at the time in the city of Fortaleza in the northeastern state of Ceará, the beneficiary of a Fulbright award. Shortly after my arrival I was reading the local newspaper when an article caught my attention. It was about a Spiritist healer. I read it, I must admit, not because of the subject matter, but because the healer's name, José Carlos Ribeiro, was my Brazilian godson's name. I soon realized that it was about a different man, but the story reminded me of what I had heard and read about Spiritist healing.

I recalled from my readings in popular books and in the Brazilian press reports of what were presented as spectacular surgeries and/or other acts of healing performed by individuals attributed extraordinary powers. According to the accounts, the person doing the healing was a medium whose body was being used by the spirit of a deceased doctor, surgeon, or other healer returning temporarily from the spirit plane to effect the cure. Possession by a spirit that did the healing procedure was the ostensible explanation for the tumors that were reported as being removed without blood or pain, the lame walking, the blind seeing, cancers being cured, and other acts of healing that defied the imagination.

My curiosity aroused, I invited my wife Eleanor and my daughter Suzanne, who were with me in Fortaleza, to accompany me in going to see what we had all heard and read about so often but had not witnessed during the may years we had spent in Brazil. The next morning we went to the address given in the newspaper where we found a large crowd waiting in line patiently in the street outside a moderately sized single family dwelling. I asked a young man who appeared to be organizing those in the street if I could speak with José Carlos, the healer. After showing him some document that identified me as a Professor of Anthropology at a North American university, he directed us through the mass of humanity that filled the house up a flight of stairs to a small bedroom that was being used for both examinations and treatment. There I introduced myself and my wife and daughter to a smiling, attractive, slender young man in his late twenties who was of mixed African and European descent. Dressed in an open sport shirt and a pair of dark trousers, he looked more like an entertainer than a religious healer.

I presented myself to him as a scholar and researcher interested in seeing his work. After asking me a few questions, the answers to which apparently satisfied him, he welcomed me saying graciously that it would be his pleasure to have us observe him. In words that reminded me of John Fuller's vivid account of the first meeting between Andre Puharich and Henry Belk, two earlier North American researchers and the famous Zé Arigó (Fuller 1974), José Carlos added: "We have nothing to hide." [1] He then informed me that I could assist him. Before I was able to ask what this would entail, a tray was placed in my hands on which there were a few ordinary scalpels, several pairs of surgical scissors, a few pairs of tweezers of assorted sizes, a syringe, some cotton, some gauze, adhesive tape and a glass of water. All of the instruments had been used previously and none were sterile. With this José Carlos turned to face a poorly dressed, dark skinned man who was accompanied by his wife.

The woman tried to tell him about her mate's problem with his vision. As she did so José Carlos directed his eyes away from the patient and the speaking woman towards the ceiling. He mumbled some words I could not understand and his body shook violently. I was told later that he had gone into trance during which Saint Ignatius of Loyola, his spirit helper, was said to incorporate in his body. An instant later he impatiently interrupted the woman who was still speaking to ask a question and to issue a command. He did this with an authority he had not previously shown and he spoke now in a sharp accent that contrasted with the soft tone he had previously used. It sounded to me as if he were a native speaker of Spanish trying to communicate in Portuguese.

He asked the man and the somewhat stunned and still mumbling woman if they believed in God. Without waiting for them to respond, he picked up a scalpel from the tray in my hands and, while ordering them both to think of God, plunged it into the man's left eye with his right hand, under the lid. With a series of jabbing and twisting motions he slid the instrument down under the eye. As he did this he substituted the back of a pair of tweezers taken from the tray with his left hand for the scalpel. While doing this he eased the eye forward, tilting it out of its socket. He then scraped the lens of the protruding eye using a side to side motion with the scalpel still held in his right hand.

The patient did not flinch. I think that I reacted more than he did, specifically to the use of the unsterilized instruments taken from the tray in my hands. My first thought, however, was: Who is going to believe me when I get home and tell my friends, colleagues and students about this? I was to ask myself the same question several more times as the days went on and I continued to assist and observe José Carlos.

There were more than 20 people (mostly friends, former patients, and patients to be seen later) watching the healer-medium perform the procedure in the small, hot, poorly ventilated room. Several of them had gasped as the scalpel was thrust into the eye, and one women was unable to stifle a scream. My wife, who had been placed directly behind the healer, felt faint. As the blood left her face, José Carlos, though unable to see her, moved his left hand quickly in her direction, leaving the tweezers dangling momentarily from its place under the protruding eye. As he did so he mumbled something I could not understand. When the blood returned to my wife's cheeks, the healer secured his grip on the dangling tweezers. After a few more scraping motions with the scalpel still held in his right hand he returned the eye to its socket and slid the tweezers, held securely again in his left hand, back to the top of the eye under the lid where he had first introduced the scalpel. As he covered the eye with gauze held down by several strips of adhesive tape, he asked the man if he had felt any pain. The patient said no and added that he had been aware of all that had happened. The entire procedure had lasted a little more than a minute.

José Carlos then wrote a prescription that seemingly flowed from the pen itself. He looked at neither the pen nor the pad, but instead off into space as he wrote. When he handed it to the somewhat startled woman, he quickly listed things the patient was to do and not do, and foods he was to eat or avoid. He then dismissed the patient reassuring him that he would be well. The man descended the stairs with complete faith in the healer.

José Carlos then turned to the next patient on whom he also performed eye surgery using the very same scalpel and tweezers that had been returned to the tray in my hands without being cleaned. Diagnosis, surgery, bandaging, writing a prescription for post-operative medication, and the dictation of a list of behavioral restrictions and a special diet took only a few minutes.

As the morning progressed, José Carlos alternated between doing other surgeries (the removal of several cysts and tumors) and the writing of prescriptions that were to cure patients or prepare them for return visits and possible surgery at a later date.

He worked almost non-stop until about 10:00 p.m., having started before our arrival at 8:00 a.m. After we returned from dinner with him and several others who were part of a group that regularly accompanied him, my wife, my daughter and I discussed the events of the day. Needless to say we were intrigued by what we had seen, but were bewildered as to how to explain it. We decided that it was worth pursuing, especially since classes had not started and I had not yet begun another research project.

We spent the next two weeks, from about 8:00 a.m. to almost midnight each day, collecting background information on José Carlos, interviewing him, assisting and observing him treat patients, interviewing those patients (occasionally before, but mostly after treatment either where they were treated or, less frequently, after they returned to their homes) while also trying to learn something about the belief system that informed what he was doing. Then one day, without a word to us, our new found friend abruptly left town. The police, we were told, had threatened to arrest him for practicing medicine without a license.[2]

Our appetites whetted, we did not wish to drop the study of Spiritist healing. We had been fortunate to come upon José Carlos. Although he had now departed, we learned early on that there were other healer-mediums who reportedly did things that were even more difficult to comprehend. A minor controversy during the first days we were with José Carlos enabled us to learn about Edson Queiroz. José Carlos had brought with him a supply of medicines made privately in the city of São Paulo that he prescribed for occasional patients. Because he collected a fee for the medicine a woman who had come to interview him for a local radio program accused him of fraud. Herself a Spiritist, she reminded him, and everyone present, that according to Spiritist doctrine, healing, including medicines prescribed, were a gift from the spirit world and that it was improper, if not sacrilegious, to charge money for them. She warned José Carlos that he might lose his powers (i.e., help from the spirit world) if he did not stop the practice.

When she finished I asked her to tell me about healer-mediums I might visit who were not frauds (i.e., did not charge for their services and/or the medications they dispensed). She immediately named Edson Queiroz who had been in Fortaleza only a few weeks before. She suggested that if I wished to see a "true" healer-medium, I should go to Recife where he lived.

I was able to do this thanks to the Fulbright program. Early on in my semester at the Federal University in Fortaleza I had received an invitation to give a series of lectures at the Federal University of Rio Grande do Sul in Porto Alegre.[3] On my way back to Fortaleza from Porto Alegre I accepted another invitation to give a lecture at the Federal University of Pernambuco in Recife. While there I went to Edson Queiroz' medical clinic and although I was unable to see him work as a healer-medium, I was able to speak at length with him and to receive an invitation from him to return at another time to observe and study him and Dr. Fritz, his spirit guide, treating patients.[4]

The Need for Visual Data

While preparing a paper about Spiritist healing after returning from Brazil (Greenfield and Greenfield 1983), I wondered whether my colleagues would believe me when I described surgeries done without antisepsis and anesthesia that, based on the sample I had, not only had no negative effects on the patients, but actually cured them? Or would I be faced with reactions of doubt and disbelief from my audiences? (and from journal editors and reviewers when I eventually submitted manuscripts for publication)?

While in Fortaleza with José Carlos I had wished that I had movies of what I had seen. The few still photographs I had taken did not do justice to the events I had witnessed. I consulted with colleagues in the Film Department of my university about the possibility of filming the events I believed I would see again when I returned to Brazil. They suggested that I practice with a Bolex camera that they would arrange for me to borrow for several weeks the following summer.

I used the Bolex to film Edson Queiroz doing surgeries in 1983. I also filmed several other healers in other parts of Brazil I visited that summer.[5] I was devastated when after my return

FIGURE 1: Edson Queiroz

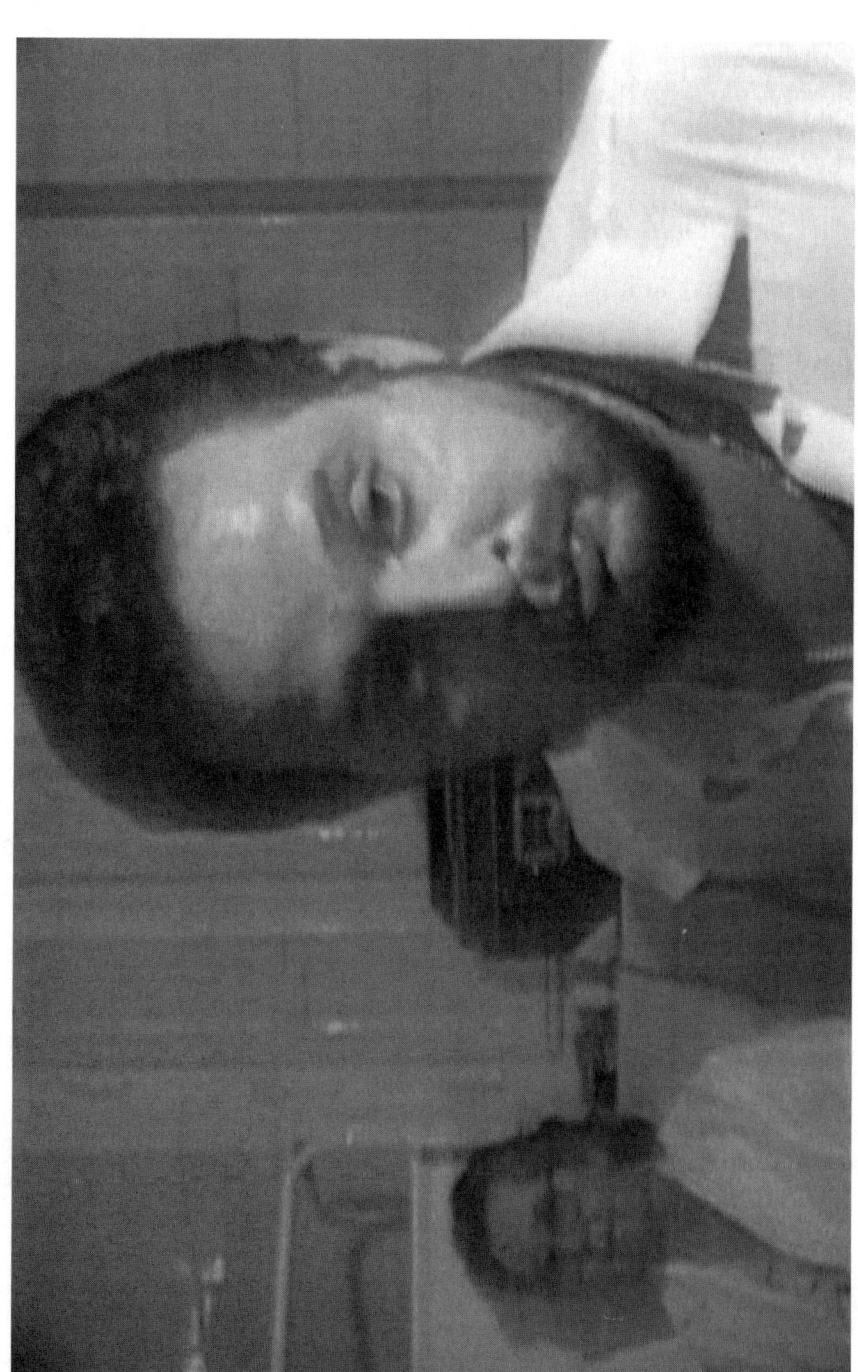

FIGURE 2: Edson in trance, after receiving Dr. Fritz

from the field I learned that none of the film had come out. Somehow I had messed up my first effort to add a visual dimension to my studies of Spiritist healers. I was beginning to believe the adage about not being able to teach old dogs new tricks when my college-age son suggested that I try videotaping.

Early in the fall of 1983 I contacted the Educational Communications Division of the university (where broadcast quality videos were made) to see if they could help me. It was there that I met John Gray, with whom I would later collaborate in the making of the RETURN OF DR. FRITZ and other documentaries. John was a video producer whose passion was ethnographic film. After I explained the research I was doing, he offered to go to Brazil with me.

Had my studies been more conventional, we probably would have applied for funds to make a video documentary. Spiritist healing and surgery, however, was not a subject funding agencies were, or are today, willing to support. Although disappointed that we were unable to raise the money for John to accompany me, he agreed instead to teach me to use a camcorder.

The instrument was easy to use and I had little difficulty deciding what to shoot. I would just focus on the kinds of events my training and experience as an ethnographer had taught me to recognize.

Continuing Research — With a Camcorder

I wrote to Edson Queiroz and arranged to spend two months during the summer of 1984 with him observing, describing and videotaping.

I also spent the spring of 1984 studying magic. Several well meaning colleagues and friends with whom I had discussed what I had seen José Carlos and Edson do warned me that, like other naive academics who had seen Philippine "psychic" surgeons, I might have been "taken in." What I thought I had witnessed, they suggested, might have been very clever sleight of hand, the kind of thing magicians do.[6]

In Recife, Edson proudly informed me that with the support of a group of followers he had recently created a foundation, the *Fundação Espírita Dr. Adolph Fritz*, which had rented a building where he now performed his mediumistic activities.

Although he had assured me that there would be no problem in my videotaping (if Dr. Fritz agreed) somehow I felt hesitant. Perhaps it was because the technology was still new to me and to the people I was observing. Furthermore, I had read and heard so much about people all over the world resisting the filming and/or videotaping of religious and other sacred rituals that I felt that I needed further assurance.

When I arrived at the Fundação Espírita Dr. Adolph Fritz that Wednesday evening, I was not the only one with a camcorder in my hand. When Dr. Fritz sent word that I could enter the inner room that had been set up with a hospital bed, I stood next to João Neves and a young man who was the "house photographer." Neither Edson, Dr. Fritz, nor anyone else paid much attention to my camcorder, although both asked me to explain to those present the research I was doing. Taking videos, it turned out, was a part of what went on at the treatment sessions at the Fundação Espírita Dr. Adolph Fritz.[7]

I should note that I did not go to Recife in 1984, or in later years, with the conscious intention to make a documentary about Edson Queiroz and Spiritist healing. That was to come later. My intent at the time was only to add a visual dimension to the research I was doing. My primary objective, I must admit, was to satisfy the doubts of those who expressed disbelief when I told them about what I was studying. In time, however, the videos were to become useful in other ways.

Although I had learned much from Edson and the others at the foundation in Recife, they had been unable to teach me what I felt I had to know about the Spiritist beliefs that informed the surgeries and other treatments I had witnessed. At the end of the summer of 1984 I was searching for someone who could teach me Spiritist philosophy and doctrine. Cicero Marcos Teixeira was to fill that role and become my mentor. Cicero at the time was, and still is, a professor in the School of Education at the Federal University in Porto Alegre. He also is a dedicated Spiritist who is very well respected among Spiritist intellectuals throughout Brazil. I returned to Porto Alegre in the summer of 1985 to study with him.

The videos I took while accompanying him became part of the body of research data I was collecting along with my field notes, interviews, published and unpublished manuscripts, etc.[8] From 1985 on I regularly added edited segments of tapes as a part of conference papers and lectures I presented on the subject. I also showed the videotapes to my students in classes I taught about Brazil.

Although John Gray and I had discussed doing a documentary on Spiritist healing from the time we first met, the project was put on hold when we were unable to obtain the funds needed to bring him and a crew to Brazil. We talked later about doing a documentary using the videos I had taken on my own. I learned then that although I had most of the video we would use and that I would write the script and most probably do the narration, we still would need several thousand dollars to pay for use of the equipment and the staff time at the Educational Communication Division of the university. In October of 1985 John and I submitted a proposal for an Undergraduate Teaching Improvement Grant to the University of Wisconsin System. We were awarded $6,012.00 in February of 1986. Work on the project was delayed, however, when I accepted a visiting appointment to teach at Barnard College and Columbia University for the 1986-87 academic year.[9]

The Making of THE RETURN OF DR. FRITZ

In viewing ethnographic films and documentaries for use in classes and as background to making THE RETURN OF DR. FRITZ and other documentaries, it appeared to me that most were primarily descriptive and provided only minimal background information and very little analysis. Even when ritual activities were shown, only the most cursory discussion of their meanings and the philosophies and belief systems on which they rested were presented to the audience. This was true especially for documentaries made for classroom use by scholars, who most often made the documentary after or while writing a book on the subject. The written materials, it appeared, would be read by an instructor who could find in them what was needed to explain the often strange and unusual behaviors and rituals shown to the students, or assigned to be read by the students prior to the showing of the visual materials. Documentaries made for general audiences might list references the viewer could consult independently for greater understanding. In brief, the documentaries told the story of a subject, but left to the printed word its in depth analysis.

When we were working on A BRAZILIAN PILGRIMAGE: THE 'FESTA DE SÃO FRANCISCO' IN CANINDÉ (1985) a few years earlier,[10] John Gray had suggested that I prepare some written materials, either for instructors who might show the documentary in their classes, or for the students to view it, to serve as background on the pilgrimage tradition and its role in Roman Catholic tradition and societies such as Brazil. Like most ethnographic documentaries, the video told a story and presented data unfamiliar to its audience. After thinking about it, I wondered why the necessary background could not be included as a part of the documentary? Why was there a need for supplemental written materials? Why couldn't whatever was necessary to understand what was being shown be included as part of the documentary itself?

Instead of writing a guide to accompany the 29 minute documentary, I prepared, and presented on camera (as Part I of what became a two part video documentary that runs 57 minutes) a history of the tradition, including its transference to Brazil (and the Americas), and an analysis of the world view that explained the establishment of the shrine to Saint Frances in Canindé and the beliefs about the role played by the saints held in contemporary Brazil. I felt that A BRAZILIAN PIL-GRIMAGE, and all documentaries, should stand on its (their) own without the viewer having to turn to another source (usually printed) to learn what is needed to know to understand what s/he is seeing. This was one of the goals I had when we made THE RETURN OF DR. FRITZ.

Writing ethnography and an anthropological monograph is generally understood to be a matter of making translations. An author begins, after introducing the subject, by describing some activity or activities usually unfamiliar to his (her) audience. The unstated assumption is that the audience will be literate North Americans, mostly scholars and their students, but also interested general readers.

After describing the exotic activities and events that in their newness and strangeness are difficult for the reader to understand, the author presents the meaning system and beliefs held by those who performed the activities in terms of which they make sense. S/he then translates, as part of what is usually considered analysis, images and meanings from the symbolic system of those about whom s/he is writing into images and ideas that can be understood by the reader. Once the translation from the exotic meaning system to that of the reader is made, the latter usually is able to comprehend the behaviors described in terms of the translated beliefs and understandings that give meaning to them. In the end the reader has a framework in terms of which the at first often strange behaviors now can be understood.

The anthropological monograph has a long history. It has been elaborated over much of the twentieth century into a specialized form of literature in which most of the data on peoples, their behaviors, and the meanings and understandings attributed to them in other parts of the world, are to be found. Students learn about peoples and cultures from them. Writing anthropological monographs, however, also has come to be the way scholars make their careers and reputations. The point is that *writing (not making films and/or videos)* is the form of presenting data, and of translating and analyzing it, that brings prestige and success to academics.

My intention here is not to question the venerable tradition of writing. But as anthropologists, the quintessential "outsiders," I wonder why, with the technology at our disposal, film and video cannot be used, not necessarily to replace the written word, but to do with words on screen what we do so well in print. That is, rather than using ethnographic film and video primarily to illustrate what we analyze and explain elsewhere in writing, to make what might be thought of as anthropological monographs on film or video that do not need anything supplemental in writing to be fully understandable.

As I worked on THE RETURN OF DR. FRITZ, therefore, I kept asking myself just how much in the way of background information, analysis and translation from one meaning system to another would it be necessary to include to enable the viewer to understand the story of Spiritist healing and surgery that was being told them without their having to go to a written text?

I tried to use the model of the anthropological monograph and modify it for the documentary I was making. The intended audience was the same as those who would read what I was writing about Spiritist healing. But, as I realized early on, there was something distinctive about the data I was presenting and the story I was telling. What I was presenting, however, al-

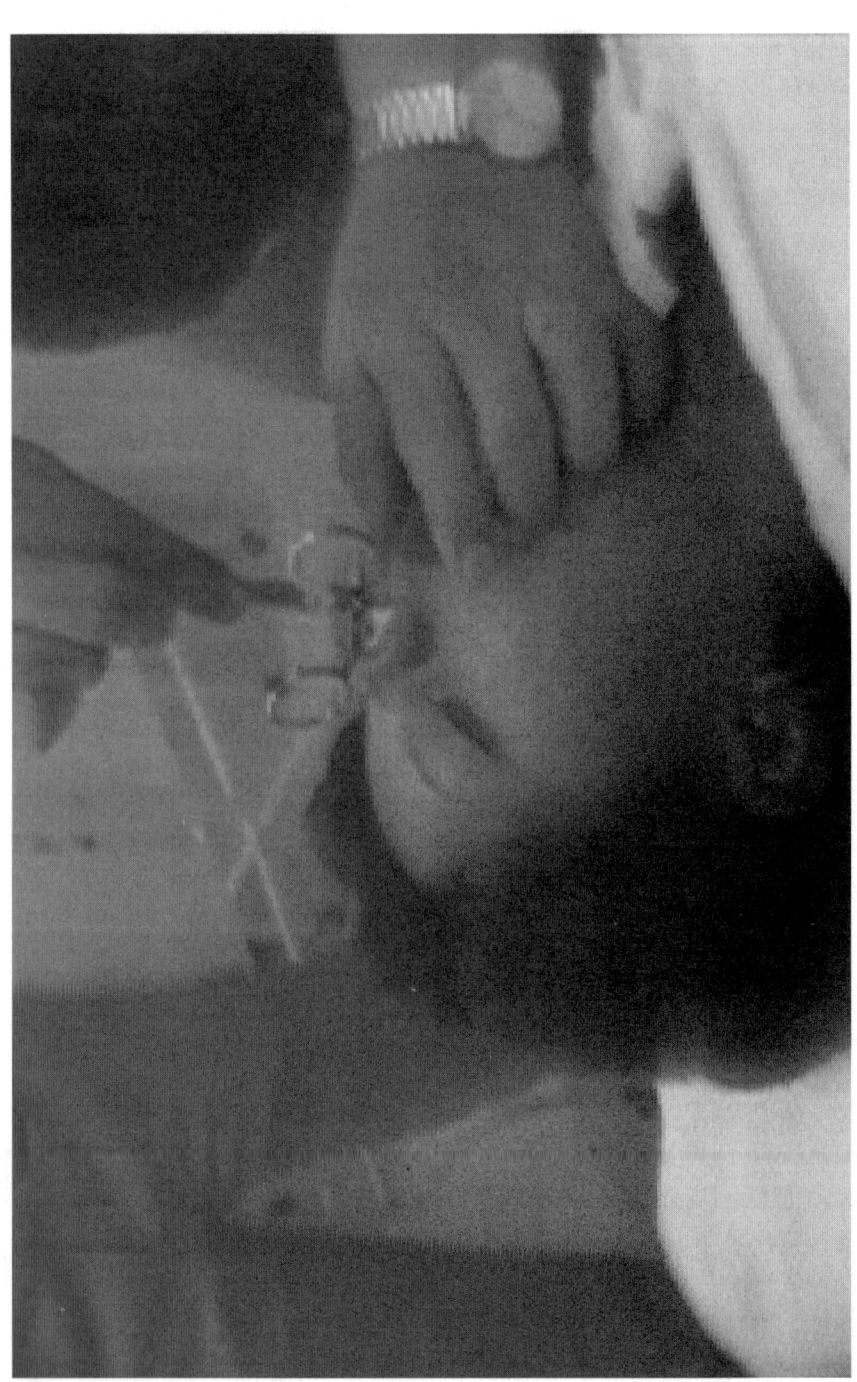

FIGURE 3: Dr. Fri͡z placing scissors into the sinus cavity of a patient (to de-materialize a growth).

FIGURE 4: Dr. Fritz placing needles in the throat (to de-materialize a growth).

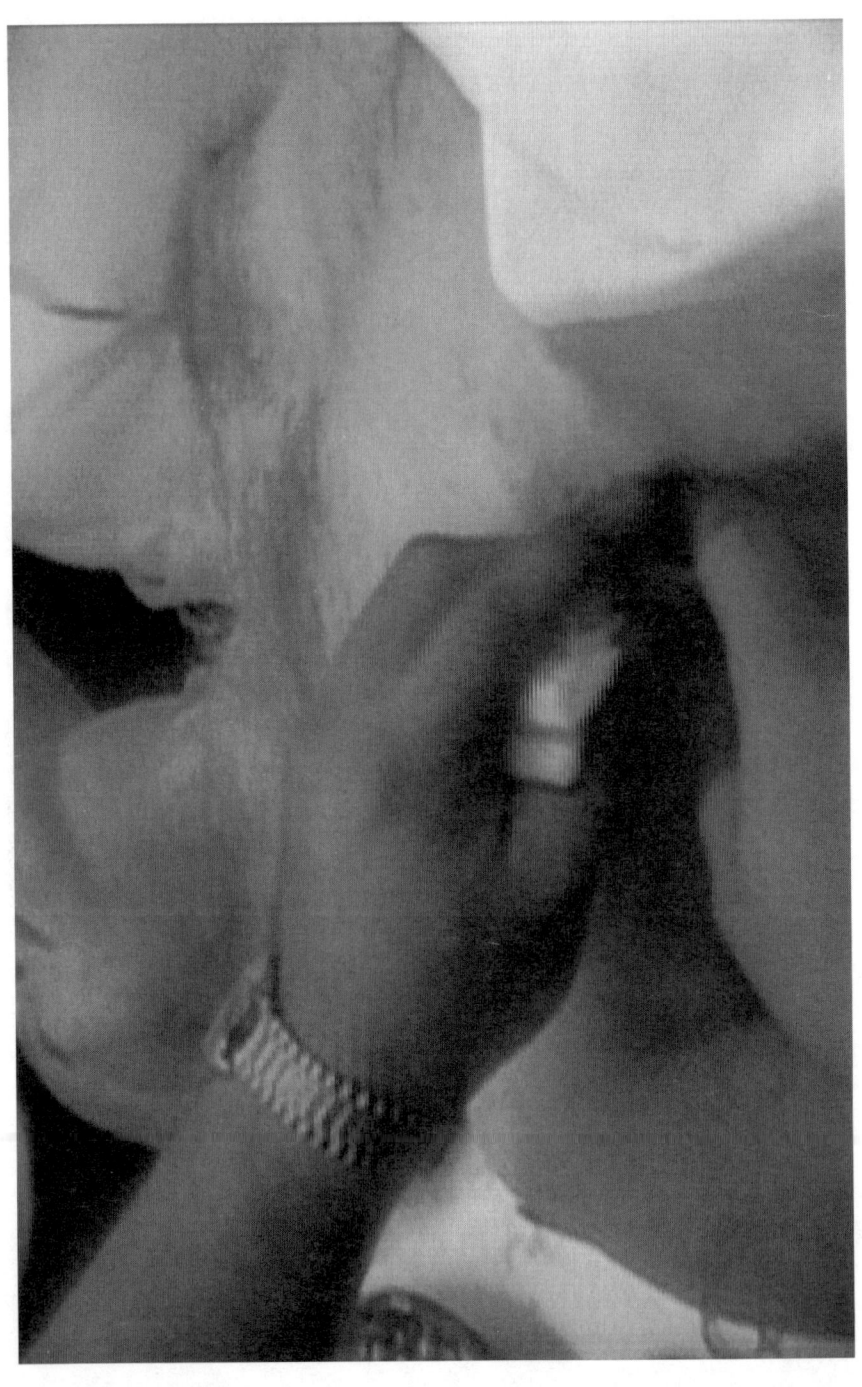

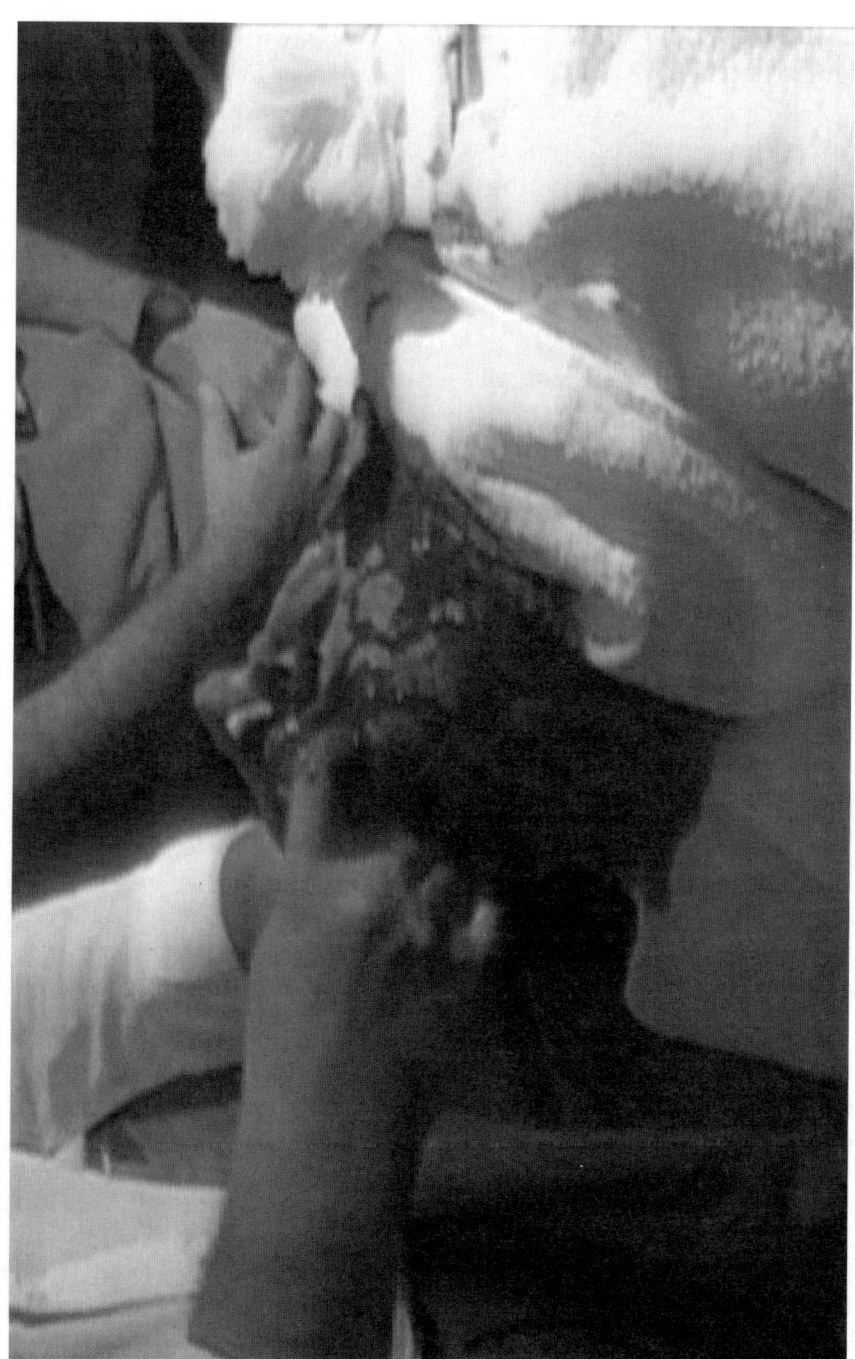

FIGURE 6: Dr. Fritz removing a lipoma with his fingers.

though shockingly different, was in part familiar to the intended audience.

Most North Americans are familiar with surgical procedures; however, most of those they have seen, especially on film or video, exclude actual cutting of patients and the flow of blood that invariably occurs. I, however, was planning to show Edson Queiroz (and/or Dr. Fritz) cutting into patients, some of whom would bleed. I accepted the fact that this might be distasteful to some of the viewers, but what was important about the surgeries I was presenting was that they were done without antisepsis and anesthesia.

To the average educated North American, the germ theory of disease is a part of their basic beliefs. To show them surgeries done in unsterile conditions, in which the person performing the surgery asks someone to spit into open wounds or otherwise introduce infection-causing contaminants, and then to see the recovering patient not suffering from complications, not only is unfamiliar, it challenges deeply held beliefs. To see patients cut into and claim to experience little or no pain casts further doubt on much that they take to be self evident. How these unusual outcomes to familiar events are to be explained had to be the central theme of the documentary.

After introducing the subject, and showing examples of surgeries, I turned to the question of explanations. I decided that first, on the model of the monograph, I should provide the viewer with a presentation of the belief system and world view that informs the work of healer-mediums like José Carlos and Edson Queiroz and gives one system of meaning that explains the surgeries they perform. The problem for me in writing a script and structuring the documentary then was to determine just how much of the vast and complex system of Spiritist belief was it necessary to present for the viewer to be able to understand this at times vaguely familiar,[11] but in fact very different view of the world.

I must admit that my thinking was primarily that of a teacher and scholar and not that of a filmmaker, although John Gray regularly instructed me in the differences. I wanted to provide on the screen as much of an understanding of the subject as I would in print. This, of course, meant that there would be long sections of the documentary devoted to Spiritist beliefs.

Were I in a position to do so I probably would have used the popular technique of asking experts, or practitioners questions the answers to which could be edited to present the system of beliefs in a coherent manner. But since I was making the documentary from videos I had taken previously, before I thought of making a documentary and before I had conceptualized what I wished to present in it, this was not possible. After some reflection, however, I decided that even had I the opportunity to go back to Brazil to do the interviews I would choose not to present Spiritism in the documentary in this way.

In writing a monograph there is ample space to present lengthy quotations of informant statements. This is one of the more valuable aspects of any monograph. However, the author then is able to comment on, add to and summarize the views presented in the quotations from informants.

The technique of presenting a belief system in the words of the "natives," even had I been able to return to Brazil and videotape additional interviews, and then translate and edit them, takes considerably more time than it would take for me to summarize the beliefs. It would take up more time than I felt we should devote to it in a documentary on Spiritist healing and surgery. We had decided to make a one hour video for use in the classroom. Presentation of the beliefs and world view of Spiritism was but one part of what we wished to present. The only way to do it in the 15 minutes I thought would be the maximum amount of time we could devote to it would be for me to summarize it in my own carefully chosen words.

It would have been nice to have been able to hire a trained professional to read what I wrote. But we did not have money to hire a narrator. So I read what I wrote myself as the camera filmed me sitting at a desk.

I wished at the time that I had been able to lay in visuals to illustrate what I was saying about Spiritist beliefs. Unfortunately, however, I did not have visual materials, other than a few diagrams and still photographs, that were illustrative of the aspects of the belief system I was summarizing. After all, where does one find pictures of spirits and their invisible world? What does one show to illustrate concepts like reincarnation and karma?

In retrospect I think that the way I presented Spiritist beliefs was a mistake. There is too much of me talking in the documentary. It is as if I were presenting a lecture in the middle of what otherwise is a documentary. I have received comments from students saying that what they referred to as my lecture detracted from their being able to follow the presentation. Although I might have done it better, I take solace in the fact that I was able to present for those interested in the subject enough of an understanding of Spiritism to enable them to comprehend how the surgeries and other procedures shown can be understood in terms that world view.

Spiritist beliefs, although interesting in their own right, however, are not sufficient as an explanation of the surgeries without antisepsis and anesthesia for the educated North Americans who are the intended viewers of the documentary. After concluding the summary of the belief system, therefore, I turned to aspects of what we think of as alternative medicine and science to summarize the state of my own investigations at the time. I reviewed some ongoing studies of hypnosis and trance states that provide a framework that complements what I had summarized of the view of the Spiritists and I used some of the videos already shown to show how some of the patients might have been induced into trance states by the setting in which they were placed. I also presented examples of individuals not exposed to the possible trance-inducing experiences feeling pain and/or bleeding profusely. This, however, injected even more of me into the documentary.

Conclusion

THE RETURN OF DR. FRITZ, as I have said, was not made to be, and therefore should not be considered, an ordinary documentary. The model I used to organize and to write it was not what I found in most documentaries made by anthropologists and other scholars. I did not want to make a film in which the viewer would have to go to a printed source for the information needed to understand what s/he is shown. The model I used to make the documentary was the anthropological monograph. I wanted to make a visual presentation that would show the extraordinary surgeries and other procedures I had witnessed and was investigating that are considered by some as scientific anomalies. I wanted to provide for the viewer the beliefs and world view of Brazilian Spiritists that informed the surgeries and other practices. Since these were foreign to the intended audience, I also wanted to include some materials on research within the framework of science and medicine that complemented rather than contradicted what the Spiritists believed.

My objective was not to take a position that represented a final statement on the subject. I was making a visual monograph on work that was still in progress. What I wished to show were some of the lines of direction the research was taking.

In this sense, THE RETURN OF DR. FRITZ was an experiment, with a form that has not really been developed. There is no such thing as a visual monograph. Anthropologists still present, examine, analyze and translate ethnographic data and its meanings almost exclusively in writing. They use film, video and other technologies to illustrate what they write about. Although there is no reason why the new visual presentations cannot include the detailed analysis traditionally presented in print, they do not. In making THE RETURN OF DR. FRITZ I tried to do so. Therefore, I should like it to be thought of as a documentary intended to stand as a self contained means of presenting, analyzing and explaining the subject.

ACKNOWLEDGEMENTS

This paper is dedicated to the spirit of Edson Queiroz who left this life in October, 1991, and to Mauricio Magalhães, the new medium through whom Dr. Fritz treats patients.

NOTES

1   I learned later, however, that he had much to hide, not from me as foreign scholar, but from anyone who might report what he was doing to the authorities. Although Spiritist healing functions in de facto complementarity with biomedicine and other healing systems in Brazil today (Milner 1980), the leaders of the formal organizations of the medical profession do all they can to eliminate these alternatives. The medical societies, for example, regularly turn to the judicial system to enforce obscure laws to stop Spiritist healer-mediums and practitioners of other alternative healing systems from treating patients (see Greenfield 1990).

2   When he departed, José Carlos left for us his home address and telephone number in the state of Goias. We have called and even searched for him in his home city, but have been unable to find him.

3   The Fulbright program would provide my transportation expenses, as they did for all award recipients when a Brazilian university provided food and lodging. I jumped at the invitation because at the time I was looking for help and possibly collaboration on a study of the descendants of European immigrants who had come to southern Brazil in the nineteenth and early twentieth centuries.

4   Before going to Porto Alegre I had met two Brazilian psychiatrists who lived in Fortaleza but had been away for several years in France completing Ph.D. Degrees in anthropology. They had returned home to

write their dissertations during the time I was living in Fortaleza. Their interest in and knowledge of traditional healing practices in northeastern Brazil and my fascination with Spiritist healing and other alternative medical forms led to a fast and long lasting friendship. I mention them because together we had our first exposure to the use of video technology in doing research. We attended and did participant observation at the 800th anniversary of the birth of Saint Francis of Assisi at a shrine to him in Canindé, a pilgrimage town some 90 kilometers to the south of Fortaleza (Greenfield 1990). Adalberto Barreto, who had been born there, told us that it was his understanding that large numbers of pilgrims came to the shrine during the festival to pay promises made to the Saint for helping them recover from illnesses. We went to see if the quest for healing really was one of the primary reasons believers made vows and whether their successful recovery had motivated them to repay their obligation by making the pilgrimage.

Adalberto arranged for a group of high school students to assist us in conducting a survey. His friend and colleague, Antônio Mourão Cavalcante, meanwhile arranged with a video cameraman, who worked for the local educational TV station, to accompany us and video the setting and interviews with the pilgrims.

None of us touched the camera but instead directed the cameraman to video what we thought was important. We had not edited the tapes by the time I was scheduled to leave Fortaleza for home. I took with me a copy of the original tapes on the understanding that when we each had the time we would edit our own documentary, mine in English and theirs in Portuguese.

Several years later, after doing my own videoing of Edson Queiroz, I made the A BRAZILIAN PILGRIMAGE with John Gray. My Brazilian colleagues and I were delighted when we eventually compared our completed documentaries to see the similarities in their orientations and in the materials we each had selected for inclusion.

5   While visiting my godson, the original José Carlos Ribeiro, in Rio de Janeiro before returning home I learned that a Brazilian television station in São Paulo had taped Edson Queiroz for a show they were doing. Through a friend I was able to meet the producer of the show who invited me to participate as a guest expert. I declined on the grounds that I had to return home before the show was scheduled for live broadcast, but I was able to obtain from her a two hour segment of the original videos. After obtaining appropriate permission, I later used that material to make SPIRITIST HEALING IN BRAZIL, my first effort at making a documentary on Spiritist healing.

6   They told me about James Randi, the magician, and the group devoted to debunking psychic surgeons and others they claimed, a priori, to be fakes and frauds. I read Randi's book, *Flim-Flam* (1983) and other materials. To guard against the possibility that he and his associates might be right, that José Carlos, Edson and the other healer-mediums I had observed were doing slight of hand and not actually cutting into their patients and removing real tissue as they claimed and it appeared to me they were, I studied magic with a magician.

When I returned from Brazil in the fall of 1984, after taking some 20 hours of videos of Edson doing surgeries and other procedures, my tutor in magic had arranged an invitation for my wife and me to attend an invocation, a convention of magicians. There I showed a group of several hundred practicing professionals some of the videos I had taken. They expressed no doubt that there was no sleight of hand and that Edson really was cutting into the flesh of the patients; but several of the magicians pointed out that the patients were in a state of trance, comparable to what they were able to achieve with members of an audience using hypnosis. This, of course, was to lead me into yet another area of study of which I at the time also knew very little. Several years later I took segments of the surgeries I videoed Edson doing with me to a meeting of the American Society for Clinical Hypnosis. My showing them to a small group of surgeons and doctors was to gain me an invitation to present a major address to the group a few years later. That, in turn, was to gain me permission to take their training program in hypnosis. Had it not been for the videos I probably would not have been directed to learn about hypnosis and eventually to be trained in its practice.

7   When Edson traveled that summer to other cities where he was invited to treat patients, I took videos copies of which became part of the archive of the *Fundação*.

8   These videos were later included in THE RETURN OF DR. FRITZ.

9   While in New York I presented several lectures on Spiritist healing at Barnard College and Columbia University that I illustrated with videos. I also illustrated with videos lectures I was invited to present at other universities in New York and nearby states. My audiences were fascinated by both the healing activities I described and showed and the belief system that informed them. I concluded, based on those experiences, that it would not be advisable to make a documentary that provided the audience with at least a basic understanding of the Spiritist view of the world.

10   Made from the copy of the videos Adalberto Barretto, Antônio Mourão Cavalcante and I directed the cameraman to take in Canindé

and paid for by another Undergraduate Teaching Improvement Grant
from the University of Wisconsin System.

11   There are many similarities between Brazilian Spiritism and "New
Age" beliefs and practices known to many educated Americans.

REFERENCES CITED

Fuller, John (1974). Arigo: Surgeon of the Rusty Knife. N.Y.: Crowell.
Greenfield, Sidney M. (1990). O Corpo Como uma Casca Descartável: O
    Médium Curador Espírita No Brasil e os Seus Críticos. IN Corpo de
    Saúde Corpo de Fé, Antonio Mourão Cavalcante, organizador.
    Fortaleza: Imprensa Universitária.
Greenfield, Sidney M. (1990). Turner and Anti-Turner in the Image of
    Christian Pilgrimage in Brazil. Anthropology of Consciousness 1:3-
    4: 1-8.
Greenfield, Sidney M. and Eleanor S. Greenfield (1983). Spiritist Healing in
    Brazil. Paper presented at the Eighth International Conference on
    the Social Sciences and Medicine, University of Stirling, Stirling,
    Scotland, 22-26 August.
Milner, Cary (1980). Gods, Saints and Spirits: A Comparative Analysis of
    Brazilian Urban Medical Systems. Unpublished Doctoral Disserta-
    tion, University of Toronto.
Randi, James (1982). Flim-Flam. Psychics, ESP, Unicorns and other Delu-
    sions. Buffalo, N.Y.: Prometheus Books.

VIDEOS CITED

A Brazilian Pilgrimage: The "Festa de São Francisco" in Canindé. 1985. A
    video in 2 parts produced by Sidney M. Greenfield and John B.
    Gray. Part I 28 minutes., Part II 29 minutes, color. Purchase $75.00
    (video); rental $25.00 from Center for Latin America, The Univer-
    sity of Wisconsin-Milwaukee, P.O. Box 413, Milwaukee, WI 53201
    (414-229-4401).
The Return of Dr. Fritz: Healing by the Spirits in Brazil. 1988. A video by
    Sidney M. Greenfield and John B. Gray. 58 minutes, color. Purchase
    $75.00 (video); rental $25.00 from the Center for Latin America, The
    University of Wisconsin-Milwaukee, P.O. Box 413, Milwaukee, WI
    53201 (414-229-4401).

from ANTHROPOLOGICAL FILM AND VIDEO IN THE 1990s
Jack R. Rollwagen (editor). Brockport, NY: The Institute, Inc.
© 1993, The Institute, Inc. All rights reserved. ISBN 0-9635206-1-X

Myth and Film

Robert Ascher
Department of Anthropology
Cornell University

ABSTRACT: Myth onto film is a series of cameraless animated films that render myths from traditional cultures. Three films are now in distribution: Cycle (1986); Bar Yohai (1988); and Blue (1991). The centrality of myth in culture is why it is a fitting subject for anthropological film. The films communicate myth across cultures in the dream mode common to both myth and film; in a mode, that is, that all people share by virtue of dreaming. The goal is to render a myth in such a way that it is comprehensible to us, but not thought to be of us. Making a film without a camera (direct or cameraless animation) described in detail, has been adapted to meet this goal. The approach described is a resolution to three issues: control over filmmaking; intrusion into other cultures; and traditional peoples making their own films.

Ideas are increasingly communicated through moving visual images. One can ignore this development. One can insist on the primacy of the written text. Particularly within a scholarly community, arguments can be made in support of writing as the legitimate form of communication. But to reach a wider community, writing is not enough. These were some of the thoughts in the back of my mind as I started to make films in the mid-1980s.

Between 1986 and the present, I completed three films and a fourth is in process. All share a common technique, theory, and approach to anthropological filmmaking (Ascher 1985; 1987; 1990). Each of them, however, draws on the mythology of a different people.

The first in the series, CYCLE (1986), is from a native Australian myth that is found in different versions across the continent. I use the Wulamba version. In outline, the myth is about a boy who runs away from home. As members of his family pursue him, he first climbs a tree and then rises into the sky where he becomes moon. Moon, when it wanes, falls into the sea and becomes nautilus shell; nautilus shell rises to become moon; moon falls back and becomes nautilus shell; rises again, falls again, and so on forever. This never-ending cycle symbolically relates people, the spiritual world, and the natural environment. The teller of the myth assumes that his hearers are already familiar with the outline. So he never retells the story in a strict sense; he alludes to it as he describes, for example, the clay-pan where the action takes place and where people collect lotus, the roots of which become evening star.

In BAR YOHAI (1988), the mythology is from THE ZOHAR, or BOOK OF SPLENDOR, a Kabbalah text. (Kabbalah means "tradition" in Hebrew.) In popular belief, Shimon Bar Yohai, a 2nd century visionary and mystic, was the author of THE ZOHAR. The book (seven volumes in English translation) contains conversations between Shimon Bar Yohai and his colleagues. They talk about nothing less than how the world got started and keeps on going. For example, in referring to the ten emanations that started the world, Bar Yohai or one of his colleagues might say "the tree" or "the candelabra." And in speaking about any one of the emanations, one of several alternate terms or a color might be used. The uninitiated reader will miss the point of the conversations. This is so because all is said in symbolic language. Still, thousands of people read THE ZOHAR and even larger numbers of people visit the tomb of

Bar Yohai in Meron, Israel, where annual celebrations are held in his honor.

BLUE (1991) is from Tlingit mythology. The Tlingit are native Americans who live in Southeastern Alaska. In just about every known culture, there is a myth in which a hero ventures forth, discovers something of great value, and then returns home with his gift. In the Tlingit version of the myth, the heroes are four brothers who go in search of the color blue. They set out on a sea journey encountering various creatures along the way. Taking shelter in a cave, they find the material out of which they can make blue. Having found and taken something so valuable, the brothers start on the return journey. On the way home, a storm develops and one of the brothers drowns. But the three surviving brothers manage to complete the journey safely and return home with the gift of blue.

CYCLE, BAR YOHAI and BLUE are about ideas held by other peoples. To visually render these ideas, I use a technique called direct or cameraless animation. This technique has been known for more than a hundred years and actually preceded live action filming by at least a decade. During the 1920s and 1930s, artists in Europe who were interested in movement, light, and the relationship between music and painting, turned to direct animation. In their films, several of which are still in distribution, one sees, for example, figures including dots, circles, and squares, growing and diminishing in size and moving in different directions across the screen. The technique flourished briefly once again in the 1950s. As in the earlier periods, cameraless animation was used mostly to make abstract, painterly, experimental, non-narrative films (Russet and Starr 1988).

As the modifiers "direct" and "cameraless" indicate, no camera is used in this kind of animation. In making a film, I sit at a table that is equipped with a light box and a magnifying glass. As I move clear 35 mm. film stock across the light box, I mark the frames, and then draw directly on the clear film, one frame at a time. There are 24 frames in each second of film. Thus, a minute of film requires 1,440 individual drawings, each one of which is not much larger than a postage stamp. BLUE, for example, is six minutes long and needed more than 8,500 drawings. All of my films are in color. The colors are applied with anything that works; pen and ink are used, but so are paper towel rolls, sponges, brushes, cloths, spray bottles, Q-tips, and my fingers. The inks chosen must permit the passage of light. They must also be composed of chemicals that adhere to the celluloid surface of the film. Using a grid placed under the film as a guide, figures are drawn and changed very slightly from frame to frame, or frames to frames, depending on the speed and direction of the motion desired. I draw directly onto the film typical filmic devices such as the wipes and fades often seen in live action film where there are, for example, changes of scene. When the film is complete, I take it to a lab where the 35 mm. original is reduced to a 16 mm. negative and prints are made. All aspects of the technique are undergoing experiment and change. For example, each of the films has been made with different inks and control over movement was worked out differently in each.

The choice of myth for the subject of my films is based on several considerations. Foremost among these is its centrality in traditional cultures. From the outsiders point of view, the importance of myth is marked by the attention paid to it in Euro-American analysis (Cohen 1969). Myth has been seen as a kind of a map that directs and guides people through everything from property rights to behavior toward the gods. It has also been viewed as an expression of the unconscious. (The interpretation of what is being expressed depends largely on the analyst.) For others, myths are problem sets in which irresolvable issues are worked out. Still others see myth as the glue which binds the people of a community. It would be easy to add other explanations of the power of myth. No one of them is sufficient. All have some truth; taken together, they complement rather than replace each other. The point is that myth is too rich to be subsumed under any of the Western attempts to account for it.

Another reason why I work with myth arises from a special relationship between myth and film. Their in common connection is dream; that is, they are related to each other through dream. At the heart of the myth-dream relationship is the setting aside of everyday logic. What seems absurd in the "ordinary" world becomes perfectly reasonable in myth and dream (Fromm 1951). For example, the boy in CYCLE is first transformed into moon and then into nautilus shell. Such sequences happen all the time in dreams. The film-dream relationship is also close (Langer 1953:411-415). On the film screen and on the dream screen (and in the words of myth), time moves freely back and forth and there are unconstrained leaps in locale. The spectator at a film sits in a darkened space in a state somewhere between sleep and wakefulness, and due to the projection mechanism, is in total darkness for one third of the show.

The relationship, through dream, of myth and film, while interesting, might be considered idle theorizing if it were not for an important finding. Studies in many diverse cultures have shown that people, regardless of culture, dream in similar ways (e.g. D'Andrade 1961; Spaulding 1981; Hall and Van de Castle 1966). Whatever the cultural and individual variation, dreaming, the structure of dreams, and interest in dreams are universal. Further, what Freud called typical dreams (for example, soaring through the air [as in the penultimate scene in BAR YOHAI]) occur in cultures widely separated in time, space, and tradition where they are often given similar interpretations.

Now, if we put together the myth/dream/film relationship with the human universals of dream, the possibility of conveying a myth across cultures through the medium of film becomes a reasonable expectation. In my work, I attempt to render a myth on film and communicate it from one culture to another in the dream mode of myth and film; in a mode, that is, that all of us share by virtue of dreaming. The anthropological goal is the fundamental one of cultural translation: to render a myth from another culture in such a way that it is comprehensible to us, but not thought to be of us.

My use of the direct, cameraless animation technique follows from the translation goal. With direct animation, I can realize comprehension without co-option. A technique once used to make abstract films has now been adapted to visualize the quasi-narrative otherworldly logic of myth. Direct animation, as I have adapted it, has recognizable figures (for example, boats and people and trees) but at the same time, my films do not "look like" other films. The wobbling figures on the screen look organic. The overall effect is spacelessness and everywhereness. It is a disservice to peoples' myths to believe that knowing the story line is to know the myth. In BAR YOHAI, there is no plot at all; in CYCLE only the barest outline of a story is indicated in keeping with the way the myth is told; in BLUE, the story is more evident in the film because it is obvious in the myth and important to it. I hope to provide an opportunity for the film viewer to step outside the ordinary and experience another cultures' myth in a way that is closer to deep appreciation than it is to facile pseudounderstanding.

A major theory of myth holds that its power rests in language. Myth is a form of poetry. I use this notion in composing soundtracks. The visual imagery in my films is accompanied by the verbal imagery in the original language of the myth. In CYCLE, the voice heard, speaking in Wulamba, recalls central figures in Wulamba mythology by using poetic devices and repeating key words: lotus, evening star, moon, and the name of the clay-pan where past and future events are played out in the present. The soundtrack in BAR YOHAI is a song, in Hebrew, sung in praise of Shimon Bar Yohai. During the first minute of BLUE, a woman's voice is heard speaking in Tlingit;

the remaining five minutes of the film proceed in silence. None of the voices narrate a myth. The verbal imagery heard is there to complement the visual imagery seen.

In preparing to make a film, I go deeply into the literature about a people and read extensively in their mythology. This takes at least a year and usually more. In preparing for BAR YOHAI, I had the added advantage of being able to participate in the rituals associated with honoring Shimon Bar Yohai. Making a direct, cameraless film takes a long time. On a good day, that is, on a day when everything goes right, I can complete half a second of film. It is easy to see that drawing a six minute film, even if one worked every day, and if every day was a good day, takes about a year. Then there is the sound track to make and the final lab work must be supervised. In the best of circumstances, the time for preparation, drawing, sound and lab work comes to almost three years to complete a six minute film. Actually, it takes a little longer.

Clearly, visualizing a myth on film using my approach requires thought, other kinds of concentrated activity, and a lot of time. Why persist in doing it this way? Theoretical and aesthetic satisfaction is a large part of the answer. The other part is that making films as I do resolves, for me at least, certain crucial concerns.

The first is control. Most filmmaking is a group effort. We insist upon naming the director of a film as its author even in the knowledge that a sound person, an editor, a cinematographer and often a writer, among others, share control through heavily influencing the final version of a film. By contract, I exercise near total control over my films. This applies even to lab work. An optical printer (basically, a camera on one side of a platform and a projector on the other) is required to reduce my 35 mm. original to a 16 mm. negative. This machine is capable of many additional cinemagraphic tricks. I request only a negative that is the truest possible rendering of my original. In my view, anthropologists and other scholars should have as much control over the films they make as they insist upon having (or should insist upon having) when it comes to the words that are published under their names. The direct, cameraless technique brings me close to this ideal.

Another of my concerns is intrusion. In the worst situation, a filmmaker and crew from a dominant culture arrive somewhere in the world with all the trappings of filmmaking (cameras, generator, sound equipment, etc.). They shoot, pack up, and go home. At home, the film is completed and shown to audiences remote from the real, living people who are now fixed on celluloid or video tape. We may recognize this extreme form of intrusion as disruptive and perhaps exploitative. But even the most carefully planned and executed live action filming in another culture is in some way intrusive. I may take missteps in my interpretation of myths, but sitting alone in front of my light box involves zero intrusion into the lives of others.

Control over one's work and the problems associated with intrusion have been apparent for several years. The final concern I raise is more recent and will have consequences well into the 21st century. Some of the peoples who have been the subjects for anthropological films throughout the 20th century now have the knowledge and equipment to make their own films. Soon enough, people in every culture will have the same. What does this mean for the anthropological filmmaker? It is perhaps too early to answer this question. In any case, the answer will be different for live action film-makers and others, such as myself, who work in what is called the ethnographic present. A staggering number of myths are now history. More than that, the myths from many cultures have become a part of world literature. I will continue to make myths on film drawing upon this rich, exciting, and lasting legacy.

REFERENCES CITED

Ascher, Robert (1981). Myth Onto Film. Anthropologia Visualis 1:37-40.
Ascher, Robert (1987). Cycle: A Cameraless Animated Film. Commission on Visual Anthropology Newsletter May: 27-28.
Ascher, Robert (1990). Approach, Theory, and Technique in the Making of Bar Yohai. Visual Anthropology 3: 111-119.0
Cohen, Percy S. (1969). Theories of Myth. Man 4 (2): 337-353.
D'Andrade, Roy G. (1961). Anthropological Studies of Dreams. IN Psychological Anthropology, Francis L. K. Hsu (ed.). Homewood: Dorsey Press, pp. 296-332.
Fromm, Erich (1951). The Forgotten Language. New York: Rinehart.
Hall, Calvin S., and Robert L. Van de Castle (1966). The Content Analysis of Dreams. New York: Appleton-Century Crofts.
Russett, Robert, and Cecile Starr (1988). Experimental Animation. New York: Da Capo.
Spaulding, John (1981). The Dream in Other Cultures: Anthropolical Studies of Dreams and Dreaming. Dreamworks 1 (4): 330-342.

FILMS CITED

Cycle. 1986. A film by Robert Ascher. 4 minutes, color. Purchase $110, rental $20 from Cornell University Audio-Visual Center, Research Park, Ithaca, NY 14850 (607/255-2091). Teaching Guide available. Rental only $20 from Cecile Starr, 50 West 96th St., New York, NY 10025 (212/749-1250).
Bar Yohai. 1988. A film by Robert Ascher. 6 minutes, color. Purchase $80, rental $20 from Cornell University Audio-Visual Center, Research Park, Ithaca, NY 14850 (607/255-2091). Rental only $20 from Cecile Starr, 50 West 96th St., New York, NY 10025 (212/749-1250). Rental only $20 from Canyon Cinema, 2325 3rd St., Suite 338, San Francisco CA 94107 (415/626-2255).
Blue. 1991. A film by Robert Ascher. 6 minutes, color. Purchase $80, rental $20 from Cornell University Audio-Visual Center, Research Park, Ithaca, NY 14850 (607/255-2091). Rental only $20 from Cecile Starr, 50 West 96th St., New York, NY 10025 (212/749-1250). Rental only $20 from Canyon Cinema, 2325 3rd St., Suite 338, San Francisco, CA 94107 (415/626-2255).

from ANTHROPOLOGICAL FILM AND VIDEO IN THE 1990s
Jack R. Rollwagen (editor). Brockport, NY: The Institute, Inc.

"Why We Cried To See Him Again": Indonesian Villagers' Responses To The Filmic Disruption Of Time

Janet Hoskins
Department of Anthropology
University of Southern California

ABSTRACT: Two films of Sumba nese rituals were shown to the people who had participated in the events, and both provoked intense displays of emotion, ranging from rage and nervous laughter to hysterical mourning. I describe these responses and interpret them in relation to problems of cinematic realism, representation, the power of filmic images, and anthropological theories about the emotional processes which are played out in ritual. Ethnographic film, like documentary (Sobchack 1984), is shown to be a powerful medium for inscribing ethical space and defining the openness or closure of an emotional process over time.

> Sometimes bodily experience exceeds intellectual un-
> derstanding. Cognitive processing and bodily experience
> produce contradictory responses that disorient the mind.
> Visceral reactions occur that are uncontained by the de-
> scriptive or explanatory gird utilized by a given film. To a
> large extent, such reactions appear as anomaly (they nor-
> mally fall within the anthropological unconscious). My
> contention, however, is that such responses indicate a
> possible direction forward, toward...a meeting ground for
> ethnographic film and those cross-cultural journeys that
> "others" have already begun (Nichols 1991: 37).

Film presents a record of visual images which plays havoc
with the flow of time. In filmic representations, events are
foreshortened, sequences are shifted around and edited out,
"natural" time is torn apart, and (because of the vivid illusory
realism of the celluloid image) the past violently invades the
present. Film seems to bring persons and events alive in a direct
and compelling manner, and can thus have a tremendous
emotional impact, especially when those who are now dead are
filmically "brought to life." The power of a documentary or
ethnographic film to play havoc with the line between the
living and the dead is familiar to us from our own society, but
may have lost much of its earlier shock value. In the intense
media activity of modern life, we may be too inundated with
films and videos of dead forebears to be moved in the same way
by the recognition of the face of someone who is now dead.

In this paper, I explore the feelings of discomfort, shock and
sorrow expressed by villagers on the Eastern Indonesian island
of Sumba when we showed them footage of rituals in which
they had participated. Interested in how the relation of representation and reality might be defined in another culture, we
did not go to Sumba expecting to explore issues relating to the
filmic disruption of time or the emotional responses to images
of dead persons. This focus was forced upon us by the intense
reactions of the local audience to ritual sequences filmed in

FIGURE 1: Filmmaker Laura Whitney and sound man during the filming of FEAST IN DREAM VILLAGE in Sumba, 1986.

1986 and 1988. I argue here that the most problematic element of the films we shot on Sumba *for the Sumbanese* was not their resemblance to real events or any "animistic" perception of soul loss, but the disruption of an emotional process of mourning for the dead. Although many people who came to see our village screenings had never seen a film before, they had no problems understanding the medium as a way of "preserving the shadows of the living" and projecting them again through a technical process of capturing images on celluloid. But they were disturbed and moved at seeing the faces of those who had died "come alive" again on the screen. I argue that this response was due to the importance Sumbanese give to the temporal process of mourning the dead, and the significance of the line between the living and dead among practitioners of a traditional religion centered on forms of ancestor worship.

As an anthropologist and filmmaker with an interest in cultural perceptions of time, I explore these issues here with particular relevance to the perception and reception of ethnographic films by the "subjects." My discussion also calls into question common assumptions about cinematic realism and the "visual translation" of culture through ethnographic filmmaking. The Kodi people of Sumba have complex and varied notions of time which I have explored elsewhere at greater length (Hoskins 1993), so here I can only touch on those aspects which bear directly on our use of film as a research tool.

Studies of emotional responses to ethnographic films have been confined mainly to the feelings of disorientation, disgust, or awe that Western students may show when confronted with the cinematic experience of other cultures (Tambs-Lyche and Waage 1989. 31-33, Martinez 1990) We know that films like THE NUER have provoked sensations of nausea, hysteria, or, alternatively, boredom and an intense refusal to identify in Norwegian and American students. But we know relatively little about how the *subjects* of such films might respond to the cinematic images constructed from their own lives. Indeed, this ignorance is largely because few ethnographic subjects have ever been given the occasion to see the films which have been made about them, or to offer any form of response.[1]

Hoping to rectify this situation at least partially, in 1988 Laura Whitney and I set off to study ritual communication on the Indonesian island of Sumba, using both film and video tape. The first stage of our project was making a "visual record" of a number of ceremonial events (feasts, funerals, calendrical rites) and then showing this footage to local people. We wanted to ask a wide range of participants and observers all the questions that could *not* be asked in midst of ritual performance: How much of the speeches did they understand? How effective was the speaker? What "worked" in the ritual and what seemed not to? What captured their attention the most? When were they bored or distracted? Our intention was to use visual materials to measure the success of ritual as communication. We wanted to test a layman's awareness of protocol and spirit etiquette, check whether there were significant differences between men and women, older people and younger people, as spectators, and probe the consequences of the semantic obscurity of ritual speech. The emphasis was on resolving cognitive problems concerning the sociology of knowledge and its distribution outside of an inner circle of specialists.

What we found, much to our surprise, was that Sumbanese villagers were mainly interested in scenes of death: the thunderous outburst from an important priest who had recently died, the scenes of mourning during a four day wake inside an ancestral house, and the protracted killing of buffalo in ritual sacrifice. The interest in sacrifice stemmed from its significance in divination, and its linkage of violence, identification and interpretation has been explored in another paper (Hoskins 1993). The scenes where people who had been mourned and buried re-appeared on the screen summoned an intense and even frightening concentration that is the subject of this article.

FIGURE 2: Jane Hoskins and Laura Whitney interviewing participants after they had watched scenes of the dead

"What It Meant to See His Face": Initial Reactions

The people of Mangganipi, a small garden community whose name means "Dream Village," were very happy to see us return to shown them the film we had made of a feast held there in 1986. Hundreds of them flocked to sit in front of the tiny video monitor we had brought to the home of our former hosts. We asked a priest who had officiated at the feast to assemble as many of the participants as possible, so they could be given places to sit closest to the monitor, and would, we hoped, be available for interviews afterward. In the confusion of setting up our equipment and beginning to show it to the crowd, we did not at first realize that one of the most important characters in the earlier film (FEAST IN DREAM VILLAGE [1989]) was missing.

When the face of Piro Pawali, the respected orator who led the rite in 1986, appeared on the screen, a hush fell on the crowd. Several small children started to scream excitedly, and our host angrily told them to be quiet.

"Don't you have any respect for the dead?" he shouted. "Let us hear his voice again, let us feel what it means to see his face!"

The children became still, and everyone sat in silence to watch the scenes which followed. Piro Pawali pronounced the opening invocations as he held his spear high in the central plaza of the village, then was replaced by shots of dancers and other orators who spoke during the first two nights, summoning spirits of the dead to return to the village and join the community of the living for the feast. On the morning of the third day, the host tried to make a small change in the order of events, and Piro Pawali flew into a rage.

"How dare you speak like that to me?" he shouted, "You're just trying to push me aside. Don't you realize that *I* am the one who sets the stages of this ritual, and *I* am the one who decides if they get changed?"

He angrily prepared to shake off the cloth mantle that he had been given to perform as the head priest, storming off to sit on the sidelines and wait for others to present their apologies. A few minutes later, the film contained glimpses of negotiations between the hosts and singers to perform a special ceremony to ask his forgiveness. At the sacrifice which followed, an unusually large share of meat was presented to him, and he stood, with a certain haughty dignity, in the center of the village to receive it. As if to express his distaste for the insult to his authority, he put on a pair of dark glasses and told the host that was feeling ill and could not attend the closing ceremony. Hiding his rage behind this mask of modern cool, he turned to stare into the camera, and this was the last image of him in the film.

When we finished showing all of the footage, we interviewed the surviving priests, host and other participants. We asked them to reflect again on the reasons for Piro Pawali's anger, and said it had often confused American audiences who did not understand why he had become so upset by a slight shift in the temporal sequence. "Piro Pawali was a great orator, but he did not get along with the singer at that feast," our host explained. "He had been complaining all night that the singer did not respond quickly enough, starting to sing when he finished speaking."

Piro Pawali died just two weeks before our arrival, and many people in the village had just recently returned from the funeral when we arrived. Before we left, they asked us if we would be willing to show the footage again to members of his family who had not been able to come on that occasion, and who could explain better the reasons for his actions in 1986.

FIGURE 3: The priest who was second in command at the Feast in Dream Village makes a point about the respect that is due to the dead. (1988)

The dramatic tensions of that first showing should perhaps have prepared us for what was to happen the second time we took film footage to a village, when we showed the people of Malandi scenes from the funeral of Ra Honggoro. Our cameras moved into the house of mourning where the corpse lay, attended by his widow and daughters, singing and wailing funeral dirges to express their sorrow. Ra Honggoro, an ever present ghost during the mourning in the house, had moved on to the status of ancestor just three months before. The return of the image of his corpse caused one of his daughters to begin sobbing profusely, shaking and swearing that she could almost smell the rotting body still hidden under the textile shroud, joining her own recorded voice in new wails and dirges. With a contagious intensity, soon dozens of the spectators were also crying and moaning, tearing at their clothes and professing to re-experience the funeral itself in its full sensory dimensions.

We were surprized and somewhat distressed at this reaction, although people later assured us afterwards that seeing these images had "lifted their hearts" and made them feel much better. All were scenes of intense emotional expression at the time of the original performance, but when they were re-examined in retrospect through visual research documents, they proved in some ways even *more* disturbing to the participants.

The complex reasons for their responses are linked, I argue, to the ways in which emotional expression in Sumba is structured in stages, and the temporal dimension within that process which was upset by the use of film and video in our research. The most disturbing part of the retrospective reviewing of these events for those we interviewed was how the filmic disruption of temporal sequence affected the ritualized stages of emotional adjustment and reconciliation which had already begun. Piro Pawali, the head priest who was so angry at the Mangganipi feast, had died just a few weeks before our return to his village. His absence was the crucial difference which prompted such a troubled re-evaluation of his volatile character. The complex that we inadvertently discovered through these interviews was centered on the dynamics of affect, the continuum of emotional responses held in a precarious balance by notions of reciprocity and obligation, and the importance of *ordering* time throughout these ritual sequences, which our filming had unintentionally violated.

The loss of an important religious leader in one case, and a beloved father and husband in another, was made particularly intense by its filmic evocation. The sensation some spectators reported of hearing sounds and starting to smell and feel other parts of the mourning experience must be interpreted in relation to the local belief that death is a gradual process, in which the spirit of the dead person hovers in the house for eight nights after death, eating with family members and only slowly coming to realize that a more definitive separation is imminent. The process that is described for the deceased in the ritual sequence must also be followed by the bereaved, but the vividness of the film record seemed temporarily to reverse time and plunge participants back into an earlier phase of mourning. To understand how these particular responses came about, I will first examine local constructions of emotion and the proper context for the display of feelings of grief.

The Cultural Construction of the Emotions in Kodi

Although Indonesia as a whole has been described as a culture area which favors emotional control and a generally reserved tenor of equanimity (Hollan 1988), the peoples of West Sumba are known for their assertiveness, daring and outspokenness. It is perhaps no coincidence that they are also defiant traditionalists in an age of modernization and conversion. Seventy-five percent of the population surveyed in the 1980 government census professed to follow the religion of their ancestors (*agama marapu*), making Sumba then the only island in Indonesia to have maintained a pagan majority. An egalitarian, competitive ethos prevails in the region of Kodi, where a population of 50,000 pastoral agriculturalists subsists on mixed gardens of rice and corn, and participates in a prestige economy based on the raising, exchange and slaughter of horses and buffalo. Personal reputation is established and enhanced by the sponsoring of large feasts, the building of lineage cult houses, and the dragging of huge stone slabs to construct megalithic tombs.

Kodi people describe their culture as obsessed with the achievement of renown: "seeking to build a name" (*kandaba ngara*) which will be remembered long after death. A system of titles, beginning as honorific "names" for a man's horse and dog, eventually culminates in the posthumous appellation of *rato*, or "great leader," to designate a man whose name must always be repeated in ceremonial invocations in his ancestral village. Such leaders are made and not born. Although certain ritual prerogatives and offices are hereditary, the titles require more than simple wealth or an impressive genealogy. A leader must become a ritual impressario, able to summon the labor, cooperation and economic contributions of hundreds of others. He must be prepared to defend himself against rivals, assure creditors that he will eventually reciprocate their gifts, and play the "great man" to the crowds.

At the same time, the sponsor of a feast, so active in organizing it beforehand, does not speak on his own behalf in a formal ritual context. Here he must be represented by ritual intermediaries, the priests, who "speak with his lips and pronounce with his tongue" in the phrases of traditional couplets. One of the most important attributes of Sumbanese leadership is the ability to summon supporters and delegate tasks. Individual success must be built on the foundation of kinship networks and and the credits and debts of exchange relationships. Social skills of establishing dependents and displaying

FIGURE 4: Members of the family gathered in front of a tiny battery powered video monitor to watch footage of the funeral.

generosity must be combined with the self-aggrandizement of feasting to allow a prominent man to follow the pathway to immortality.

Anger is an emotion which is given a moral dimension in the context of Kodi ritual performances. Justifiable anger stems from a sense of grievance, which assumes that the other "ought" to act differently (Tarvis 1982), and if someone has not fulfilled his role appropriately (as either a leader or a follower) it is considered legitimate for others to seek redress through public protest. Grief is also a "public" emotion, in that it is assigned its proper place and time for expression in the context of funerals, where it is assumed to be most intense at the moment that the body is moved from inside the house to the procession which leads to the grave. While anger could be said to be used as a means to seek redress, grief seeks reincorporation. The bereaved person is initially angry at the deceased for deserting the family. Once he or she has accepted that the desertion is final, grief takes the place of anger, and the ritual sequences begins to reincorporate the deceased, not as a man or woman but as an ancestor. Anger assumes that reciprocal expectations are shared; grief proceeds from the realization that this can no longer be so. Thus Kodi "emotion talk" (Heelas 1986) sorts the two forms of intense response that we observed into moments on a temporal continuum, and sees one as the preamble to the other.

Interview Data on these Responses

In our study of the audience perception of ritual, we spoke to different categories of people, "positioned subjects" (Rosaldo 1984) with varied responses to both the ritual itself and the screening of a filmed record.

One daughter reflected on her outburst on seeing the scenes from the funeral in these terms:

> When I saw my father's body lying inside the house again, with all of us gathered around him, it was as if he were still there: I could smell the decaying flesh as I heard the dirges, I could feel the textiles under my hands as I caressed the mortuary bundle. We say that the dead person doesn't realize he is dead until four days after the burial. When I saw the film, I was back on the veranda with him, holding his body in my hands and whispering to his ghost who could still hear my voice.

The illusion of immediacy evoked complex reactions in other spectators, not always in the same way. A second daughter re-lived earlier feelings of rage at her father's desertion:

> I was angry when I saw his body there. It made me remember how we felt when we got the news of his death. He should not have left us like that, when we still needed him to finish so many things. My marriage negotiations were left hanging. So much that he had promised to do may never be finished. Our songs are about the helplessness we feel faced with his death. If he had been killed by another person, and not by a *marapu* (ancestral sanction), we could take revenge. But now he is shattered like a glass jar, and can never be mended again. I thought I had accepted it by now, but the film made me return to this rage.

Several of his daughters and daughter-in-law sobbed profusely at the screening, but those with the most important structural roles in the ceremony, his widow and mother, did not do so. The widow explained her reaction in terms of the responsibilities she had to bear during and after the ceremony:

> My husband is already buried, and I have to go on, taking care of all these children: six from my sister (his first wife, who died ten years ago) and five of my own. We did the proper ceremonies to separate his ghost from the house, so it should not return. I am trying to build a new life for us, to think of our future. The film showed he was an

important man, a man of consequence. Many people came
to his funeral, and cried. But that time is past, and he will
not return to speak with us unless he is angry himself, if he
is unhappy with his tomb or the ceremony. We need to go
on. I felt far away from these events when I watched them,
though it was only four months ago. I have had to change
my life so much since then.

His mother expressed similar feelings, noting the ritual
constraints on her during the rite and their effect:

This is the third child that I have buried. Two others
died when they were young. Ra Honggoro was a man who
already had achieved a lot. He had held feasts, he had a
name, a stone tomb, two wives and eleven children. He
hadn't finished it all when he died, but he had earned the
respect of others. I was the official mourner at the funeral,
and observed taboos on leaving the house, bathing and
speaking. My spirit was with my son then. But now we
must separate.

Both women stressed that at this funeral, they were mourning a loss which repeated other, earlier experiences, which fit
into a pattern. Each had played a clearly specified role in the
funeral sequence. The mother's role as mourner structured her
grief into a series of specific restrictions for four days after the
burial, miming the state of the corpse which still symbolically
present in the house. After she fed his soul a final meal on the
fourth day, the final prayer of farewell was spoken. By the time
they watched the events on film, both the bereaved wife and
mother had gone beyond the most intense stage of mourning.
If they were not as deeply affected, it seems that it was in part
because they were not moved back into the earlier time frame.
They were not re-immersed, as the daughters were, in an
illusion of shared time, shared sensations, even a tactile fantasy
of closeness to the body.

Reported feelings of distance from the recently deceased also occurred with the footage of the priest's quarrel in FEAST IN DREAM VILLAGE. Piro Pawali's recent death and burial made an already imposing figure into an even more dangerous invisible presence in the village. In effect, *marapu* belief posits that certain persons become more important after their deaths. So the commentary of our host, the priest who was second in command and his son who performed the sacrifices, emphasized their understanding of his earlier rage and its present repercussions:

> Piro Pawali was angry because he said people did not respect him enough, and did not respect his position. He was exhausted from speaking to the deities all night long, and he was right to insist that the payment not be delayed to suit outside guests. We were sorry he did not return for the closing ceremonies, and we had to perform the final offerings without him. To show our respect, we brought a buffalo to his funeral feast.

His son concurred with this evaluation, adding the following commentary:

> What if his ghost were to see all this rushing around, the chaos of the children rushing around, screaming at his image? He would be angry again. The anger of the dead is worse than that of the living. He was angry at the sponsor because he did not know the proper protocol, the hierarchy of ritual specialists. These children do not know that we must fear the dead. He was a great man, a great speaker who stood up for tradition. He wouldn't accept compromises which were not the way of our ancestors. We should fear him in death because of what he knew.

Commentary centered on responses to seeing a filmic representation of a man who had since died. The emotional outburst which had offended some American audiences, finding it overwrought and undignified, was considered justified by local viewers. His anger took on a new meaning because of the possibility that it could reach beyond the grave.

Piro Pawali's outburst has its rightful place in ongoing debates about the role of traditional ritual in the modern world. Mangganipi now has an influential Christian community (30% of the total population). Many of these are schoolteachers and government officials who would be attending Catholic Mass on Sunday morning. Their arrival at the feast was therefore delayed by attendance at a rival form of worship. Piro Pawali refused to allow the sponsor of the feast to delay the public payment of the orators until after guests had arrived. He argued that waiting for them would have privileged the visible audience of spectators over the invisible audience of ancestral spirits and local deities.

If the ritual performance could be said to have two audiences (one visible and one invisible) it nevertheless has only a single "stage" on which all attention is focused. Therefore, the leaders of the village community and the leaders of the ceremony had to agree on the priorities in performance, and especially the timing of stages. The other priests argued that Piro Pawali's temper tantrum was justified because he was defending the traditional schedule against those who would disrupt it. Their perspective on these events was altered by the temporal distancing of watching the quarrel as it was recorded on film, after the composition of the visible and invisible audiences had shifted, since the protagonist himself had gone over to the invisible world.

These ideas that "stage" and "audience" can shift, as they did here, is related to the still further shifting involved in watching a filmed ritual, where participants become spectators to their own emotional outbursts. It allows for a new kind of reflexivity and self-consciousness, which brings into question classic anthropological approaches to the expression of emotion in ritual, and its relation to temporal sequence.

FIGURE 5: A priest points to the image of the man who had since died on the video monitor as others watch with amazement and some distress.

Theories and Problems: Emotional Responses to Ritual

Symbolic anthropology has grappled with issue of emotions in ritual in several ways. One tradition, stemming from the work of Durkheim and Radcliffe Brownn, maintains ritual "creates" collective sentiments and makes them come alive within the participants. Correct attitudes are not merely mimed or simulated, but actually experienced in the ritual process. The idea of emotional intensity and sharing in ritual was behind Victor Turner's much paraded notion of *communitas*, which has now been extensively questioned as a general paradigm. Not all rituals involve a stage of liminal anarchy, shared effervescence, or "anti-structure," and even those that do cannot guarantee that such states are actually experienced. As Geertz has famously observed, often "ritual is not a 'free expression of the emotions' but a disciplined rehearsal of 'right attitudes'" (Geertz 1973).

But where do the right attitudes come from? Some writers have suggested that ritual can be "expressive" of private sentiments, a vehicle for the externalization of feelings formed outside of the ritual context and only carried there for specific reasons. Rosaldo (1984) argues that the "cultural force of the emotions" develops in everyday situations, and rituals serve as "busy intersections," a crossroads where ideas, practices and experiences intersect rather than being encapsulated (1984: 190). The crisis of enraged grief or turbulent envy which lies behind Ilongot head-hunting leads to a catharsis, but the process and postions of different participants are quite distinct. Subjects evaluate their own involvement differently. The confluence of social processes is effective and overwhelming for some, not for others.

Models of the role of emotion and affect in ritual have tended to focus on key moments of transformative emotional experience, which are supposed to occur through a process of suggestion and dramatic enactment in which individual subjects are drawn into a collective process. Scheff (1977) revamps the Aristotelian notion of catharsis, distress re-experienced to produce an emotional discharge, as a key mechanism of ritual efficacy. Turner, using the model of the "social drama," redistributes affectively charged moments more evenly over the stages of breach (a symbolic transgression), crisis, redressive action and reintegration (1967).

The interaction between public suggestion and private expression is a complicated one, with much movement back and forth, between collective scenarios and individual responses. The presence of a ritual stage, of a category of participants who are defined as "performers" and others who are defined as "spectators" provides a frame in terms of which actors situate themselves and explain and account for their own behavior. To study the effect of a filmic representation on an audience of former participants, we must examine the frame of audience and spectator not only in the metaphoric sense (where ritual is often investigated as having dramatic or dramaturgical elements) but also in its operational effects: the problems that we suggest in English by asking whether certain emotions are "staged" or "performed" instead of being "real."

Members of the audience at both screenings stressed that their responses to the film provoked a genuine state of temporal confusion, which was signaled by a repetition of ritualized forms of mourning (at the funeral) or respect (for the feast footage). These are *expected* responses within a ritual frame, but they were *unexpected* at a screening, and so may open a window onto the process which constructs a sequence of expected stages of grief or mourning. Emotional reactions which are *not* part of the prepared script, which deviate from formal expectations and appear disorderly and disruptive, are also culturally constructed, and require their own explanations.

Sumbanese villagers accepted the fact that film was a medium of representation, and did not naively confuse the "reality" of our footage with actual events. But they did react intensely to both the scenes of the priest's rage and the mourning on the veranda. I believe that clues to these reactions lie in the ability of film to mime "ordinary time," to repeat a sequence so it can be re-lived *as if it were happening again*, and to then bring spectators out of the experience and back to daily life with a somewhat altered perspective. Given the importance that ancestors assume in Sumbanese daily life, accommodations with them carry more than a simply "emotional" weight. They can also have consequences on group life and the vast shared project of bringing the authority of the past to bear on the present.

Analysis: What Film Brings to Life

Film was not an unknown medium to our audience of Sumbanese villagers, even if many of them had never seen a film before. Government teams from the Department of Information screened films related to development projects (agricultural intensification, family planning, sanitation) in a number of villages, and many of the younger men and children had seen such films. The Kodi language of West Sumba translates "film" as *nggambaro mopiro* or "living pictures," but films are believed to be "alive" only in the mechanical sense that they move. Although official statistics define members of the *marapu* religion as "animists," their interpretation of filmic images was not "animistic" in the traditional sense. They did not believe that cameras could steal souls, or that the colored shadows we projected for them were anything more than a clever piece of technology.

It is true that I had at times been approached by older men who received a snapshot portrait of themselves as a gift, asking if I could "bring it to life" (*pa mopiroyaka*) and make it move for them. But none of them believed that we manipulated images of them for any nefarious purposes, and everyone was enthusiastic about the prospect of appearing in a film. Sumbanese traditional exchange involves an elaborate system of "shadows" (*magho*) of gifts given to represent a gift to be actually conveyed later, and their interpretation of the film itself was that it represented a "shadow" of their customs to be shown to people in the West. It was not technical aspects of film which disturbed them, but its effect on an internal psychological process.

Ritual is composed of carefully delineated stages, so an upsetting of sequence is a violation of the ritual process. Those who were most distressed at our screenings (the daughters of the dead man) related their distress to an immediate re-experiencing of the earlier state they had been in at the funeral. Those who remained distant and more in control spoke of having gone through the stages earlier, and thus feeling securely "on the other side" of certain important hurdles. The spirit of forgiveness and reconciliation which typified reactions to the images of the angry priest contrasted strongly with the anger and reproaches reserved for the recently departed father.

In sum, stages of mourning are ordered by a cultural process of letting go which was complete for some of the viewers, but not for others. The screening of images of the deceased was dangerous because it tore at the boundaries of the visible and invisible worlds, upsetting the balance between the two audiences of Sumbanese ritual and obscuring the edges of the "stage" which frames the performance. But (at the same time) this new and unexpected catharsis was acknowledged to be therapeutic, to "lift hearts and soothe sadness," because it came as part of an effort to honor the dead concerned and allow their names to live on in memory. While the filming was an unorthodox commemoration, it could serve to complete the mourning process for those who wanted a further stage to confront their own feelings for the dead man. For others, it was only an homage, and thus not as involving. It was in this spirit that we wanted to offer them these colored shadows suggesting, however briefly, the vitality of persons now lost.

Rosaldo has suggested that ritual mourning involves "catalysts that precipitate processes whose unfolding occurs over subsequent months or even years" (1984:189). The viewing of these scenes was a new unfolding in this process, one which provoked initial feelings of both pain and anger, but also a new adjustment to the realities of bereavement. Since the world of the living and the dead is structured in Sumbanese life by complex forms of reciprocity, the film itself entered into these patterns and mediated between those who had been most involved in the ceremonial processing of death and those who may have felt left out. In the temporal process of Kodi mourning which begins with anger and moves into grief, this return to an earlier moment offered a chance for those who were not given direct ritual roles to acknowledge their feelings and work through them again.

The argument that anger in Kodi society is paired with grief in a relationship at times sequential and at times dialectical is reminiscent of other culturally sensitive studies of anger in cultural context, such as those of Scheifflinn (1983) and Myerss (1989). If Kaluli anger is related to violations of reciprocity and Pintupi anger to lapses in compassion, this suggests that there may be a more general underlying oppositional "logic of emotions" which Myers proposes as universal. If anger is defined as a reaction to "unjustifiable harm to the self" (1989:606), then the anger which occurs in the process of mourning must be further contextualized in terms of local notions of when exactly the deceased is fully separated from the living and thus from the "self" which experiences bereavement.

The ability of film to produce dislocations in time; (to show scenes which vividly project us back into the past, or hurl us uncertainly across space) can also disrupt sequences in emo-

tional processes, and provoke reactions which bring the catharsis theory of ritual response into question. In a society like Kodi,
where the dead may hover as invisible presences in the world
of the living, the celluloid image of the "living dead" is particularly unsettling.

Thus, I argue that what film "brought to life" in those
Sumbanese villages was an awareness of the passage of time,
and of the weight of past generations and their impact on
present life. One woman who sobbed at the sight of Ra
Honggoro's body put it better than I could:

> When we mourned him on the veranda, we didn't want to
> realize he was dead. We saw his image on the screen, we
> went back to that time, but when his image had disappeared
> from the screen, we knew he was gone. We prayed, using
> the phrases of verse passed down from our ancestors:
>
>> "We stand only for a moment on this earth
>> We barely catch our breath as we sit
>> Soon the tide rises to sweep us away
>> And the river flows on without us
>> The span of one life is soon over
>> And new generations are born to breath in his
>> place."
>
> This is what the film has shown us.

Indeed it has.

NOTE

1   An important exception to this general rule are the films made by
        Tim Asch, Patsy Asch, and Linda Connor on Jero Tapakan, a Balinese
        healer, which include one film (JERO ON JERO) in which the subject
        watches herself in trance and reflects on the experience before the
        camera. For further discussion of this case, see Asch, Asch and Connor
        (1985).

REFERENCES CITED

Asch, Timothy, Linda Connor, and Patsy Asch (1985). Jero Tapakan: Balinese Healer. Cambridge: Cambridge University Press.

Geertz, Clifford (1973). Religion as a Cultural System in The Interpretation of Cultures. New York: Basic Books.

Heelas, Paul (1986). Emotion Talk Across Cultures. IN The Social Construction of Emotions, Rom Harre (ed.). London: Blackwell, pp. 234-266.

Hollan, Douglas (l988). Pockets Full of Troubles. Ethos 16(1): 52-72.

Hoskins, Janet (1993). The Play of Time: Kodi Perspectives on Calendars, Exchange and History. Berkeley and London: University of California Press.

Lutz, Catherine (1987). Unnatural Emotions. Chicago: University of Chicago Press.

Martinez, Wilton (1990). Critical Studies and Visual Anthropology: Aberrant vs. Anticipated Readings of Ethnographic Film. Commission for Visual Anthropology Review, Spring, 1990: 34-47.

Myers, Fred R. (1989). The Logic and Meaning of Anger Among Pintupi Aborigines. Man (n.s.) 23(4): 589-610.

Nichols, Bill (1991). The Ethnographer's Tale. Visual Anthropology Review 7 (2): 31-47.

Rosaldo, Renato (1984) Grief and a Headhunter's Rage: On the Cultural Force of Emotions. IN Text, Play and Story: The Construction and Reconstruction of Self and Society, S. Plattner and E. Bruner (eds.). Proceedings of the AES. Washington, DC: American Anthropological Association, pp. 178-195.

Scheff, Thomas C. (1977). The Distancing of Emotion in Ritual. Current Anthropology 8(3): 483-505.

Schieffelin, Edward L. (1985). Anger and Shame in the Tropical Forest: On Affect as a Cultural System in Papua New Guinea. Ethos 11: 181-91.

Sobchack, Vivian (1984). Inscribing Ethical Space: Ten Propositions on Death, Representation and Documentary. Quarterly Review of Film Studies 9(4): 283-300.

Tambs-Lyche, Harald and Kjellaug Waage (1989). Intimacy, Recognition and Nausea: Reflections on the Perception of Ethnographic Film by Norwegian Youth. Commission for Visual Anthropology Review, Fall 1989: 31-33.

Tavris, Carol (1982). Anger: The Misunderstood Emotion. New York: Simon and Schuster.

FILMS CITED

Feast In Dream Village. 1989. Produced and directed by Janet Hoskins and Laura Scheerer Whitney. 27 minutes, color. Purchase $500 (16 mm), $250 (video),rental $45 (video only) from University of California Extension Media Center, 2176 Shattuck Avenue, Berkeley, Ca. 94704 (510) 642-0460. Study guide available in short (5 page) and longer (30 page) format.

Horses of Life and Death. 1991. Produced and directed by Laura Scheerer Whitney, with anthropologist Janet Hoskins. 26 minutes, color. Purchase $500 (16 mm), $250 (video), rental $45 (video only) from University of California Extension Media Center, 2176 Shattuck Avenue, Berkeley, Ca. 94704(510) 642-0460.

The Nuer. 1970. Produced by Hillary Harris and George Briedenbach. 75 minutes, 16 mm, color. Rental $40 from Pennsylvania State Audio-Visual Services, Division of Media and Learning Resources, University Park, PA 16802 (800) 826-0132.

from ANTHROPOLOGICAL FILM AND VIDEO IN THE 1990s
Jack R. Rollwagen (editor). Brockport, NY: The Institute, Inc.
© 1993, The Institute, Inc. All rights reserved. ISBN 0-9635206-1-X

Everybody's A Critic: Video Programming With Guatemalan Maya Refugees In The United States

Allan F. Burns
Department of Anthropology
University of Florida

ABSTRACT: The immediate presence and the apparent transparent style of ethnographic film and video invite criticism and commentary during production as well as after the release of a documentary. As ethnographic film and video become more and more involved in discussions of critical theory, post-modern ethnography, and even applied anthropology, criticisms also become an issue to be confronted as part of the work of visual anthropology. Four ethnographic video projects with the over 20,000 Guatemalan Maya refugees in Florida and the work that went into making them over the past six years are used to explore how critics and their criticism affect the shape of the programs. Criticism within the refugee community, criticism within the crews working on the projects, criticisms by different screening audiences within and without the refugee community, and finally criticism from the professional world of reviews are described as they affected each succeeding program. While producers and directors are quick to dismiss critics as unskilled and unwanted nuisances, criticism is part of the work of ethnographic video.

Everybody who watches an ethnographic film or video finds it easy to be a critic. Criticisms of film and video are common, whether elicited or not, and although most producers and directors dislike them, they are a fact of life in the field. One thing that is seldom talked about publicly among producers of visual anthropology is how to deal with critics. This is especially surprising because producers and directors often talk about critics among themselves, sometimes cursing them and other times wondering if the critics might just be right.

This essay is about the reviews, criticisms, and comments that have grown up around five video programs I have produced on Guatemalan Maya refugees in Florida. Over 15,000 Maya people came to Florida in the 1980s to escape the political and cultural violence that began in Guatemala in the 1980s (Burns 1993). An estimated half of the eight million people of Guatemala are Maya, although more people would claim Maya identity if it were valued instead of a mark of prejudice and subjugation. The difference between a Maya and non-Maya person in Guatemala is not so much biological as it is a question of language, behavior, and history.

The guerilla insurgency of the 1980s and counter- insurgency campaign by the military in Guatemala resulted the destruction of hundreds of Maya towns and villages, farmlands, and networks of communication and commerce. By the 1990s more than 400,000 Guatemalans, both Maya and non-Maya had become displaced. The Maya of the mountainous area in northern department of Huehuetenango where the guerilla forces found refuge were caught up in an uprising that left them most vulnerable: they could not quickly leave their lands and villages like the insurgents and could not defend themselves against the guns and helicopters used by the Guatemalan army. Those who did escape now find it very difficult to return; fear and a great deal of violence remain in the 1990s.

Most of the 15,000 Maya people who have come to Florida are from the Northwestern highlands of Guatemala and are Q'anjob'al Maya (sometimes spelled "Kanjobal"). These Maya people fled the municipal center and surrounding aldeas of San Miguel Acatán in the department of Huehuetenango beginning in the early 1980s. Tens of thousands crossed the border into Mexico. There they were subject to Guatemalan army attacks while living in squalid refugee camps. In 1984, the Mexican government moved many refugees to the inhospitable tropics of Campeche. But thousands more headed north until they came to the relative safety of the southwestern U.S. border states. In 1983 a few came to Florida to pick oranges, and

FIGURE 1 :Migrant farm worker housing for Guatemala Mayas in Florida (photo by Paula Horvath Neimeyer).

quickly established themselves in an agricultural community with the unusual name of "Indiantown."

Indiantown, Florida, a town named after a Seminole encampment, is a place where the Q'anjob'al Maya are very visible: they make up the majority of the migrant workers who come to the town each year seeking temporary work. They live in apartment houses known as "camps." One is called "Blue Camp" where rooms are divided by curtains so that two or three families can pay the high rent in a town with few housing opportunities. Another is "Yellow Camp," which used to be called "the Roach Palace" because of the large population of bugs before publicity forced the owners to clean it up. A few Maya have rented homes because they fear for their families living in the crowded conditions of these and other "camps." In the camps life is dangerous. Robberies are common as men whose families are still in Guatemala carry their wages with them so they can send money orders back home. Other people know this and attack the Guatemalans. The population of Indiantown is just over 6,000, although the actual number of residents is close to twice that figure during the harvest season from October through May. The inland area of this part of Florida is rich in agriculture and the migration of rich retirees has created a building boom on the Florida coast near Indiantown. These two industries need a great deal of unskilled labor which traditionally has been met through migrant laborers from Mexico, the Caribbean, and now, from Guatemala. When farm work is available, it is sought out. When it is not, landscape work, day labor in construction, child care, salvaging, and other informal jobs become the way to survive. As unofficial refugees and often undocumented immigrants, the Guatemala Maya are unable to receive many social benefits, so many are reduced to the extremes of poverty when work is unavailable.

FIGURE 2 : Maya refugees perform a ceremony of arrival in Florida.

The lives of these de facto refugees have been traumatic and difficult. In 1983 I met an activist refugee who has made helping this new Maya community in Florida his work. Jerónimo Camposeco is a Jacaltec Maya who has received political asylum status and at that time was organizing an indigenous association of Maya refugees, Corn Maya. Camposeco had training as an anthropologist and native language teacher in Guatemala before fleeing for his life, and now in the United States was involved in legal and educational work with the Guatemalan Maya. One of the first things we talked about when we met was making a video program for public television and other outlets about the case of the Maya in Florida. This initial conversation has grown into a series of applied projects and video programs that colleagues and I have carried out with the Maya of Indiantown. Two of these video programs, MAYA IN EXILE (Burns and Saperstein 1985) and MAYA FIESTA (Burns and Saperstein 1988), have been shown on public television, and two, SALUD ENTRE DOS CULTURAS (Health Between Two Cultures) (Rocha and Burns 1991) and LA MUJER MAYA: SALUD PRENATAL (The Mayan Woman: Prenatal Health) (Cameon and Burns 1991) are used in homes and clinics in the Maya communities of Florida and California. I have discussed the working conditions of making these programs elsewhere (Burns 1993). Here I examine the broader issue of the criticism of ethnographic film and video and how it affects producers and their work.

Margaret Mead wrote that one of the problems with visual anthropology, especially the use of video in research, was that it is situated in a "discipline of words" (Mead 1975). The power of the written word and its history in anthropology have relegated visual documents to a secondary role as either a fieldwork technique or illustrations of a written ethnography. Video and film are very transparent because most of the time the visual productions have an intuitive "truthfulness" about them, a kind of direct look into the functioning of a group of people or a society that communicates many things without too many words. Ethnographic film and video arose from a tradition of documentary work (MacDougall 1991, Ziller 1990:16), so that a seemingly clear view into another way of life is attained through film and video. This makes visual anthropology, and ethnographic film and video especially, a field where everybody who looks at a production has something to say about it. This is not the case with written ethnographies: they can be well written or poorly written, but it is usually assumed that a great deal of scholarly effort is needed to review and criticize. The best of written works in anthropology are complex, demanding, and multi-leveled explorations into the history of theory, fieldwork, representation, and literary skill. Many readings are often needed before sense can be made of them, and the aesthetics of good anthropological writing are that readers are challenged. In contrast, videos and films in anthropology seldom are expected to be this complex. A few are, such as REASSEMBLAGES by Trinh Minh-ha (1982). In that film, Minh-ha uses the scenes of life in Africa as a kind of artifact to focus on the nature of anthropological representation and colonial thinking. David and Judith MacDougall (personal communication) have argued for increasing the complexity and work needed by viewers to understand ethnographic film, a point made by Howard Becker in the mid 1970s who argued that photographs in sociology and anthropology should be given the same kind of attention that is given to articles and books (Becker 1975). Becker, as well as Collier and Collier (1986) suggest that any photograph used in anthropology and sociology should be studied for ten to fifteen minutes and scrutinized for sociological method, theory, and bias. But few viewers of anthropological pictures take the time to do so; fewer still examine ethnographic films or videos in the same way that they do a written ethnography. Ethnographic films and videos are still received more like illustrations than theoretical statements or analytic discussions, even though producers and directors make them with goals far more complex than mere illustration. Ethnographic films and videos are also sometimes seen as a metonym for all of anthropology, so that the relative superficial nature of film and video information is assumed to also be true of ethnography as a whole.

But while producers and directors are quick to point out that there is much more to a picture than meets the eye, the transparency of ethnographic film and video is also one of the great strengths of the media. Video is especially remarkable in this regard because the instantaneous feedback that is possible with video gives the subjects of a program the chance to review and criticize what is being documented a few moments after it is recorded. At first glance these people who are the subjects of a video seem distant from the professional critics who review work in newspapers and journals, but it is instructive to look at them in the same light. The subjects of a video may have a stronger reason to review parts of a program or a final video with greater interest because of their own presence in the piece, but they share with the public, students, and professionals an assumption that the media is immediately accessible. Video, like all photography, invokes meaning through the interaction of three features: the activities of the person behind the camera, those of the subject, and the impressions of the viewer (Ziller 1990:22). While critics are usually just found in the last of these, they can at times be the subjects, and, on crew productions, also in the first category. In this sense, everybody really is a critic.

The series of video programs on Guatemalan Maya people in Florida have each become better as a result of the criticisms of the previous one. I will turn now to a discussion of the kinds of critics and criticisms of each program and how the criticisms informed these evolving video projects. Criticisms are not just made after a program is done; they are a continual part of the film or video crew's work, and the immediate results of video filming make criticism part of the ongoing production of a show.

Few people in places like Florida knew that there were refugees from Guatemala in their midst, and fewer still realized the reasons why they fled their homeland or how they lived in the United States. The first program, MAYA IN EXILE, was made with a crew consisting of a filmmaker-director with experience making documentaries as well music videos for MTV, a videographer from Venezuela, and an assistant videographer and narrator who had made several feminist programs and other documentaries. The other members of our crew were a student who had worked in the community for a year and the Mayan activist, Jerónimo Camposeco.

During the course of taping, we reviewed each days' results and each of us became critics of the others: I told the cameraman how to shoot scenes; he in turn suggested many things for me to ask in the interviews I did. The assistant videographer told me to bring more women into the video. Camposeco was doing interviews for political asylum applications and allowed us to

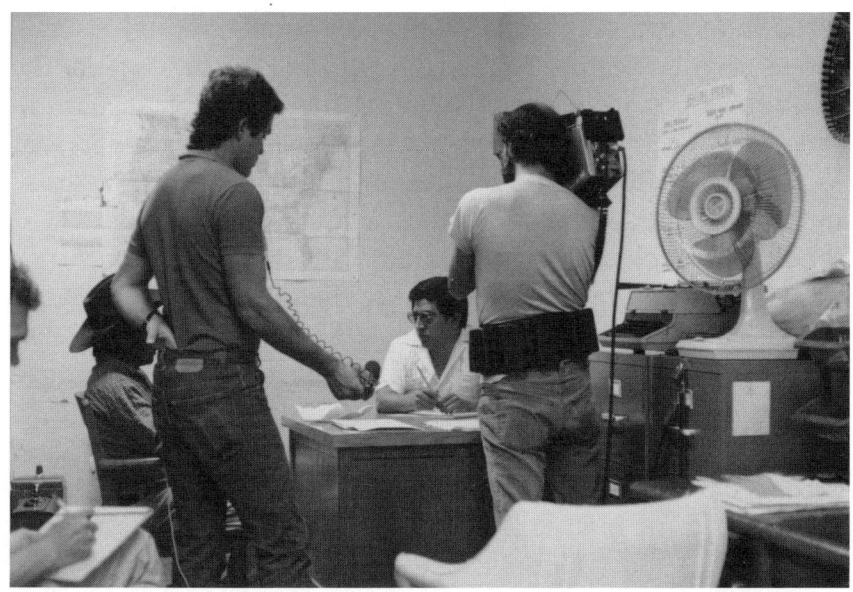

FIGURE 3 : The crew of MAYA IN EXILE tape a political asylum interview.

tape one interview. This later became the cornerstone of the program MAYA IN EXILE because of the eloquent and straightforward story that the refugee told. A few months later, while we were trying to edit the program, we held a fund-raising showing of part of the video in a university community. For a reason I could not quite verbalize, I had become enthralled with a soccer match we had taped. Perhaps it was because the videographer had a background in sports programming and so the shots were exciting and well executed, and perhaps because I was curious and intrigued about the organization of the Mayas vis-á-vis other immigrant groups in South Florida through soccer.

I put in about four minutes of the match in the rough cut of the program that was shown to a public audience. The audience was made up of people who had an interest in Central America, peace research, and in political advocacy. They donated their admission price so that we could continue to edit, and so were invited to be the first critics of the video from the standpoint of uninvolved viewers. They did not hesitate to make their criticisms known. Several people complained that we had not dealt with the U.S. involvement in Central America and so had missed a chance to make a kind of exposé about American involvement in Guatemalan life. We had not videotaped in Guatemala, and instead relied on still photographs that the Guatemalan anthropologist had taken before he fled the country. The goal of the program was to show what refugee life was like in the United States. My interest in the soccer game was not shared by the audience. Everyone thought the soccer sequence was too long and boring, a point that the director had already told me many times while we were editing. The final program has some soccer in it, even though the importance of soccer still intrigues me. I am waiting for someone interested in the anthropology of sport and immigration to work on the soccer clubs of South Florida.

A final criticism arrived in the mail a few days after we showed the rough cut. I was accused of being chauvinistic because we had left a scene in the video where a woman turns the tables and begins to interview me. She asked in Spanish if I had children, using the masculine form, hijos. I answered that I had a son and she asked if I had any daughters, I said that I did, and we went on talking. While this is a common discourse strategy in Spanish, in our English translation it appeared that I did not want to mention my daughter. The criticism was not justified, but it still alerted me to the importance of translation in the programs, translation not only of words, but also styles of speaking and listening. This became an important lesson to me, and as we edited the section with the refugee, I made a point to include the idea that the way people talk about things changes when they switch languages. This led us to put in sections of the program showing animated talk in Mayan and subdued, quiet talk in Spanish. Although this was far from the point of the criticism, it suggested an important conceptual point that might not have been included in the final program had not the criticism been made. On a more direct level, the criticism made us realize that many of the people who would watch the program with sympathy would often be activists and feminists, and so we became careful to show the lives of refugee women as we did refugee men.

As soon as the program was completed, it was publicly shown in Indiantown at an open screening. A Guatemalan who briefly appeared in one of the scenes did a simultaneous translation of the video into Q'anjob'al as it was shown. The response to the program was positive and enthusiastic. After the screening we asked if there were questions or comments on the video. The first question asked was "where can we buy a copy." I had made fifteen copies available without cost to the community and left them with a Catholic service center to distribute. We also used the local Maya non-profit association as the distributor for the video, although later conflicts and factionalism in the community led some Maya to criticize the imagined profits that were made through selling the video through this organization.

The second question was more of a criticism: we were asked if we would make a version in Maya. The program was in English as it was aimed at a general U.S. audience, but the question was important. The program used extensive narration throughout as we had made a decision to limit it to under thirty minutes so that it could be easily shown on local public television and cable channels as well as to schools and other groups. Versions in other languages meant considerable work in translation and studio recording, something that we had no budget for in this first program. It was not until several years later that we were able to begin making programs with alternative sound tracks in Maya, Spanish and English.

A third comment that came out of this initial screening had to do with the politics of refugees and of Guatemala. In the program we carefully focused our attention on the experiences of people now that they were in the United States, but still, mention of the civil war and the guerrilla movement in Guatemala were necessary. One refugee who had escaped from the guerrilla groups was angry that we had even mentioned the word "guerrilla" in the video. I did not understand the shifting political alliances and commitments that people make in times of social and political violence in places like Guatemala, and so was surprised at his reaction. Still, this concern led me to learn more about what it means to be forced to take sides under such situations, and as a result we were much more careful in subsequent programs about presenting the insurgency or counterinsurgency in simple terms.

When the program was reviewed by the American Anthropologist (McKee 1988), it was given a sympathetic viewing, as did the second program in the series, MAYA FIESTA (Earle 1991). At the time we made the first program in 1985, we used an editing studio at the local television cable company, so we were forced to make the video without dissolves or any effects other than titles and keys. The straight cuts between scenes gave the video a jumpy feel which was noticed by the reviewer. We had also used still photographs of Guatemala in the program to evoke the "timelessness" of the past (as well as because we did no filming in Guatemala). I did not want to use the still photographs, but other members of the crew convinced me to do so. I waited to have this device criticized, but instead it was mentioned in the review in a positive way. When I have asked colleagues about the use of the stills, they invariably have said that it was a good idea as it showed how Guatemala looked when people left it as well as slowed down the pace of the program. In this case, as my own critic I found out that I was wrong.

When we made the first video program, one refugee we had videotaped was adamant about not wanting to be shown in the final video program. We did not use him, but when the program was shown in the community, he was very pleased with it and made a point to congratulate us on the work and offer his help making the next program. He suggested that something that showed the culture of the people would be important to portray, especially as so many young people had now spent five or six years in the United States and knew only of the life of migrant workers. He suggested a video about the Maya calender and its use today or about traditional rituals. As it turned out, we did not make a program about either of these things, but instead used the occasion of a traditional community festival as the focus of the next program.

MAYA FIESTA was made to show the interaction of Maya with other people in the community and to present a side of these refugees to audiences as people with an ongoing and interesting culture. We also wanted to make a program that showed more of the new community of Indiantown, as we had concentrated on individuals in MAYA IN EXILE with few shots of the agricultural community of Indiantown. Our initial idea of following a few people from year to year was still with us as we filmed, but we quickly found that many of the people who had been memorable in the first video had now left Indiantown and had gone to other parts of Florida or other states to work. A few came back to celebrate the patron saint of their community in Guatemala, San Miguel. We did a few interviews with these people, and showed others who had been in the first video in some of the crowd scenes of the program, but we were unable to make the kind of video that would result in a life history documentary project. Instead of an overt continuity between the two programs, I decided on using a few of the people who had been in the background of the first program as key subjects in the second. This included one of the marimba musicians who is only seen playing in the first program, but is interviewed about the reasons he and his family fled Guatemala in the second program.

One example of criticism during the filming of MAYA
FIESTA that helped the final program was made by a Catholic
nun who was working at a social service center for migrant
workers. I was standing next to her in the church when many
babies were being baptized, as the patron saint of the village
festival day is a valued time to baptize children. She turned and
said that we had filmed the church before, but why weren't we
filming now during the baptism ceremony which was both
beautiful and important for the people. I went out and got the
camera and a sound assistant and came back in the church to
film the baptism of the children. This proved to be an especially
evocative part of the video, and was warmly received when the
video was shown to the community later.

The public screening of MAYA FIESTA in the community
was well received. The most common reaction during the
showing was delight and laughter by people who saw themselves in some of the public scenes. Between the time we filmed
and the year later when we showed the video, a second wave
of mostly young men had come to Indiantown, so most people
who saw the program had not been present during the festival.
They watched in silence, and had little to say after the program
was over, except to inquire about the availability of the video,
as did the audience of the first program. A new priest had been
assigned to the parish of the community, and he took on the role
of spokesperson for the community during this public screening. He said that the video was good, but it did not show how
people worked for a living. During the late 1980s the ever
increasing number of Guatemalans who came to Indiantown
were seen as a threat to the rest of the community. The Guatemalan Maya had become more and more resented by the
Anglos of the community (Burns 1989), and the perception that
there were thousands of Guatemalans in the community who
did not work but instead lived off of welfare was common. The
priest wanted a video that showed the contribution of these
immigrants to the local economy. Our working group appreci-

FIGURE 4 : Migrant housing for Guatemalan Mayas in Florida (photo by
        Paul Doughty).

ated this issue, but permission to film in the orchards and other
industries, especially in light of the controversies about the
ability of qualifying for the Immigration Reform and Control
Act (IRCA) of 1986 made it very difficult to develop this as a
focus of a later program.

MAYA FIESTA had both sadness and humor in it, and in
general was criticized less than MAYA IN EXILE. The local Maya
organization used the video to apply for several grants, and at
least one relief agency official told me that the video was a
deciding factor in their decision to fund the association. The
video was also shown in Mexico at a meeting of representatives
of the officially recognized refugees living there in 1990. There
a surprising reaction to the video occurred. One person at the
screening was delighted to see a friend in the video who had
been assumed to have been killed in Guatemala. The video was
seen as a kind of letter or communication between the Mayas

living in Mexico and those who had immigrated to the United States.

In 1990 I was approached by a representative of the Presbyterian church in Florida and asked if I could make a program about prenatal health among the immigrants. As more and more women in the Maya refugee communities in Florida began having children, it was apparent that educational programs were needed both for the women and for the medical people who treated them. Unfamiliarity with the U.S. health system and the routines of prenatal care and birth resulted in a growing concern for the health of young mothers. Indiantown is some forty miles from the nearest hospital, so many women waited until labor started and then called an ambulance. As a result, more and more babies were being born in ambulances or at home in the community. Likewise, public health workers in Florida and elsewhere knew that traditional midwives were working in Florida immigrant communities, but saw them as a hindrance to health care. A graduate student in Latin American Studies at the University of Florida, Maria Rocha, and I met with the church peace and social welfare representatives. We were asked to submit a proposal for making a video that would be useful for both the Maya women and health workers. After we received funding, I was also contacted by the a south Florida March of Dimes representative who discussed the interest by the foundation to make a pilot video tape program with a high degree of community involvement about prenatal care. A friend who was receiving her advanced degree in public health who had been active in women's health for more than twenty years, Randi Cameon, and I proposed a second video program to the March of Dimes. We received funding for that project as well, in part because of the record of programs that we already had completed and in part because of the skill and reputation my colleague had in organizing women around health issues. We decided to make each video useful for both groups (the women and the health workers), but to use the

Presbyterian foundation project to make a program that stressed the day to day lives of women in the community and their own systems of nutrition, health care, and use of midwives, and use the March of Dimes project to make a more educational program about the functioning of the U.S. rural health care system.

The more ethnographic of the two programs, SALUD ENTRE DOS CULTURAS; (Health Between Two Cultures) was made primarily in Spanish and then given both a Spanish and English narration, using one sound track on the final video master for each. When the representatives of the church saw it, they were unhappy with it for two reasons. First of all, they thought that the program should show more scenes of women using the clinics and other facilities. Secondly, they wanted a version with a sound track in Mayan, something that we had put in our original proposal, but had decided not to do because the program had evolved into an educational tape more for clinic workers than for the women themselves. The first criticism was easily dealt with, as we had the other video, LA MUJER MAYA: SALUD PRENATAL (The Maya Woman: Prenatal Health) which was more like a traditional health education video in that it explained clinic procedures and pre-natal concepts. That video had been made with both a Spanish and Mayan narration, each recorded from the same woman from the Maya community. We decided to add a Mayan narration to SALUD ENTRE DOS CULTURAS. This was in response to the criticism of the church foundation, but it also made us realize the importance of a Mayan version so that women in the community would understand what the clinic workers were learning about them.

There are at least five different Mayan languages spoken in the community, and even among the Q'anjob'al, there are dialectical differences that make understanding difficult between people of different communities. When the videos were screened with local people, several complained that they could not understand the particular dialects of the women who recorded the narration. So while the Mayan versions were an important addition to our project, the complexity of languages in the community make it difficult to decide on which Mayan language or dialect to use. We chose the most common Mayan, but it is not spoken by more than a half of the community. The Spanish version, spoken with a recognizable Mayan accent, became the most useful version even though it excludes many of the women who speak only Mayan.

These two health videos are distributed together as a set, and are being used in the many states that have Guatemalan immigrants living and working in migrant communities. While they are localized to one community in Florida, similarities in migrant communities throughout the United States make them more generalized. These programs are not intended to be classroom or college anthropology course material, and so criticism of them outside of migrant worker communities will not occur.

The series of four video programs made with Maya refugees in Florida represent a collaboration between different parts of the community and the anthropologists, filmmakers, and other specialists. There is no doubt that the Maya people themselves will be making their own video programs in the future about their experiences as refugees and undocumented aliens in the United States as younger people in the community gain expertise and resources to do so. There are already several families with camcorders in the community, and so documenting events like the fiesta of San Miguel or family ceremonies is an activity that the Maya do just as other people throughout the world find interesting. The evolution of skills in videography and production of programs is not something that will replace the kind of work I have described here. In this sense, I am arguing that indigenous media need not be something better or an alterative to ethnographic film and video as some writers suggest (Ginsberg 1991; Asch et al 1991). The role of anthropology, whether in print or in film and video (Elsass 1991) is to use the perspective of the discipline, the concepts, theories, approaches, and traditions, to construct a view of the world which sometimes approaches that of local actors and other times is quite different from the world as seen from a local community. In a post-modern sense, the "voices" that are heard through indigenous media are not just speaking in the open to the sky. They belong to people who may want to continue a relationship of collaborative video. Collaborative video is more like a dialogue or conversation between local people and anthropologists and other documentary filmmakers. Sometimes the role of the local people is much stronger than that of the anthropologist, as in the case of the baptism video described earlier. Other times the voice of the professional filmmaker is stronger, as in the case of MAYA IN EXILE. Sometimes one side or the other seems almost completely absent from some aspect of production, be it planning, filming, editing, or post production. Other times the line between who is really "local" and who is the "outsider" is blurred, especially if collaboration continues over several years.

This is why the concern within culture theory and among some anthropologists over who are the subjects and who are the objects of anthropology is often misguided. While some anthropologists and filmmakers do "one shot" studies and programs, many others are engaged in a long term relationships with the communities they research, write about, and film. Under these circumstances anthropologists do not necessarily "go native," but they do become part of the cultural and social landscape so as to make talk about "the other" as opposed to "the anthropologist" something of an anachronism or at least out of place. Bill Nichols, in an article "The Ethnographer's Tale" (1991), argues that visual anthropology, and anthropology as a discipline, is in a crisis brought on by the increasing importance and authority of the voices of the "others" (a term many writers put in quotations to signal the artificial construction of the world into academic elites and the people they write about) and the criticisms these "others" make of the ethnographic representations of their lives. Nichols also notes that increasingly the creation of more and more refugee communities result in people who are neither "here nor there in terms of a fixed location" (Nichols 1991:40). Traditional ethnographies and films that rely on the idea of traveling to an exotic location in search of cultural difference cannot do justice to these and other changes in today's world. He hopes for a move from representation to evocation to capture these changes, and suggests that ethnographic film and video will become for new filmmakers from indigenous and other oppressed communities something of the "representational residue they may chose to adapt, ignore or redress" (Nichols 1991:44).

Long term work in visual anthropology is far more complex than writers like Nichols comprehend. The study of transnational communities and communities under severe stress is a part of anthropology, and from them a different perspective of the criticisms of "the others" can be understood. Criticism by the "others" is expected, and the intricacy of criticism within the reality of refugee lives often is not easy to follow. After six years of working with and making videos with the refugee community of Indiantown, I was surprised to hear complaints about anthropology as well as the intrusiveness of film crews who, as one refugee said, "looked at us like we were in a fishbowl." But as the time drew near for the yearly festival of San Miguel, I received several calls from of the most vociferous critics, asking if students and I at the university would come and make another video of the festival as we did in MAYA FIESTA. I was surprised at the request, since the criticisms had seemed a personal attack. I made arrangements to make a new fiesta video, this time locating a young refugee who worked with us as a way to learn film and video.

What were the reasons for the earlier criticisms, and why had some of the critics from the local community reversed their position? One aspect of this criticism was that it was directed at

FIGURE 5: Allan Burns with Maya refugees learning video production.

the popularity and notoriety of the community among journal-
ists, anthropologists from other universities, students doing
term papers, social workers, religious groups, foundations,
lawyers, medical workers with a concern for immigrants as
well as myself. The people were quite simply tired of always
being photographed, interviewed, and in other ways pestered
by a curious public. A second aspect of the criticism was that
complaints about the "helping community" of church and
social workers in the town were endemic, and as my own work
often included working with local clinics and agencies, we
were subsumed under this general complaint. A third aspect of
this criticism was that it was part of a public message that was
different from the personal relationships we had established
over many years. A distinction was made between our work as
an example of the "gaze of anthropology" and our work that
was part of the "inside" workings of the refugee community. In
other words, the public criticism was a general one, not neces-

sarily directed at the work that we did in the community. But the criticism was ambiguous, so that it was easy for someone like myself to read into it a personal attack when one was not meant. The criticism of anthropologists is part of the discourse of oppressed people in the new world, made famous by Vine Deloria's CUSTER DIED FOR YOUR SINS (1969) and continuing through the present. "Anthropologist bashing" is something that has been taken up by many people in culture theory as well, often as a way for culture theorists to align themselves with the concerns of subjugated people. Finally, criticism is constant within the refugee community, as personal attacks, both verbal and physical, condemnation, and factionalism are facts of life. When I commiserated with one refugee about this he said, "Well, criticism is everywhere. It is something we live with both from the anglos and from each other." Criticism of visual anthropology and anthropology in general in a way showed that we were part of the general discourse of this community undergoing the stress of war, migration, and regular dislocation.

This project differs from many ethnographic film and video productions in that it has continued for over six years and will continue into the future. The criticisms of the people in the videos, people who watch the videos and do not have any personal acquaintance with the refugees, professionals in film, video, or anthropology all contribute to the evolution of the project. The early idea of documenting one or two people over a ten year period has been dropped, in part because of the difficulties of keeping track of anyone in such a rapidly changing context like the refugee community. People come and go, moving between migrant labor towns throughout the United States, official refugee camps in Mexico as well as unofficial communities of refugees there, as well as to Guatemala as clandestine returnees. My first vision of a ten year documentary of a few immigrants fell victim to the realities of the critics. The critics within the community wanted programs that reflected their concerns with surviving in the United States. These were at times cultural and at other times focused on issues like health and work. Other critics, including colleagues and reviewers of the programs within the discipline of anthropology also influenced the direction of the project. I had always felt the need to work with professionals in film and video so that some of the programs would be what is called "broadcast legal," or made to standards that allow for transmission over public television channels. In all cases, the professionals involved in the overall project gave each program except the family baptism video a legitimacy that could not be achieved with home-video equipment. The technical quality of the editing, post production, and other aspects of the programs meant that the content of the programs would be paid attention to, and the style would be both professional and transparent. Sometimes colleagues who were not experienced with video or visual anthropology tended to misjudge the technical quality. The review of MAYA FIESTA by Duncan Earle (1991), for example, gives high marks to the content of the program, but as a parting shot, says that the program is useful and good, "recognizing that the project was not done on a high budget nor with top-of-the-line equipment" (Earle 1991:256). The budget was indeed minimal, but the equipment was indeed broadcast quality, and the post production studio was professional.

The saying "everybody's a critic" reflects film and video makers' displeasure with the kinds of things that are said and written by people who "were not there." At the same time, the beauty of video as a method in anthropology is that it allows everyone to be a critic, or at least have a direct and important role in the evolution of a visual anthropology project. Sometimes the critics are wrong, but very often they say what a producer or director needs to hear.

REFERENCES CITED

Asch, Timothy, with Jesus Ignacio Cardozo, Hortensia Cabellero and Jose
    Bortoli (1991). The Story We Now Want to Hear is Not Ours to Tell:
    Relinquishing Control Over Representation: Toward Sharing Vi-
    sual Communication Skills with the Yanomami. Visual anthro-
    pology Review 7(2): 102-106.
Becker, Howard (1975). Photography and Sociology, Afterimage, May-
    June, 1975, pp. 22-32.
Burns, Allan (1993). Maya in Exile: Guatemalan Refugees in Florida. Phila-
    delphia: Temple University Press.
Burns, Allan (1989). Internal and External Identity Among Kanjobal Refu-
    gees in Florida. IN Conflict, Migration and the Expression of
    Ethnicity, Nancie Gonzalez and Carolyn McCommon (eds.). Boul-
    der, CO: Westview Press, pp. 45-59.
Collier, Malcolm, and John Collier, Jr. (1989). Visual Anthropology. Albu-
    querque: University of New Mexico Press.
Deloria, Vine (1969). Custer Died for Your Sins: An Indian Manifesto. New
    York: The MacMillan Co..
Earle, Duncan (1991). Review of MAYA FIESTA. American Anthropologist
    93: 255-56.
Elsass, Peter (1991). Self Reflection or Self Presentation: A Study of the
    Advocacy Effect. Visual Anthropology 4: 1-13.
Ginsburg, Faye (1991). Indigenous Media: Faustian Contract or Global
    Village. Cultural Anthropology 6(1): 92-112.
MacDougall, David (1991). Whose Story Is It? Visual Anthropology Review
    7(2): 2-10.
Manz, Beatriz (1988). Refugees of a Hidden War: The Aftermath of
    Counterinsurgency in Guatemala. Albany: State University of New
    York Press.
McKee, Lauris (1988). Review of MAYA IN EXILE. American Anthropolo-
    gist 90: 240-241.
Mead, Margaret (1975). Visual Anthropology in a Discipline of Words. IN
    Principles of Visual Anthropology, Paul Hockings (ed.). The Hague:
    Mouton, pp. 3-10.
Nichols, Bill (1991). The Ethnographer's Tale. Visual Anthropology Review
    7(2): 31-47.
Ziller, Robert (1990). Photographing the Self. Beverly Hills: Sage Publica-
    tions.

FILMS AND VIDEOS CITED

Maya in Exile. 1985. A video by Allan Burns and Alan Saperstein. 28 minutes, color. Purchase $45 (no rental) from CORN MAYA PROJECT, P.O. Box 147, Indiantown, FL   34956 (407/597-4151). Teaching guide available.

Maya Fiesta. 1988. A video by Allan Burns and Alan Saperstein. 25 minutes, color. Purchase $45 (no rental) from CORN MAYA PROJECT, P.O. Box 147, Indiantown, FL   34956 (407/597-4151). Teaching guide available.

La Mujer Maya: Salud Prenatal ("The Mayan Woman: Prenatal Health"). 1991. A video by Randi Cameon and Allan Burns. Not for sale or rent. For information, contact South East Florida March of Dimes Foundation, 2831 Exchange Court, West Palm Beach, FL   33409.

Salud Entre Dos Culturas ("Health Between Two Cultures"). 1991. A video by Maria C. Rocha and Allan Burns. Not for sale or rent. For information, contact Presbyterian Church Peace and Social Justice Program, 100 Witherspoon Street, Louisville, KY   40303.

Disassemblages. 1982. A film by Trinh Minh-ha, Minh. 40 minutes, color. Purchase (16mm) $800. Rental (16mm) $90 from Women Make Movies, Inc., 225 Lafayette, Suite 212, New York, NY   10012 (212/925-0606).

SUGGESTED FILMS ON THE MAYA

Todos Santos Cuchumatan . 1977. A film by Olivia Carrescia. 58 minutes, color. Purchase $685 (16mm), $400 (video); rental $85 from First Run/Icarus Films, 153 Waverly Place, 6th Floor, New York, NY   10014 (212/727-1711).

Todos Santos, The Survivors. 1989. A film by Olivia Carrescia. 58 minutes, color. Purchase $895 (16mm), $450 (video) rental $125 (16mm only) from First Run/Icarus Films, 153 Waverly Place, 6th Floor, New York, NY   10014 (212/727-1711).

from ANTHROPOLOGICAL FILM AND VIDEO IN THE 1990s
Jack R. Rollwagen (editor). Brockport, NY: The Institute, Inc.
© 1993, The Institute, Inc. All rights reserved. ISBN 0-9635206-1-X

Beyond Ethnographic Film: Hypermedia And Scholarship[1]

Peter Biella
Department of Anthropology
Temple University

ABSTRACT: Anthropological literature has sought to legitimate ethnographic film by creating in it parallels with ethnographic writing. Faulty logic and incomplete theorization of writing have resulted in inadequate prescriptions for ethnographic film style.

A more adequate description of ethnographic writings is needed. The definition of such concepts as "ethnographic," however, is subject to intense debate. This essay plunges only so deep into the fray as to identify eight attributes of scholarship which all of the debating anthropological factions acknowledge to be valid. Three attributes are rules of argument and presentation. The remainder describe properties of the medium in which a scholarly work must be inscribed.

Because film must be viewed linearly and at the pace established by its makers, it very incompletely meets scholarship's demands. Indeed, one essential criterion can never be met. Filmmakers often rightly conclude from this fact that they should ignore other criteria as well. Film has therefore remained marginal to the theoretical struggles which have shaped anthropology.

Computer technology now allows film to be integrated fully into the scholarly apparatus. As works of hypermedia evolve, film will make increasingly substantive theoretical contributions to the discipline, adding insistently empirical and aesthetic contributions to the major debates.

"..the understandings communicated by film
may always be radically different
from those of anthropology
and equally unacceptable to anthropologists."

David MacDougall

Introduction

For more than forty years, efforts have been made to develop strategies and to prescribe criteria for making ethnographic film. Many shooting and editing styles have been
proposed which seek to emulate attributes of written ethnographic texts. This essay first discusses weaknesses that are
shared by the majority of such proposals. Their error is to
identify and propose a cinematic equivalent to a single attribute
of textual ethnography while ignoring all other, equally important, attributes. The proposals thus fail to define properties
of ethnography with thoroughness. Notably absent is recognition of the importance that scholarship has in the ethnographic
enterprise.

Ethnographic film presents profound, compassionate views
of people and cultural worlds which are otherwise unimagin-
able. It combats racism more effectively than argument. Yet
despite its beauty, profundity and power, ethnographic film
has a secondary status in the field. It will continue to remain at
the edge of the discipline until it becomes integrated into the
universe of scholarship. Although anthropology is wracked
with theoretical disputes about its purpose and nature, surprising unanimity exists concerning the requirements of good
scholarship. A discussion of the unanimity which underlies
anthropological debate comprises the second section of the
essay. There, attributes of the scholarly apparatus are defined
in a way that seeks to be acceptable to anthropologists regard-

less of their theoretical orientation. The groundwork is thus laid for a discussion of scholarship in ethnographic film, the precondition for its service in anthropology's theoretical debates.

Most features of the scholarly apparatus are prohibitively difficult to realize in film or video. This fact, analyzed in the third section of the essay, has kept ethnographic film outside of the major debates which have shaped the field. Crucial among attributes of scholarship is the requirement that readers may subject ethnographic material to thorough investigation. This preeminent activity of the scholar is only possible when the material to be investigated is inscribed in a medium that allows non-linear study, a requirement that is not met for viewers of the film medium.[2] Rapid, unlimited and repeated searches through film material are always difficult and often impossible. The vast majority of viewers see, and indeed are expected to see, a film only once. Because of this, makers do not often attempt to present serious scholarship in their works. Infrequent cases of scholarship that interpret ethnographic films are therefore very different from those based on ethnographic texts: films are treated more as foreign artifacts of the culture they depict than as vocal participants in the shared cultural and intellectual heritage of scholarship. Yet even if such elements of the apparatus as the defense of theses and the critique of rival schools were to occur in film, limitations of the viewer's memory and the inability to take adequate notes render the medium inappropriate for scholarship.

A means to overcome the impasse between a rapid-fading medium like film and the requirements of scholarship has been developed through computer technology. Videodiscs and CDs, which can store an enormous amount of audiovisual and textual material, may be accessed through databases to form instructional, hypermedia programs. Because audiovisual material is stored digitally, the experience of viewing need no longer be linear, unrepeated and brief. Non-linear access and vulnerability to repeated study, properties necessary for adequate scholarship and once exclusive to text, are now permanent properties of ethnographic film.

The implications of this development for audiovisual anthropology are enormous. With debilitating restraints on scholarship released, makers and users will be free to integrate the traditional apparatus into their films and their investigations. The fourth section of this essay suggests new paths which hypermedia will permit visual ethnographies. The opportunities opening for artistic and scientific expression can only be glimpsed, but one point at least is certain. The empirical bases of anthropological fieldwork will come to be more thoroughly shared and more deeply appreciated through hypermedia's introduction of scholarship to anthropological filmmaking.

I. Existing Proposals for Ethnographic Film

In an earlier essay (Biella 1988), I analyzed the epistemological assumptions which underlie dominant theses about how ethnographic films ought to be made. Here, I begin by investigating the implicitly syllogistic legitimation on which such theses base their claim. The epistemologies and the understandings of "ethnography" held by many authors on anthropological film theory could not be farther apart. Yet the syllogistic structure of the arguments, and the logical errors to which the arguments succumb, are the same.

Dyhrenfurth (1952), for example, argues that "scientific" anthropological films must condense time through editing. Thoroughness of description in ethnographic film is, for Dyhrenfurth, an attribute legitimated by the demand for "completeness" in ethnographic texts. This demand may no longer seem credible, but the search for justification in a single attribute of texts continues. Goldschmidt (1972), working with more contemporary assumptions, proposes that only "representative" cultural practices should be filmed: the attribute of ethnography which legitimates his argument is anthropology's commitment to the study of normative behavior. Ruby (1975, 1980) suggests that anthropological films should concentrate "reflexively" on the methodology used in their production: his legitimation is the fact that textual ethnographies must include a section on methodology. In a parallel effort, Karl Heider (1976) prescribes a strategy for ethnographic film to achieve "holism," an attribute of ethnography which many anthropologists consider to be legitimate in print. Again, Sorenson and Jablanco (1975) pursue textual anthropology's research orientation, and suggest a filming strategy which is legitimated in the standard commitment to data presentation for reanalysis. Stylistic proposals offered by MacDougall (1975, 1978, 1991) for multitextual filmmaking share concerns with written anthropology for attributes of discursive experimentation. Similarly, Marcus (1990) advocates the use of techniques which problematize traditional representation, arguing that the style which will best express the postmodern, textual ethnographic vision in the cinema is montage.

These proposals for filmmaking strategies have more in common than the fact that they all quest legitimation in anthropological paradigms which have been established in print. Each of the proposals favors a particular attribute of ethnographic writing, and champions it as essential for anthropological film. Each prescribes a particular filming-strategy, and argues that it brings to film that favored attribute. Most interestingly, each argues syllogistically.

Texts on ethnographic film also disagree. The premises of their syllogisms are alike in form, but not in content. Authors differ concerning the particular ethnographic attribute which should be championed (call it attribute "a") and concerning the particular filming-strategy which should be prescribed (strategy "s"). Yet all seek legitimation of a Conclusion, how films should be made, with the logic outlined below. The syllogism is not made *explicitly* in the essays cited, but it is their moving force.[3]

Theories of ethnographic film seek legitimate in the following syllogism:

Premise 1:   Ethnographic films must have attributes of ethnographic texts.

Premise 2:   Ethnographic texts have attribute *"a."*

Premise 3:   Ethnographic films made with filming-strategy *"s"* have attribute *"a."*

Therefore:

Conclusion: Ethnographic films must be made with filming-strategy *"s."*

The syllogism is flawed. Its practical implications for film-making are not definitive and its truth-value is formally doubtful.[4] Two ambiguities can be identified. First, granting that strategy *"s"* is one means to introduce attribute *"a"* to ethnographic film, it logically may not be the *exclusive* means to do so: other strategies may be equally capable of performing the task, and may be superior in other ways. A second ambiguity is present: granting the premises, the logical possibility exists that attribute *"a"* is *insufficient:* ethnographic texts may contain many additional, necessary attributes (*"a-prime," "a-double prime"* and so on) which must also be introduced to a film if it is to incorporate everything necessary for a competent ethnography.

In regard to the first ambiguity, exclusivity, some authors acknowledge that their recommended filming-strategy exists among others which are equally capable of transmitting anthropological knowledge. Marcus, for example, writes that his cinematic "requirements [for multitextualism] .... are by no means exhaustive" of valid alternatives (1990: 6). Marcus'

Conclusion, therefore, is to be interpreted particularistically: "Some ethnographic films must be made with filming-strategy 's.'" Marcus seeks to expand the repertoire of expression in anthropological filmmaking without forbidding other strategies,[5] without false exclusivity.

Heider (1976) leaves no room for the possibility of alternatives: he claims that his prescribed strategy, to shoot "whole-bodies in whole scenes, with long takes, in wide angle with sync-sound," is the exclusively-valid means to achieve "holism" in ethnographic film.[6] Heider's Premise 3, then, is intended to be interpreted universalistically: "*Only* ethnographic films made with filming-strategy 's' have attribute 'a.'" It follows that Heider's Conclusion is to be interpreted in the same way: "*All* ethnographic films must be made with filming strategy 's.'" Formally, Heider's logic is unassailable: when the middle term of a syllogism is distributed, the conclusion *is* universal. Of course, formal truth in a syllogism does not indicate that the premises are true. Indeed, when interpreted universalistically, Heider's Premise 3 and Conclusion are factually *incorrect*. Alternative filming-strategies can also communicate "holism," and in more satisfactory ways. The formal truth of Heider's syllogism distracts attention from the first type of ambiguity: his insistence on universalism and exclusivity introduces unwelcome limits to the search for appropriate ethnographic film styles. This negativity outweighs the usefulness that Heider's prescriptions have in certain contexts (Biella 1991: 40).

The attribute of ethnography which is championed by Ruby (1975, 1980), reflexive exegesis of methodology, flounders on the second ambiguity, insufficiency. Ruby states: "Being reflexive is virtually synonymous with being scientific" (1980: 165). Despite the fact that reflexivity is necessary, it is not sufficient in science. Ruby's statement is therefore misleading or incorrect. Scientific practice in anthropology and elsewhere demands far more of a practitioner than reflexive method.

Other attributes are necessary for the attainment of an ethnography, adequately defined.

Existing syllogistic prescriptions for ethnographic film are incomplete and limiting. Yet when the middle term of a syllogism is true and fully distributed, the conclusion is also true. Thus, if a filming-strategy "s" could be designed to duplicate, exhaustively, all attributes of written ethnography (and assuming counter-factually that there were universal agreement about what a written ethnography ought to be!), then the filming-strategy would be "ethnographic" in a comprehensive sense.

The next section of this paper does not attempt so ambitious a course as to propose universal attributes of ethnography, although such a course may not be futile. (Despite arguments to the contrary [e.g., Barrett 1984], contemporary paradigms of cultural anthropology are not "radically incommensurable.") The purpose here is to identify necessary attributes of anthropological *scholarship*, the intellectual foundation of the discipline. In this, the present argument maintains the structure of the syllogism and of the literature on ethnographic film discussed above: attributes of anthropological scholarship will be identified and, ultimately, proposed for inclusion in film.

II. The Scholarly Apparatus in Anthropology

The list of attributes of scholarship presented below was compiled from texts on the subject of writing for the social sciences, articles about normative criteria and peer review in scholarly publications, reviews in anthropology, and diverse works of ethnography, ethnology and sociology. The first three criteria described here are requirements for proper scholarly *argumentation*. The remaining five are attributes of the *medium* in which a scholarly work must be inscribed: without the latter five, research and other scholarly activities would be extremely

difficult or impossible. Before the computer age, these attributes were only available in some sort of printed form: stone,
clay tablets, or paper provided scholars with a "hard-copy"
necessary for their work.

A number of authors have focussed on the means by which
ideology and bias are expressed through a seemingly-neutral
glass of scholarship (Gouldner 1971; Hindess 1973; Denich
1977; Bauer 1990; Dolch et al. 1990). These works, like those on
ethnography as text (Marcus and Cushman 1982; Hutnyk 1987;
Geertz 1988; Myers 1989), demonstrate conclusively that the
content of scholarship, however rigorously it is conducted, is
neither politically neutral nor value-free.[7] The present essay
pursues a different goal. Here, the concern is to describe the
formal attributes of scholarship and of scholarly media that are
acknowledged and employed by *all* scholars, regardless of their
theoretical orientations, political commitments or truth-claims.

In anthropology, a field otherwise torn with hostile perspectives, presence of the scholarly apparatus is universally
acknowledged to be a major indication of professionalism.
Basic agreement about the apparatus exists among paradigmatic alternatives. This is true, for example, with regard to the
demand for originality, clarity and adequate bibliographic
support. The moment that an original thesis is clearly expressed, of course, agreement across paradigmatic lines is
likely to end. The apparatus thus provides means by which
authors have agreed to disagree, a "Robert's Rules of Order"
within scholarly anthropology.

If a printed work is evaluated as worthy of attention in the
discipline, the eight attributes of scholarship described below
will almost certainly be represented in it. Improper argumentation, the inadequate articulation of the first three attributes,
provides grounds to question an author's professionalism,
credibility and usefulness. Failure of the medium to provide for
the latter five attributes renders a work impractical to study. As
such, the attributes of the apparatus are an important part of the

intellectual and logical bulwark of contemporary anthropological discourse.

The scholarly apparatus is largely unavailable to viewers of
the ethnographic film in the darkened room. Because films are
linear and brief, complex arguments, footnotes and citations
are inappropriate; cross-references in the service of research
are futile; rapid searches are impossible; and repeated study
and note-taking are extremely difficult at best. Indeed, by far
the strongest effect of the apparatus on ethnographic film,
beyond the influence of funding agents and ethnographic
consultants, has occurred within print anthropology, the "discipline of words" (Mead 1975). Yet even in the rare case of films
which have textual scholarly companions, the texts are often
unavailable to film viewers.

Following are essential components of the apparatus of
scholarship. They developed from centuries of scholarly practice in the medium of print, and their transferability to film
cannot occur without a profound restructuring of that medium.

(1) The scholarly work must be articulated within or in clear
    response to an established intellectual paradigm.

As a rule, individual publications strive to attain comparatively limited objectives which are recognized to be valuable
because they exist within the much larger goals of a disciplinary framework or paradigm (Kuhn 1962). The first criterion of
the scholarly apparatus, which peer reviewers weigh heavily
when considering a work for publication, is the prescription
that the objectives of the work do in fact further existing goals
(Lindsay 1978. 19, Berardo 1981. 771). Authors must demonstrate
adequate familiarity with the relevant paradigmatic literature,
to earn the right to be heard in a forum with stringent entrance
requirements, to show the place of their own contribution, and
to demonstrate originality (Berardo 1981: 775-776; Berry 1986:

1). When the purpose of the work is to critique a paradigm, exceptionally detailed exposition of its assumptions is required.

(2) The work must adhere to standards of clarity and argument within that paradigm.

Once having insured that an essay will contribute to the historical project of a paradigm within the discipline, peer reviewers must also consider its immediate project: they insist on adherence to a number of standard components of "good writing." For example, the objectives and purposes of the work must be established at its outset and consistently maintained (Berry 1986: 39; Fischer 1970: 3; Almackk 1930: 11; Smigel and Rors 1970: 21), definitions should be provided to minimize ambiguities in vocabulary (Fischer 1970: 25; Knop 1967: 90), and the research method must be in accordance with accepted canons (Bouju 1989: 160).[8] Despite factional disputes between competing paradigms in anthropology, majority and minority positions agree on the need for standards of intellectual integrity. Foremost among these according to the majority view are Merton's (1973a [1942]) criteria of "universalism" and "organized skepticism." These rules state that final judgements of evidence must be made independently of the social attributes of individual scholars and must await adequate evidence.[9] One theoretician states that peer reviewers must judge whether an author:

> was a bad observer, whether he was credulous, suffered from illusions, prejudices, etc., whether the author's condition was such as to preclude him from objectivity and truthful reporting, and whether he was habitually negligent or indifferent (Subrahmanian 1980: 169).

Peer review is generally anonymous, in order to further remove personality from evaluation (McGiffert 1988: 46). One author within the majority position even suggests that scholars should pretend that their own works were written by a stranger, in order to criticize them more objectively (Berry 1986: 46)!

In contrast, minority positions hold that the social and personal attributes of observers cannot coherently be removed from an understanding of the achievements of science. Variants range from the post-neo-Kantianism of Rorty (1983), and radical empiricism of Stoller (1989) to the ineluctable historicization of knowledge in praxis (Rigby 1985, 1992; Laclau and Mouffe 1985).

Regardless of paradigmatic positions, it is universally acknowledged that an author in the social sciences must not shirk debate. Just as scholars are required to cite intellectual forebears, they must also anticipate and answer the criticism which their arguments are likely to receive (Berardo 1981: 777). Authors are expected to cite and counter opposing conclusions (Gilbert 1977; Kaplan 1965: 181). The young scholar is told that he should "'bend over backwards' to prove himself wrong before accepting hypotheses" (Knop 1967: 91).

In contrast to scholarship's extreme pressure for adherence to tradition and conformity to rules of "good writing" is its parallel insistence on originality. Paradigms cannot remain vibrant and attractive without the infusion of new ideas. Thus, original work, properly grounded in tradition, is highly valued and rewarded (Almack 1930: 223; Wolff 1970: 637; Subrahmanian 1980: 168; Berardo 1981: 773; Chase 1970: 262; Bannerr 1988: 109; Lindsay 1978: 19). Plagiarism is considered as improper as the falsification of data (Merton 1973b; Banner 1989).

Within important quarters, the quest for originality is understood to promote scientific progress in Popper's (1972) sense. Although many others view progress to be an illusion, they nevertheless conform to disciplinary pressure for original ideas and publications (e.g., Kuhn 1962; Rorty 1983). The work of Tyler (1986) is noteworthy in this regard because it exemplifies stringent, albeit unusual, standards of literary craftsmanship, originality and rigor, yet sees ethnography as a cite for therapeutic evocation rather than scientific progress.[10]

(3) The work must be comprised of standard sections which are cross-referenced and partially-redundant.

Scholarly books almost always include the same standard sections: title, publication data, acknowledgements, table of contents, introduction, statement of the problem, thesis, argument, data, quotations, figures, tables, photographs, conclusion, footnotes, appendices, index and bibliography. Articles may add an abstract to this list and dispense with the table of contents and index.

Because all scholarly works have the same standard design components, experts as well as users with only a modest background in scholarship are able to approach an unfamiliar work and quickly find those sections in which the information that they need is contained. Regularity in the scholarly apparatus leads to regularity in scholars, permitting "identical tasks [such as finding information] to be performed by different persons at different times" (Subrahmanian 1980: 6).

Scholarly works include partial-redundancy between sections in order that one idea may be presented at different degrees of brevity and difficulty. Internal cross-references and the author's self-monitoring reports provide another type of functional, non-linear redundancy in scholarly works. Strong essays give running summaries of data and arguments as well as conclusions when goals are met. Such reports are intended to render a work highly vulnerable to critique by others, since a demonstrated failure of any claim or self-evaluation may be fatal to an argument. Thus, the formal property of scholarly works which obliges writers to express themselves clearly in regard to premises, goals, milestones and results not only helps to keep them honest in the short term of authorship but also provides a basis for critique by future scholarly readers.

(4) The work must be inscribed in a medium which allows rapid, non-linear access to all of its components.

The mandatory table of contents and index sections of lengthy scholarly works, along with cross-references within the text, use page numbers and page headers to allow rapid, accurate, non-linear access to specific locations or information. Non-linear navigational facility is essential because readers bring needs, questions and criteria to scholarly works which were not the principle concern of the author (Knop 1967: 91). Most information cannot be discovered rapidly from a reading that begins on the first page. An intelligent and rapid evaluation of a book also requires judgement based on non-linear sampling. Random-access navigation is often attributed exclusively to electronic media, but it is clearly a property which facilitated scholarship in books long before the computer revolution.

(5) The medium must allow users to spend any amount of time in recursive study of any part of the work.

The opportunity for repeated, non-linear study, combined with redundancies that are calibrated in degrees of difficulty, permit persevering beginners to become increasingly sophisti cated. The reader may return as often as necessary to difficult passages, gaining insight into the implications of earlier, simpler descriptions. Advanced readers speed ahead to advanced material.

Authors anticipate non-linear reading. Even the best-intentioned authors, who write in the anticipation of extended critical review, cannot present an argument which is sure to be completely clear and self-explanatory on the basis of one reading. Many factors mitigate against the success of comprehension on the basis of one linear reading. Among them are the possibilities that the scholarly reader may grow fatigued, be ignorant of vocabulary or of bibliographic prerequisites, or be prejudiced sufficiently against an idea to require repeated exposure to persuasive argument.

(6) The medium must allow users to take unlimited notes.

If texts were not frozen in time, constantly available to the reader, accurate note-taking, one of the principle requirements for scholarly practice, would not be possible. Without notes, current scholarship could not accurately recall, preserve and develop past work. Notes introduce a further element of non-linearity to research. They permit readers to decipher an author's point, to distill and rearrange distant portions of a text, and to create new or clearer interpretations.

Essayists on techniques of scholarship recommend that simple, one-idea notes be recorded on single, one-idea note cards (Subrahmanian 1980: 156-9). This practice allows non-linear, original combinations of many authors' ideas to be created, long after reading, through the rearrangement of cards. Insofar as the most compelling aspect of an argument is its overarching structure or vision, notes which encapsulate this vision in terms which are most inspiring to the note-taker can be more helpful than the physical presence of the original text.

Original ideas are spawned in familiar paradigms and inspired by the ideas of others. But readers cannot always anticipate which of a scholar's ideas should be remembered or will later be useful. Readers must take far more notes than they will use: as one author puts it, "Waste is inescapable from research" (Berry 1986: 31); another adds, "A scholar must have many items of information at his command; he is constantly in need of adding to his store of information" (Almack 1930: 223). An essential feature of note-taking for scholarship, then, is that it compensates for the inevitable failure of human memory in an endeavor the success of which requires accurate acknowledgement and the precise reproduction of detail (Coyle 1971: 18).

Scholarship is a tradition in which note-takers are the authors of that from which others will later take notes. Readers are writers. In both capacities, scholars can only meet their responsibilities because text provides the patience of print, a constant accessibility to note-taking, an openness to repeated, non-linear study.

(7) The medium must allow authors to make unlimited foot-
    notes.

Scholarship has been dubbed "ordeal by footnote" (Coyle 1971: iii), and it may sometimes be locus for the arcane to digress into the obscure. But an author's footnotes, like a reader's notes, serve important functions as non-linear, digressive arguments. Footnotes allow an author to suggest fertile alternatives to the flow of an idea without compromising its original logic or coherence (Garraghan 1946: 383): through the footnote, time is made to stop in the march of a sentence while an alternative path is suggested for exploration.

Footnoted digressions, like parenthetical remarks, may temporarily cause readers to lose track of an argument in the main text. The confusion is easily cleared, however, and is justified in light of the benefits of these addenda. In disciplines where finickiness about words must sometimes predominate, footnotes permit authors to guard against being misunderstood. Clarifying remarks in a footnote may serve only the needs of a few experts for extreme precision. When such information is seen to reside in a footnote, less technical readers know that they may ignore it without danger of losing the main thrust of a thesis.

Yet theses are often not linear arguments. In some works, such as Weber's PROTESTANT ETHIC (1958), footnoted digressions are so integral to the thesis that it is doubtful whether the author's vision could have been communicated in any other way. Derrida's GLAS (1976), too, is an extended experiment in non-footnoted, non-linear argument, with as many as four half-autonomous texts vying for attention on one page. Like Adorno's footnotes which recapitulate the dialectic and are home in time for tea, like poetry, these works provide oceanic insight.[11] Digressive footnotes serve to humanize the rigid structures of the scholarly apparatus. They show that ambiguity, anecdote and playfulness have a serious purpose, a fact to which this essay will have reason to return.

(8) The medium must allow authors to make unlimited bibliographic references.

Bibliographic references bring to the scholarly text its greatest non-linear achievement. Scholarship's principle raisons d'être are a provisional commitment to the traditions of the past and an overriding commitment to serve the future. A crucial requirement of bibliographic citations, therefore, is to situate the current work and justify it as part of a living intellectual heritage. The citation of sources contributes to this task as well as establishing in the minds of readers the important information of what literature was not employed (Gerraghan 1946: 391). Scholarly readers scan the bibliography of a work in order to establish whether its author has adequately explored the intellectual territory that the work is supposed to expand.

Scholars also recognize that another function of the bibliography is purely "ceremonial" (Oromaner 1981: 235), to praise the proper ancestors (to "shine in the reflected glory" [Gilbert 1977: 116]) and to obtain peer approval "by contesting published results which the intended audience believes to be false" (Gilbert 1977: 121). Bibliographic homage is a necessary part of scholarly survival: as such, it does not always guarantee the value of the text that is cited (Mander 1989) or assist readers in ascertaining "truth." As one author suggests, "scholars worry a lot about which 'school' they belong to, with good reason, for many fields, highly factionalized, reward or punish people by the allegiances they display" (Becker 1986: 38).

The all-too-human side of bibliographic citation is further demonstrated by the function that references serve in laying claim to intellectual property (Gilbert 1977: 116). In a field with intense pressure for original contributions, from one author's perspective a bibliography serves only as:

> a social device for coping with problems of property rights and priority claims. Only incidentally do these citations serve as a careful and accurate reconstruction of the scholarly precursors of one's own contribution (Kaplan 1965: 181).

Yet conventional wisdom is correct that citations also verify the accuracy, or enhance the plausibility, of statements in a text (Gerraghan 1946: 383) and allow "a future reader to check on the researcher" (Berry 1986: 33). In the case of citations from fieldwork, standards for authenticating and contextualizing informants' reports are comparatively high because the possibility of recognizing fraud is comparatively slim (Meillassoux 1991: 163; Fox 1990: 68).

Finally, bibliographic citations provide assistance for scholars or students who want to explore a new topic more fully (Coyle 1971: 37; Kaplan 1965: 182). The discovery of a large bibliography in a specialized field saves the tedium of repeating a search which has been conducted before.

In sum, scholarly practices in anthropology, and the medium in which scholarly material can be inscribed, allow readers and authors to protect the discipline's heritage as it is transformed through debate. Scholars cut a path between conformity to intellectual antecedents and the innovations of their own intellectual ambition. In order for scholarly ambitions to be achieved, texts must be available to be read and reread, written and rewritten. Texts await recognition of merit just as they lie vulnerable to critique. The accessibility of the printed text, footnote, and citation to repeated, non-linear scrutiny and note-taking is thus essential for readers to benefit from or critique the validity of an argument. Scholarly readers and writers can therefore only meet their fundamental responsibilities because the medium in which scholarly works are inscribed has the availability and the patience of print.

III. Incompatibilities of Scholarship and Ethnographic Film

Scholarship can only exist in an appropriate medium and with proper argument. Because, with rare exceptions, films can only be viewed linearly and at the pace established by their makers, properties of the *medium* of film hinder the scholar's work. As a consequence of this intransigent linearity, makers generally design films which minimize the *argumentative* attributes of scholarship as well.

Most ethnographic films exist without any specific scholarly support. A few makers, however, have used the only method available to integrate the scholarly apparatus into film, the publication of textual ethnographic companions. Such works can only be written with the aid of generally-unavailable slow-motion projectors or editing machines, which permit recursive analysis. Among such works are Bateson and Mead (1942), Collier (1972), Heider (1972), Worth and Adair (1972), Rundstrom, Rundstrom and Bergum (1973), Sorenson (1976), Connor, Asch and Asch (1986), Chagnon (1986), Rollwagen's edited collection (1988b), and Taussig-Lux (1993).

Textual companions satisfy three of the criteria of scholarship. Because they are written by the filmmakers, they can present the film's anthropological paradigm (Criterion #1) as well as provide the film with appropriate footnotes and citations (#s 7 and 8). Before hypermedia existed, the satisfaction of these three criteria in textual companions served anthropological film scholarship in the most responsible way. As will be shown, the remaining criteria could not be met satisfactorily for film: although the text could have standard components and be studied rapidly and recursively, properties of actual films continued to frustrate scholarship.

Despite the importance of ethnographic companions written by filmmakers, from the perspective of critical scholarship, the author of a work should not be its only critic. The vibrancy of any discipline requires original and competitive views. In rare cases when a single film has been subjected to analyses by different scholars, the scholars' paradigms, purposes and successes have varied dramatically. This is true both when a single film has been analyzed diachronically (e.g, Canudo 1927; Calder-Marshall 1963; Danzker 1979) and synchronically (Freedle, ed. 1989). Ultimately, the value of a scholarly work can only be judged from a perspective that is comparative and historical.

Ethnographic companions, written by the makers of anthropological films, do not exhaust films' *potential* use. Yet anthropologists are relatively indifferent to the opportunities provided by ethnographic films; scholars rarely frequent ethnographic film archives. Indeed, film has remained outside the ambit of scholarship and standard scholarly resources for the two reasons mentioned at the outset of this section.[12] First, the film medium is not conducive to research: without preventing scholarship, it places upon it severe limitations.[13] Second, as a consequence, anthropological filmmakers restrain their creative experimentation with the medium to the extent that they take advantage of properties which are most likely to assure communication with single viewings. Scholarship flourishes in texts which are designed to reward repeated, lengthy, nonlinear research.

In the following, these assertions are argued in regard to companionless ethnographic films, and to films whose companions are unavailable. The final sections of this essay show that the limitations of such films can be removed when the material is integrated into hypermedia.

(1) Established relationship to an intellectual tradition

On occasion, glimpses of an ethnographic film's commitment to its anthropological school or paradigm may be given in the narration. Rarely, though, are the requirements of Criterion #1 met with the stringency demanded of textual scholarship. Rarely are a film's objectives specified or is the articulation of its objectives within a paradigmatic framework discussed. Rarely do filmmakers demonstrate their familiarity with significant literature. Rarely do filmmakers show that they are not about "to rediscover the wheel" (Lindsay 1978: 26), or to repeat discredited or clichéd theories. Almost never do ethnographic films attempt criticism of existing films, texts, theories or paradigms. Anthropologists' "felt need" for theory, described by Rollwagen elsewhere in this volume, is rarely satisfied in film.

At one point of the ethnographic film production process, however, a genuine effort is made by the scholarly community to contend with the demands of Criterion #1. Film collaborations with qualified fieldworkers are increasingly common, and agencies require scholarly documentation before funding an anthropological film (Biella 1989). The scholarly and theoretical credentials thus established, however, virtually disappear in the finished work. This is true because filmmakers (and funding agencies) know that the product is to be viewed only once. They know that any verbal argument will be rapid-fading and that viewers will necessarily suffer from limited attention spans. Theoretical discussion must be minimized. Thus, the effort of funding agencies to respect Criterion #1, although sincere, contributes little to the mandatory requirement that a scholarly work should acknowledge its assumptions and lay itself bare to the vulnerabilities entailed by the commitment to an intellectual paradigm.

With theoretical discussion minimized in anthropological film, the historical practice of scholarship (the capacity to conduct a critical analysis of a work's objectives in relation to its paradigmatic assumptions) is effectively terminated. A double standard therefore exists between anthropological film and the rest of the discipline. To appreciate the inconsistency, one need only imagine the reaction of scholars to a textual ethnography which, like the majority of ethnographic films, justifies its theoretical laxity with the following excuse:

> Do not object to the minimization of theory in this work because anonymous reviewers for the agency which funded it have declared it to be based on adequate theoretical foundations.

If failure to satisfy Criterion #1 has previously been acceptable in ethnographic film, one can only assume that film images are so valuable to the field that the failure has been justified. Nevertheless, the omission of theory is poison to legitimate scholarship. Unarticulated theory, covert justification with unknown arguments, and approval by anonymous reviewers can never be the foundation of judicious, critical thought. Fully "anthropological" films have the obligation to discuss theory, evaluate competing interpretations, and argue the relation between event and abstraction (Rollwagen 1988a: 305). A compelling demonstration of this case for film is made in Vered (this volume).[14]

Anthropological scholarship, in all schools of thought, has purpose: its self-imposed goals. Paradigms historically define and organize goals. Criticism transforms them. As long as films remain removed from criticism, they will play only a marginal paradigmatic role.

(2 and 3) Standards of argument, format and redundancy

Significantly absent in films are scholarly standards of "good writing" and argument, as well as a standard, hierarchical and partially-redundant format. Anthropological films strive for organization and clarity, but the standards that they employ are not those of texts. Films are not designed with the expectation of receiving extended, non-linear analysis. As a result, most of the normal sections of the scholarly apparatus (from acknowledgements to appendices) are absent. Films have no adequate means to contend with the fact that their viewers represent different levels of expertise: filmmakers therefore cannot take advantage of educational redundancies at different levels of difficulty.

Standard, argumentative engagement with other experts in the discipline virtually disappears: assertions in films usually are made without reference to, or benefit of, contradiction. Although quotation is the fundamental acknowledgement of scholarly tradition, anthropological films almost never refer to texts or to other films. Indeed, many ethnographic films convey a sense of "timeless reverie" (Nichols 1981: 292). The clichéd vision in many films, of untouched cultures which are forever isolated from ourselves, suggests cultural worlds *sui generis*, without their own histories, without previous efforts of comprehension. A less scholarly attitude could hardly be imagined.

Small wonder that a maker of profound ethnographic visions still expresses the concern: "understandings communicated by film may always be ... unacceptable to anthropologists" (MacDougall 1978: 421). The abandonment of the culture of anthropological scholarship may allow filmmakers more completely to convey the culture of non-Western people. Films sustain the vital pulse of compassion. Indeed, from the perspective of praxis, compassion must be considered a ninth criterion for legitimate scholarship! Yet passionate and evocative visions, however valuable, often fail to conduct necessary critique. Only when transformed can films provide service to all domains of scholarship.

(4) Rapid, non-linear access

The film *medium* also hinders processes of scholarship. Films have no equivalent to pages that can be easily skipped, marked and found. Non-linear retrieval, extremely important for efficient research, is impossible.[15] The absence of tables of contents and other standard sections of print conspires with the lack of page numbers to frustrate the normal practices of scholars. Linear retrieval is paralyzingly slow. Rapid exploration of a film, to determine whether it is worthy of further investigation, is very difficult to conduct.

Because anthropological films are generally viewed in a classroom group rather than by an individual scholar, when a section of film *is* replayed, the purpose is usually "closed" in Collier's sense (1988: 86): that is, it provides a demonstration rather than allowing for an open-ended exploration. Exploration "wastes" time, a requirement that may be "inescapable from research" and scholarly note-taking (Berry 1986: 31) but is hard to justify in group process.

(5) Recursive study

The mandatory linearity of film and the pace determined by filmmakers negatively affect many aspects of film scholarship. It has been argued above that the amount of time which a viewer needs to understand a difficult idea in a film constrains the film's design. In contrast, the difficulty of written ideas is largely irrelevant to the design of scholarly texts. When a reader judges that a difficult written passage merits repeated study, the reader will commit the necessary time. Films are rarely studied recursively. Only when a filmmaker decides that certain footage is sufficiently important that it should be re-peated, shown in slow motion, or frozen, do viewers experi-ence the capacity of recursive exposure that is always available to them in print media. Yet even in such cases, viewers are dependent on the one filmmaker's judgement of importance: authentic scholarship cannot be satisfied with such prejudgements.

Because the experience of viewing a film is brief, makers are reluctant to expend precious screen-time on materials that require intense study. Because the experience is linear, stan-dard features which assume that study will be recursive (such as theoretical discourse, definitions, discussions of method, calibrated redundancies, cross-references, demonstrations of originality, and posted milestones and summaries) are gener-ally considered more distracting than instructive, and appro-priate only in publications.

Such features reward scholarship but are lost in a medium that resists academic investigation. As a result, many anthro-pological films seek to achieve that equilibrium point between difficulty and comprehensibility which is established by broadcast television. Many television producers apparently hold the theory that only the lowest common denominator of a target audience's intellectual capacity should be addressed. The trend in broadcast programming is to place downward pressure on the equilibrium point. A paucity of intellectually stimulating broadcast offerings and low viewer-expectations reinforce each other. Indeed, comparative research in educational media suggests that the very fact that information is presented on a television screen indicates to many viewers that the information is not important (Hannafin and Phillips 1987).

(6) Unlimited note-taking

Notes permit scholars accurately to associate, evaluate and represent texts by others in their own scholarly productions. Before hypermedia, even under the most ideal conditions for film analysis, no satisfactory means was available for scholarly note-takers to represent or quote film adequately. The film scholar's notebook was limited to sketches and words force-pressed into representing a phenomenon that is photographic, kinetic and acoustic. Past authors on film, using the best techniques available, were only able to publish representative photographs. Sound and motion were lost. To quote a motion picture well (and to take notes about it well) one must present motion pictures. The quality of film scholarship has suffered as a result of these technical limitations.

(7 and 8) Unlimited footnotes and bibliographic references

Finally, the potential of scholarship can only be achieved with non-linear footnotes and bibliographies. Although these two features are separated physically from the text to which they are linked, they may rapidly be found. The *separation* of the two features prevents confusion that might otherwise result from an overload of information in the main text. The *rapidity* with which separated features may be found insures both that the time consumed in search will not be more valuable than the information gained by it, and that readers will not be likely to forget the ideas which originated their search by the time that it has achieved its purpose. Readers return to the main text knowing that it, like everything else on the printed page, always awaits their attention with equanimity and undiminished intelligibility.

In contrast, film cannot both separate features and allow rapid access between them. Filmmakers have no functional equivalents to the footnote and bibliographic reference, which optionally may be read or ignored. In film, makers must choose whether to situate these features in the main text (like parenthetical remarks in print that everyone is obliged to read) or to eliminate them completely. The choice is not usually difficult. In film, time is at a premium and comprehension must be achieved from linear viewing: thus, when an idea in a film is not precisely to the point, the presumption is that it ought to be eliminated. The filmmaker is thus denied the valuable opportunity for inspired digression, an opportunity always provided by the play between text and footnote.

Scholarly readers of texts are anticipated to bring a wide variety of expertise, interests and purposes to their reading. As a result, footnotes that address a wide variety of concerns are commonplace in print, and are perfectly legitimate. In film, however, the variety of digressive remarks that are considered legitimate and feasible is far more circumscribed, its potential growth stunted by an hypothesized lowest common denominator of the audience.

Indeed, it is not a secret that film's proclivity to eliminate digressions always threatens to expand into the elimination of ideas that are merely *difficult*. Ambitious editors of educational films are warned that they can achieve but limited goals with the time that they have on screen: "It's only public television. Try to keep it simple."[16] The world of scholarship, with its difficulties, is not welcome.

The Flight from Scholarship to Film

The absence of "difficulties" of scholarship in anthropological film is an important loss to the discipline. Reasons for the flight away from academic concerns by ethnographic filmmakers cannot be explained entirely by the technical and pragmatic arguments presented above. Psychological and ethical issues are also involved. To show why this is true, the contrast of text and film concludes with a last appraisal of footnotes and bibliographic references, scholarship's greatest feats of non-linear communication.

Textual scholarship increases the pertinence of argument, centers concentration on problems, and challenges deviant points of view. Embedded in the midst of this sobriety, footnotes and references serve contradictory functions. On one hand, they set a limit on the impact of the ideas that they express, preventing them from boiling into profusion and chaos. On the other hand, these non-linear addenda serve the field precisely because they are artistically, even uncontrollably, suggestive: they permit authors to give a glimpse into the fecundity and pertinence of issues which might otherwise escape attention.

The scholarly apparatus exerts its limiting control over the footnote and bibliographic citation iconically. Small print and relegation to the end of the page or the text suggest that a footnote is of minor importance. The brevity of the bibliographic citation within a text likewise conceals its power: to call forth distant genius, perhaps betray the author, seduce and kidnap readers. From their terminus in the hinterland, footnotes and bibliographies announce to all who hear the next-ships-out to unknown ports-of-call. Scholars' complacency is ever-vulnerable to their challenge.

Beyond the sobriety and demands of scholarly publication, then, lies scholarship's functionally-disruptive, exciting instabilities: of resonance, digression and contradiction. Instability gives clues to the transformation of bestowed wisdom. There, too, is the source of poetic and eidetic knowledge, a source with strong appeal to makers of film.

In the past, ethnographic filmmakers have had no equivalent to textual footnotes and bibliographies. Visual ethnographers could not take advantage of many opportunities for creative instability which these attributes provide to textual scholars: opportunities for the play of ideas and theory, for resonant anecdotes, and for time-and-concept bending digressions which add refinement or point out contradiction.

Footnotes give unlimited opportunities to break from the disciplines of logic and bestowed wisdom, to serve textual anthropology as legitimate vehicles for movement beyond paradigmatic confines. In contrast, film's best available means to present fecundity while maintaining coherence is simply to return often to one idea, to demonstrate facet upon facet of its implications in linear display. But even this technique must cut its concepts into bite-sized bits, clipping them to size for the postulated short-term mental power of the lowest common denominator.

Many ethnographic filmmakers who rebel against a theory of predigested education are left in a dilemma. The choice of an artistic profession suggests a penchant for ambiguity, but the commitment to anthropology indicates respect for scholarly discipline as well. Some filmmakers resolve the problem by renouncing all together the use of artistic ambiguity, "unscientific" impressionism: they canonize their inflexibility in one-dimensional, prescriptive film styles. Others take the opposite extreme, fleeing false visions of science as well as serious scholarship. In the knowledge of anthropology's need for compassionate understanding, and buoyed by an awareness that legitimate attributes do exist within scholarship to serve equally humanizing functions, they have turned to the presentation of oceanic, cultural insight. Benefits of their flight have been profound, but they have been achieved at the high price of reinforcing ethnographic film's distance from the practice of scholarship and the discipline's ultimate foundation in theory.

The price no longer needs to be paid. With the innovations of interactive hypermedia, film can remain intensely aesthetic while also serving in the universe of debate. Obstacles which once inhibited use of the scholarly apparatus no longer need inhibit the invention of new strategies for ethnographic film.

IV. Hypermedia

The development of multimedia computer technology and software in the last decade will presently bring an end to the marginalization of ethnographic film in the discipline of anthropology. With the new medium, filmmaking anthropologists need no longer limit the understandings communicated by film to ideas which are comprehensible on the basis of brief, linear viewings. The full apparatus of textual scholarship can now be brought to bear. Motion pictures can now be stored as digital information on a hard drive, CD-ROM or other device, and any frame can be instantly available for unlimited viewing. Images, played on the computer, can be stopped, shrunk or slid to a side of the screen, beside analytical text. Film and text may both be given electronic buttons (like automated footnote asterisks) which, when clicked, call forth the other to the screen. A multitude of texts may have reason to access a single piece of film. A single image may require the creation of many buttons to call up different texts. Users interactively click on and follow these electronic links, either at the lead of the ethnographic media designer, or on the basis of their own search-techniques and research goals.

Enhancing hypermedia's capacity for rapid, non-linear search of film and text is its enormous storage capacity. One CAV laser disc can store 108,000 photographs at the quality of a normal television screen, or one hour of live-action television, or sixty hours of low-resolution sound. Text, too, can be stored on laser disc, but, at least until very recently, it could not be searched conveniently. CD-ROM provides a storehouse for easily-searchable texts: an entire encyclopedia can be held on one compact disc. In 1991 it became feasible to store photographs and moving pictures on disc, as well. At the present (late 1992), a CD-ROM can hold 2,000 full-screen, color photographs of moderate quality or one feature-length film of relatively poor quality. Improvements are announced almost weekly: the quantity and quality of images that can be stored on disc will certainly increase.[17]

Despite this promise, relatively little has been written on the subject of hypermedia and ethnographic film.[18] Howard's (1988) discussion of these topics is very useful because of its broad range of creative and practical suggestions for ethnographic hypermedia makers. Ironically, the thrust of Howard's argument is opposite to that presented here: Howard argues compelling about the limitations of textual scholarship. My point is to show that without the scholarly basis in text, anthropological media will remain in the sidelines of the discipline.

Hypermedia technology allows the eight criteria of scholarship to be met in the study of film. Because text can be appended to any frame or frames, the demonstration of a film recording's relationship to an established intellectual tradition, Criterion #1, is assured. Hypermedia links intellectual antecedents, difficult arguments of theory and method, quotations from the print literature and other media, the logical derivation and defense of new concepts (indeed the entire theoretical component of the scholarly apparatus) to presented audiovisual recordings. The goal of integrating particularistic empirical recordings into scholarly debate becomes closer, because the recordings can be thoroughly, and collectively, studied. Fundamental questions of the relationship between observation and construct will take on unprecedented significance.

Any argument or footnote which can appear in print can appear as hypermedia: Criteria #s 2 and 7 are therefore met. Like print scholarship, ethnographic hypermedia also serves readers of different levels of expertise. As the user becomes increasingly knowledgeable about stored audiovisual documents and the instructional design, he or she may progress through material which is increasingly difficult. Hypermedia has the patience of print: it attends the user, forgives fatigue, is fresh when needed again.

Criterion #3, the requirement for standard sections of published works, redundancies and pagination can easily be made a part of anthropological hypermedia. Film frames, shots and sequences are all identified numerically and may be coded for content so that they are easily searched and linked to text in multiple ways. The numbering system permits efficient use of a table of contents, intertextual cross-references, and an index. Because, in hypermedia, ethnographic recordings are always ensconced in the context of written analyses, all of the partial redundancies of print can be brought to bear upon them. The user may return to important recorded passages and their attendant analytical texts at will, may review passages or images indefinitely.

Rapid, non-linear access and unlimited opportunities for recursive study, Criteria #s 4 and 5, are available with access to a computer. Ethnographic film recordings of great length may be stored on disc and be as available for use as is any digital information. Intransigent linearity disappears when film and sound are digitized.

The scholar's need for unlimited note-taking, Criterion #6, is also satisfied in hypermedia. Users will be able to quote films, visually and acoustically, with frame accuracy, using the familiar computer technique of copy-and-paste. Verbal notes and sketches can easily be appended to these quotations with keyboard and mouse manipulations.

Finally, the capacity of makers to append unlimited bibliographic references to film satisfies Criterion #8 and adds greatly to the significance of film for scholarship. Engagement in the time-tested tradition of citation-homage, along with unprecedented engagement in the theoretical clashes of the discipline, will provide anthropological media-makers with the standard opportunities for full citizenship (for professional survival, recognition, and advancement) too often unavailable to makers of profound, but non-scholarly, ethnographic films.

V. Conclusion

All ethnographic filmmakers agonize over the loss of clarity and complexity which results when shaping a film into a half-hour, hour, or even longer format. The huge storage capacity of hypermedia will resolve this dilemma: edited film and rushes can all be included for review. Of course, films which are very long (like those which will be stored in the computers of the future) still provide only a small sample of cultural behavior. Repeated viewings do not increase sample size any more than sample size determines the importance of events that are sampled on film. It is clear that the introduction of hypermedia to the tools of critical anthropology leaves unchanged its basic theoretical questions and ethical dilemmas.

On a personal note, I have spent a great deal of time in the last twelve years contemplating and writing about twenty hours of audiovisuals that I recorded among Tanzania Ilparakuyo Maasai in 1980 (Biella 1984, 1988, 1989, 1991; Biella and Cross 1981). The experience of working with "raw" ethnographic footage for such a long period of time is currently available only to filmmakers. It may be difficult for others to appreciate why such long-term study of the same material might continue to be rewarding. In my case, rewards have stemmed from the ethnographic richness of the original events, the audiovisual fidelity, length and variety of the recorded scenes, and the changing theoretical interests which I have brought to bear on them.

When ethnographic recordings of comparable length begin to appear as hypermedia, other anthropologists will find similar rewards and challenges. Elsewhere in this volume I describe how I have applied the eight criteria of scholarship to an interactive CD-ROM which contains many hours of the Ilparakuyo Maasai material.

Hypermedia will invigorate theoretical questioning of ethnographic footage and film. The first section of this essay mentions strategies for filmmaking which champion different attributes of ethnography: the impulse to holism, the demand for methodological reports, the attractiveness of a large sample size, and the commitment to multifaceted montage. Through application of the scholarly apparatus to hypermedia, these and many other approaches can easily be brought to bear on the same audiovisual material. All of these approaches might coexist or indeed receive criticism in a single ethnographic hypermedia publication.

Hypermedia can exploit the scholarly advantages of text. But if scholarship is the greatest unifying strength of print anthropology, ethnographic film also brings to the discipline its own unique powers. Chief among these is the ability to communicate a compelling sense of intimacy with the subject, an oceanic insight into something new and startlingly important. Through ethnographic imagery, the viewer gains an unprecedented, privileged sense about people who would otherwise remain unknown. To foster this sense is anthropology's best strategy to combat ignorance, indifference and racism. It will not be lost. In time, hypermedia will allow film and scholarship to join forces in the service of compassion and critique.

NOTES

1   David MacDougall's "Beyond Observational Cinema" (1975) provides inspiration to this essay in more than name. To Sarah Elder and
Paul Stoller I owe thanks for impassioned comments on an earlier
version of this paper. David Plath kindly pointed to the lasting importance of the pencil in the computer age. Richard Chalfen discovered
for me many of the CD-ROM visual ethnographies cited below, in
footnote 18. Special thanks are owed Peter Rigby for his profound
example of *praxis* in scholarship.

2   Unless otherwise specified, I will use the words *film, motion picture*
and *video* interchangeably.

3   In the literature cited, proposed strategies for ethnographic film are
unintelligible without attributing to them this syllogism and Conclusion. The syllogistic structure is nowhere explicitly articulated: I have
triangulated it from the context.

        In different variants of the syllogism, attribute *"a'"* is given such
definitions as "multitextualism" or "holism," while *"s"* receives definitions including "cinematic montage" or "attributes of
ethnographicness."

4   In the following discussion, I depend on McCall's BASIC LOGIC
(1969).

5   Rollwagen is among the rare advocates of diversity. He writes:

        The framework [of anthropological films] should be
        based in anthropological understandings but should per-
        mit a wide variety of approaches to filmmaking in order to
        allow for a wide variety of filmmakers, purposes and
        audiences (1988a: 299-300).

        Chiozzi (1989) is another important proponent of stylistic diversity.

6   I demonstrate that Heider's (1976) prescriptions for ethnographic
filming, although inconsistent, are universalistic and rigidly exclusionary in Biella (1991).

7   Both this model of the scholarly apparatus and the application of it
to film are value-laden and political. Scholarship, like film, is a battle-

ground of ideas and values which are often in strong competition. Sometimes, the stakes in human welfare are high. To resolve questions of fact, the scholarly apparatus involves tradition, argument and methods which facilitate discovery and agreement. To resolve questions of value, the apparatus is silent. Through it, however, arguments and pleas concerning values are often made.

Though the apparatus itself is relatively neutral, its machinations provide the only valid reasons for a scholar to accept that one intellectual tradition is superior to another. The effort here, as before (Biella 1984, 1988), is to establish a territory within anthropology that uses cinematic images and is both intellectually committed and compassionate. By showing how film may be inducted into the apparatus of scholarship, I hope to raise its intellectual contribution. With the tools of a more powerful intellectual tradition and therefore with increased respectability, film can contribute more meaningfully to epistemological and theoretical battles. At the same time, it can preserve intense awareness of human lives and values.

8   It bears repeating that the universal insistence by peer reviewers that publications should serve established paradigms and meet accepted methodological canons does not mean that peer reviewers agree universally with one another. Disparities between paradigms and methodologies are enormous. In sociology, where these linens are washed more openly than in anthropology, the following observations are made: "Accumulated evidence suggests that agreement among peer reviewers is the exception rather than the rule" (Bakanic and Simon 1987: 632). "Slightly more than one quarter of the [peer reviewers'] judgements involved serious disagreement" (Smigel and Rors 1970: 21).

In a related vein, an ethnographic study of scholarly publishing houses found editors repeatedly to insist: "The ingredients of a successful book are not known.... Objective measures hardly exist" (Powell 1978: 227).

9   See Berardo (1989) for a contemporary critique of Merton's (1973a) criteria.

10   Polier and Roseberry (1989) and O'Meara (1989) provide very different critiques of the Tyler (1986) phenomenon.

11   Jameson describes the method of Adorno's *opus* as an extension of his use of the footnote:

In [*Philosophy of the New Music*], the footnote as a lyrical form allows Adorno a momentary release from the inexorable logic of the material under study in the main text, permitting him to shift to other dimensions, to the infrastructure as well as to the wider horizons of historical speculation. The very limits of the footnote (it must be short, it must be complete) allow the release of intellectual energies, in that they serve as a check on a speculative tendency that might otherwise run wild....

[Adorno's] essays are thus the fragments of or footnotes to a totality which never comes into being....For what as fragments they share in spite of the dispersal of their raw material is the common historical situation itself, that moment of history which marks and deforms in one way or another all of the cultural phenomena which it produces and includes, and which serves as the framework within which we understand them (Jameson 1971: 9, 52).

12   Rollwagen (1988a: 287-8) offers two different reasons, complementary to whose which I believe actually predominate, as explanation of the absence of theory in anthropological filmmaking. They are, he suggests:

> (1) a high percentage of the most visible writers on "ethnographic" filmmaking are not anthropologists by training and cannot be expected to deal in their writings with anthropological theory in any sophisticated manner; and (2) a high percentage of the anthropologists who write on "ethnographic" filmmaking for classroom and / or general-audience use reflect a position common in anthropology in general that the primary task for anthropologists is the collection of data (through ethnography or, in this case, through "ethnographic" filmmaking) and that the collection of this data should be based on the nature of that which is observed, not on theory. Theory is thus viewed as one product of data collection rather than a framework within which ethnography proceeds. As a result, the literature on anthropological filmmaking is, for the most part in terms of anthropological theory, sterile.

Rollwagen's first argument is telling, but it must also be acknowledged that a large number of writers on ethnographic film do have doctorates in anthropology. The second argument, essentially that ethnographic film theory is dominated by a reductive materialist epistemology, has great explanatory power (Biella 1988, 1991). Rollwagen does not discuss the incompatibilities of the film medium with the scholarly apparatus.

13   Since the work of Marshall McLuhen (1964), the idea that different media foster and inhibit the communication of certain messages has often been abused. Baudry (1974-75), for example, applies this idea in his questionable argument that the Renaissance perspective of a "normal" camera lens is essentially ideological. Henderson (1976) similarly suggests that deep-focus cinematography is inherently, irreducibly "bourgeois." Like claims by anthropologists which I critique in the text above, that only one camera style can be "scientific" or "ethnographic," the arguments of Baudry and Henderson are essentialist and ahistorical. (For more detailed critiques, see Rothman [1976] and Biella [1984]).

In contrast to arguments based on reductionist essentialism, when I state that the medium of film places severe limitations on scholarship, I am concerned only with the practicalities of *efficient* communication. Calf-skin scrolls served scholars for many centuries, yet scrolls, like film and video, provide only slow, linear access to their resources. Many attributes of the scholarly apparatus (including labyrinthine expositions such as this footnote) are quite *possible* to include in film. Their use in that medium, however, would be so unwieldy that it would not occur. If scholars wanted to fast-forward a video in order to read each footnote or citation which appeared at the end of a tape, they would not be prevented from doing so by the essence of film. Good sense, not essences, has kept footnotes and citations in textual ethnographic companions. Thus my argument is not essentialist. It *is* historical: the major premise of the essay is that recent innovations in digitized film technology have removed previous limitations.

14   Neither Rollwagen (1988a) nor Vered (in this volume) attempts to show how scholarly obligations realistically can be met in a linear, rapid-fading medium like film.

15   My thesis that film exposition is irreducibly linear may superficially appear to be in conflict with that of Rollwagen (1988a: 313-314), in which *all* comprehension is argued to be achieved through non-linear processes of thought. I would stipulate that Rollwagen is correct but that some media serve non-linear analytical processes more effectively than others. In this sense, film is far more linear than print.

16   The advice was given by David Othmer, Managing Director of Philadelphia's PBS affiliate WHYY, to Laura Jackson, Producer/director of an ambitious television documentary on El Salvador, in August, 1992.

17   Market forces will continue to stimulate advances in digital image compression. Since its release to the public last year, Apple Computer's software for digitized movies, QuickTime, has been upgraded twice. With the upgrades, the memory consumed by digitized photographs

and movies is now 1/100th of that required only a year ago. Of great importance to educational media makers also is Apple's decision to include a CD-ROM port in new Macintosh computers. A proliferation of the means to *play* CDs will not go unnoticed by text publishers: a large market will be opening for the new medium. Finally, the cost of creating a CD master from digital information stored on a hard drive is less than $1,000. CD copies of the master cost as little as $1 each! The video revolution has thus been continued by that of the computer: production and distribution costs are falling significantly. With lower costs and the fact that the apparatus of scholarship now has a permanent place in film hypermedia, funding agencies will come to recognize the fact that interactive video is as cost-effective and as beneficial to the field of anthropology as is text-based research. Agencies and publishers will begin to seek out visual anthropologists to produce works for distribution on CD. Since this impetus will be for educational distribution irrespective of the standards required for television profit-making, stultification in fields of visual communication is sure to be reduced.

18   A number of works exist on non-visual computer applications to the discipline. Despite advances in technology since the time it was published, Hymes' THE USES OF COMPUTERS IN ANTHROPOL-OGY (1965) presents a wide range of issues that are still significant. Boone and Wood (1992) provide a contemporary account, including a chapter on anthropological education through computer, a large bibliography and a list of available software. Richard Wagner has been instrumental in translating the Human Relations Area Files to CD-ROM. See Wagner (1989) for a useful bibliography and a list of newsletters and software. The monthly *Anthropological Newsletter* of the American Anthropological Association now includes brief computer notes in a column, "Soft.Where." A group at the University of New Mexico publishes the *MacAnthropology* newsletter.

The 1987 issue of *Senri Ethnological Studies* (Vol. 20) is dedicated to hypermedia and computer-based visual education in anthropology. MacFarlane (1990) discusses a laser-disc visual encyclopedia, created under his direction, about the Naga people of the Assam-Burma border. Another interactive disc, on Andean culture and the Quechua language, has recently been announced: contact Dr. Rosaleen Howard-Malverde; Institute of Latin American Studies; University of Liverpool; P.O. Box 147; Liverpool, England, L69 3BX. THE FIRST EMPEROR OF CHINA, a searcher-friendly double laser-disc concerning an archaeological site, is available from Simmons College. PERSIUS 1.0 is probably the most impressive hypermedia work, an interactive library on ancient

Greece. It includes a CD-ROM and videodisc, and is available from Yale University Press.

Outside the domain of cultural anthropology, more than fifty journals are dedicated to computer-based educational media. Some of the most imaginative work comes from Brown University's IRIS project (e.g., Yankelovich et al. 1988). Landow's (1991) "rules" for hypermedia authors are particularly helpful to anthropological designers. See also his excellent HYPERTEXT: THE CONVERGENCE OF CONTEMPO-RARY CRITICAL THEORY AND TECHNOLOGY (1992) for a discussion of post-modernism and the computer revolution.

REFERENCES CITED

Almack, John C. (1930). Research and Thesis Writing: A Textbook on the Principles and Techniques of Thesis Construction for the use of Graduate Students in Universities and Colleges. Boston: Houghton Mifflin Co.

Bakanic, Von, Clark McPhail, and Rita J. Simon (1987). The Manuscript Review and Decision-Making Process. American Sociological Review 52(5): 631-642.

Banner, James A. (1988). Preserving the Integrity of Peer Review. Scholarly Publishing 19: 109-115.

Banner, James A. (1989). Guidelines for Peer Review of Sponsored Book Manuscripts. Scholarly Publishing 20(2): 116-122.

Barrett, Stanley R. (1984). The Rebirth of Anthropological Theory. Toronto: University of Toronto Press.

Bateson, Gregory, and Margaret Mead (1942). Balinese Character: A Photographic Analysis. Special Publications of the New York Academy of Sciences, 2. New York: New York Academy of Sciences.

Baudry, Jean-Louis (1974-75). Ideological Effects of the Basic Cinematographic Apparatus. Allen Williams, trans. Film Quarterly 28: 39-47.

Bauer, Henry H. (1990). Barriers Against Interdisciplinarity: Implications for Studies of Science, Technology and Society. Science, Technology, and Human Values 15(1): 105-119.

Becker, Howard, with a chapter by Pamela Richards (1986). Writing for Social Scientists: How to Start and Finish Your Thesis, Paper or Article. Chicago: University of Chicago Press.

Bedaux, R.M.A. (1991). Review of "Dogon Restudied: A Field Evaluation of the Work of Marcel Griaule" by Walter E.A. van Beek. Current Anthropology 32(2): 158.

Berardo, Felix M. (1981). The Publication Process: An Editor's Perspective. Journal of Marriage and the Family 43(4): 771-779.

Berardo, Felix M. (1989). Scientific Norms, Research Publication Issues and Professional Ethics. Sociological Inquiry 59(3): 249-266.

Berry, Ralph (1986). How to Write a Research Paper [2nd ed.]. Oxford: Pergamon Press.

Biella, Peter (1984). Theory and Practice in Ethnographic Film: Implications of the Ilparakuyo Maasai Film Project. Ph.D. Dissertation, Anthropology, Temple University.

Biella, Peter (1988). Against Reductionism and Idealist Self-Reflexivity: The Ilparakuyo Maasai Film Project. IN Anthropological Filmmaking: Anthropological Perspectives on the Production of Film and Video for General Public Audiences, Jack R. Rollwagen (ed.) Chur and London: Harwood Academic Publishers, pp. 47-72.

Biella, Peter (1989). Trouble Shooting: Overcoming Problems of Collaboration with Filmmakers. New York Folklore 15(3-4): 41-64.

Biella, Peter (1991). Criteria for Style and Content in Ethnographic Film. CVA Review, Spring: 37-41.

Biella, Peter, and Richard Cross (1981). Maasai Solutions: A Film about East African Dispute Settlement. Philadelphia: Contemporary Historians (limited edition).

Boone, Margaret S., and John J. Wood (eds.) (1992). Computer Applications for Anthropologists. Belmont, CA: Wadsworth Publishing.

Bouju, Jacky (1991). Review of "Dogon Restudied: A Field Evaluation of the Work of Marcel Griaule" by Walter E.A. van Beek. Current Anthropology 32(2): 159-60.

Calder-Marshall, Arthur (1963). The Innocent Eye: The Life of Robert Flaherty. London: W.H. Allen.

Canudo, Ricciotto (1927 [1971] Another view of Nanook. IN The Documentary Tradition: From Nanook to Woodstock, Lewis Jacobs (ed.) New York: Hopkinson and Blake, pp. 20-21.

Chase, Janet M (1970). Normative Criteria for Scientific Publication. American Sociologist 5(3): 262-4.

Chiozzi, Paolo (1989). Reflections on Ethnographic Film with a General Bibliography. Denise Dresner, trans. Visual Anthropology 2(1): 1-84.

Collier, John (1967). Visual Anthropology: Photography as a Research Method. New York: Holt, Rinehart and Winston.

Collier, John (1972). Alaskan Eskimo Education: A Film Analysis of Cultural Confrontation in the Schools. New York: Holt, Rinehart and Winston.

Collier, John (1988). Visual Anthropology and the Future of Ethnographic film. IN Anthropological Filmmaking: Anthro-pological Perspectives on the Production of Film and Video for General Public Audiences. Jack R. Rollwagen (ed.) Chur and London: Harwood Academic Publishers, pp. 73-96.

Connor, Linda H., Patsy Asch, and Timothy Asch (1986). Jero Tapakan: Balinese Healer. New York: Cambridge University Press.

Coyle, William (1971). Research Papers (3rd ed.). New York: Odyssey Press.

Danzker, J.A. Birnie (ed.) (1979). Robert J. Flaherty: Photographer / Filmmaker. Vancouver: Vancouver Art Gallery.

Denich, Bette (1977). On the Bureaucratization of Scholarship in American Anthropology. Dialectical Anthropology 2(2): 153-157.

Derrida, Jacques (1975). Glas. John P. Leavey, Jr. and Richard Rand, trans. Lincoln: University of Nebraska Press.

Dolch, Norman A., Mary Frank Fox, Anthony M. Orum, Gary Alan Fine, Richard L. Simpson, Sheldon Stryker, and Joseph W. Schneider (1990). Symposium: Ethical Issues in Scholarly Publication. American Sociologist 21(1): 67-95.

Dyhrenfurth, N.G. (1952). Filmmaking for Scientific Filmmakers. American Anthropologist 54: 147-152.

Fischer, David Hackett (1970). Historians' Fallacies: Toward a Logic of Historical Thought. New York: Harper and Row.

Fox, Mary Frank (1990). Fraud, Ethics and the Disciplinary Contents of Science and Scholarship. The American Sociologist 21(1): 67-71.

Freedle, Roy O. (ed.) (1989). Collegial Discourse: Professional Conversation Among Peers. Norwood, NJ: Ablex Publishers.

Garraghan, Gilbert J. (1946). A Guide to Historical Method. Jean Delanglez (ed.) New York: Fordham University Press.

Geertz, Clifford (1988). Works and Lives: The Anthropologist as Author. Stanford: Stanford University Press.

Gilbert, G. Nigel (1977). Referencing as Persuasion. Social Studies of Science 7(1): 113-122.

Goldschmidt, Walter (1972). Ethnographic Film: Definition and Exegesis. P.I.E.F. Newsletter 3(2): 1-3.

Gouldner, Alvin W. (1971). The Coming Crisis of Western Sociology. London: Heinemann.

Hannafin, Michael J., and Timothy L. Phillips (1987). Perspectives in the Design of Interactive Video: Beyond Tape versus Disc. Journal of Research and Development in Education 21(1): 44-60.

Heider, Karl G. (1972). The Dani of West Irian: An Ethnographic Companion to the film Dead Birds. Andover, MA: Warner Modular Publications, Module 2. (1976). Ethnographic Film. Austin: University of Texas Press.

Henderson, Brian (1976). Toward a Non-Bourgeois Camera Style. IN Movies and Methods, Bill Nichols (ed.) Berkeley: University of California Press, pp. 422-437.

Hindess, Barry (1973). The Use of Official Statistics in Sociology: A Critique of Positivism and Ethnomethodology. London and Basingstoke: MacMillan.

Howard, Alan (1988). Hypermedia and the Future of Ethnography. Cultural Anthropology 3(3): 387-410.

Hutnyk, John (1987). The Authority of Style. Social Analysis 21: 59-79.

Hymes, Dell (ed.) (1965). The Uses of Computers in Anthropology. London and the Hague: Mouton.

Jameson, Fredric (1971). Marxism and Form. Twentieth Century Dialectical Theories of Literature. Princeton: Princeton University Press.

Kaplan, Norman (1965). The Norms of Citation Behavior: Prolegomena to the Footnote. American Documentation 16(3): 179-184.

Knop, Edward (1967). Suggestions to Aid the Student in Systematic Interpretation and Analysis of Empirical Sociological Journal Presentations. American Sociologist 2(2): 90-92.

Kuhn, Thomas (1962). The Structure of Scientific Revolutions. Chicago: University of Chicago Press.

Laclau, Ernesto, and Chantal Mouffe (1985). Hegemony and Socialist Strategy. London: Verso.

Landow, George P. (1991). The Rhetoric of Hypermedia: Some Rules for Authors. IN Hypermedia and Literary Studies, Paul Delany and George P. Landow (eds.). Cambridge, MA: MIT Press, pp. 81-103.

Landow, George P. (1992). Hypertext: The Convergence of Contemporary Critical Theory and Technology. Baltimore: Johns Hopkins University Press.

Leach, Jerry W. (1988). Structure and message in *Trobriand Cricket*. IN Anthropological Filmmaking: Anthropological Perspectives on the Production of Film and Video for General Public Audiences, Jack R. Rollwagen (ed.) Chur and London: Harwood Academic Publishers, pp. 237-251.

Lindsay, Duncan (1978). The Scientific Publication System in Social Science: A Study of the Operation of Leading Professional Journals in Psychology, Sociology and Social Work. San Francisco: Jossey-Bass Publishers.

MacDougall, David (1975). Beyond Observational Cinema. IN Principles of Visual Anthropology, Paul Hockings (ed.) The Hague: Mouton.

MacDougall, David (1978). Ethnographic Film: Failure and Promise. Annual Review of Anthropology 7: 405-425.

MacDougall, David (1991). Whose Story Is It? Visual Anthropology Review 7(3): 2-10.

MacFarlane, Alan (1990). The Cambridge Experimental Videodisc Project. Anthropology Today 6(1): 9-12.

Mander, Peter (1989). The "Double Life" in Academia: Political Commitment and/or Objective Scholarship. Dissent 36(154): 94-99.

Marcus, George (1990). The Modernist Sensibility in Recent Ethnographic Writing and the Cinematic Metaphor of Montage. Society for Visual Anthropology Review 6(1): 2-12, 21, 44.

Marcus, George E., and Dick Cushman (1982). Ethnographies as Texts. Annual Review of Anthropology 2: 25-69.

McCall, Raymond J. (1969). Basic Logic: The Fundamental Principles of Formal Deductive Reasoning. New York: Barnes and Noble.

McGiffert, Michael (1988). Is Justice Blind? An Inquiry into Peer Review. Scholarly Publishing 20(1): 43-48.

McLuhen, Marshall (1964). Understanding Media. New York: McGraw-Hill.

Mead, Margaret (1975). Visual Anthropology in a Discipline of Words. IN Principles of Visual Anthropology, Paul Hockings (ed.) The Hague: Mouton, pp. 3-10.

Meillassoux, Claude (1991). Review of 'Dogon Restudied: A Field Evaluation of the Work of Marcel Griaule', by Walter E.A. van Beek. Current Anthropology 32(2): 162-3.

Merton, Robert K. (1973a). The Normative Structure of Science. IN The Sociology of Science, Norman W. Storer (ed.) Chicago: University of Chicago Press. pp. 267-278.

Merton, Robert K. (1973b). Priorities in Scientific Discovery. IN The Sociology of Science: Theoretical and Empirical Investigations, Norman W. Storer (ed.) Chicago: University of Chicago Press, pp. 286-324.

Myers, Greg (1989). Persuasion, Power and the Conversational Model. Economy and Society 18(2): 221-244.

Nichols, Bill (1981). Ideology and the Image: Social Representation in the Cinema and other Media. Bloomington: Indiana University Press.

O'Meara, J. Tim (1989). Anthropology as Empirical Science. American Anthropologist 91(2): 354-369.

Oromaner, Mark (1981). The Quality of Scientific Scholarship and the "Graying" of the Academic Profession: A Skeptical View. Research in Higher Education 15(3): 231-239.

Polier, Nicole, and William Roseberry (1989). Tristes Tropes: Post-Modern Anthropologists Encounter the Other and Discover Themselves.

Economy and Society 18(2): 245-264.

Popper, Karl (1972). Objective Knowledge: An Evolutionary Approach. London: Oxford University Press.

Powell, Walter W (1978). Publisher's Decision-Making: What Criteria do they Use in Deciding which Books to Publish? Social Research 45(2): 227-252.

Rigby, Peter (1985). Persistent Pastoralists: Nomadic Societies in Transition. London: Zed Books.

Rigby, Peter (1992). Cattle and Capitalism. Philadelphia: Temple University Press.

Rollwagen, Jack R. (1988a). The Role of Anthropological Theory in "Ethnographic" Filmmaking. IN Anthropological Filmmaking: Anthropological Perspectives on the Production of Film and Video for a General Public Audience, Chur and London: Harwood Academic Publishers, pp. 287-315.

Rollwagen, Jack R. (ed.) (1988b). Anthropological Filmmaking: Anthropological Perspectives on the Production of Film and Video for a General Public Audience. Chur and London: Harwood Academic Publishers.

Rothman, William (1976). Against "The System of the Suture." IN Movies and Methods, Bill Nichols (ed.) Berkeley: University of California Press, pp. 451-468.

Ruby, Jay (1975). Is Ethnographic Film a Filmic Ethnography? Studies in the Anthropology of Visual Communication 2(2): 104-111.

Ruby, Jay (1980). Exposing Yourself: Reflexivity, Anthropology and Film. Semiotica 30(1-2): 153-179.

Rundstrom, Donald, Ronald Rundstrom, and Clinton Bergum (1973). Japanese Tea: The Ritual, the Aesthetics, the Way. An Ethnographic Companion to the Film *The Path*. Warner Modular Publications, Module 3.

Smigel, Erwin O and H. Lawrence Rors (1970). Factors in the Editorial Decision. The American Sociologist 5(1): 19-21.

Sorenson, E. Richard (1976). The Edge of the Forest: Land, Childhood, and Change in a New Guinea Proto-Agricultural society. Washington: Smithsonian Institution.

Sorenson, E. Richard, and Allison Jablonco (1975). Research Filming of Naturally Occurring Phenomena: Basic Strategies. IN Principles of Visual Anthropology, Paul Hockings (ed.) The Hague: Mouton.

Stoller, Paul (1989). The Taste of Ethnographic Things: The Senses in Anthropology. Philadelphia: University of Pennsylvania Press.

Subrahmanian, N. (1980). Historical Research Methodology. Madurai, India: Ennes Publications.

Taussig-Lux, Karen (1993). God's Mother is the Morning Star: The Life and Art of Joseph Mender. Ph.D. dissertation, Department of Folklore and Folklife, University of Pennsylvania.

Tyler, Stephen A. (1986). Post-Modern Ethnography: From Document of the Occult to Occult Document. IN Writing Culture: The Poetics and Politics of Ethnography, James Clifford and George E. Marcus, eds. Berkeley: University of California Press, pp. 122-140.

Vered, Karen Orr (1991). Feminism and Ethnographic Filmmaking as Political Praxis. Masters Thesis, Department of Anthropology, Temple University.

Wagner, Richard A. (1989). The Rise of Computing in Anthropology: Hammners and Nails. Social Science Computer Review 7(1): 418-430.

Weber, Max (1958). [1930] The Protestant Ethic and the Spirit of Capitalism. Talcott Parsons, trans. New York: Charles Scribner's Sons.

Wolff, Wirt M. (1970). A Study of Criteria for Journal Manuscripts. The American Psychologist 25(7): 636-639.

Worth, Sol, and John Adair (1972). Through Navajo Eyes: An Exploration in Film Communication and Anthropology. Bloomington: Indiana University Press.

Yankelovich, Nicole, Bernard Haan, Norman Meyrowitz, and Steven Drucker (1988). Intermedia: The Concept and the Construction of a Seamless Information Environment. IEEE Computer 21: 81-96.

from ANTHROPOLOGICAL FILM AND VIDEO IN THE 1990s
Jack R. Rollwagen (editor). Brockport, NY: The Institute, Inc.
© 1993, The Institute, Inc. All rights reserved. ISBN 0-9635206-1-X

Feminist Ethnographic Films: Critical Viewing Required

Karen Orr Vered
Critical Studies of Cinema and Television
University of Southern California

ABSTRACT: Do women make better feminist films than men? How do we identify and characterize a feminist ethnographic film? Questions like these have been the focus of many heated debates among those concerned with both issues of feminism and filmmaking. Among anthropologists there is a growing concern and demand for investigative standards. Explanatory standards should also follow. This chapter approaches these issues from three positions.

First a discussion of the groundings of different feminist epistemologies is presented. Secondly these philosophies generate recommendations for production and evaluation of feminist ethnographic films. Five criteria for assessment of feminist ethnographic film have been developed from this discussion. The five criteria correspond to scholarly standards of anthropology and are interpreted for film production application. They include: Documentation, Material Explanation, Advocacy, Geo-Political Contextualization, and Political Statement. Finally, a case study evaluation of the popularly screened film MASAI WOMEN is offered as an example of how the criteria may guide an informed viewing of a film.

Feminism and Ethnographic Film

Amid the disparate claims to victory and cries of defeat from various actors one can be certain that feminism, in its many guises, is vital. Nothing more clearly indicates the health of feminism than recent attacks against certain theories and their proponents. The popular media's recent attention to theoretician in-fighting, with spotlight on Camille Paglia and her detractors, has served to both inspire the young and revitalize the theory-weary. The debates are raging in all fields, especially those in which women are increasingly out-numbering men, like cultural anthropology.

The development of feminist theory and criticism, the increasing number of women in anthropology, and a re-thinking of the "ethnographic other" have brought to anthropology an acknowledgement of gender as an organizing principle of social order. The variety of theoretical and methodological perspectives which constitutes "feminist anthropology" reflects distinctions among feminist theorists in literary criticism, Marxist feminism, and post-structuralism. Though "feminist anthropology" is not a univocal field, feminist anthropologists have reached a consensus when expressing a common concern over lack of theory and product with respect to feminist ethnographic film.

Feminist anthropology does not attempt merely to analyze women's positions within particular societies to demonstrate their status. Rather, feminist anthropology seeks to develop social change through the practice of anthropological inquiry and dissemination of those findings. The concept of studying gender theory, on the other hand, does not contain the purposefully political essence which is demanded by any effort to secure social change.

Conflicting recommendations for the design and constitution of feminist or gender acute ethnographic film reflect current debates about the writing of ethnography in general (ie.Marcus and Fischer 1986) as influenced by the works of feminist film theorists. This fact makes the discussion of feminist ethnographic film all the more controversial. As well, film has been treated historically in science as a secondary rather than primary tool of both investigation and explanation. Ironically, though film in anthropology, and specifically the sub-discipline of visual anthropology, has been treated like the proverbial "stepchild," education in the last twenty five years (at all levels) has increasingly made use of audio-visual aids, specifically film and video. This fact, coupled with current concerns about the role of gender in social order form the basis for anthropologists to call for critical assessment of gender analysis in anthropological films.

A recent article by Kathleen Kuehnast stands as an example of the nature of prescriptions for feminist ethnographic film (1990). Kuehnast, following a popular line of reasoning, perceives the problem as one of interpretation as she argues that "looking is not a representation of reality, but an interpretation" (1990: 22). She further asserts:

> The camera, if used consciously as a tool to understand different interpretations of a culture and not as a tool to reproduce objective exotic proofs, can assist not only in revealing to ourselves our own cognitive and cultural constructions, but it can also allow others to tell their stories in their own voice, with their own views (1990: 26).

To make better use of existing ethnographic films and to improve the quality of future films, Kuehnast makes two recommendations. The first is that ethnographic filmmakers develop a set of criteria "whereby anthropologists can critically evaluate gender inclusivity in visual ethnographic texts" (1990: 22). "Gender inclusivity," as Kuehnast uses the term, is an explicit acknowledgment of gender as an "analytic category," with which an anthropologist assesses social organization through an analysis of gender construction (1990: 24). Kuehnast's second recommendation is a change of filmmaking personnel: "women [should] make visual images of the world according to their own viewpoint ... reconstructing the female voice" (1990: 25).

Kuehnast's two proposals are examined here. Arguments about how to reconstruct the female voice are examined within the broader discussion of feminist epistemologies. Within this context, the relative value of Kuehnast's recommendation for a personnel change is addressed.

Secondly, I have developed a set of criteria for evaluating gender inclusivity in existing ethnographic and anthropological films derived from the "feminist standpoint" (Hartsock 1983). Though Kuehnast suggests such criteria are needed she does not provide them. I take this opportunity to extend her work in two specific areas. I have applied my criteria in a case study assessment of the film, MASAI WOMEN (Llewelyn-Davies 1974). Kuehnast's critical mention of MASAI WOMEN prompted a detailed investigation of this film.

Kuehnast's recommendations, however valid, are incomplete because they are the product of a particular epistemological position which is itself flawed. Furthermore, her recommendations do not aid resolution of conflict among feminist anthropologists from varying theoretical schools. Though anthropologists who study gender theory agree that gender does structure and mediate experience, they do not agree on *how* this operates.

Feminist Epistemologies

Kuehnast's position, as outlined above, subscribes to a naive empiricism which does not fully transcend the dominant conceptions of scientific objectivity but which still claims to be a liberating praxis. The basic error is one of logic which has the effect of weakening any platform for change at the level necessary to improve ethnographic film production to the degree Kuehnast apparently desires. Her prescriptions for ethnographic film provide the opportunity to expose her implicit epistemological assumptions. In light of the works of feminist theorists Jane Flax (1983), Sandra Harding (1986), and Nancy C. M. Hartsock (1983), who explicitly discuss feminist epistemology and concomitant methodological implications, Kuehnast's particular brand of feminism and its applications and implications for ethnographic filmmaking are discussed.

Nancy Hartsock's "feminist standpoint epistemology" (1983) provides a powerful tool to critique the domination of women under Western patriarchy. The "feminist standpoint" is based on the methodology and model of Marx's proletarian standpoint described, for example, in THE COMMUNIST MANIFESTO. The argument is not that Marx's critique of capitalism is the best model for feminist theoreticians. Rather, it is the adoption of Marx's meta-theoretical claim that "a correct vision of class society is available from only one of the two major class positions" (1983: 284). Hartsock asserts that there is a "privileged vantage point" from which women may critique androcentric institutions and ideology *because* their lives are experienced in materially different ways than men's (1983: 284). This statement may at first appear to confirm Kuehnast's recommendation for a "change of personnel." However, Kuehnast, unlike Hartsock, does not explicitly link a woman's position to subjugation or domination. Kuehnast asserts:

> the camera acts more as a magnifying glass, emphasizing the ethnographer's world view, than it does as an objective lens documenting another culture's world view (1990: 24).

This statement seems to be the cornerstone upon which Kuehnast sets her recommendation that women, not men, make films about women. The naivete of this position becomes increasingly clear when one discusses films about women from cultures outside that of the filmmaker, regardless of the filmmaker's gender. MASAI WOMEN provides a good illustration of this point. Though Kuehnast does describe women as "silenced," she does not provide elaborate reasons for a personnel change.

Hartsock's argument rests on the knowledge that production entails *"both* social relations *and* relations to the world" (Hartsock 1983: 285). This argument is parallel to Marx's description of the proletarian standpoint. In THE COMMUNIST MANIFESTO , Marx and Engels write of bourgeois ideas that they

> are but the outgrowth of the conditions of your bourgeois production and bourgeois property, just as your jurisprudence is but the will of your class made into law for all, a will whose essential character and direction are determined by the economic conditions of existence of your class (1848: 26).

Thus, the feminist standpoint enables one to confront the ruling group's control of the means of mental production to challenge dominant (androcentric and patriarchal) ideology because both individuals and theories of knowledge develop under material conditions and limitations (1983: 288;283). Hartsock's position can most easily be understood as a parallel equation of "bourgeois" to "androcentric" wherein the subjugated proletariat is replaced by the subjugated female.

Clarifying Hartsock's position, Sandra Harding compares the feminist standpoint to a concept of "feminist empiricism." Harding summarizes feminist empiricism as the argument

> that women (or feminists, whether men or women) *as a group* are more likely to produce unbiased and objective results than are men (or nonfeminists) as a group (1986: 25).

Kuehnast's recommendation for a change of personnel at the production level in filmmaking is just such a feminist empiricist approach. Kuehnast's recommendation to improve film content by means of changing personnel constitutes a sort of methodological reform. Locating standards at the production level, Kuehnast imitates the empiricist practice of monitoring methodological norms to increase scientific rigor. Kuehnast *assumes* that women will make "better," "more objective," "more true" ethnographic films. The personnel change implies naive empiricism because Kuehnast *links the gender of the filmmaker with objectivity* and scientific knowledge in general. Ironically, this linkage, in some ways the embodiment of empiricism, is also in direct conflict with a primary empiricist assumption that the observer's identity is irrelevant since adherence to methodological standards insures objectivity. Kuehnast attempts to add the gender of the scientist/filmmaker to the list of methodological standards. This addition is unnecessary within the logical parameters of empiricism and certainly irrelevant from the feminist standpoint. Furthermore, commitment to arbitrary standards of objectivity usually limits one's ability to act as advocate or defense for the poor, the outcast, or the female (Biella 1991, personal communication). Harding and supporters would argue that this personnel change "leaves unchallenged the existing methodological norms" of ethnographic filmmaking (1986: 25). A man or a woman can make gender insensitive films. It is not the gender of the filmmaker that determines the film's content and form. Rather it is the philosophy of filmmaking held by the filmmaker which (among other constraints) determines the film's content and form.

Harding further argues that women's subjugated position within patriarchal power relations and social life challenges the knowledge of the dominant group as "partial." Defining the dominant knowledge as "partial" implies the possibility of expanding knowledge. Logically expansion can be provided by a non-dominant, subjugated point of view. Harding conceives the project:

> not [as] a switch of epistemological and political commitments from one gender to the other but a commitment to understanding the world from the perspective of the socially subjugated (1986: 149).

Harding's position does not, however, imply that one is eternally or fixedly more objective. She states:

> A feminist epistemological standpoint is an interested social location ("interested" in the sense of "engaged," not "biased"), the conditions of which bestow upon its occupants scientific and epistemic advantage (1986: 148).

The object of study is thus restricted to issues of liberating capacity, engaged and interested directly with the circumstances and struggles of the subjugated.

"Engaged" means connected to real material conditions of production and existence in production. The feminist standpoint thus makes apparent the inseparability of epistemology and ontology. Kuehnast assumes that a woman's life circumstances differ from those of a man. However, she does not offer an explanation of how that difference will effect a change in ethnographic film production.

Kuehnast lacks both an adequate theory of the power of imagery, and a theory of political action to guide her recommendations for improving ethnographic filmmaking. I address these two points in their respective order.

Theories about the power of filmic imagery are complex and conflicting at best. Michele Barrett (1985) examines the potential political power of filmic images of women in an analysis which posits film as analogous to literature. For the purposes of my argument, Barrett's emphasis on the production of gender differences in literature and film highlight the most significant issues. She argues that the *meaning* of gender in contemporary capitalism be understood "as *not* simply 'difference', but as division, oppression, inequality, internalized inferiority for women" (1985: 83). The implications of Barrett's analysis for film are twofold. First, the construction of meaning through film "cannot be divorced from its material conditions in a given historical period" (1985: 83). Secondly, and most importantly for the consumption of film in particular, Barrett states:

> since there is no one-to-one relationship between an author's intentions and the way in which a text will be received, the feminist artist cannot predict or control in any ultimate sense the effects of her work (1985: 83).

Barrett concludes these two points define rigid limitations for political art in production and distribution.

Kuehnast's project is also in need of a political theory. Brian Fay provides the foundations of such in CRITICAL SOCIAL SCIENCE (1987). Most important for Kuehnast is Fay's concept of the "activist being." Fay defines the "activist being" as engaged in a relationship in which self-perceptions exert a degree of control over social relations. This understanding is made clear in a feminist practice which advocates the demystification and de-naturalization of social relations. It is argued that mystification and naturalization are products of false conceptions of self and society.

Combining Fay's concept of "activist being" with the feminist standpoint, provided by Hartsock and Harding, forms a theoretical foundation for explicitly political, gender-sensitive and feminist film production.

The feminist standpoint argues that one's knowledge derives from experience and that ultimately this knowledge is applicable to another's experience. This concept underpins the common call for the expression of a "women's voice." When

Kuehnast requests to hear from the "women's voice," she implicitly claims that the voice will be more objective. The idea of objectivity directly conflicts with Hartsock and Harding's concept and analysis of "engaged" reasoning. Harding argues that scientific inquiry, method, and application be guided by moral and political goals. In the forthcoming pages I argue that ethnographic filmmaking must also be guided by moral and political goals.[1]

The feminist standpoint does not allow for the separation of moral and scientific concerns. It does not allow for the separation of fact and value. Scientific inquiry is thus politicized and, consequently, "value neutral" science is rejected as an impossibility. Feminist theorist Jane Flax traces the historical roots of the detrimental separation of fact and value in philosophy: "...being (ontology) has been divorced from knowing (epistemology) and both have been separated from either ethics or politics" (1983: 248). This "divorce" creates a "rigid distinction between fact and value" which has silenced philosophers on "issues of utmost importance to human life" (Flax 1983: 248). Not only have philosophers been silenced but scientists have been socialized to understand scientific research as distinct from, rather than engaged with, political activity.

A wide range of experience has thus been excluded "from the realm of the known, of the rational," most importantly women's experience, blinding social science to gender theory (1983: 270). Flax argues that patriarchal social relations will only be changed when

> the development of theory is seen in relation to practice
> and knowledge itself is demystified, traced back to the life
> histories and purposes (conscious or not) of those who
> produce it (1983: 270).

Feminism seeks to change social relations. The achievement of social change demands a theory of education and politics designed specifically to alter social relations. Brian Fay (1987) cites feminism as a

> "critical philosophy" informing the practice of critical so-
> cial science(1987: 112).

Fay demands that a critical social science acknowledge the dialectical nature of the relationship between ideas and social conditions. Contrary to the Platonic concept of knowledge, which holds knowledge and its application distinct from one another, critical social science seeks to synthesize knowledge with its application. Fay summarizes this position:

> ideas are a function of social conditions, but also...they do
> in turn play a causal role in creating and sustaining particu-
> lar social structures...(1987: 25).

Clearly, feminist empiricism does not qualify as *critical* in Fay's sense. The feminist standpoint, however, does.

Feminist empiricism does not challenge the practices of science nor does it acknowledge the patriarchal base of much scientific knowledge. Feminist empiricism falsely assumes an increased number of women involved in the production of scientific knowledge increases objectivity. The feminist stand-point, however, like Fay's critical social science, advocates the process of consciousness raising. Fay in fact cites the feminist consciousness raising activities since World War II, along with "halfway houses, drug clinics, [and] certain prison-reform programs...," as settings in which successful social change has occurred (1987: 111).

Fay, like Flax, Harding, Hartsock, and Marx and Engels, implies that social science must be conducted dialectically. Knowing must be treated as activity, constituted in social relations. Flax calls for an analysis of material circumstances of life to inform the production of theory. This analysis is also necessary to inform the production of ethnographic film. Carrying Flax's analysis to the realm of film production highlights the insufficiency of Kuehnast's recommendation for a personnel change.

In his eloquent history of the development of social scientific inquiry, Peter T. Manicas (1987) critiques methodological individualism. Methodological individualism for Manicas is part of a philosophy which holds that "facts about society or human action are to be explained solely in terms of facts about individuals" (1987: 271). These individuals, however, are necessarily members of structured social units. Manicas elaborates with a citation of Bhaskar's distinction:

> We can say that a person is hungry or in pain, just as we can say that a lower animal is hungry or in pain. But the moment we say that the person is a tribesman or a revolutionary, cashed a check, or wrote a sonnet, we are presupposing tribes (a social order), a banking system, and a literary form (Manicas 1987: 271).

Quite clearly the critique of methodological individualism indicates insufficiencies in Kuehnast's personnel change proposal. Her assumption, that women will necessarily produce better ethnographic films, denies the validity of Barrett's statement that limitations for the production of feminist ethnographic film exist within the contexts of production and distribution.

Manicas emphasizes the dialectical relationship between behavior and social structure: "...society is incarnate in the practices and products of its members" (1987: 272). Manicas considers society both as medium and product, the form of expression and the statement. So conceptualized, the reproduction of society is achieved through practices. Fay's conception of the activist being echoes Manicas' criticism by pointing out that successful consciousness raising aimed at change has been achieved at an individual level. The concept of the production of "engaged" scientific knowledge, shared by Flax, Fay, Manicas, Marx and Engels, assumes the application of knowledge to have real consequences for how we live whether in public policy, such as the formulation of immigration policies at the turn of century, law, as evidenced in the formulation of status for an individual in the court system, or, as argued here, ethnographic film.

Kuehnast correctly states, "visual ethnographies are viewed by more people than any written ethnography will ever have the chance to be read" (1990: 25). Therefore, distribution of anthropological knowledge, especially through film, contributes to the formulation of ideas not only in the classroom setting but to the general population. Publicly broadcast anthropological films are sources of information, often the *only* information on a people that reaches the general population outside classroom settings. As such, the responsibility of the filmmaker, to adhere to reliable ethnographic detail and to produce a document which does more than merely "other" the subjects, is immense.

Assuming a degree of agency within any given structure, Fay and Manicas both assert the inseparability of epistemology and ontology to prove that knowledge derives from existence within structure. The political challenge to feminists, similar to that of any minority opinion, is to make obvious the union of epistemology and ontology through practice. The project for feminists, both anthropologists and filmmakers alike, is to revive the notion of the "interested" or "positioned" science which negates the myth of value neutral science, knowledge, and experience.

Implications for Ethnographic Film

The feminist standpoint offers the anthropologist the necessary epistemological basis for conducting politically oriented social science. Indeed, the feminist standpoint gives rise to the criteria merely wished for by Kuehnast. These criteria are outlined in the following pages demonstrating through critical example that subscription to the feminist standpoint insures feminist ethnographic film production will be "interested" praxis, purposefully acknowledging the real life existence of women within the structure of the greater society in which they live.

Criteria for Gender Inclusivity in Ethnographic Film

The feminist standpoint provides the epistemological basis for criteria which constitute a check list for the production of "gender inclusive" ethnographic film as called for by Kuehnast. The criteria constitute guidelines for film production as well as points for critical analysis of films which already circulate within academic settings and generalized distribution.

In light of Biella's criticism (this volume) of many ethnographic film theoreticians who "isolate" *particular* attributes of written ethnography to form a basis for filming strategies, I now reiterate the parameters of my criteria. The problem I am tackling is gender inclusivity, one important aspect of an anthropological or ethnographic film. I do not claim to identify or recommend *universal* properties of filmic ethnography. Employing any particular production strategies which grow out of the criteria does not guarantee a "holistic" filmic representation of a culture or society. In the vocabulary of anthropological fieldwork, these criteria may be considered part of the "methods" employed in response to a specific research "problem" or "question" related to gender.

FIVE CRITERIA

1. Documentation of Actual Life Processes;
2. Material Explanation of "Subjugation of Women";
3. Speaking from the Engaged/Interested Position;
4. Broad Geo-Political and Ideological Contextualization;
5. Political Statement.

1. Documentation of Actual Life Processes

The film must document the actual life processes of women in relation to specific material limitations and conditions. This criterion demands ethnographic accuracy, a judgment which must be determined by scholarship and praxis. Such films will elaborate in clear detail material conditions and relations of production as they relate to women as part of a larger society. The film must explain these relations of production through detailed example rather than simple assertion.

2. Material Explanation of "Subjugation of Women"

A film which claims women are subjugated must elaborate how the domination is structured within the particular set of relations specific to that society. The film must document material and ideological conditions which create, foster and sustain the claimed subjugation of women, since the subjugation of any group or individual is based in relations of production and rarely achieved by brute force alone. Specifically this project may include explanation of the relative autonomy women have in particular spheres of activity. This information may enlighten the viewer to the values held by society with regard to power.

3. Speaking from the Engaged/Interested Position

Speaking from the engaged/interested position is achieved in different ways, depending upon the position of advocacy taken by the filmmaker. Recalling the advantage of the feminist standpoint, it allows the filmmaker to advocate for a non-dominant understanding of the issues addressed in the film. There may be more than one non-dominant perspective which the filmmaker may advocate. I offer two examples here.

If the film's project is to document subjugation of women in the society examined by the film, and the material conditions supporting that subjugation have been demonstrated (per criterion point two), the filmmaker must provide information explaining emic conceptions of subjugation and inequity held by the women and others of that society. This explanation must include emic concepts of freedom which are understood as the opposites of concepts of subjugation. It is insufficient to apply only those conceptions held by the documentarist or ethnographer. The latter are generated from social relations and a personal history situated in another social structure. Meeting this criterion ensures that the documentarist has fulfilled the requirement of speaking from the engaged/interested position which provides the epistemic advantage attributed to the feminist standpoint.

The second example relies upon the filmmaker advocating examination and change in her own society. Through a comparison of Western and non-Western concepts, the filmmaker can point out how other forms of social organization give rise to different values and how those values influence the construction of gender and representative roles. In this way, for example, the engaged position of the ethnographer/documentarist may be elaborated as part of a project which compares and contrasts different social structures in an effort to highlight points about Western society.

4. Broad Geo-Political and Ideological Contextualization

The documentarist must include acknowledgment of social systems which influence (or have influenced) the society in question. The national political and ideological systems, in which the society in question is situated and through which that society has developed, must be integrated into the analysis. Furthermore, distinctions among groups within the same linguistic community must be noted since they may be of significance. James Clifford makes these points most eloquently:

> Other groups can less easily be distanced in special, almost always past or passing, times—represented as if they were not involved in the present world systems that implicate ethnographers along with the peoples they study. "Cultures" do not hold still for their portraits. Attempts to make them do so always involve simplification and exclusion, selection of a temporal focus, the construction of a particular self-other relationship, and the imposition or negotiation of a power relationship (1986: 10).

Since ethnographic films are often viewed by students with limited knowledge of the geography and politics of the anthropological settings, the filmmaker must provide some of this information.[2] This ensures that the system/society addressed by the film will be contextualized within broader, non-idiosyncratic categories of analysis, in terms of geography, politics, and ideology. If statements made in a film are idiosyncratic, this too must be acknowledged and explained in relation to the more standard or familiar forms of relations expected in that setting.

5. Political Statement

The moral and political demands of engaged praxis must be explicitly stated. This requires the advocacy position of the filmmaker to be stated clearly. Following Flax, not only the development of theory but also the production of film must be connected to the history and purposes of those who produce it. A concomitant effect of this explicit statement of political purpose will be to advocate change, if necessary, fulfilling the spectrum of political action required by the feminist standpoint. As with criterion point three, the change advocated may be directed at the filmmaker's own society through discoveries made in comparative analysis between very different systems.

Biella (this volume) has described film as "rapid-fading." Due to this quality of the film medium, the values espoused by a film are often difficult to identify as are the theoretical positions taken by the filmmakers. Precisely because of this insidious quality of film construction and viewing practices I argue that the political statement of the film be made consciously and explicitly. Biella claims, that "[t]heoretical subtleties are necessarily lost on viewers" when they are not able to view a film repeatedly. I agree with this assessment but contend that this is not an immutable quality of film nor film viewing. Since film is viewed linearly, as Biella correctly states, it is the responsibility of the filmmaker to repeat important political and theoretical positions. This enables the viewer to rehear important conclusions as one would re-read an important printed passage.

Discussion of Criteria

Application of these criteria to assess a film does not limit one to excluding or preferring analysis of one filmic element over others. For instance, there is no analytical necessity (nor advantage) to separate the discussion of visual elements from the discussion of narration (voice over), interview, or natural sound elements. In the following analysis, both audio and visual elements are considered, individually in some instances and jointly in others.

Additionally, the criteria do not prescribe production details for the filmmaker in the same sense as Karl Heider's (1976) "criteria of ethnographicness" indicate. For example, none of my criteria limit the cinematographer to particular framing or focal length standards. Nor do they prescribe the use of certain editing techniques such as uninterrupted natural sound, interrogative inclusive interviews, or other such style considerations.

Though the criteria do not directly advise on style, consequent to criterion point five, the criteria require that the filmmaker explicitly state political goals. This can be facilitated in some cases through certain stylistic maneuvers, such as the inclusion of questions which prompt interview responses. However, the criteria are not intended as exclusionary proscriptions through which style dictates content.

Case Study: MASAI WOMEN

MASAI WOMEN provides valuable and unique ethnographic information about women of a Maasai homestead and some of their activities. The film production unit and consultant anthropologist, Melissa Llewelyn-Davies, have captured many events and activities which elsewhere have not been visually documented in such detail (Rigby 1991, personal communication). The production unit is commended for this achievement. However, the film attempts more than this: it claims to be a feminist ethnography. In this regard, it fails to meet the criteria demanded by the feminist standpoint. The result is a film which is neither an addition to feminist theory and practice nor an accurate presentation of how Maasai women live within Maasai society. The analytical content of the film echoes the substance of Llewelyn-Davies' written works on Maasai women (1979 and 1981). The same ethnographic details appear in both her writing and film credits.[3]

The film received a mixed review by Beidelman, in AMERI-CAN ANTHROPOLOGIST, stating that the film would be "difficult to employ in a classroom." He specifically criticizes the film for not offering

> scenes of women involved in domestic matters such as fetching water, milking, preparing food, cleaning, fashioning clothing and jewelry, tending babies (1976: 959).

While Beidelman compliments the films' visual beauty and the "refreshing" and "provocative" approach, he looks forward to Llewelyn-Davies providing "us with films of a more anthropological nature" (1976: 959).

The following assessment may be valuable for teachers of anthropology, film, and women's studies precisely because MASAI WOMEN is ethnographically unique as well as idiosyncratic.

The film MASAI WOMEN is not informed by the feminist standpoint epistemological position nor its criteria for application to film production. My analysis is derived from an historical materialist approach. The benefits of this perspective are twofold. First it provides a thorough method for analyzing the numerous and varied influences on issues of gender as they effect social organization. Second, the particularities of Maasai society, in its current encounter with capitalism, are best understood by an explanation which includes the analytic categories of historical materialism.

Below I argue that the film exhibits three basic limitations: ethnographic inconsistencies and inaccuracies, inappropriate use of capitalist categories of analysis, and lack of clarity with regard to purpose and intent, both morally and politically. The ethnographic inconsistencies and capitalist categories of analysis directly conflict with criteria points one, two, and four. Points three and five relate specifically to the moral and political concerns of the film, as directed by the anthropologist.

I have identified these limitations three ways. I elaborate inconsistencies within the film itself, between the film and available anthropological writings on Kenya and southern Maasai, and conclusions issuing from the overall tone of the film. For clarity sake, examples are presented following the sequence of the criteria and limited in number.

1. Documentation of Actual Life Processes: MASAI WOMEN

The first instance of ethnographic inconsistency occurs in the initial segment of the film, as the narrator (Llewelyn-Davies) describes Maasai life generally:

> *A man needs a woman to build his house for him,* milk his cows and do the household chores. But a woman needs a man far more because women can never have rights of ownership over any living animal. To survive they must attach themselves to some man with cows(emphasis added).

Later, Nol Paiaya, a middle aged Maasai woman and wife of a Laibon, is interviewed.[4] The subtitled translation of her words reads: "...when you marry you build your own house, and sit on your own bed." This statement indicates that the Maasai wife in fact does not build a house *for* her husband but rather for herself and her children. Rigby (1985: 147) argues that young men do not have their own homes. They live with parents until they become *ilmurran* ("warriors") and later, when they marry, are permitted to sleep in the house of their wife or wives. The physical structure of the homestead is such that with the addition of each co-wife there is another house built on alternating sides of the cattle paddock gate (Rigby: 1985: 141-147).

Clearly the houses are the domain of the women. Within the film itself, between the narration and the interview material, there is an inconsistency. Other ethnographic literature indicates that the interview material is the more accurate. The credibility of the narration and narrator are consequently drawn into question.

In addition to the inconsistency and ethnographic inaccuracy of this narration, there is also a tone of denigration associated with the statement, "To survive they [women] must attach themselves to some man with cows." The implication is that women, *more than men*, are reliant upon kin relations of production for survival, when in fact, for Maasai society as a whole to exist, both women *and men* must remain "attached" through kinship ties. There is no ethnographic evidence to suggest a Maasai woman is more bound or limited by these relations than a man is.

The editorial decision to include an interview with two young married women on the subject of wife abuse suffers from a similar prejudice. The interviewees supply extensive information about the consequences of adultery for a married woman who is found to have had "a lover." These consequences include "beating," according to the young women. However, the narration fails to include any statement regarding the retribution suffered by a man who has beaten his wife. Nor does the film describe the penalties a man suffers for an adulterous offense. In fact, the practice of having extra-marital love relations is so common among Maasai that they have developed a strict and elaborate system of penalties and punishments for offenders. Kipuri points out that "a man who has committed 'adultery' (or incest) with a classificatory daughter may be both fined and physically chastised by women" (1985: 15). MASAI WOMEN, however, leaves the viewer with a misconception of Maasai society in that women appear to lack any form of recourse in such instances. This one-sided presentation is ultimately due to Llewelyn-Davies' prejudice, but in practice results from the questioning procedure of the interviewer and the editorial decision to exclude additional information. Llewelyn-Davies, both in her writings (1979, 1981) and the film MASAI WOMEN, selectively presents evidence which creates an image of Maasai women as victims of the social organization of their own society. Llewelyn-Davies' victims are powerless either to change their society or leave it.

MASAI WOMEN misrepresents the daily activities and responsibilities of women vis-á-vis those of men. Llewelyn-Davies makes two arguments. The first is that women are subjugated by Maasai social structure. The second, an extension of the first, is that domination of Maasai women is enforced through the division of labor, restrictions on women's participation in important rituals, and a Maasai system of justice which maintains a double standard based on gender. To argue these claims MASAI WOMEN presents evidence which does not meet the demands of criterion point one with regard to documentation standards. The evidence is contradicted within the film and in reference to independent ethnographic literature, as I have shown. The material conditions of Maasai life presented in the film are not substantially nor convincingly documented in the film.

With regard to women's limited participation in ritual, the narrator states that "after their own circumcision, women *only* participate in ceremonies through their children"(emphasis added). This statement is made with a tone which implies that women are purposefully and unjustly excluded from ceremonies unless they participate as "mothers" rather than as women within many different social relationships. In addition to connoting limitations on women's participation in an important part of Maasai life, the statement reflects the Western capitalist denigration of motherhood, which is not a Maasai sentiment.

The discussion of criterion point three will provide further exposition on the inappropriateness of this position. The point I am making here, in terms of ethnographic accuracy, is that there is no sense either in the content or delivery of the narration that, for Maasai men and women, there could be no greater joy than to participate in a child's ritual ceremony. Llewelyn-Davies does not seem to object to men participating in the rituals of their sons as much as she objects when women "participate in ceremonies through their children."

Prior to the statement that women only participate in rituals through their children, there is a scene in which a new bride (i.e. a circumcised woman) is ritually greeted by her new co-wives and other women of her new husband's homestead. In this greeting, which the narrator herself describes as a "dramatic ritual," *only* women participate. These women are neither mothers nor daughters to one another. The narration is clearly contradicted by the visual and supporting narrative evidence in the bride greeting sequence. This is another instance of supplying inconsistent, apparently inaccurate, information to the viewer.

Arguing against Llewelyn-Davies, Kipuri demonstrates that women are not denigrated in the age-set system through processes of exclusion from rituals. Rather she points out that "there is hardly a rite of passage that can be performed without the active participation of a daughter, wife or mother of the candidate" (1990: 96). MASAI WOMEN confirms Kipuri's statement with the evidence that women play important roles in *eunoto* through the blessing with milk. The film also shows that the parallel women's initiation is highly valued by the community as evidenced in the elaborate celebration and blessings. Kipuri concludes,

> Although ritual interdependence does not necessarily imply a balance in status, the point we are making is that an assessment of rituals alone suggests complementary roles

for men and women, and not an inherent denigration of
women (1990: 98).

Therefore, it is difficult to convincingly argue that the age-set
system is responsible for gender asymmetry.

An examination of rights of inheritance necessarily sheds
light on concepts of "ownership" and distribution of means of
production relative to relations of production. Maasai relations
of production and the distribution of the means of production
are inseparable from kinship relations. The implications for
gender relations are tremendous and must necessarily be addressed in any film attempting to represent those relations.
Related to concepts of distribution of the means of production
in cattle is the value Maasai place on children. The film mentions that women will often give a child away to a barren co-
wife, sister or even to her own mother. The film states that a
woman will do this to provide companionship for the barren or
lonely woman. The fact that a woman has the right and power
to unilaterally give a child away without the consent of her
husband, who may or may not be the father of that child, is
quite important yet not addressed in the film. Instead of elaborating the implications for inheritance and the potential change
in status for the barren woman who receives the gift of a child
the film merely states that women make these gifts because
they value companionship and sympathize with a barren
woman. Even if one were to remain within the logical parameters
offered in MASAI WOMEN, this should not have been overlooked since, according to the narrator, "women and children
are wealth in themselves." Following from the information
provided by the film itself, this is an instance of a woman giving
away a form of wealth. Additionally, if she gives the child to her
mother, that child no longer even "belongs" to the extended
family of her husband since the film tells us that women go to
marry men in distant homesteads, far from their own mothers.
MASAI WOMEN does not analyze the ability of women to

unilaterally create lines of descent through which inheritance is determined by maternity. This surely is one of the highest forms of power in Maasai society yet MASAI WOMEN does not mention this fact. I contend that inclusion of this evidence would further highlight the inappropriateness of Llewelyn-Davies argument that women are victims of Maasai society.

It is difficult to say what effect the presentation of conflicting information has on the viewer but suffice to say the contradictions cannot be justified by an appeal to any standards of ethnographic or documentary truth. The viewer, noticing the inconsistency, is left to weigh which statement is the more accurate. Though for some, "seeing is believing," even the most naive viewer may begin to doubt the credibility of the visual images in light of contradictory evidence of other ethnographic sources.

As previously stated, the film interprets ethnographic information through inappropriate Western capitalist categories of analysis heavily laden with ideological implications for the interpretation of ritual, economics, and concepts of motherhood. This practice often is the root of the contradictions highlighted in the preceding analysis. It is clear from this introductory critique that use of the film MASAI WOMEN in classroom settings must be judicious so as not to replicate in the students' understandings the ethnographic inaccuracies and ethnocentric conclusions of the film.

2. Material Explanation of "Subjugation of Women"

Point two demands the assertion of subjugation of women be supported by evidence documenting that subordination within the specific social and material relations which exist in the society in question. It is clear from the discussion of point one that MASAI WOMEN misrepresents these social and material relations and weakens the plausibility of the assertion of subjugation.

Kipuri argues that Llewelyn-Davies locates the cause of women's subordination in the age-set system, which Llewelyn-Davies argues excludes women from the highest levels of cultural activity ("moranhood"). Kipuri maintains Llewelyn-Davies combines this notion with a perception of Maasai women as property (1990). In part Llewelyn-Davies achieves this by documenting and discussing women and their activities vis-a-vis men, while she defines men's activities as independent of influence by similar social bonds. Kipuri succinctly identifies Llewelyn-Davies' error when she states:

> The problem with such comparisons is that they tend to misinterpret both pre-capitalist and capitalist systems. Capitalism as a mode of production is not defined by the existence of capital but by specific relations of production vis-a-vis the generation and distribution of community resources (1990: 68).

It has already been illustrated how a woman has rights of distribution over her own children. Also, her access to livestock is prescribed by custom. Both of these instances qualify as part of the "generation and distribution of community resources."

Llewelyn-Davies conflates two non-equivalent terms, "subjugation" and "exploitation." Exploitation requires the appropriation of surplus product by a group of non-producers from direct producers. Llewelyn-Davies' analyses, in written and filmic forms, attempt to show that elders in the age-set system, which is said to exclude women, appropriate surplus from women in a way which is parallel to class exploitation in capitalist systems. However, Maasai elders do not constitute a group of non-producers. In fact, among Maasai, everyone is a producer and consumer of the collective products and resources, to varying degrees throughout the life cycle. Though the "potential" for exploitation may be great, as Kipuri points out, Llewelyn-Davies does not substantially establish its existence in her written works, which, as has been noted, reflect the analytical frame and ethnographic evidence in MASAI WOMEN (Kipuri 1990: 114). Furthermore, exploitation from the production level is only one means of subjugation.

Llewelyn-Davies further tries to demonstrate subjugation of women through linguistic evidence. The Maa word Llewelyn-Davies translates as "wealth" (and "wealthy" in the adjective form) actually has two forms in Maa. The appropriate masculine or feminine form is applied when one refers to a man or a woman respectively. Both words, "*olkarsis*" and "*enkarsis*" Rigby translates as "successful, respectable, good person" (Rigby 1991 personal communication). Llewelyn-Davies has ignored the feminine form of the word. She has translated it to mean "wealthy" when applied to a man but then states that a woman cannot have "wealth." Indeed, how could someone who is in fact "property" be "wealthy"? It appears that in fact Maasai either do not use the word to indicate wealth in the Western sense or that they believe both men and women are entitled to that description. Either interpretation indicates a serious analytical error in MASAI WOMEN.[5]

The assertion of subjugation of women in Maasai society is thus not supported with incontrovertible ethnographic evidence of exploitation either within the film or between the film and other ethnographic literature. Additionally, the linguistic evidence presented does not constitute proof as ideological sustenance for practices of subjugation of women in Maasai society.

What does not get mentioned in the film is how women feel about the degrees and types of power they do have in relation to production and distribution. As point two suggests, an investigation of Maasai women's opinions of the customs which prescribe the number and sex of their cattle could be valuable. For MASAI WOMEN, this may have exposed different information through which Llewelyn-Davies' argument may have gained support. Additionally, more information from Maasai women about the consequences of giving away a child or receiving a child may have elucidated notions of subjugation. The film discusses the barren woman but never offers an interview with one.

Llewelyn-Davies' analysis in MASAI WOMEN is limited by her foregone conclusion that it is the age-set system which subjugates Maasai women. Marriage to this idea has restricted investigation of particular points of the age-set ideology. Since the film represents the subjugation of women as a "package deal" there is no avenue available to explore the individual aspects of that ideology which may be perceived by Maasai women as significantly contributing to any domination or subjugation. Thus the *assumption* of subjugation has limited any actual documentation which would prove that subjugation.

3. Speaking from the Engaged/Interested Position

Speaking from the engaged or interested position may be achieved in different ways. I provide examples of two such ways. Either the conceptions of subjugation used in the analytical framework of the documentary must replicate those of the film's subject society, or they may, for the purposes of comparison, represent the conceptions of subjugation in the documentarist's society (or that of the potential audience).

MASAI WOMEN errs on two levels with respect to criterion point three. First, there are two instances in which Western distinctions are applied to Maasai social/psychological organization inappropriately. These applications are inappropriate since there is no clear sense that the film is attempting to address issues of inequity in Western society. The thesis of the film is that Maasai women are subjugated within Maasai society according to endemic cultural constructions of the age-set system. Secondly, there is one instance in which contradictory ethnographic information is presented within the film, between the narration and a subtitled translation, calling attention to the possibility that the narrator incorrectly interprets Maasai concepts of subjugation.

The two questionable Western distinctions are:

(1) the previously discussed notion of "wealth" and its associated concept of "property rights," and
(2) the distinction between "public" and "private" domains.

The narration begins: "These Maasai are animal herders. Land is held in common and animals are the only form of wealth." In less than one minute the narrator contradicts this statement continuing: "Women and children are wealth in themselves. Wealth involves rights over people as well as rights over things." Thus it is immediately established that women are wealth and therefore cannot possess wealth. These statements set the tone for the argument that women are permanently subjugated *as property* within Maasai society. It has already been pointed out that the translation of the term for "wealth" is questionable because it is ethnocentric. Additionally, the analytical weight of the concept of "property" in MASAI WOMEN is Western. Contradicting this Western notion of property the narrator states that, for Maasai, "Land is held in common" with no further elaboration of this point. The viewer is led to believe that Maasai have a practice of sharing land, commonly understood to Westerners as property, but that they also *count* "women and children" as a Westerner would count money, or other property.

Continuing this discussion of property, in one segment (series of scenes) about "warriors" (*ilmurran*) the narrator states, "...girls *belong*, as a group, to the warriors" (emphasis added).

However, later, when explaining the female circumcision ceremony, the "female equivalent of male circumcision," the narrator contradicts this notion of ownership when describing the female circumcision celebration as

> an occasion for rejoicing, *especially for the parents. They are proud and happy* to announce to the world that *they have a daughter* and that she has grown without mishap into a woman (emphasis added).

Now if the young girls *belonged to* (read: "were the property of") the *ilmurran* then one would expect that the *ilmurran* in fact would be sponsoring the ceremony and that they would be the most "proud and happy." The mention of the girls belonging to the *ilmurran* is never elaborated further and is only contradicted in following statements. An important question is whether the viewer remembers that young girls are owned by young men or that it is the parents and guests who are pleased, because, as the narration states, "the ceremony marks the emergence of an adult who will increase the fertility of the *whole community.*" Llewelyn-Davies conflates mutual dependence with domination in her analysis of how kinship relations structure relations of production and rights of distribution. This example illustrates both the ethnographic inconsistency within the film and the inaccurate application of Western concepts to an analysis of Maasai practices and beliefs. The film does not claim to be addressing issues of gender inequity in Western societies. Therefore it is impossible to claim that the film's project is to use Maasai women's lives to illustrate points about Western social organization. Additionally, since the ethnographic details of Maasai life are, as I have shown, equivocal, the film does not speak from the position of Maasai women. Thus, neither of the example positions I have suggested are achieved in accordance with criterion point three.

Though the narration attempts to present the status of women as property there is an important element which is not addressed; that is the value of that alleged property, the nature and degree of the value Maasai place on wives and mothers. As discussed previously, the film informs the viewer that a woman must "attach herself to a man" for security. This statement is presented with the negative connotation of dependency which is sustained throughout the film. However, it is also stated that women are property by which a man's wealth is gaged. If one takes just these statements, ignoring for the sake of argument any ethnographic invalidity, it is clear that a man's status in terms of wealth is also judged by his attachments to, or relationships with, people: "women and children are wealth in themselves." However, as stated previously, the fact that men's wealth is associated with social relations and bonds is not presented in the same denigrating fashion. The critical viewer might wonder why it is that "what's denigrating for the gander is not for the goose."

MASAI WOMEN treats women as negotiable property in terms of exchange value. Clearly other ethnographic evidence of Maasai economic structure indicates that use value has been the more dominant form. For example, MASAI WOMEN claims that subjugation of women is evident in the fact that women are not allowed to dispose of their cattle. In a society in which cattle are the means of production it would be foolish for anyone to dispose of a significant portion of the main means of subsistence production, the milk cattle which feed the community. It is a gross error to translate a Western capitalist notion of wealth and property to a non-capitalist or marginally capitalist society. The scenario of a Maasai woman wishing to sell any significant portion of her milking herd is misleading at best. Not only would she be selling the community's means of production but she would also be selling her son's future inheritance, the next generation's means of production, and her own means of subsistence through her son's future prosperity. It is simply invalid to compare the latitude a Western woman may have with regard to the sale of jointly owned property with that of a Maasai woman's rights to sell her family's milk cattle. Endangering a child's welfare in the United States through either denying the child food or shelter is also impermissible. Speaking from the engaged position requires the ethnographer/filmmaker's statements to be contextually relevant and adequately informed, representing the emic perspective.

The Western distinction between nature and culture has been extended in feminist criticism to include the domestic and public domains respectively. Llewelyn-Davies employs this distinction between public and private when discussing spheres of control in Maasai communities with respect to gender differences. To reiterate her argument, she holds that the age-set system is the highest level of Maasai culture. Since it excludes women, according to her interpretation, women have no access to the highest levels of Maasai culture. This creates a problem for her subsequent analysis since within Maasai society first of all there is very little elaboration of such a distinction (Rigby 1985: 59-63). The structure of labor relations for subsistence is determined by sets of both familial and age-set bonds. Inheritance is always relevant to work since each worker is an "owner," if the Western metaphor is to be extended. In its application to Western capitalist societies, work has been deemed part of the public sphere. For Maasai, work does not occur separately from private (familial) relations.

Secondly, what by Western-capitalist societies has been considered labor of the private sphere, reproducing the labor force or bearing and rearing children, has not been highly valued. However, in Maasai society this duty is highly valued as noted in the film through the lengthy blessing of children, fertility and parenthood. For Maasai living in extended family communities, the public is the private and vice versa. Through age-set, marital, and maternal ties, the labor force is a family and the family members (workers) are owners of the means of production. Kipuri points out that

> the "nature/culture" dichotomy and the associated "do-mestic/public" spheres of operation are not universally recognized and indeed even in western thought, it cannot be resolved into a single dichotomy (1985: 47).

If MASAI WOMEN held as its thesis that Western women are subjugated because capitalism does not acknowledge its systematic denigration of women (vis-a-vis mothering) through the separation of the public and private domains, a comparison with the Maasai system would have been fruitful for an argument advocating change within Western society. Since the film does not examine, let alone advocate change, of Western family structure, the comparison does not qualify as speaking from the engaged position of the Western woman.

4. Broad Geo-Political and Ideological Contextualization

Point four requires the presentation of the society in question to be contextualized within the broadest range of geographical, political and ideological considerations possible. This includes discussing the pertinent effects of both proximate social systems, and encompassing social systems. In the case of the Maasai this indicates a consideration of the national political and ideological systems in which the Maasai are living as well as those systems which have had developmental effect on the Maasai, most importantly the colonial era. Without acknowledgment of the historical development of the current national government policies and their effects on the Maasai any analysis of Maasai society is incomplete and, potentially, erroneous. There are several levels at which contextualization can be achieved. Ethnographic evidence within the film intimates the necessity for further elaboration and contextualization but seems to have been ignored.

MASAI WOMEN centers its exposition of Maasai society on the activities of the homestead of a *Laibon*, a man distinguished among Maasai by his powers of divination. Kipuri states that many aspects which are now considered "traditional" of Maasai probably developed during the mercantile capitalist period between 1640 and 1890. During this time the concept of an "army" developed as well as the "institutionalization" of the diviners in one lineage(1990: 22). The homestead is atypical of Maasai because it is a Laibon's homestead rather than one of a more common family. Kipuri states that control of women's sexuality is far greater in the groups that have "close association with the diviners, especially Loita and Wuasin-Kishu" (1990: 144).

The film does not intimate that this homestead is anything but average with the exception of its "wealth" which is stated as "many cattle and many wives and children." It is not clear from the film that in fact the many wives may be treated differently than other Maasai wives in less distinguished homesteads.

To maintain the hierarchical structure which privileges *Iloibonok* lineages, women of these lineages are restricted from visiting their natal families in order that control over their reproductive capacities can be maintained (to keep them from breeding with others). This control of reproduction is of course achieved through control of sexuality (Kipuri 1990: 145).

Comparing the economic autonomy of women from *Ilomet* and *Iloibonok* groups, Kipuri explains that since juniors of the *Iloibonok* lineages will receive their herd from gifts to their father by others, the mother hardly contributes to her son's means. She has thus lost input into the process of inheritance which recreates an important aspect of the social structure. Through this exclusion the woman loses status. Kipuri notes that it is in times of crisis that this practice has the most significance because it is then that economic manipulation through inheritance rights can be executed depending on one's inclination and relationship with a particular son (1990: 152). Additionally, in the diviner lineages women are excluded from the processes of arranging marriages for their sons. This not only limits the women's participation in the structuring of the next generation but it also alters the relationship between mother and son, marginalizing the mother in relation to the adult son and his responsibilities to his mother.

Kipuri concludes, and I am as before in agreement, that the ideology of the *Iloibonok* lineage conflicts fundamentally with the concepts of age-set ideology and practice. It is here, among the *Iloibonok*, that one encounters the most seriously subjugated women, not in association with age-set ideology but rather in association with the diviner system.

It is clear that MASAI WOMEN does not contextualize the economic or ideological distinction of the Laibon's homestead but rather represents the case as normal or average. The conclusions drawn about these women and their collective position within society cannot be generalized for all Maasai women, though that is the implication of the film's title. A more responsible presentation would have clearly acknowledged the special situation of the *Iloibonok* lineages in relation to other Maasai and also in relation to the historic circumstances which privileged the *Iloibonok* during the colonial mandate.

As mentioned before, if the special case or "worst" case were chosen to make clear the point that capitalism, even in its most nascent forms, tends to subjugate women, MASAI WOMEN would have made a stronger, more reputable argument. However, the important information about the *Iloibonok* lineage was left out of the film and the viewer has no basis for making the judgment that subjugation of *Iloibonok* women is due to the developmental pressures of capitalism during the colonial period. Without consulting other sources the viewer may not even be aware of this possibility since the film does not even mention current economic pressures on the Maasai, let alone historic ones.

The implications for assessing gender inclusivity among the Maasai are greatly jeopardized by the film's complete lack of recognition of pressures on the Maasai imposed by the Kenyan government. The Maasai are a people with a distinct social organization but who live within limitations structured by another social order, that of the national government and its position within the world economy. The women of MASAI WOMEN surely are effected by the policies and procedures of the national government either directly or indirectly, but there is no acknowledgment of this fact in the film. MASAI WOMEN represents the Maasai as somehow immune to all of these realities. They appear removed and self-sufficient, uninfluenced by the outside world. This depiction is simply inaccurate. Since it is inaccurate to represent the Maasai society, as a whole, as insulated, it is equally erroneous to make statements about Maasai women from such a flawed perspective.

Thus MASAI WOMEN does not present the historical development of the *Iloibonok*, which some anthropologists argue is essential to an exposition of women's status in Maasai society. The current market economy is alluded to but never mentioned directly nor positioned in relation to the Maasai. Finally, even the interview material which is probably quite respectable comes into question because of the restricted context. In these ways, MASAI WOMEN does not meet criterion point four's demand for broad contextualization with regard to both the grand issues of history and ideological development, as well as the specific issue of interview sources.

5. Moral and Political Agenda

The overall impression left by MASAI WOMEN is that these women are hard working and never reap any rewards from their efforts. The blame seems to fall solely to the "patri-archal" system of age-set and its male representatives. The viewer is left with the impression that there is no potential for change which will improve women's positions, short of de-stroying the Maasai system as represented in the film.

The critical viewer is left to wonder what the filmmakers' purposes were in producing the document other than to draw a distinction between the position of Maasai women and West-ern women. Is one to understand from MASAI WOMEN that *all* women are subjugated? Or is one to believe that Western women are somehow more fortunate than Maasai women, in that they are less subjugated? The filmmaker's position is unclear.

The educational/ethnographic information offered is not accompanied by an explicit frame for interpreting the material. It is difficult to say how the filmmaker intended the material to be understood. There is no framework which may be consid-ered the filmmaker's political or moral agenda.

Conclusion for Feminist Ethnographic Film Production

In the preceding analysis I have shown how the film MASAI WOMEN, through its inaccuracies, lack of clear political state-ment, and direction by inappropriate ethnocentric, capitalist categories does not make an independently valuable contri-bution to feminist theory and practice as demanded by the feminist standpoint which I defined at the outset. MASAI WOMEN does not, as the distribution company claims, offer an "accurate, enlightening portrait in which the people, their values, and their behavior...speak for themselves." Nor does the film qualify as feminist praxis under the guidelines de-manded by the feminist standpoint. MASAI WOMEN implic-itly argues that the subordination of Maasai women is the

result of an immutable patriarchal age-set guided social structure, a tenuous theoretical position to argue at best.

This criticism is not offered with the intention of completely
excluding the use of MASAI WOMEN in classroom settings. To
the contrary, I advocate screening the film in concert with
critical reading of other ethnographic literature as well as in-
depth discussion of points similar to those I have made in the
preceding pages.

NOTES

1   The distinction between "moral" and "political" goals is Jane Flax's
         (1983) and is here maintained for the sake of consistency between the
         literature and my application of the concepts.
2   Wilton Martinez (1990) discusses the impact of ethnographic film
         viewing on undergraduate students. Martinez finds that film viewing
         may reinforce ethnocentric beliefs. Addressing the study's findings on
         Masai Women Martinez quotes excerpts from female student responses:

> The film was good and interesting...The women were treated
> unfairly...I was shocked by the role of women...I am strongly
> against the pre-arranged marriages and that men were allowed to
> have many wives...I felt sympathy, they do not realize how
> poorly they are being treated(1990:43).

3   Films Incorporated Video of Chicago, a distributor, presently cir-
         culates the following description of *Masai Women*:

> This enlightening program looks at the women of the tribe-
> from childhood through marriage to old age- and examines their
> role in a completely male-dominated society." Further they quote
> Granada Television International's statement that "film crews
> worked in close association with anthropologists who have done
> extensive fieldwork living with the societies concerned. The
> academic strength of this series is heightened by the stature of the
> anthropologists involved..." They conclude: "The result is a
> series of accurate, enlightening portraits in which the people,
> their values, and their behavior are allowed to speak for them-
> selves."

4   *Laibon* (pl.*Iloibonok*) is the Maa word variously translated to mean "diviner" or "prophet." The *Iloibonok* are a distinct lineage. Collectively, the other lineages are known as *Ilomet*. The *Laibon* is highly atypical, representing a tiny minority of Maasai. Among other differences, the *Iloibonok* are exceptionally wealthy and have many more wives than most Maasai.

5   Kipuri elaborates several examples of this type in her unpublished critique of Llewelyn-Davies, "Gender Relations Among the Maasai of East Africa" (1985). It is redundant to cite similar instances here.

REFERENCES CITED

Barrett, Michele (1985). Ideology and The Cultural Production of Gender. IN Feminist Criticism and Social Change: Sex, Class, and Race in Literature and Culture, J. Newton and D. Rosenfelt, (eds.). New York: Methuen.

Beidelman, Thomas O. (1976). Review of: MASAI WOMEN AND MASAI MANHOOD. American Anthropologist 78(1976): 958-959.

Biella, Peter (1984). Theory and Practice in Ethnographic Film: Implications of the Ilparakuyo Maasai Film Project. Unpublished Ph.D. Dissertation, Temple University, Department of Anthropology.

Biella, Peter (1988). Against Reductionism and Idealist Self-reflexivity: The Ilparakuyo Maasai Film Project. IN Anthropological Filmmaking: Anthropological Perspectives on the Production of Film and Video for General Public Audiences. Jack R. Rollwagen (ed.). Studies in Visual Anthropology, No. 1. Chur, Switzerland: Harwood Academic, pp. 47-72.

Clifford, James (1986). Introduction: Partial Truths. IN Writing Culture, James Clifford and George Marcus (eds.). Berkeley: University of California Press, pp. 1-26.

Fay, Brian (1987). Critical Social Science. Ithaca: Cornell University Press.

Flax, Jane (1983). Political Philosophy and The Patriarchal Unconscious: A Psychoanalytic Perspective on Epistemology and Metaphysics. IN Discovering Reality: Feminist Perspectives on Epistemology, Metaphysics, Methodology, and Philosophy of Science, Sandra Harding and Merril B.

Hintikka (eds.). Dordrecht, Holland: D. Reidel Publishing, pp. 245-281.

Harding, Sandra (1986). The Science Question in Feminism. Ithaca: Cornell University Press.

Hartsock, Nancy C.M. (1983). The Feminist Standpoint: Developing the Ground for a Specifically Feminist Historical Materialism. IN Discovering Reality: Feminist Perspectives on Epistemology, Metaphysics, Methodology, and Philosophy of Science, Sandra Harding and Merril B.Hintikka (eds.). Dordrecht, Holland: D. Reidel Publishing, pp. 283-310.

Heider, Karl (1976). Ethnographic Film. Austin: University of Texas Press.

Kipuri, Naomi N. Ole (1985). Gender Relations Among the Maasai of East Africa. Unpublished paper, Temple University, Department of Anthropology.

Kipuri, Naomi N. Ole (1990). Maasai Women In Transition: Class and Gender in the Transformation of Maasai Society. Unpublished Ph.D. Dissertation, Temple University, Department of Anthropology.

Kuehnast, Kathleen (1990). Gender Representation in Visual Ethnographies: An Interpretivist Perspective. Commission on Visual Anthropology Review Spring: 21-29.

Llewelyn-Davies, Melissa (1974). Masai Women. Disappearing World Television Series. London: Granada Television, producers. 52 min.

Llewelyn-Davies, Melissa (1979). Two Contexts of Solidarity Among Pastoral Maasai Women. IN Women United, Women Divided, Patricia Caplan and Janet M. Bujra (eds.). Bloomington: Indiana University Press, pp. 206-237.

Llewelyn-Davies, Melissa (1981). Women, Warriors, and Patriarchs. IN Sexual Meanings, S. Ortner and H. Whitehead (eds.). Cambridge: Cambridge University Press. pp. 330-358.

Manicas, Peter T. (1987). A History and Philosophy of Social Science. Oxford, England: Basil Blackwell, Ltd.

Marcus, George E. and Michael M.J. Fischer (1986). Anthropology as Cultural Critique: An Experimental Moment in the Human Sciences. Chicago: University of Chicago Press.

Martinez, Wilton (1990). Critical Studies in Visual Anthropology: Aberrant vs. Anticipated Readings of Ethnographic Film.

Commission on Visual Anthropology Review Spring: 34-47.

Marx, Karl and Frederick Engels (1970). The German Ideology. Trans. by Lawrence and Wishart, Ed. by C.J. Arthur. New York: International Publishers.

Marx, Karl and Frederick Engels (1969). Manifesto of the Communist Party. Ed. by Frederick Engels. New York: International Publishers Co., Inc.

Rigby, Peter (1985). Persistent Pastoralists: Nomadic Societies in Transition. London: Zed.

APPENDIX A: FEMINIST ETHNOGRAPHIC FILM CRITERIA

(1) Documentation of Actual Life Processes. The film must document actual life processes of women in relation to specific material limitations and conditions, including relations of production which affect the entire society, and women as they exist within social structures. Detailed examples are required, simple assertions are not acceptable.

(2) Material Explanation of "Subjugation of Women"
If a film claims women are subjugated, it must be demonstrated how domination is structured within relations, both materially and ideologically. Explanations of autonomy and definitions of power taken from the subject society are significant for this task.

(3) Speaking from the Engaged/Interested Position
The filmmaker must be clear about her position of advocacy. To insure that the filmmaker is not inappropriately applying categories of analysis, foreign to the social relations of the people in the film, the audience must know from which perspective the filmmaker speaks (especially in the voice of the narrator). If a film argues that women in culture "X" are subjugated, there must be evidence provided which comes from within culture "X" to substantiate the definition and designation of subjugation.

(4) Broad Geo-Political and Ideological Contextualization
The film must acknowledge social systems which have or have had influence on the society studied. The society under examination cannot be viewed as insulated from international, national, historic, linguistic, economic, and other systems of development. This contextualization will ensure that non-idiosyncratic categories of analysis are used.

(5) Political Statement
Film production, like the development of theory, must be connected to the purposes and history of those producing it. This demands a moral and political statement by the filmmaker, to be stated clearly.

from ANTHROPOLOGICAL FILM AND VIDEO IN THE 1990s
Jack R. Rollwagen (editor). Brockport, NY: The Institute, Inc.
© 1993, The Institute, Inc. All rights reserved. ISBN 0-9635206-1-X

Anthropological Visualization Of The Huichol In Ethnographic Film: A Discussion Of The Problem Of Contextualization

Jay Courtney Fikes
Institute for the Investigation of Inter-Cultural Issues
Carlsbad, CA

ABSTRACT: The problem of ethnographic contextualization is elucidated by evaluating films portraying Huichol Indian peyote use. Reconstructing and interpreting Robert Zingg's footage on Huichol rituals, and researching how HUICHOLE: PEOPLE OF PEYOTE (48 minutes) was produced from 42,000 feet of footage, informed the author's conclusion that four criteria are essential to insure adequate ethnographic contextualization in Huichol documentaries.

Huichol culture and ethnohistory are summarized. Aboriginal temple-oriented peyote hunts (i.e., those portrayed in HUICHOLE: PEOPLE OF PEYOTE and in MILLENNIUM, TRIBAL WISDOM AND THE MODERN WORLD) are distinguished from anomalous peyote hunts led by Ramón Medina Silva and his widow, Guadalupe. Films depicting peyote hunts organized by such refugee Huichol leaders (e.g., TO FIND OUR LIFE: THE PEYOTE HUNT OF THE HUICHOL INDIANS OF MEXICO and HUICHOL, SACRED PILGRIMAGE TO WIRIKUTA) ignore or camouflage considerable differences in acculturation. Because such films disregard the diverse ways in which refugee Huichol "shamans" differ from Huichol singers or *cahuiteros* affiliated with ceremonial centers within the Chapalagana Huichol homeland (Fikes 1993), they provide insufficient ethnographic contextualization for scholarly purposes. Making study guides and outtakes indispensable companions to every ethnographic film increases contextualization for viewers and scholars and may enhance filmmaking.

Introduction

I first viewed about 50 minutes of archival footage shot in 1934 by Robert Zingg in August, 1988. Zingg's footage was shot in the Huichol Indian community of Tuxpan with what must have been a hand-wound 35mm camera. It had been deposited at the Smithsonian Institution without a scrap of annotation. In fact, Zingg's Huichol footage was mixed up with some Tarahumara Indian film footage which had not yet been identified. The idea of reconstructing and interpreting Zingg's unedited footage seemed more daunting than enticing at the time. Besides, there was almost 42,000 feet of color film footage shot during the mid 1970s at and around the Huichol ceremonial center of San Andrés Cohamiata. This more up-to-date color footage was accompanied by considerable annotation as well as ambient sound. After a cursory review of Zingg's 1934 footage and the 42,000 feet shot in the mid 1970s, I decided to seek funding to study the ethnographic clues this archival material contained.

I examined exhaustively the 42,000 feet during my postdoctoral fellowship in anthropology at the Smithsonian, from July, 1991 to July, 1993.[1] With the encouragement and advice of John Homiak, then Director of the Smithsonian's Human Studies Film Archives, I reconstructed Robert Zingg's unedited footage, wrote a narration to accompany it, and finished a 45 page study guide to make this documentary more serviceable to college students. We will begin marketing this 30 minute film about Huichol rituals, with the study guide, after we complete the sound track.

This recent interest in ethnographic film evolved out of my long-standing commitment to document the Huichol Indian ritual cycle (Fikes 1985). This essay explains how I grappled with the issue of contextualization, both in reconstructing Zingg's footage, and in evaluating the merits of ethnographic films about the Huichol. I conclude that four criteria are essential to evaluate whether ethnographic films about the Huichol peyote hunt have sufficient contextualization to recommend them for educational use. I will briefly address the problem of ethnographic contextualization in general before offering some suggestions which may improve the quality of ethnographic filmmaking. The obvious prerequisite to this discourse is an concise outline of Huichol culture and ethnohistory.

Summary of Chapalagana Huichol Culture

Although some Huichol scholars question the accuracy of 1990 Mexican census estimates, most will agree that at least 8,000 Huichol Indians live in rugged mountain and canyon country in northwestern México, about 150 miles north of Guadalajara. The 4,107 square kilometer homeland reserved by Huichols inhabiting the Chapalagana river basin is half the size it was before Spanish conquest. Traditionally, slash and burn horticulture was supplemented by hunting, fishing, and gathering of wild plants such as prickly pear cactus, maguey, and mesquite.

Huichols believe the environment they inhabit was originally established by precedents set by deified ancestors such as Grandfather-Fire, Father-Sun, and *Caoyomari*. Greatgrandmother-germination, Rain-Mothers, and other personifications of natural phenomena are sustained by Huichol temple officers. By performing rituals which honor and feed their ancestor-deities, Huichol temple officers maintain the ecological order which has always provided adequate subsistence. The well-known Huichol peyote hunt is but one of at least ten subsistence-oriented rituals. This annual cycle once encompassed hunting of rabbits and deer, fishing, and maize horticulture. Ritual rabbit hunts are gone. Cattle are sacrificed as substitutes for deer, whose numbers have declined drastically in the past 45 years. In addition to collecting peyote, a yellow root for face-painting, and sacred water from shrines of various Rain-Mothers, Huichol temple officers provide cattle to be sacrificed, and food to be distributed to attenders of aboriginal rituals. Such duties comprise the cargo of each of 26 aboriginal temple officers. The cargo-holders, known as *huahuauïte*, are obligated to perform rituals for five consecutive years at a particular ceremonial center. During this time each temple officer represents, serves, and embodies a particular ancestor. During their term of office they call each other by the names of the ancestors they represent. At Santa Catarina, nine out of 26 temple officers represent Rain-Mothers. By replicating in ritual the world-organizing precedents their ancestor-deities set, temple officers dispose them to protect human health and provide abundant subsistence for all Huichols.

Data obtained by Phil C. Weigand (1981, 1985a, 1985b) and I suggest that temple officers active at any of the 19 or 20 Huichol ceremonial centers discovered by Lumholtz (1900: 9-10, 1902: 27) are heirs to a system of regional trade and ceremony which began about 200 A.D. My research among the most traditional of the Chapalagana Huichol (Fikes 1985), revealed that an individual's prestige is determined largely by community service. To qualify as a healer five years of service as a temple officer is required. To qualify as a singer, or ritual leader, takes ten years; two terms as a temple officer. Elders or ritual specialists are called *cahuiteros* (Fikes 1985, 1993).

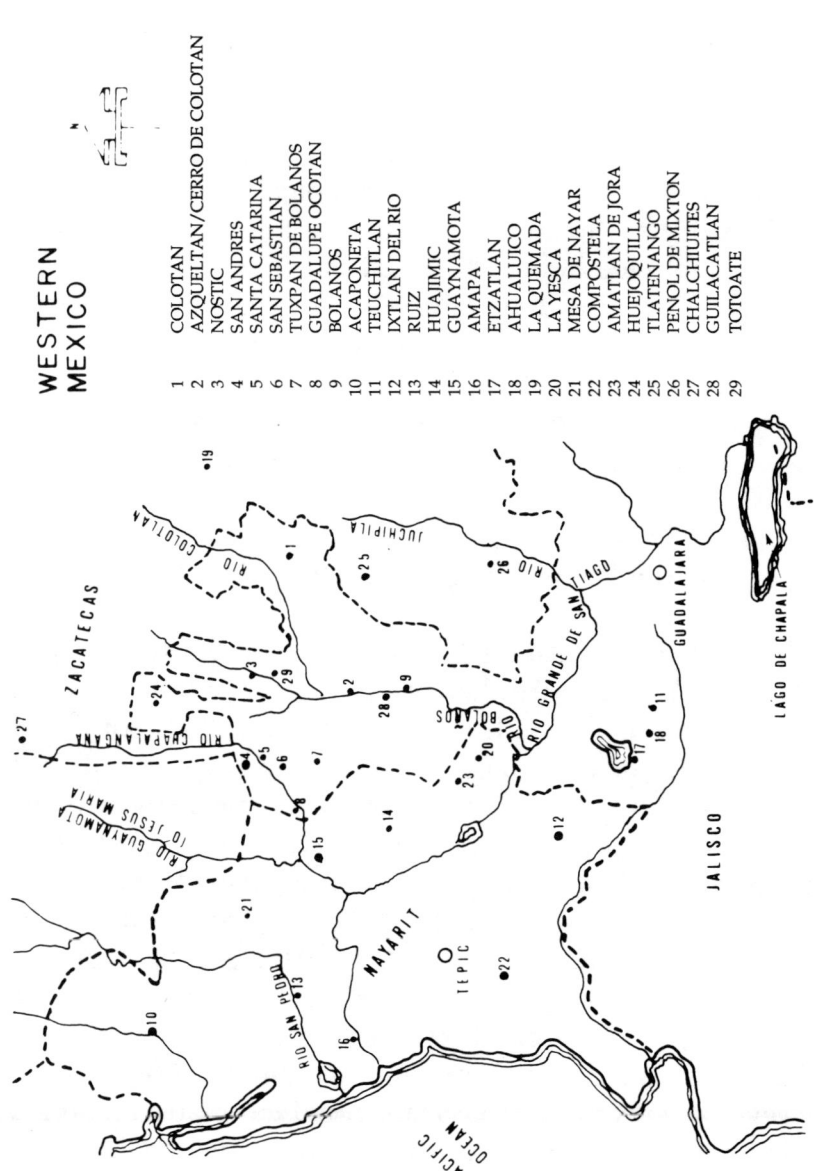

WESTERN
MEXICO

1   COLOTAN
2   AZQUELTAN/CERRO DE COLOTAN
3   NOSTIC
4   SAN ANDRES
5   SANTA CATARINA
6   SAN SEBASTIAN
7   TUXPAN DE BOLANOS
8   GUADALUPE OCOTAN
9   BOLANOS
10 ACAPONETA
11 TEUCHITLAN
12 IXTLAN DEL RIO
13 RUIZ
14 HUAJIMIC
15 GUAYNAMOTA
16 AMAPA
17 ETZATLAN
18 AHUALUICO
19 LA QUEMADA
20 LA YESCA
21 MESA DE NAYAR
22 COMPOSTELA
23 AMATLAN DE JORA
24 HUEJOQUILLA
25 TLATENANGO
26 PENOL DE MIXTON
27 CHALCHIUITES
28 GUILACATLAN
29 TOTOATE

FIGURE 1: Map of Western Mexico, with major locations in Huichol territory.

To escape from the violence of the Mexican revolution, which began in 1910, many Huichols migrated from their homeland in the Chapalagana river basin to Mexican cities such as Tepic, Nayarit. Other Huichol refugees founded enclaves outside their homeland, in rural areas controlled by Mexicans. Most urban and refugee Huichols quickly abandoned participation in the aboriginal ceremonial centers and were thereby subjected to greater acculturation. Among the several thousand refugee Huichols, a few, such as Ramón Medina Silva and his widow Guadalupe de la Cruz Rios, have been glorified as shamans. They have proven to be less knowledgeable about the meaning of aboriginal Huichol ritual than *cahuiteros* or singers affiliated with ceremonial centers within the Chapalagana Huichol homeland (Fikes 1993).

Reconstructing Robert Zingg's Huichol Film Footage

In 1934 Robert Zingg began one year of ethnographic research in the Huichol Indian community of *Tuxpan de Bolaños*. His ethnographic research at Tuxpan, located on the southeastern boundary of Chapalagana Huichol territory, resulted in publication of the first monograph on Chapalagana Huichol culture. This 800 page book, THE HUICHOLS: PRIMITIVE ARTISTS, was supplemented by an unpublished book-manuscript called HUICHOL MYTHOLOGY. Zingg's ethnographic writing, like the fifty minutes of film footage he shot, was predicated on a Boasian commitment to document and survey the full range of aboriginal activities, from material culture to myth and ritual. Zingg's unedited documentary film footage surveys the spectrum of Huichol ritual, both aboriginal and Catholic. It provides a well balanced portrait of Huichol religious life, and represents an implicit indictment of the highly sensational coverage Huichols have had since the dawn of the psychedelic sixties.

In organizing Zingg's film footage I respected the analytic framework Zingg chose for his monograph. Thus the sequence of aboriginal Huichol rituals filmed by Zingg are depicted before presenting the three Catholic-Spanish inspired rituals: the *cambio de las varas* (i.e., the changing of political authorities, symbolized by their sacred staffs or *varas*), the Carnival, and Easter Week ceremonies. The sequence of aboriginal rituals follows the aboriginal Huichol year, starting in October with the pre-harvest ritual called *Tatei Neixa* and ending with summer rain-making ceremonies.

Robert Zingg's 1934 film footage included small samples of the most salient features of all rituals performed among Tuxpan Huichols (except perhaps the "ceremony to prepare the soil for seed"). He filmed portions of all three Catholic-Spanish inspired rituals: the *cambio de las varas*, the Carnival, and Easter Week ceremonies, as well as several aboriginal Huichol rituals: i.e., the pre-harvest ritual, the parching of corn, the Peyote Dance, and rain-making rituals. Here we shall consider only how Zingg and I, in interpreting his footage, portray Huichol sacramental peyote use, the subject for which Huichols are best known.

The opening scene, which depicts Huichol men walking single file across an open field, is not inserted in actual chronological sequence. The narration accompanying this footage implies that these men are returning from a peyote pilgrimage. In reality they are returning from the same deer hunt which reappears, at its proper time, during the pre-harvest ritual held at Ratontita. Viewers are also likely to conclude that the footage of Huichols painting their faces with the yellow pigment was filmed during a peyote hunt. In reality, these Huichols are preparing to participate in a pre-harvest ritual, *Tatei Neixa*, at a village.

A bit of artistic license is invoked here. In the anthropological visualization of the Huichol the peyote pilgrimage predominates. Indeed a procession of Huichols has become a filmic icon for their culture. In this regard, the opening scene was intended to be a filmic establishing shot. Presenting a cultural stereotype for openers may seem slightly hypocritical. This strategy is partially justified by my admitting, in the study guide, that it was contrived, and by including in the rest of the film a wealth of information and images unknown to all but those of us who have done fieldwork at one of several Huichol ceremonial centers which also feature Catholic-inspired ceremonies. This banal beginning is also offset by the fact that I conclude that Huichols with whom Zingg was in contact probably used peyote, an assertion which contradicts some of what Zingg wrote.

Because Zingg obtained thirteen peyotes (which I photographed in June of 1992), and provided some circumstantial evidence for its use in his film footage and in his book, I concluded that peyote was probably present at some pre-harvest (*Tatei Neixa*) rituals, and at the Peyote Dance performed on May 11, 1934 at the ceremonial center of Ratontita.

The yellow face paint evident on participants in this pre-harvest ritual, as well as the singer's tobacco gourds, led me to assert that the bowl he held contained peyote.

According to Zingg, this ceremony at Ratontita was "given as if there had been peyote" and included "the ceremonial procession releasing husbands and wives from their vows of continence, just as though the husbands had been away on a peyote pilgrimage" (1938: 410). Zingg also remarked that this Ratontita ceremony was more elaborate than a nearby ceremony at which Lumholtz had observed peyote being used nearly forty years before (Zingg 1938: 410). Although it is possible that Huichols concealed their sacramental peyote use from Zingg, there is considerable evidence suggesting that Zingg knew about it, but decided to conceal it out of respect for their aboriginal culture. Indeed, Zingg helped vaccinate Huichols against smallpox and served as their political advocate (1938: lvii, 15-16, 51). Perhaps Zingg's circumspect handling of this issue was related to the violent political turmoil in which Tuxpan was still immersed in 1934.

Zingg's research may be the most comprehensive of any Huichol ethnographer. The scope and overall accuracy of his ethnographic investigation greatly facilitated my reconstruction and interpretation of his film footage. It also contributed significantly to shaping my criticism of other ethnographic films.

Examining Ethnographic Film Portraits of Peyote Hunting

During the mid 1970s Kalman Muller shot about 42,000 feet of color film at and around the Huichol ceremonial center of San Andrés Cohamiata. Muller's footage, evidently produced for E. Richard Sorenson, then Director of the National Anthropological Film Center at the Smithsonian Institution, is the raw material from which a 48 minute film called HUICHOLE: PEOPLE OF PEYOTE was produced. As the title suggests, the film emphasizes the Huichol peyote hunt. However, it also includes data about Huichol subsistence, social organization, and rituals, both Christian and aboriginal. This film generally lacks clarity and consistency, probably because the producers had yet to grasp the principles underlying the apparent complexity of Huichol culture. It often lapses into a travel log style, focusing on the feel of events, even those which are trivial. For example, film depicting the Carnival or *Las Pachitas* ritual features dogs fighting, Biblical Jews clowning, people eating food, and people sleeping on the ground after becoming intoxicated with alcohol. Meanwhile, the meaning of vital ritual activities, symbols, and songs is inadequately interpreted. Many statements in this film are simply wrong, e.g., that Huichols refer to themselves as *Huerica*, which supposedly means healers. Ethnographic researchers have learned that their word, *Huixárica*, is singular, and denotes a person who speaks the Huichol language.

Although Easter Week ceremonies are portrayed in Muller's archival footage,[2] they were absent in the film HUICHOLE: PEOPLE OF PEYOTE. The scope and significance of connections between the peyote, the temple officers who collect it, and their participation in Christian ritual was ignored. Christian symbolism in the peyote hunt was misinterpreted. For example, when pieces of fresh peyote were used to anoint or consecrate the sacred staff, the staff was mistakenly referred to as the cross of money. The meaning and use of the cross of money, which had been glimpsed some two minutes earlier, was never mentioned. Nevertheless, there is more contextualization in this documentary film than in the two segments about the Huichol included in the ten-part series called Millennium: Tribal Wisdom and the Modern World. In HUICHOLE: PEOPLE OF PEYOTE the crucial role that *cahuiteros* (elderly ritual specialists) and ceremonial centers play in Huichol culture is conveyed more clearly than in Millennium: Tribal Wisdom and the Modern World.

The peyote hunt portrayed in HUICHOLE: PEOPLE OF PEYOTE begins and ends from the ceremonial center of San Andrés Cohamiata. This film's recording of the peyote hunt conforms closely to the sequence of events integral to peyote hunts described by Fernando Benítez (1968, 1975) and Ramón Mata Torres (n.d.), each of whom is a Mexican writer who accompanied the Huichol temple officers from the ceremonial center of San Andrés. It appears that the first and last segments of the peyote hunt depicted in HUICHOLE: PEOPLE OF PEYOTE were made on foot. Government vehicles are visible in Muller's archival footage, but were not seen or mentioned at all in HUICHOLE: PEOPLE OF PEYOTE. This film suggested that the peyote hunters had become tired from fasting and walking. That they walked some of the way is attested to by the footage depicting peyote being cut and dried on strings in the sacred high-desert country where peyote is collected, *Huiricüta*. Drying removes water and thus makes peyote lighter to carry. The temple officers probably carried it back on foot to San Andrés from the last Mexican town accessible by vehicle, which at that time was at least two or three days away on foot. Using modern transportation to complete part of their peyote pilgrimage probably explains another omission in this film. After the peyote collectors left the Huichol sierra viewers are suddenly shown a huge metal cross, which Huichol scholars can identify as belonging to a place near the Mexican town of Matehuala. As we view this town, near where peyote is hunted, we are told, but not shown, that the peyoteros confessed their sexual transgressions to purify their hearts before ingesting peyote. The only other crucial omission is that viewers are not shown the first peyote being shot with arrows, as prescribed by Huichol mythology. The footage depicting peyote collectors making offerings at the sacred springs of *Tatei Matinyeri* and praying for rain there is excellent and well explained. The footage of peyote harvesting is excellent but the narration about why peyote is a sacrament is superficial. In that connection it is stated, incorrectly, that the peyote cactus has "poisonous tufts."

The connections between peyote hunting and the deer hunting ritual which follows it were illustrated and briefly explained. But the primary purpose of the Peyote Dance, which is performed essentially to solicit rain, was not conveyed at all. Instead viewers are shown very bizarre dissolving colors accompanied by loud and discordant music blaring in the background. This segment is certainly a flashback to the psychedelic sixties.

The Millennium television series recently aired on PBS contained a one hour segment called "Touching the Timeless" which included about thirty three minutes depicting a peyote hunt which departed from and returned to the ceremonial center at San Andrés Cohamiata. Because trucks transported the San Andrés temple officers, certain sacred places were not visited. The sequence of events corresponding to this slightly abbreviated peyote hunt seems authentic otherwise. One event which is clearly out of sequence is the food being eaten by Huichols riding in the truck. Richard Meech, one of the Millennium producers, told me it did not violate the fasting required of peyote seekers because the food viewers see Huichols eating was actually consumed after the peyote had been collected, during their return to the sierra. Unfortunately, the connections between the peyote hunt, other aboriginal rituals in the annual cycle, and Christianity were not explained. The amount of contextualization was insufficient for an ethnographic film. Clarification of the Huichol perspective on peyote, which is revered as the Creator's heart (Fikes 1993), would have been desirable. Millennium's treatment of peyote use made it seem awesome or glorious. It was reminiscent of the early 1960s, when peyote and mescaline were widely credited with having the power to cleanse the doors of perception. Both Millennium's hyper-reverent tone and the grotesque feeling conveyed by the Peyote Dance segment included in HUICHOLE: PEOPLE OF PEYOTE seem to pander more to the expectations of non-Indian audiences than ethnographic films should.

Within the 33 minutes on peyote hunting nearly two minutes are devoted to the temple officers' public confessions of their sexual transgressions. The reason for making public confessions was briefly stated: to purify the heart prior to arriving at sacred places, and to avoid punishment sent by offended ancestors. The emphasis on the would-be Catholic priest, Chaliyo, and how his confession resembles that given privately to a Catholic priest, does little to explain Huichol religious identity. Far worse are the statements attributed to the Huichol shaman: "This man Chaliyo is the future of the Huichol. ... Where will he take us? What is his cargo?"

Asking such questions about Chaliyo implies that his cargo is simply his destiny or future. As every bona fide Huichol shaman knows, Chaliyo's individual choices are irrelevant to his obligation to provide service to the ancestors and the community during his five year cargo in the aboriginal Huichol ritual cycle. A related problem is the overly ecumenical suggestion, that "we are all pilgrims." This statement is first attributed to the shaman as he brushes the non-Huichols and the vehicles accompanying them. It is repeated again, allegedly by the shaman, near the end of the segment. This perspective, which I suspect may be more congruent with the beliefs of the producers than with those of the Huichol shaman, may encourage a viewer to equate his/her spiritual searching with the duties of Huichol temple officers. It is wrong to imply that Chaliyo and other Huichol peyote hunters are only individual pilgrims. Huichol peyote collectors are not pilgrims. This English word carries connotations which mislead. The Huichol word for temple officers is *huahuauüte*. Chaliyo and all other temple officers represent and serve particular ancestors. During their five years in office they fulfill an institutional role which has been embedded in Huichol culture since 200 A.D. Traditional Huichol temple officers intend to follow in the footsteps of the ancestors they represent. In doing so, they recreate the world established by those ancestors. Their goal is to renew and maintain this world rather than to discover something new about themselves. In addition to bringing peyote back for rituals performed in the sierra, temple officers should return with sacred water from at least three sacred springs. This sacred water, the yellow root, and the peyote are items required for the Peyote Dance which summons the Rain Mothers at the end of the dry season. This ritual is performed at the end of the dry season, primarily to bring rain, which for Huichols is the greatest collective benefit imaginable. With the coming of the summer rain Huichols are saved; they can plant their corn, beans, and squash again. Instead of individual salvation, or pilgrimages for self-discovery and transformation, it is group survival which underlies aboriginal Huichol rituals such as the peyote hunt. The Millennium producers do not express the uniquely Huichol sense of reverence for and devotion to an ecological order inhabited and established by their ancestors.

Discussion of Ethnographic Contextualization

Despite their deficiencies, the two documentary films discussed above have enough ethnographic contextualization in them to be used in university or college classrooms. Neither Peter Furst's 1969 film, TO FIND OUR LIFE: THE PEYOTE HUNT OF THE HUICHOL INDIANS OF MEXICO, nor Larain Boyll's 1991 film, HUICHOL SACRED PILGRIMAGE TO WIRIKUTA, will be reviewed here. Both of these films present abbreviated versions of peyote hunts which are totally unconnected with any aboriginal Huichol ceremonial center. What they do offer, peyote hunts organized by refugee Huichols adapting to modern Mexican culture, is not contextualized sufficiently to be of value to scholars. I have already identified (Fikes 1993: 80-85) numerous deficiencies and anomalies in Furst's film, and am planning to analyze Boyll's film in the near future. The Furst and Boyll films are unacceptable to scholars because, among other things, they present peyote hunts led by refugee Huichols as if they were indistinguishable from the traditional peyote hunts organized by aboriginal temple officers at Huichol ceremonial centers such as San Andrés.

My perspective on ethnographic films about the Huichol has been guided by four criteria, each of which is an indicator of ethnographic contextualization. The extent of contextualization increases to the degree that a documentary film fulfills all four of these criteria, which include: (a) interpretation of how Christian ritual elements interface with aboriginal elements, (b) describing how peyote hunting is embedded in the annual aboriginal temple ritual cycle, (c) understanding the proper sequence of peyote hunt activities, and (d) depicting sacramental peyote use with dignity, reverence, and reference to Huichol belief.

It seems evident that films constructed without comprehensive understanding of the aboriginal Huichol temple ritual system (that larger context in which particular rituals, such as the peyote hunt, are embedded) are likely to encourage misconceptions about Huichol culture. Familiarity with fundamental themes and principles permeating the entire ritual cycle could have helped prevent most problems diagnosed in filmic depictions of rituals involving peyote, which Huichols revere as the heart of their "tutelary spirit" and Creator, *Caoyomari*. One way to prevent viewers from interpreting ethnographic films in ways "that reinforce ethnocentric stereotypes of nonwestern cultures" (see El Guindi, this volume) is to present images and narrations which help elucidate those key symbols and central characters who foster integration or unity within a particular liturgical order. My suggestions about the significance of the simultaneous dimension in the Huichol ritual cycle (Fikes 1985: 160-164) and the profound meaning *Caoyomari* has among Huichol singers (Fikes 1985: 99, 244-256) might provide the basis for constructing films with adequate ethnographic contextualization. Identifying and interpreting key symbols (i.e., those underlying and connecting all rituals in a given liturgical order such as the Huichol use of bird feathers in every ritual and in healing, and evoking the numbers seven and forty in all life-cycle Egyptian rituals [see El Guindi in this volume]) should contextualize ritual activity enough to effectively counteract ethnocentric stereotypes held by viewers.

Much of my analysis of film portraits of Huichol peyote hunts has focused on the temporal context of ritual: completing a prescribed sequence of inter-dependent activities to fulfill a specific objective. Consistent with this emphasis is the assumption that the invariance of events embedded in individual rituals is a universal feature of ritual process, as Van Gennep,

Turner, Rappaport (1979) and others have recognized. More-over, intra-ritual invariance is, in many cultures, reinforced by convictions to the effect that performing a particular ritual according to its prescribed sequence is essential, either to secure subsistence, or to promote human health and matura-tion. Whenever invariance in intra-ritual sequence has such compelling cultural justification, as it does among the Huichol, filmmakers would do well to respect it.

Neglecting to mention, or minimizing, the scope and sig-nificance of Christian elements in the Huichol ritual cycle, a problem particularly obvious in films about Huichol peyote hunting produced by Boyll and Furst, exemplifies a type of ethnographic decontextualization which may be widespread among anthropological filmmakers. Rosaldo's discussion (1989: 68-71) of "imperialist nostalgia" as a form of mystification seems highly applicable to this genre of filmmaking. As Rosaldo implies, even when it is done with the best of intentions, concealing the impact historical changes have on "primitive cultures" may be deceitful.

Most scholars of ethnographic films would agree that rec-reating or staging an extinct ritual, without mentioning that it is no longer being performed, would give viewers an errone-ous idea about the culture, perpetuating the illusion that the ritual was still alive. To what degree did Edward Curtis do this in his classic film, IN THE LAND OF THE HEADHUNTERS? Filming people dressed in exotic costumes which are rarely if ever worn, without mentioning that fact, or without showing them in their everyday apparel may also be misleading. All such practices tend, in varying degrees, to camouflage the contexts in which the people portrayed in film really live. The question of what would motivate documentary filmmakers to conceal rather than inform viewers about the economic condi-tions or material culture in which their "informants" live is beyond the scope of this essay.

Concealing ethnographic context may, in certain cases, such as that of Carlos Castaneda (Fikes 1993), violate scholarly standards. Simulating reality, or faking authentic contexts by skillful use of sets, props, and fronts, is obviously an essential element in most Hollywood movies. But, because we all know they are fiction, and are made primarily to entertain us, we need not denounce them for their indifference to ethnographic context. Ethnographic filmmakers are obliged to follow rules rather distinct from those which guide production of Hollywood's feature films. When, if ever, are ethnographic filmmakers justified in substituting a set or using props to offer viewers well-crafted illusions instead of ethnographic truth?

Conclusion

The process of reconstructing Zingg's footage involved putting several Huichol rituals, and the various activities included in each ritual, in the proper sequence. In producing my documentary film from Zingg's unedited footage I became convinced that study guides are indispensable companions of ethnographic films. Study guides can help viewers understand the complex relationship between visual images, native explanations of behavior captured on camera, and the film narrator's explanation of both the images and the natives' explanations. Providing information about this inter-cultural context, in which all filmic productions are embedded, is also essential to encourage honest ethnography. Unlike Hollywood's fictional films, documentary films produced to interpret other cultures are obliged to inform viewers about when, how, and why events seen on screen were taken out of their "real life" contexts.

Comparing images and narration contained in the 48 minute film, HUICHOLE: PEOPLE OF PEYOTE, with the 42,000 feet of raw material available to the producers convinced me that evaluation of ethnographic films may be enhanced significantly by study of their outtakes. Without access to outtakes, our judgments about somebody else's ethnographic film are likely to be based primarily on what we already know about that culture. Our judgments will have a firmer foundation to the extent that we as viewers-critics are enabled to know more about the culture being portrayed on film, whether as a result of reviewing outtakes, or, by reading a study guide.

My research on the relationship between archival film footage and documentary film, and my production of a documentary from archival footage, lead me to conclude that there is no compelling reason for not providing a study guide for every anthropological film and unrestricted access to outtakes for other scholars. Making outtakes and a study guide escorts of every ethnographic film would provide viewers and scholars with additional information about the context in which the film was produced. In doing so we will empower our viewers and help keep ourselves honest.

NOTES

1   This essay is a longer version of a paper, "The Anthropological Visualization of the Huichol," presented at the 91st annual meeting of the American Anthropological Association in San Francisco, California on December 3, 1992. I wish to express my gratitude to John Homiak for his insightful comments on that paper, and to thank William Sturtevant, William L. Merrill, Candace Green, JoAllyn Archambault, and Ann Kaupp for facilitating my research at the Smithsonian. Research from July, 1991 to July, 1992 was fully funded. My second year of research at the Smithsonian was unfunded.

2   Information on Easter Week ceremonies at San Andrés can be obtained by viewing Kalman Muller's Mullerarchival footage at the Smithsonian's Human Studies Film Archives: see "Huichol 1973" and rolls four and five of "Huichol 1975." It should be noted that the methodology Muller used in making ethnographic research films was significantly influenced by E. Richard Sorenson. Several years later,

Muller's foootage was used by Steve Dreben and others to produce the film.

REFERENCES CITED

Benítez, Fernando (1968). En La Tierra Mágica de Peyote. México: Biblioteca Era.

Benítez, Fernando (1975). In the Magic Land of Peyote. Translated by John Upton. New York: Warner Books.

Fikes, Jay C. (1985). Huichol Indian Identity and Adaptation. Doctoral dissertation, University of Michigan.

Fikes, Jay C. (1993). Carlos Castaneda, Academic Opportunism and the Psychedelic Sixties. Victoria, B.C. Canada: Millenia Press.

Lumholtz, Carl (1900). Symbolism of the Huichol Indians. New York: American Museum of Natural History, Memoirs 1 (2).

Lumholtz, Carl (1973). Reprint. Unknown Mexico, Vols. 1 and 2. Glorieta, New México: Rio Grande Press.

Mata Torres, Ramón (n.d.). Peregrinación del Peyote. Guadalajara, México: Edición de la Casa de las Artesanías del Gobierno de Jalisco.

Rappaport, Roy (1979). Ecology, Meaning, and Religion. Richmond, CA: North Atlantic Books.

Rosaldo, Renato (1989). Culture and Truth. Boston: Beacon Press.

Weigand, Phil C. (1981). "Differential Acculturation Among the Huichol Indians." IN Themes of Indigenous Acculturation in Northwest México, P.C. Weigand and Thomas B. Hinton (eds.). Tucson: University of Arizona Press, pp. 9-21.

Weigand, Phil C. (1985a). "Considerations on the Archaeology and Ethnohistory of the Mexicaneros, Tequales, Coras, Huicholes, and Caxcanes of Nayarit, Jalisco, and Zacatecas." IN Contributions to the Archaeology and Ethnohistory of Greater MesoAmerica, William J. Folan (ed.). Carbondale: Southern Illinois University Press, pp. 126-187.

Weigand, Phil C. (1985b). Evidence for Complex Societies During the Western Mesoamerican Classic Period. IN The Archaeology of West and Northwest Mesoamerica, Michael S. Foster and Phil C. Weigand (eds.). Boulder: Westview Press, pp. 47-91.

Zingg, Robert M. (1938). The Huichols: Primitive Artists. New York: G.G. Stechert.

Zingg, Robert M. (n.d.). Huichol Mythology. Unpublished manuscript on file at the Laboratory of Anthropology, Santa Fe, New Mexico.

FILMS CITED

Huichole: People of Peyote. A film by Steve Dreben and Tom Perry. 48 minutes, color. Purchase for $59.95 plus $5 postage through Tom Perry, Hollywood Home Entertainment, 1505 Washington Avenue, Santa Monica, CA 90403 (310/393-7677).

Huichol Indian film project, 1975. 35 hours (42,000 feet) of archival film footage, color, shot by Kalman Muller are deposited at the Human Studies Film Archives, E-307 National Museum of Natural History Building, Smithsonian Institution, Washington, D.C. 20560 (202/357-3349).

Huichol Sacred Pilgrimage To Wirikuta. 1991. A film by Larain Boyll. 29 minutes, color. Purchase VHS copy for $45.00 from Larain Boyll, Four Winds Circle, 7 Annie Lane, Mill Valley, CA 94941 (415/381-2373).

Millennium, Tribal Wisdom and the Modern World. 1992. A ten-hour color film series produced by KCET and Biniman Productions. Purchases for educational use, with teacher's guide, are $350 plus $8.50 postage from PBS Video, P.O. Box 791, Alexandria, VA 22313-0791 (800/328-PBS1). Individual two-hour VHS tapes in this series are available for $50 each plus $8.50 for postage. Purchases for home use are $150 plus $10 for postage from KCET Video, 4401 Sunset Blvd., Los Angeles, CA 90027. Individual two-hour tapes in this series are $30 each plus $4 postage to KCET. Purchases of this series *within Canada only* are $130 (Canadian) plus $12 postage and are available from New Vision Media, Suite 150 12140 Horseshoe Way, Richmond, B.C. V6A 4V5 Canada (604/275-7910). Individual two-hour tapes are $40 each plus $5 postage.

Robert Zingg's Huichol footage, 1933-34. Fifty minutes of Zingg's archival film footage, black and white, are deposited at the Human Studies Film Archives, E-307 National Museum of Natural History Building, Smithsonian Institution, Washington, D.C. 20560 (202/357-3349).

To Find Our Life: The Peyote Hunt of the Huichol Indians of México. 1969. A film by Peter T. Furst. Film *formerly* distributed through the University of California, Berkeley Media Center, 2176 Shattuck Avenue, Berkeley, CA 94704 (510/642-1340) and through the University of California Los Angeles Instructional Media Library, 405 Hilgard Avenue, Los Angeles, CA 90024 -1517 (310/825-0755).

from ANTHROPOLOGICAL FILM AND VIDEO IN THE 1990s
Jack R. Rollwagen (editor). Brockport, NY: The Institute, Inc.
© 1993, The Institute, Inc. All rights reserved. ISBN 0-9635206-1-X

"Visual Resources For University Audiences And Adult Education": Video Modules For University Classrooms, And Beyond

Jack R. Rollwagen
Department of Anthropology
SUNY College at Brockport

ABSTRACT: This article explicates the concepts behind the production of the videotape series "Visual Resources for University Audiences and Adult Education" (hereafter VRUCAE), including discussions of the anthropological context of the production process, elements of the production process, and the business aspects of pre-production, production, post-production, and distribution. The article concludes with a discussion of examples of a VRUCAE series in production: the series TZINTZUNTZAN IN THE 1990s; and a description of the forthcoming AMERICAN ETHNIC GROUPS PROJECT.

Definitional Preface: "Film" and the Transition from Linear to Non-Linear Access

The coming-into-being of the personal computer industry in the 1980s and the consequent development of mediums of mass storage with non-linear access, and the increasing integration between the previously separate fields of (magnetically stored) video and (magnetically stored) computer information has begun the process by which the term "filmmaking" will cease to have its former accepted meaning. Non-linear access to whatever information the user desires places that user in the position to select from the information available as stored digital material what he/she wants, and in whatever order he/she wants it. Although "filmmakers" may continue to record material through the use of machines which record information onto formats which record that information linearly (e.g., onto film or video), once that information has been recorded and transferred to digital storage media which can be accessed non-linearly, the previous relationship between the viewer and the order in which that information was originally stored will have been changed dramatically.

Because viewers will no longer think of themselves as having to wait passively for the "film" to unfold (with only the possibility of stopping the "film," freezing a frame, rewinding it, or leaving the room), they will assume a more active role in accessing (only) that data which they wish to see out of that which is available to them. Previously, the filmmaker had to make the assumption that a "film" had to be of "reasonable" length: long enough for the purpose of the film, but short enough to retain audience interest. Since these considerations were mostly based upon assumptions about audiences of more than one, the assumptions that filmmakers made about audiences did not allow for much diversity in the use of that film. In non-linear access, with each individual viewing as much as he/she wants and in the order that he/she wants to access information, many of the assumptions that "providers of information" make will change. The amount of information to be provided will, on the one hand, be linked to assumptions about individual usage by a much greater variety of people, each with his/her own intentions in accessing that information; on the other hand, the access to the information will be constrained in one way or another by the mechanical means available, and the relatively high costs of information access and storage (for the immediate future, at least).

Within this quite different universe, those who wish to be "information providers" (e.g., the former "filmmakers") must reconsider their purposes and functions. One cannot make one film for all people. However, one can attempt to provide sufficient information to allow many individuals to find in it what they wish. In this way, information (both visual and aural) provided through non-linear (and at this point, magnetic means) can be likened in its use to a library, in which users approach the collected information with their own purposes, determine an approach to the information, sample, select, accumulate, consume, and transform themselves in the process.

To continue the analogy above one step farther, in the past viewing a "film" was like someone reading a book to an audience comprised of a variety of individuals with different abilities, interests, and goals. In non-linear access, each individual in the former audience in pursuit of his/her own ends is much more in control of his/her own destiny and the means to it. In that sense, non-linear access places an individual in a library wherein individuals can navigate through that collection in much more individualistic terms. This is not to say that the information which is made available will not be selected by an information provider(s); but only that a much broader base of information can provide alternative means to its use, and in this way allowances can be made for the varying goals and abilities among those who use it.

This article is an attempt to explain the evolving rationale for the on-going development of a set of "visual (and aural) resources" amenable to both linear and non-linear access, in the hope that those who wish to begin the transition between perspectives which concentrate on the linear collection and display of information will have at least one example of the goals that I have outlined above. In this transition, I will continue to use the terms "film" and "filmmaking" because (a) some of the visual resources that I will be making will conform to what it is that people think of when they use the word "film"; and (b) because the use of those terms provides a point of departure in the transition between linear production and access, and non-linear production and access.

Introduction

In this article, I will describe an approach to filmmaking[1] which I have been developing over a period of nearly twenty years. This approach combines: (1) elements which relate to the film's intended audience (e.g., university instructors, their students, and proactive adult learners) and potential uses of these films, and (2) elements which relate to the production of those films (e.g. social science frameworks for filmmaking, production and post-production concepts and practices, and business aspects of filmmaking). In my view, the importance of the series VISUAL RESOURCES FOR UNIVERSITY CLASS-ROOMS AND ADULT EDUCATION (hereafter "VRUCAE") is that it is a set of materials produced by social scientists for social scientists, a set of films produced (at this time) on video cassette for distribution to a very specific market. This production strategy is opposed to that which dominates the arena of films produced by non-social scientists for distribution by broadcast television to a much more generalized audience. It also stands in marked contrast to those films which are independently produced in the tradition of which I will herein call "works of art" whose relationship to social science is not as central as the VRUCAE materials. The tradition of social science filmmaking (and its conceptual frameworks) stands in contrast to the two above traditions because the overriding concern of the VRUCAE project is to produce films which are based upon social science approaches to their subject matter, and which concentrate centrally on social science concerns.

There are ten key concepts that are important in the explication of the concepts behind the VRUCAE series. These are: (1) Meeting "Felt Needs"; (2) Market-Driven Production Strategies; (3) Learning Modules; (4) Simultaneous Production of Several Films; (5) On-Location Filming; (6) Integrating the Interests of the Social Scientist/Filmmaker with the Interests of the Social Scientist/Classroom Instructor; (7) Cooperative Arrangements Between the Social Scientist/Filmmaker and the Scholars who Appear in the Films; (8) Alternative Possibilities in the Development of Future VRUCAE Films; (9) Empowering the Social Scientist/Filmmaker; and (10) Incorporating Aesthetic Considerations. After treating each of these in turn, I will conclude with (1) a discussion of an example of a VRUCAE film project in production (the VRUCAE film series TZINTZUNTZAN IN THE 1990s), and (2) a discussion of the forthcoming AMERICAN ETHNIC GROUPS PROJECT.

In this discussion, my intent is not only to inform, but (1) to empower social scientists by outlining a means by which social science instructors (and others) can obtain films by social scientists for use in classrooms, and (2) to encourage those social scientists who, like me, are dissatisfied with the majority of films for classroom use to produce films for themselves and for others.

Ten Key Concepts in the Production of VRUCAE

1. Meeting "Felt Needs"

My desire to produce a set of visual resources on social science topics arose out of my increasing frustration with the visual resources that are available for teaching social science in university classrooms. Although it may be true that there are many films available for use in university classrooms, in my experience the majority of them do not do what a social scientist wants them to do. In general, the production of most such films are controlled by people who are not themselves social scientists, are not interested in social science (because they feel that it "restricts" their ability to do what they want in films), and do not believe that it is important that social science concepts are integral to the conceptualization of films for social science uses.[2] Rather, they argue, the nature the of production process itself and the necessity for producing for a mass (broadcast) audience determine what must be filmed and how it is to be presented. In this article, I will argue that it is precisely these two points which makes their films of less value to university social science instructors.

It is my experience that the vast majority of social scientists do use films in their classroom, and that they would be receptive to the availability of a new series of films provided that those films directly addressed their needs. In my long academic career, I have been involved in many discussions with colleagues about films and other visual resources as aids to instruction. I have frequently heard colleagues say (1) that they are unsatisfied with the films that are available for use in teaching their courses; (2) that they wished that they could find something better that they could use in their classes; and (3) that they hoped such films could incorporate elements of the important controversies that are so much a part of social science learning.

To me, these statements indicate a "felt need" (if you will, a market) for a particular variety of film. I must hasten to add at this point that it is a small market, one that would stand in stark contrast to broadcast television market and to the strategies used in the production of most of those films and series which are screened on broadcast television in the United States, England, or on other national broadcast televisions. Yet I feel that the number of social scientists and proactive adult learners is large enough to justify the creation of a set of visual materials which is intended to fill that "felt need." In attempting to do so, however, there is always the possibility that the prospective film producer's evaluation of the felt need of audiences is not accurate or "on target." Only time will tell if VRUCAE will be useful in satisfying some small part of that felt need.

2. Market-Driven Production Strategy

Once I decided that I would set about producing a set of visual materials for university instruction, it became apparent that many of the constraints that existed for producers of broadcast television programs and series were removed. The whole framework of university learning is quite different from that of the broadcast mass audience composed of individuals who chose programs during leisure hours in their own home (with the exception, of course, of academic course materials specifically produced for educational broadcast, such as "Classrooms of the Air.") The use of films in university social science education is embedded within a variety of conceptual frameworks quite different from that of casual viewing. For example, films are shown in university classrooms in the context of: (a) a university quarter or semester which usually consists of 10 to 15 weeks of instruction; (b) university libraries which contain materials (e.g., books, professional journals, VCRs, possibly computer-based data bases, etc.) supplementary to the contents of films; (c) discipline-derived and problem-focused courses which are frequently geographically, culturally, or political economically oriented; (d) the expectation on the part of the instructor (and at least some of the students) that the goal of a university education (and of the social science courses within it) is to provide students with a better conceptual framework within which to evaluate the world of human beings as participants in various social entities and processes; (e) the expectation of both instructors and (some) students that taking the courses would involve university level understandings of the subject matters covered in the course; (f) the hope by the instructor that some of the students would become as captivated with some of the materials of the course as much as he/she is; (g) the involvement of the course instructor in his/her own discipline and individual fields, with their own histories and key personalities, "schools" of thought, and a variety of well-known and lesser known examples, case studies, etc.; (h) the history and current condition of university education in America, both in the private sector and in the public sector, such that in the 1980s and 1990s university instructors can expect to teach larger classes, often more classes, students who are frequently not well prepared for the level of instruction in classes in which they are enrolled, a shortage of money for new equipment or new "films," and so forth.

It is to these (and other) elements of the university context that the strategy behind VRUCAE was developed. The strategy in VRUCAE is a market-driven production strategy. It assumes that university instructors want to have available to them a set of visual resources to supplement their own instruction. It assumes that they will want to show students films of "cultural systems" (see Rollwagen 1980a for a discussion of the difference between a "culture" and a "cultural system") around the world which are important in the explication of social science understandings of the world. It assumes that they will want to present interviews with or comments by social scientists who have been important in the explication of particular cultural systems talk about them. It assumes that they will want to present interviews in which acknowledged social scientists talk about their work and the way that they came to particular insights. Finally, it assumes that this audience is segmented in a variety of ways into categories of instructors and categories of material to be learned such that any particular film would be sold into a (perhaps small but) particular market; whereas, for example, each of ten videos in the same series might be sold into a number of slightly different markets but overlapping markets. Examples of this will be presented below in the discussion of the series on Tzintzuntzan, and in the discussion of the American Ethnic Groups Project.

From a business perspective, a market driven production strategy for university classrooms assumes that not many copies of any one tape will be sold (in comparison to the number of copies of a major motion picture released on video-cassette, for example). However, by contrast to the relatively expensive production strategy of producers in broadcast educational television (with all of the costs of buying and maintaining studio equipment, supporting numerous personnel, and paying for studios, vehicles, etc.) who must offer programs and sell videotapes derived from them to a very large audience in order to pay for their production costs (or depend upon corporate sponsorship or grants which may change the nature of what is produced), it is my opinion that a production strategy can be created to produce high quality films for university audiences that will be scientifically based, visually stimulating, and produced at moderate cost. Copies of these films can be sold at a price which is well within the range of most university budgets, they can be professionally produced and nicely packaged, and still provide sufficient returns to keep the production process going.

In short, I feel that a prospective social scientist/filmmaker can and must reject the standards of the broadcast television producers and substitute for them a set of standards which will allow the production of high quality social science films judged by social science standards.

Consciously setting about to produce a series of films in this manner transforms the "landscape" of film production. The intent of the VRUCAE series is: (1) to choose a set of topics that are important to social scientists, (2) to select locations in a variety of countries and in a variety of cultural systems that are visually and intellectually interesting, (3) to incorporate interviews with social scientists (hopefully from the cultural systems that are the subject of the films) who will offer insights into these cultural systems, and (4) to employ camerapersons who love their craft and proficient editors to produce a set of tapes which will be appreciated and used by social scientists and students alike.

As the development of a market-driven production strategy for VRUCAE evolved, I eventually arrived at the decision to produce for three major (and obviously overlapping) audiences: (a) courses at the introductory level in anthropology (which may contain materials from cultural systems not included in those visual resource materials to follow); (b) courses in four major world culture areas: Latin America, Asia, Europe, and the U.S.; and (c) courses which focus on agriculture, health care, aging, and women's work. Each of these audiences comprise a sufficiently large market into which to sell any particular video so as to expect that the expenses of the video would be paid by the returns on sales. Because of the modular design of the films (and the ability to add new modules on successive videotapes), it is possible to add new dimensions to any series as new opportunities arise. Also, any series can be modified by the addition of new modules so that they support the modules in other series. In this way, cross cultural comparisons between modules becomes a way to market into audiences that would not be interested in the resources in any one series.

For example, the proposed series on Tzintzuntzan begins with (1) an ethnographic overview, the kind of videotape that would be useful for courses at the introductory level (and which would also be useful in higher level courses as an introduction to other tapes in the Tzintzuntzan series). However, my expectation is to produce additional modules on other tapes that will provide: (2) life histories, of men, of women, of older people, of migrants from Tzintzuntzan into the United States, in two versions (Spanish originals or translated into English); (3) modules on anthropological research methods that Foster and Kemper have used in their study of Tzintzuntzan; and (4) modules on Tzintzuntzeño migrants to the U.S. This set of tapes (and the individual modules therein) would thus be useful to (1) introductory courses; (2) courses on peoples and cultures of Latin America; (3) courses on Mesoamerica and/or Mexico; (4) courses in Spanish language and (oral) literature, folklore, etc.; (5) courses on life histories; (6) courses on cross-cultural aging; (7) courses on culture change; (8) courses on multiculturalism; and (9) courses on immigration, ethnicity or race in the U.S. The Tzintzuntzan series is now in full production, with the first tape distributed in March, 1993. I returned to Tzintzuntzan in February, 1993 to gather additional video footage on life histories, and the fiesta complex; and I also travelled to Washington state in July-August 1993 to gather additional video footage on Tzintzuntzeños who had migrated there to live and work.

At the same time, the first (ethnographic) tape on (a village called "Fengjia" in) China is in full production and may be ready for distribution in late-1993. This video may be used in introductory courses, but, in addition, will also be of interest to quite a different set of instructors. The Fengjia tape(s) will include the following modules: (1) an introduction to the village; (2) agriculture in Fengjia; (3) the family; (4) health care; (5) rural industry in the village; and (6) the increase in the number of draft animals after the breakup of the communes.

The modules on this first tape will include (1) on-location interviews with anthropologist Shu-min Huang, and (2) narration of the introductory module, and narration and slides for the module on draft animals by Stewart Odend'hal, a veterinarian who is conducting research on livestock in Fengjia.

Thus, the first Tzintzuntzan tape and the Fengjia tape would be useful to an instructor in an introductory course who wishes to screen village life in two different cultures. As video production continues, I expect to produce a series on Poland (production already well underway) and Polish-Americans in the U.S. Thus, VRUCAE is positioned to fulfill felt needs in a variety of markets each of which appears to be large enough in and of itself to support the production of and sale to at least one major market in the social sciences and related disciplines.

3. Learning Modules

Each videocassette produced in the VRUCAE series will include one or more "modules." A "module" is a learning unit, normally between 15 and 35 minutes long, which is self-contained and sufficient unto itself and which may be shown during one class period. My decision to create a series of videotapes in which there were a set of "modules" shorter than a typical university classroom was, in part, based upon a theory of learning that I evolved over the years. The fundamental idea behind this theory was that individuals learned about a particular complex topic by understanding how one aspect of that topic functioned and how it was connected to other aspects of a complex whole. For example, in conducting my first filmmaking project on Puerto Rican spiritism in Rochester, New York, I assumed that I would be producing the usual kind of documentary film, which included diverse material integrated into one 50 minute film. Soon, however, I began to realize that for a student to understand how Puerto Rican spiritism "worked," there must be some coverage of the differences between individual spiritist sessions throughout the year; the differences between different spiritists who performed in the area; the process of becoming a spiritist and how individuals became different kinds of spiritists; the existence and functioning of institutions (such as "botanicas") which supported, complemented, and contrasted to the spiritist sessions; the relationship between spiritists who held regular sessions, and others (such as the owner of the botanica who provided "cures" upon demand, taro card readers, and other "performers" in the same neighborhoods); the relationship between the spiritist and the Catholic Church in Rochester; the relationship between those who attended the spiritist sessions and the various fundamental and Pentecostal churches in Rochester; the relationship between spiritists in Rochester and spiritists in other areas to which the Rochester spiritists went (e.g., Buffalo, New York, etc.); and so forth. Although it is easy to say that in any project the researcher must delimit his/her research, it seemed to me that one of the things that made social science research so interesting was the incredible complexity of human life, the way that any activity or process is so embedded in its matrix, and the interrelatedness of all activities and processes within a cultural system (however chosen). Not to give students some idea of this complexity of human cultural systems was to leave them with a simplistic view which was no true indication of the reality. Not to provide them with some way of understanding and evaluating those activities in terms of their own needs was a dereliction of duty in education.

After thinking this over, I decided that the problem for me was my view of what constituted a "film." I began to realize that, particularly for university education purposes, a set of "modules" about related topics might be better than one "film." It seemed to me that students did well by learning about one aspect of a cultural system at a time, but also by concentrating on one cultural system long enough to realize the complexity of that system and how its components were interrelated. In carrying this idea one step further, I began to realize that if one produced a set of "modules" included in one "film," that other sets of modules included in other films about the same topic (perhaps produced much later) could always be added through the production of an additional videotape.

Finally, a word about the medium itself. Although VRUCAE was produced on Super VHS (hereafter "S-VHS") videotape (a "linear" format), my intent was to produce a product that would be amenable to a variety of non-linear formats such as videodisc, and material stored on computer mass storage devices. These formats will undoubtedly gain an enormous segment of the educational media market in the very near future. My solution to this problem of current linear production for a soon-to-arrive non-linear market also lead me to orient the production of films that were composed of "modules." Since the primary use of the films was to be for university instruction, and since most classroom periods in universities are 50 or 60 minutes, I decided early that I would try to limit the modules of each film to less that 50 or 60 minutes to allow ample time for discussion of that module before or after its showing.

Somewhat later in the process of developing VRUCAE it became apparent to me that these modules could also be incorporated into the instructor's plans for the course outside of the classroom proper. My expectation now is that the university instructor may screen only one or two modules of any particular film (or series of films) in a VRUCAE series and then place the remainder of the modules on reserve in the university library (for example, in a "special materials" section of the library where VCRs are available for viewing videotape materials) or at some other location on campus where such material could be used. Once the university has purchased a VRUCAE "film," it would be possible for the instructor, for example, to make individual copies of the modules on that film so that a number of students could be viewing and working with different modules from the same film at the same time. (This procedure is somewhat similar to what university libraries do with multiple copies of books "put on reserve," or what software companies have done with the "site licensing" of computer programs for use in a particular university.)

As non-linear storage devices for magnetic media become more widely available, university instructors could also transfer the modules from the VRUCAE series onto videodiscs, computer disks, optical disks, and/or other mass storage devices. Non-linear access to such materials by students would enhance individual research projects on materials not screened in class, and adds to the justification of my argument for much more VRUCAE material in a series than any one instructor could screen during the limited amount of class time that any one semester holds.

4. Simultaneous Production of Several Films

Given the discussion of "modules" above, it should be relatively easy to understand another advantage of the "modular" approach to film production. If "modules" in one series are about both places and people, and if places and people for any one module are scattered about the world (as they most often are), a producer who wished to maximize limited production funds and limited time for production would work on several series of films at the same time, collecting materials for those films when budget and time permitted, and then working on the post-production in between. Actually, the model for this kind of production arose in my own life not out of film production but rather out of my experience as editor of an international quarterly journal for more than 20 years. Planning for the production of a quarterly professional journal often required the solicitation of manuscripts for "special issues" of the journal well in advance of the actual publication of that issue. This was so much the case that it would not be unusual for me to be working on the solicitation, editing, and publishing of manuscripts of from four to six issues of the journal URBAN ANTHROPOLOGY and STUDIES OF CULTURAL SYSTEMS AND WORLD ECONOMIC DEVELOPMENT (hereafter "UAS") at any one time. I learned how to work on one set when something could be done with it, how to put aside that set when nothing was happening and work on another, and how to schedule my own time so that I could be doing a number of quite diverse tasks over periods of time stretching from year to year. I also learned how to budget money, and how to establish schedules for the integration of contributions from others into my own work schedule.

Given my experiences in working on a variety of issues of UAS at the same time, and my decision to distribute videotapes comprised of modules, it seemed natural to me to establish a videotape production schedule in which I tried to produce a number of "modules" for a variety of videotape series all at the same time. I collect materials for several modules and perhaps different films when I go on a trip (in order to maximize funds and time). For example, I have been collecting material for modules for films on Mexico, Poland, China, the U.S., and Costa Rica over the past four years. When I travel to collect material on one module for one film series, I try to arrange that trip so that I can also collect material for another module and thus save money and eliminate the need for making two trips. During the summer of 1991, for example, I spent six weeks in Poland, three weeks in China, and two weeks in Mexico. In each of these projects, I collected material on agriculture, health, and local community and national policy. The process of working in several different cultural areas in one short time also helps one to see filmmaking and anthropology quite differently.

Also, the conceptualization of films may change quite drastically in the process of their production. With the more usual conceptualization of a film this could be a disaster. With the idea of a film of modules as I have described them, change is not only not a problem but actually a benefit. The later modules thus reflect changes from the baseline of the first modules. The changes provide contrasts from the social scientists who are interviewed in the films to comment upon. The changes bring individuals to the fore who were perhaps not apparent when previous modules were produced. For example, in the film production work that I have been doing in China, during the time that I have been working there the communal system model has been replaced by the responsibility system model, the relationship between the national government and that of the provinces has changed to allow more choices at the local level, and China has been increasingly more integrated into the international economic system, in some regions much more so than others. All of these changes have been productive of new insights into China, and of new possibilities of modules not apparent to me when I first began to work on the China "films."

5. On-Location Filming

One of the major reasons why I think social scientists will find the VRUCAE films valuable is that they will be oriented toward filming "on location." When I first thought seriously about producing a set of films, my original intent was to prepare films about topics which I, myself, knew well and for which I would then write a script. That approach to filmmaking probably would be, in many ways, preferable to the one which I have chosen because it would be less expensive (in terms of travel), and it would unify my anthropological research on one cultural system with my filmmaking efforts. However, during my career I have also decided that I am interested in how specific cultural systems relate to larger (national or interna-tional) cultural systems, an approach which is political economic in general and perhaps "world systems" in particular. (See Rollwagen 1980a for a discussion of my own use of the concept of "cultural system and world system.") Having adopted a political economic approach in general and a world system's approach in particular allows me to return in a new way to what the forefather's of anthropology called "ethnology." Ethnology is an integrative science (as opposed to "ethnography" which is a particularistic approach used to derive information about particular "cultural systems"). As such, ethnology urges anthropologists to deal with questions in a way that is more amenable to other social scientists.

In the last few years, I have become interested in the transformations that are taking place in the socialist and post-socialist world. I have come to believe that it would be possible to make a set of films that would deal with topics that would be of interest to a wide range of scholars. In that regard, I have collected footage in Poland and in China for a forthcoming set of modules. Since that footage and the footage which I have begun to collect elsewhere deals to a great extent with the topics of agriculture, health care, aging, and women's work, it will be possible to plan a overall film production strategy in which comparisons will exist between film series, and perhaps at some time to integrate footage from different parts of the world into one "film."

In any case, one of the features which is central to the production strategy for VRUCAE is on-location filming. My intent is to provide modules incorporating social scientists in those locations about which they have written discussing their research and its findings. In that way, the viewers have a much better grasp of the circumstances of field research, the conditions in which the people in that cultural system live, and how the processes that are described in words appear visually. In addition to recording the social scientist, I hope to include major visual segments about some aspects of the lives of individuals in that cultural system (e.g., pottery-making in

Tzintzuntzan), and biographies of individuals from that culture which illustrate major processes (e.g., Tzintzuntzeño migrants to the United States talking about their lives in Tzintzuntzan and in the United States; elderly Tzintzuntzeños talking about aging in Tzintzuntzan).

6. Integrating the Interests of the Social Scientist/Filmmaker with the Interests of the Social Scientist/Classroom Instructor

In describing my decision to concentrate upon particular social scientists and the cultural systems/processes for which their description/analysis is well-known, I hope that I do not give the impression that my own desires and perspectives are unimportant in this process. Obviously, any selection of topics for films by any individual producer is only a small set of possibilities among a much more extensive set. In choosing to concentrate upon those cultural systems, processes, and social scientists that are (and will be) in the VRUCAE series, I have chosen those cultural systems, processes, social scientists, and perspectives which are and who are (1) acknowledged leaders in a particular social science field, and (2) newer researchers in areas so far neglected by filmic social science.

The focus of topical attention in VRUCAE is, and continues to be, on agriculture, health care, aging, and women's work in their local, national, and international contexts. The concentration on agriculture came about because all three of the individuals who comprised the original production team (myself, Louise Stein, and Tim Jones, the original cameraman) were interested in and have been trained in some aspect of that subject. Louise and I shared an interest in health care and health care delivery. Louise was interested in aging and women's work and argued very effectively that these would be important subjects for the production of a set of videos. Our choice of geographical areas/cultural systems was likewise a mixture of training, experience, desire, and opportunity, along with the suspicion that these would be important arenas for the production of series of "films." I had conducted research in Mexico. Louise had conducted fieldwork in Poland. Louise, Tim and I had the opportunity, as a film crew, to accompany a joint French/People's Republic of China field research team into Hainan Island in 1988. Tim and I had begun film work in Costa Rica in 1987. My own perspectives in teaching had lead me to conceptualize almost all research and teaching within my own version of the World Systems approach (see Rollwagen 1989, 1988, 1981, 1980a and 1980b).

Similarly, we chose the individuals whom we wanted to invite to be the key individuals in our "films." We wanted them to be the spokepersons for what we felt to be the best film series that we could produce. In making the films about these cultural systems, social scientists, and perspectives we created something that spoke about us as individuals as well as about those who appeared in the films. The first tape produced (TZINTZUNTZAN IN THE 1990s: A LAKESIDE VILLAGE IN HIGHLAND MEXICO: TAPE #1: An Ethnographic Overview), for example, is about anthropological research in Mexico (the country of my own dissertation fieldwork). In it, three anthropologists discuss aspects of their work in Tzintzuntzan. George M. Foster, whose writings are central to a number of fields in the evolution of cultural anthropology, discusses the economy of the village (agriculture, fishing, craft production, and migratory labor), changes in the village since he began work there in the 1940s (including the transformation of the population from "peasantry" to non-peasantry), and other topics for which he has become well-known in anthropological theory and ethnography. Robert V. Kemper discusses the emigration of Tzintzuntzeños and the lives of Tzintzuntzeño emigrants in other places, and provides a framework for looking at Tzintzuntzan's continuing economic evolution as a a center for tourism and the production on touristic goods. Stanley H. Brandes and George Foster discuss the religious calendar in Tzintzuntzan and the importance of fiestas in Tzintzuntzan.

Because the VRUCAE series is specifically produced for educational purposes and for university-level audiences, we assume that they will be incorporated into a learning situation in which (1) a social scientist will be present to help learners understand the implications of that which is presented in the "films," and/or (2) that there will be other materials available to the learner (e.g., books and articles available in a library). It is for that reason that we intend to provide accompanying materials (e.g., a paper copy of a bibliography relating to the subject matter of that film or possibly a computer diskette which might include a bibliography, and perhaps a HyperCard stack with maps, music, etc.). Since the films are produced for educational purposes, providing supplementary materials in addition to the films themselves increases the value of those films for classroom instruction and independent learning.

7. Cooperative Arrangements Between the Social Scientist/ Filmmaker and the Scholars who Appear in the Films

The entire structure of VRUCAE is based on cooperative arrangements between those scholars who appear in the modules (and others who provide me with information but do not appear in the films) and the film production team. This cooperation, in each case, requires a working out (hopefully as much as possible during the pre-production phase) of the "rules" by which that particular project proceeds. In general, I will try to determine before I begin filming on any particular individual who I think should be featured in the modules that comprise that "film." This selection is based on two types of information: (1) my evaluation of written materials on that topic; and (2) a process of evaluation in which I make contacts in the scholarly community and ask my contacts about particular individuals as potential participants in the modules. Only then do I contact the scholar who may appear in one of the modules and discuss the project with him/her. In that process I will also begin to isolate possible topics for modules, and perspectives which that person may use in the module. Since this process is being applied to several potential contributors to the series, the discussions usually begin to identify quite different topics and approaches to those topics, as well as dealing with the question of locations for filming.

Because the filming of modules require complicated logistical arrangements (e.g., release time for camerapersons, planning a production schedule including the arrangements for airline tickets and housing arrangements, scheduling of several participants in different modules) within a restricted budget, one of the next tasks that must be addressed is the negotiation of dates when I can maximize the arrangements about my own time with respect to the availability of the participants in the modules. In that sense, the production of a film of modules is quite a bit more complicated than the traditional "ethnographic" film. The usual view that people have of an anthropologist and a film producer going out to live among the Umgawah for three months and filming whenever they can (however valuable that is for some people) is NOT the blueprint for the filming of VRUCAE. Rather, the way that VRUCAE films are produced is much more of a series of negotiations in which the questions are:

1. **Who** to choose and ask to appear in the films;
2. **Which topics** to ask that person to discuss;
3. **Which locale** to select as the best for the filming
   a. based on the visual interest of the surroundings;
   b. based on the willingness of the individuals to have us film there;
   c. based upon the ability of the scholar to appear in the film to be there;

4. **When** the participant(s) can meet me and spend a few days in filming.

Once questions such as these have been dealt with initially, it then becomes necessary to deal with the particulars of that person's appearance in that module. If the modules are to "work," the social scientist who is to be featured in any particular module must select four of five major aspects of the topic which he/she will discuss on camera, hopefully in a location in which the context relates directly to what they are discussing. This approach prepares them for the actual filming of those topics by letting them know (a) that they will not be expected to talk for 30 minutes straight in front of the camera without notes; (b) that changing the camera position is an important part of the process of filming, since it provides for "visual refreshment" of the audience.

8. Alternative Possibilities in the Development of Future VRUCAE Films

Having evolved the approach to producing VRUCAE films that I have described does not in any way suggest that films in one series will be very much like films in another series. Each of the variables can be changed. The first film ("An Ethnographic Overview") of the series TZINTZUNTZAN IN THE 1990s was made using only American anthropologists as the subjects of our filming (that is, "outsiders" speaking about "others"). As will be indicated, my hopes are (as much as I can) to produce films that include social scientists from the cultural group (country or nation) that is being filmed. For example, I intend to produce a set of films about African-Americans using primarily Afro-American social scientists to discuss Afro-Americans. I will also strive to include as social scientists from the country within which the cultural system being filmed exists, and interviews with and segments by individuals from those cultural systems. For example, in the proposed VRUCAE videotape on Peruvian migrants to Patterson, New Jersey (discussed briefly in the latter part of this paper in the section on the American Ethnic Groups Project) I hope to use a social scientist from Peru to discuss the situation of Peruvians in the U.S.

"TZINTZUNTZAN IN THE 1990s: TAPE #1: An Ethnographic Overview" concentrated on one village in Mexico and was videotaped to indicate the views of three anthropologists who had examined different aspects of life in a village in Mexico. It was oriented to a potential audience of individuals (primarily of cultural anthropologists in the United States) who might wish to illustrate village studies in anthropology, peasants, culture change, village life in Mexico and Latin America, and George Foster's life and writings (which are widely recognized as seminal to many different aspects of American cultural anthropology). The proposed project on Afro-Americans in the U.S. will be oriented to a somewhat different potential audience, since it can be assumed that this topic will not only be appealing to cultural anthropologists in the United States with interests in Afro-American life and culture in the U.S., but also to sociologists and scholars in ethic studies, Afro-American studies, multicultural education, and others both in the United States and in other countries around the world. Thus, each series, each videotape, and perhaps each module may be oriented toward, and will therefore be appealing to, the needs of quite different audiences. My hope is that as production continues, I will be able to satisfy both my own emotional and academic desires, and those of a wide variety of university instructors and audiences as well.

9. Empowering the Social Scientist/Filmmaker

In my opinion, the system of funding for films which most prospective filmmakers look to is, in general, destructive of their goals and of their self image. Academics are not well paid in comparison to people with comparable education in the "professions." In that sense it is difficult for them to accumulate sufficient funds for filmmaking out of their own salaries. Films, in many cases, are made with borrowed monies, and social science filmmakers hope to earn sufficient monies out of the sale and/or rental of films to repay themselves for the production. They are often dedicated people who try to exist within a larger framework that is often hostile to their efforts and which often appears to them to demean their skills and insights.

Anthropologists who wish to make films about topics that would be of interest to university audiences must confront the attitude of potential funders that topics chosen and approaches used must satisfy relatively large audiences. These attitudes work against the social scientist who wishes (a) to satisfy his/her own desires to make a film from a particular perspective which may or may not be amenable to the administrators making decisions about funding, (b) to satisfy his/her needs to produce films on topics and approaches needed in his/her classroom, and (c) to satisfy his/her needs to produce films for other instructors who also cannot obtain such films for their own classrooms.

It is my belief that social scientists must find some way to produce films which does not subject them to the "judgement" of funders, funders whose views on filmmaking are often quite different from that of a university instructor and who quite frequently produce for audiences very different from that of university classrooms and/or university-level learning. VRUCAE is such an attempt. It seems reasonable to assume that if VRUCAE does satisfy a need in the scholarly community, it should provide enough resources to sustain production.

The history of my own entre into video production may be interesting, but will probably not provide a model for others. Yet it does demonstrate that individuals with few resources can evolve a means by which they can produce films over which they have complete control. As I indicated above, by 1993 (the date of the writing of this article) I have been the editor of the journal UAS for 22 years. Contrary to most academic editors, I founded the journal myself, and it was self-supporting right from the beginning through subscription revenues. I did much of the work in the beginning by hand, and purchased those services (e.g., typesetting, printing) which I could not perform myself. For the same reasons that I encourage filmmakers to fund their own filmmaking, I began the journal as a private venture, contributing hours of my own time every week to solicit articles, solicit evaluations of those articles, typeset articles, paste them up for phototypesetting, prepare the printed journals for mailing, and conduct all of those activities related to the management of a small business (e.g., record keeping, tax preparation, purchasing and maintenance of equipment, etc.). To make a long story short, I created a labor-intensive business that barely made ends meet for nearly 15 years. Then, in the mid-1980s, with the arrival of personal computers and desk-top publishing, I secured a small business loan and purchased the equipment necessary to publish the journal, distribute it, and take care of the business end of the operation as well.

In 1993, it is clear that the same computers that facilitate desk top publishing will also facilitate desk top video production. Shot logs and edit decision lists can be kept quite nicely on the same computer which sets the type for a journal. By 1988, I began to see what the real impact of the fact that computers and video were digital systems and relied on magnetic media. I began to buy video production equipment with the money that was saved by typesetting my own journal and doing all of the other activities necessary to produce a journal myself. At this point, I have most of the equipment necessary to create an edit decision list for the VRUCAE modules and prepare them for final mastering onto 1" videotape. I had originally intended to master onto 3/4" SP in my own edit suite from the S-VHS footage shot in the field. However, my own editing skills are not comparable to those of a professional video editor, and my equipment is really not comparable to that in a fully equipped professional studio. At the last moment, I decided to master onto 1" videotape at WSKG, a regional public broadcasting corporation which offered editing services and equipment at a very reasonable price. I also found a regional private firm ("Univisions") which offered similar facilities at a comparable price.

At this point, then, I have produced the first film (comprised of 5 modules) on Tzintzuntzan and I am working on the second film (comprised of at least 3 modules) on Fengjia, China. My intent is to continue to do the preparatory work on my own equipment and then to master onto 1" tape at WSKG and/or Univisions. I have been able to pay for the production expenses as they arose, to pay for the post-production at WSKG and Univisions, and to distribute the first tape. The funds from the journal have supported this second venture. I have never paid myself anything in salary from the receipts of the journal. Rather, the returns from the business have been invested in some aspect of video production (e.g., equipment, travel, and per diem expenses in the field for the production team). It is not the epitome of successful entrepreneurial capitalism. But it has allowed me to do what I have always dreamed of doing.

10. Incorporating Aesthetic Considerations

In a recent article (1991), Nichols argues that anthropological filmmakers disavow aesthetic intent in their film production. Nothing could be further from the truth. Given the confusion and mis-(re)presentation in the argument of Nichol's article in general, it would not be difficult to argue whatever one wished. However, since the article represents the first venture of a major figure of the world of narrative film criticism into what I have called here "anthropological" film and filmmaking, it requires a somewhat more lengthy response than otherwise. My response is that aesthetics in anthropological filmmaking should be focused precisely upon the subject matter of anthropology itself, the area in which Nichols is not competent to judge and the area which (as I have argued in an earlier article [Rollwagen 1988]) distinguishes anthropological film from "ethnographic" film made by non-anthropologists.

For an anthropological filmmaker, aesthetic intent is ultimately based on that filmmaker's ability to meet the conditions of anthropological argument (an area in which Nichols is, judged on the comments in his above-mentioned article, almost totally ignorant, much to the detriment of the explication of his argument). That is, if aesthetic norms are to be satisfied not only do "facts" have to be "correct," but data must be joined to some "theory" or "perspective" which gives them meaning. What an interviewee says in response to a question in a video interview becomes the basis for the next question (and for an interview with another informant [the etic approach]). The questions that the interviewer asks is, to a great extent, based upon years of experience in a discipline which comprises tens of thousands of practitioners conducting research throughout the world. Thus, if the subject matter of the interview has to do with life in a village of small farmers in Mexico, the framework for the interview is not only earlier "ethnographic" research conducted on that same village, but also ethnographic research conducted throughout that culture area (Mesoamerica or Latin America), and cross-cultural research on small farmers conducted throughout the world (including in my case China and Poland, for example). Furthermore, the investigations of anthropologists are corroborated and supported by social scientists from other disciplines and perspectives (such as sociology, economics and political science from the traditional disciplines on the one hand, and political economy [which cross-cuts those disciplines] on the other). If Nichols is going to argue that anthropology, as a social science discipline, is worthless because it is positivistic and empirical in its approach (which is true only to the extent that Nichols knowledge of it makes it seem that way to him) then he must also take on the much larger task of arguing that social science as a whole is also worthless (which he intimates). Unless he wishes to offer some alternative to social science that has more value than the arguments in his above-mentioned article, then he should confine his arguments to narrative film where (presumably) he has something to offer. The arguments that Nichols introduces in his 1991 article are confused, illogical, and ultimately not very insightful. However, since he has raised the issue of aesthetic intent, let me reply in short below.

When an anthropologist is in control of the filmmaking, his/her first duty is to the integrity of the presentation of the subject matter. That is why the film COWS OF DOLO KEM PAYE is such a gem in anthropological film production whereas to non-anthropologists is might appear to be an amateur production (since the filmmaker runs out of color film two-thirds of the way through the production and has to proceed with black and white film). Correspondingly, although the work is beautifully filmed, THE NUER (and other films of that ilk) is ultimately of little anthropological value. THE NUER is more like a great-grandchild of The March of Time than it is a coherent anthropological argument. The VRUCAE films are anthropologically informed films which integrate with a huge written literature and, indeed, articulate with that written material in theory, concept, argument, and data. It is in this sense that the VRUCAE films do not have to confront "a well-formulated television documentary aesthetic" (Nichols 1991:35) which, in reality, they oppose. Since the VRUCAE films are specifically produced for classroom audiences and are distributed by cassette, they do not have to "confront" (broadcast) television standards, an argument that many of the non-anthropological "ethnographic" filmmakers still do not accept or incorporate into their world view. (In a conference at American University in Washington, DC several years ago, critics of anthropological film attempted to quash any arguments such as those I am arguing with the response that the panel of "experts" from broadcast television who were in attendance would agree with them that such films would not be accepted for broadcast.) In my view, it is important that the aesthetics of anthropology be used to determine whether a particular argument or perspective is to be included in an anthropological film. It is precisely for this reason why so many films made by non-anthropological filmmakers fail.

If the explication of an informed anthropological argument if central to anthropological filmmaking, then the inclusion of sufficient material to support that argument is also essential. It is in this sense that the VRUCAE concept of filmmaking differs most from that of the majority of ethnographic and anthropological filmmakers. The "argument" of the VRUCAE film *project* is that people learn by immersion in a great variety of programmed and integrated "visual resources." In the Tzintzuntzan series, overviews of the village of Tzintzuntzan by anthropologists will be followed by Tzintzuntzeños talking about their lives and work (the title of the second tape in that series). Future tapes in that series will provide insights into the craftmaking tradition of the village, into the lives of the elderly, and other topics. In this way, viewers of the films will have sufficient materials to gain an insight into the lives of the Tzintzuntzeños themselves, and in that sense can have their "aesthetic of knowledge" sense satisfied. As in the argument immediately above, a VRUCAE videotape series (unlike that of broadcast television) can be premised upon the proposition that college students who have a semester's worth of time can invest much more time in viewing visual resources than a casual viewer of broadcast television documentaries is willing to do.

Thirdly, the visual aesthetic sense in anthropology is extremely important. Most anthropologists actively pursue a film-as-product that "looks good." However, that usually means employing somebody as a filmmaker who has skills that the anthropologists himself/herself might not have. For example, I do not consider myself a photographic artist. Furthermore, I can no longer see well enough to do the photography myself even if I were willing to base my films on my own photography. Therefore, if I am to produce films which are based on anthropological and political economic argument and evidence (which the photographic artist whom I hire presumably does not have), then I must find someone who is willing to photograph what I want and understand that I will be the person to edit it and organize it. In this way, I can maintain those aspects of argumentation and evidence which I feel are central to the nature of the film(s) and achieve that level of visual aesthetic that I want to achieve in those films.

Just as hiring a photographic artist to film the materials that I wished filmed depends upon having the financial means to do so, so does the ability to finance the filmmaking endeavor itself. In his discussion of (the lack of) anthropological aesthetic, Nichols provides two key examples for his argument that anthropologists are not concerned with "aesthetics." Both examples (1991:35) he provides are, of course, total misinterpretations, misinterpretations based upon a desire to prove his own point but disregarding the intent of the author. The intent of the first example is to say that (a) the event which was being filmed was of short duration, and (b) that the anthropologist could only afford to be there for that one time to collect that footage. I do not read it as a lack of desire to film aesthetically, or a lack of ability to do so (as Nichols does).

Likewise, the intent of the second example is to indicate that the anthropologist did not "arrange" any of the circumstances of that which was filmed (as some non-anthropological "ethnographic" filmmakers have done because of their own vision of "aesthetic intent"). Part of the "anthropological aesthetic" is that subject matter is to be described/analyzed ("filmed") as it is found, and not to be arranged so that it conforms to the standards of the analyst/filmmaker/photographer.

As one step further in this direction, for the VRUCAE films I have endeavored to not only find the anthropologist whose analysis is "best" (most insightful, most penetrating, most beautiful) but I have also attempted whenever possible to locate someone from that culture. In my filmmaking in Fengjia, Shandong Province, People's Republic of China, I enlisted the help of Chinese born, American educated anthropologist Huang Shu-min. In collecting material in Poland, I found a Polish Gypsy, Andrzej Mirga, an ethnographer at Jagiellonian University in Cracow, who accompanied me to collect footage in the village in which he grew up. For future filmmaking endeavors, I hope to continue this strategy wherever possible. An accompanying strategy is to supplement these ethnographic materials with analyses of regional, national, and international topics (e.g., health care delivery policy at the national level) which provide the context for the ethnographic materials at the village level. In this arena, it is often more desirable to have the analyses of scholars from outside of that particular cultural system, scholars whose futures are not dictated by the "political correctness" of their analyses. Thus, contrary to what Nichols indicates in his article, choosing an informant is not necessarily always as straightforward as simply choosing anyone from the culture being examined (in opposition to choosing an anthropologist). Most of Nichol's arguments are as simplistic at their core as this one.

In short, there is an aesthetic intent in (truly) anthropological filmmaking. The aim of the VRUCAE films is to present a set of films that are aesthetically pleasing as they can be. Just as I try to select those anthropologists whom I think will best (re)present the culture of the cultural system upon which I am focusing, so too do I try to choose the subject matter which best achieves the goals that seem to me need to be achieved. Although I have tried to find the best artistic photographer that I could afford to hire, the visual aspects of "visual resources" are clearly secondary to the presentation of a well-structured argument and compelling evidence. From my conversations with other anthropological filmmakers, I would conclude that their position is much like my own. So much for the argument of the disavowal of aesthetic intent.

The Example of the Tzintzuntzan Filmmaking Project

The modular approach which I have adopted in the VRUCAE tapes came into being in order to respond to a number of constraints and/or possibilities in university education.

First, most university classrooms are constrained by a limited amount of time in classroom sessions. Because I initially decided to produce VRUCAE for university classroom audiences, I decided to distribute an end product containing a number of related "modules" any one of which could be shown during a class period of 50 to 60 minutes and still leave some class time for discussion. The five modules in the first video tape in the first series that I have produced are all shorter than 40 minutes, several much shorter.

Second, the pedagogical imperative which I adopted in the VRUCAE tapes is that education proceeds best when students appreciate and understand the complexity of a cultural system through the process of seeing it from a number of different perspectives. In most non-social science documentary films (and in many social science documentary films as well) the "complexity" of the subject matter is explained in the voice-over written by the documentary filmmaker. As in the case of contemporary entertainers, it is not enough to sing well, or play well; the top entertainers are those who create the music that they sing or play. In documentary filmmaking, it is too often the case that the recognized filmmakers are those who are the best script writers,[3] and it is the script (accompanied by visuals) which provides the continuity and the complexity. I wanted to experiment with another approach. A film (in this case, the first videotape) can be constructed to offer a number of sources of information to the viewer so that he/she learns about the cultural system from a number of perspectives and individuals whose voices and ideas are within the video footage.

Third, VRUCAE recognizes that "social science" relies upon both (a) an approach in social science which in anthropology is called "an emic approach; and (b) an approach in social science which in anthropology is called "an etic approach" (see Rollwagen 1988 for an earlier statement on the importance for that in creating a framework for anthropological film production). Basically, in an emic approach a social scientist checks the accuracy of his/her investigations with some members of the community under examination against his/her investigations with other members of that same community. In an etic approach a social scientist tests that accuracy of his/her findings and the value of the interpretation based on those findings within his/her disciplinary community (and perhaps outside of it) by explicating the findings and the interpretations within some social science framework.[4]

In VRUCAE my focus of attention in the first videotape ("An Ethnographic Overview") in the first series ("Tzintzuntzan in the 1990s: A Lakeside Village in the Highlands of Mexico") concentrates its attention on the work of three anthropologists who have conducted fieldwork in Tzintzuntzan: George M. Foster, Robert V. Kemper, and Stanley H. Brandes. After a series of shots which provide an overview of the physical features of the region around Tzintzuntzan and of some of the activities of the residents, there are five "modules" which present different anthropological perspectives on the village and on the municipio ("county") of which it is a part:

1. An introduction, by George Foster, to the village and to his long-term (47 years) anthropological fieldwork there (from the beginning of the film to the enc of module 1 comprises 22 minutes).
2. A discussion, by George Foster, of culture change in the village between 1946 and 1992, with comments on how the discipline of anthropology has changed in the same period of time (module 2 comprises 33 minutes).
3. A two part discussion ("Religion in Tzintzuntzan") on aspects of religion in Tzintzuntzan: the first ("The Religious Calendar in Tzintzuntzan") by George Foster (14 minutes) and the second ("Fiestas As Folk Religion and as Social Control") by Stanley Brandes (16 minutes).
4. A discussion ("Tourism in Tzintzuntzan"), by Robert V. Kemper, of the importance of tourism to the changing economy of Tzintzuntzan (18 minutes).
5. A final module, by Robert Kemper ("Emigration from Tzintzuntzan"), which focuses on the out-migration of many of the inhabitants of Tzintzuntzan and their lives in other places. In particular, for this module, I concentrated on Kemper's description of emigrants from Tzintzuntzan in Mexico City and in Chicago (20 minutes; for a total of 126 minutes on the tape).

There are other modules in this series about Tzintzuntzan in production. One of these (tentatively titled "Tzintzuntzeños Talk About Their Lives and Work") will be comprised of a number of statements by Tzintzuntzeños about their lives, in Tzintzuntzan and as workers and/or residents away from Tzintzuntzan. This tape expands upon and adds depth to the material presented in the first tape. It provides personal examples of the material in the first tape, and adds to the complexity required in the pedagogical approach which I have chosen. In this second tape, I will record statements in Spanish (which will then be translated into English for English-speaking classrooms) and in English where possible. In transferring this material to the master tape during editing, I will record the Spanish on one linear sound track and the English on the other linear sound track. Proceeding in that manner means that, during the duplication process, the master tape can be easily used to produce either (1) an English language version (with the Spanish original faded out in the distribution tape) or (2) a Spanish version for use in university Spanish language classes or for distribution to Spanish-speaking audiences in the United States or abroad.

Another proposed film module in the Tzintzuntzan series ("Long Term Collaborative Fieldwork") directs its attention to the topic of cultural anthropological field research, specifically to the long-term collaboration between anthropologists in projects, like the study in Tzintzuntzan, which provide opportunities for two or more anthropologists to conduct fieldwork and share ideas and information about one field site. In that tape, George Foster and Robert Kemper explain how what originally started out to be two different (but related) studies of Tzintzuntzeños increasingly became a shared research effort.

Since the entire conceptualization of VRUCAE is "modular," additional modules of whatever nature can be added as a film containing one or more modules to any of the series at any time.

Written Materials to Accompany the Videotapes

Because these modules were developed specifically for university classroom use (and for proactive adult learners), it was important in the selection of the project itself, and the development of its component modules (a) to choose a project which I thought would be important to and interesting for a wide variety of anthropologists (and other social scientists); (b) to choose a project for which there was an abundance of written materials; and (c) to choose topics and / or approaches to examine which other anthropologists would find useful in discussing the "film."

The Tzintzuntzan project satisfies all of these criteria to a high degree. Without a doubt, George Foster and Tzintzuntzan are extremely well known in anthropological literature. Most cultural anthropologists have read Foster's work on Tzintzuntzan (or in theoretical papers about other topics based upon his research in Tzintzuntzan) at some point in their career. Foster's work in Tzintzuntzan is and has been for some time essential reading in a number of arenas: the anthropology of Latin America, village studies, peasant studies, culture change, medical anthropology, and (more recently) aging. Robert Kemper's studies of migrants from Tzintzuntzan, on urbanization, and on tourism (in which Tzintzuntzan serves as a major example) are widely known in urban anthropology. Brandes' treatment of fiestas in Tzintzuntzan examines a community in which, unlike that of many communities in Mexico, fiestas have remained important in the lives of both its residents and those of its citizens who have emigrated to other locales. (See, for example, in the references cited section of this paper the selection of works by Brandes, Foster, and Kemper.) Beyond the works of these three anthropologists, there is a wealth of anthropological studies of communities in the immediate ("Tarascan") region of Mexico. These factors were an important consideration in selecting Tzintzuntzan for a filmmaking site since university professors would feel confident that in showing TZINTZUNTZAN IN THE 1990s, they could direct students to additional materials for in-class discussions, for term papers, and for satisfying those students whose curiosity had been aroused by what they had seen in the film itself. My expectation is to send either (1) a paper copy, or (2) a computer diskette in ASCII format of that bibliography along with each tape sold in the future.

Filmmakers who are social scientists (in contrast to documentary filmmakers who are not social scientists) must look for subject matters for their filmmaking that are well documented by written materials. It is the relationship between insightful written materials and well-constructed films which will differentiate good social science filmmaking from non-social science filmmaking about similar subjects. Good social science filmmaking of course is, in an important sense, based as much upon what the social scientist brings to the filmmaking as it is upon what is in front of the camera. In this sense, Margaret Mead's comment (1975) that "anthropology is a discipline of words" is a positive comment. VRUCAE as a series will depend upon the fact that anthropology is a discipline of words. Most social scientists will agree that film cannot do as well what written materials can. To introduce a series such as VRUCAE is not in any way an attempt to substitute for written material. These films can do what they do (and what written materials cannot do) precisely because they complement the written materials. As the possibilities for incorporating BOTH written and visual materials (and audio materials) expands (such as in the case of inexpensive and large capacity non-linear storage devices driven by computers) visual materials such as VRUCAE will increasingly integrate the two so that learners can select from a broad range of materials stored on the same medium whatever they wish to use to learn about a particular subject.

How VRUCAE May Be Used for University Classes

In adopting a modular approach to filmmaking, I assumed that these films could and would be used in a number of ways. The first way (and the one which instructors most often consider) is screening in the classroom. Projection of documentary films in classrooms became the established way of using films because in those days when films were actually made of celluloid: (a) the cost of purchasing the film was relatively high and the film's usable life was extended by only making the film available to the teacher in classroom situations (and NOT to students to view them as individuals); and (b) duplication of that film (or portions of it) was a costly technical procedure. The emergence of video, a magnetic media (at least in its present configuration) removed those restrictions. Because video is a magnetic media, because VCRs are almost ubiquitous equipment both for institutions and in private households, and because many people know how to make a copy of a videotape (or portions of it) video films and access to them can be much easier than for celluloid films.

In deciding to produce VRUCAE I assumed that there would be a sufficiently large number of instructors who would have classrooms equipped with (a) a video cassette recorder (VCR), and (b) a large screen television set, or video projector. I also assumed that instructors would either (a) run the purchased tape in the cassette to the point at which they wished to begin during that day's class, (b) make a copy of the particular module that they wished to play for that day, or (c) have their university audio-visual department play that portion of the tape for that class over closed circuit television.

A second way in which the modular films such as VRUCAE can be used in university instruction is in providing student access outside of the classroom. Some instructors will not wish to show all of the modules in a particular set of VRUCAE. They may show the introduction to that set and perhaps one other module and discuss them in class. They may then place the tape containing the remainder of the modules in an audio-visual lab with VCRs where students can view one or more of those modules in preparation for in-class presentations or as material to be viewed in conjunction with reading written materials in the preparation of a term paper about a topic of interest to them.

A third way in which modular films will be used in the near future was apparent to me from the beginning of my decision to adopt a modular approach. The linear nature of video tape has one major limitation: it takes too much time to get from any one point in a two hour tape to another point. My hope in designing the modular approach to social science filmmaking, of course, was that it would not be long until some satisfactory non-linear means of storing and accessing these modules would be available. Non-linear storage of materials, of course, means that both instructors in class and students outside of class can adopt non-linear means of access to the materials. Such an approach implies more equipment than most classrooms have at present (e.g., a computer with which to access the non-linearly stored material and, at this time at least, a mechanism with an extremely large storage capacity to hold the two hours worth of material on only the first of many tapes on Tzintzuntzan). Given the rapid advances in computer and video technology, I do not think that it will be long before visual materials produced in modules will be in high demand precisely because they were produced to contain a sufficiently large amount of material (visual resources) to appeal to the diversity that exists in every classroom. Modular films (available through non-linear means) will be used to complement in-class instruction, and (with the addition of computer-based indexes to the material) will be used by students outside of classrooms to navigate through the modular materials to locate aspects of the film which interest them. (I am including this discussion now only because I feel that the movement to modular visual resource films has a bright future.)

Production Strategies and Marketing into Segmented Markets

Because the markets into which any particular film is to be sold are relatively small, part of the production strategy of any series of films that I will make is to attempt to target at least two markets for each film. One of these two markets will be the same for that series. The second market may be quite different between films in a series. For example, my expectation is that the series TZINTZUNTZAN IN THE 1990s will be attractive primarily to anthropologists who teach (a) introductory courses in general anthropology or cultural anthropology; (b) courses in Latin America or Mexico; or (c) courses in peasant society or culture change. This variety of subject matter in the series and the depth of resources which it provides would allow individual anthropologists (who might teach their courses quite differently from another anthropologist) to select from the series (a) general modules, and (b) additional modules which treat topics which are of particular interest to them. Those modules not discussed in class become valuable supplemental resources for additional viewing by students and/or materials for research viewing.

In the Tzintzuntzan series, the first videotape is an ethnographic overview: an introduction to Tzintzuntzan, an introduction to some of the topics that will be covered in the series, and an introduction to the three anthropologists who are at the center of the anthropological studies of Tzintzuntzan. My expectation is that this module will be purchased by almost everyone who buys tapes in the series, since it is the ethnographic bases of the other modules.

However, in the modules that follow on Tzintzuntzan, there will be a variety of strategies which will be interesting for a variety of other audiences and uses. In the modules which will present life histories, for example, the distribution tapes may be bought in either the translated English version (with the Spanish barely audible in the background), or in the Spanish

FIGURE 1: Jack Rollwagen (left) and Robert V. Kemper in
Tzintzuntzan, Mexico discussing an interview.

version (with no English present). There is a tradition in anthropology which values life history materials and, consequently, there are a number of anthropologists who would use life history materials in their classrooms (regardless of whether they teach peoples and cultures of Latin America or Mexico). Given the recent emergence of Cultural Studies as a major interdisciplinary framework for inquiry and use of life histories, my expectation is that scholars from disciplines other than anthropology would find such life histories useful as well. Finally, in addition, I hope to capture some of the market in foreign languages, hopefully in the more extensive high school market as well as in the university market. Life histories recorded "in the field" are important to language learning because (a) they are reality based (in that they arise out of an individual's life experience) and not fictitious or "docu-drama"

FIGURE 2: An interview for a forthcoming TZINTZUNTZAN IN THE 1990s videotape: "Tzintzuntzeños Talk About Their Lives and Work."

re-created situations which mimic reality; (b) they present interesting material; and (c) they exemplify dialectical and cultural features that are frequently absent from the "professionally" prepared material.

As a second example, one of the other foci of the Tzintzuntzan series will be on the elderly in Tzintzuntzan. Since the United States has large and rapidly growing population of elderly (many of whom are and will be Latinos), my hope is that one of the tapes which I hope to produce on elderly Tzintzuntzeños (which I expect to contain both ethnographic, that is analytical, materials and life history segments) will be of interest to (a) instructors in ethnic studies, and multiculturalism, (b) aging and health care, as well as the previously mentioned (c) life history enthusiasts. In this module, I will also gather life history materials from elderly women as well as elderly men, with the

FIGURE 3: Doña Mica looks at her interview footage.

hope that some of the modules which comprise this film will be of interest to and will be purchased by instructors interested in women's studies.

Similarly, other modules in the Tzintzuntzan series will attempt to incorporate (in addition to the university anthropological market) other segments of the academic market and/or markets quite different than (and hopefully larger than) anthropology. Additional comments on the production of VRUCAE for a variety of markets will be presented in the material below on the American Ethnic Groups Project.

Example 2: The American Ethnic Groups Project

The idea for the American Ethnic Groups Project arose in my mind only after I had shot a considerable amount of footage in Mexico, Poland, China, and Costa Rica, and was heavily involved in negotiating to return to China for research and filming among the Chinese Hmong. One of the major concepts behind VRUCAE was to collect comparable footage in agriculture, health care, aging, and women's work across four cultures (two socialist and post-socialist, that is China and Poland; and two capitalist, that is the U.S. and Costa Rica). In that context, when the opportunity to film in Tzintzuntzan arose the Tzintzuntzan project was "outside" of that system of four cultures. However, I chose to do it (and to complete it first) because of the market value that I thought it would have. The Tzintzuntzan project, almost by necessity (given the heavy involvement of one of the anthropologists in the study of migration) included a module on the migration of Tzintzuntzeños to Mexico City and to the United States. When I started editing the Tzintzuntzan footage, I gradually began to think that the Tzintzuntzan material (with footage shot both in Mexico and on Tzintzuntzeños in the U.S.) filled another role. I had initially thought of the Tzintzuntzan material as primarily about a village in Mexico that happened to have a module on migration to the U.S. However, when I started to think about the Tzintzuntzan materials from a marketing point of view, I realized that there was a great opportunity to market a set of modules on Tzintzuntzeño migrants to the United States to instructors of courses such as Chicano studies, Latino studies, ethnic studies, and so forth.

Once I began to think in such a way, I began to think of similar modules in the proposed series on Poland. Since I assumed that this ethnic studies and multicultural studies market was potentially much greater than that in anthropology, I started to focus my attention on what it was that ethnic studies (rather than anthropology) instructors might want. It then occurred to me that instructors in ethnic studies would find the tapes on Tzintzuntzan as a whole extremely valuable because they not only depicted Mexicans from Tzintzuntzan in America, they also provided a great depth of material on the village in Mexico from which they came. At that point, I decided to try to collect material for each foreign location in which I would film on both the local (foreign) cultural system (e.g., village) and on migrants from that cultural system to the United States. Thus, those tapes and modules about migrants from the foreign locations to America would, collectively, comprise a set of modules about ethnic groups in America, each of which would have a great deal of material about the culture (and perhaps about the particular village or city) from which those migrants came.

Finally, for the purposes of this article, I also began to think of domestic and overseas markets for these videos in different ways. My original intent was to produce in NTSC and perhaps duplicate some copies into PAL for distribution into England, Australia, and other countries that used PAL. However, in November, 1991, I attended the American Anthropological Association meeting in Chicago and very purposefully attended the business meeting of the Society for the Anthropology of Europe (hereafter "SAE"). Because of my involvement in the production of films on Poland (including some material shot in a Gypsy village in southern Poland), I wanted to see what was going on in the SAE (which I had not visited for some time). I was indeed surprised to find that the number of people involved in the SAE had skyrocketed in this last decade. And with the continuing evolution of the socialist states into the era of post-socialism, the number of (mostly younger) anthropologists with involvements in the previously socialist countries had increased as well. This fact not only suggested new filming opportunities, but also a very sizeable market into which to sell the Polish tapes. It also raised the possibility of new projects in Europe specifically to sell into that SAE market with, hopefully, ethnic groups in the United States from that society.

In any case, the more than I considered the variety of markets that existed during the early 1990s in anthropology

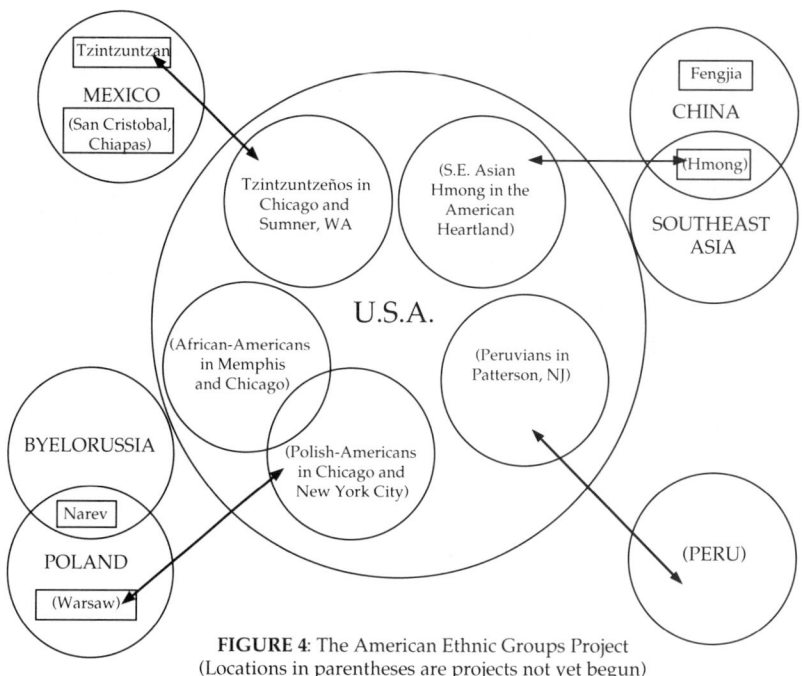

FIGURE 4: The American Ethnic Groups Project
(Locations in parentheses are projects not yet begun)

and in other disciplines, the more that I concluded that I would integrate (where possible) the two strategies. I would, first, continue to produce tapes on cultural systems that were important to anthropologists, and in which there had been anthropological research which could become the basis of the first modules in the series. Because of my own involvement in anthropology over the years, I felt fairly confident that I could identify topics and markets that would provide sufficient returns to support video production on the first tapes.

Secondly, I felt that if I could choose some populations for which there were a significant number of migrants to the United States (and for which there was a market not only in anthropology but in other disciplines), I could also link the modules shot specifically for anthropologists to those which would be appealing to instructors who were teaching courses in immigrants to the U.S., ethnicity, multiculturalism, Latinos, Asian immigrants, etc. Hopefully, the modules on ethnic groups in America might also be of interest to individuals and social agencies outside of academia as well. It was in this manner than The American Ethnic Groups project evolved. Figure 1 is a graphic representation of how the American Ethnic Groups project appears to me at this point. It is, perhaps, a enormous project; and it may never eventuate. But the concept that it suggests has a great impact upon how I view video production for VRUCAE and thus serves as a model for my production at this point.

Conclusion

In this discussion of VISUAL RESOURCES FOR UNIVER-SITY CLASSROOMS AND ADULT EDUCATION, I have attempted to provide an overview of why the VRUCAE series was begun, where they seem to be headed from my current view of them, and how the pre-production, production, post-production, and related management processes are structured. If all goes well, there will be much to discuss as the various series and videotapes evolve, particularly as the advances in non-linear formats become available and sufficiently inexpensive to use for the purposes outlined in this article.

NOTES

1   In this article, I will follow the commonly accepted practice of using the word "filmmaking" to denote those activities which result in a film whether the medium upon which the image and sound is recorded is a light sensitive emulsion (e.g., 16mm or 35mm film stock) or material which responds to magnetic fields (e.g., video tape, video diskettes) or,

more recent technologies (e.g., optical disks). (See, for example, Rabiger 1987: 3.)

2   Some documentary filmmakers and some documentary film critics feel that the concept of "good social science filmmaking" is a contradiction in terms. For such elitists and self-congratulatory individuals, there can be no good social science filmmaking because, it is contended (a) social science cannot be interesting, (b) social scientists cannot themselves produce films of any value, and/or (c) social scientists do not know enough about filmmaking in order to make a worthwhile film. It should be apparent that I do not believe that there is any value in this position. It should also be apparent that the reverse could also be argued, to wit: (a) social science is too interesting to allow it to be treated by those who do not have the faintest idea of what it is about; (b) social scientists can produce films which may satisfy felt needs precisely because they know both the specific framework for the subject matter of that film and the larger social science framework within which that example is treated by other social scientists; and (c) filmmaking is, like nearly everything that human beings do, a learned set of behavior and attitudes. There is nothing about the physical brains of social scientists which is any different from that of non-social scientist documentary filmmakers. If social scientists devote themselves to learning documentary filmmaking and expanding its rather narrow conceptualizations of what is "good," they will be able to empower themselves and satisfy the need for good social science filmmaking.

3   Obviously, there are major exceptions to this rule. Frederick Wiseman's films are not scripted, but they certainly manifest Wiseman's "voice." Nichols defines "voice" in the following way: "By voice I mean something narrower than style: that which conveys to us a sense of a text's social point of view, of how it is speaking to us and how it is organizing the materials it is presenting to us. In this sense, voice is not restricted to any one code or feature, such as dialogue or spoken commentary. Voice is perhaps akin to that intangible, moirélike pattern formed by the unique interaction of all a film's codes, and it applies to all modes of documentary" (1988:50).

4   If non-social scientist filmmakers want to apply their non-social science framework and "art" to the description and analysis of a particular set of people in film, that is fine, and I encourage it. However, they should not be allowed to pretend they they are social scientists because (in their mind) (a) they are recording "reality" through the use of a device that "captures reality" (see Byers 1977 article "Cameras Don't Take Pictures"); or (b) their belief that their ability to interpret a cultural system other than their own on film and get positive audience

response makes them a social scientist. Most non-social science film-makers want the "social science" to reside in the subject being filmed. (That is, the "reality" being filmed is what is important to social science, and for this reason they like the concept of "ethnographic film" which they like to think of as "film recorded by a camera about people in their daily lives." For my own response to this, see Rollwagen 1988.) However, as most social scientists would agree (see Harris' [1968] discussion of this topic), social science is a particular disciplinary framework which is available only to those who know it, and it is apparent which films are produced within that framework and which are not. More importantly, it is even more apparent whether there is any social science involved when non-social scientists write about the production of films. (In this regard, see the written works by both Nichols and Mac Dougall, particularly their most recent works in which they try to insist that anthropology's vision is limited [by the discipline of anthropology], whereas their own is NOT limited because they are not so bound. This argument is, of course specious, precisely because they themselves are limited by their own particular training, a topic which they refuse to discuss, trying to maintain that they are unlimited in the perspectives which they bring to film.)

I would not spend so much time on this topic if non-social scientists were not so hostile to the production of social science films by social scientists. Since, as I have tried to explain elsewhere, social scientists are interested in the production of social science films primarily for class-room purposes (and are not in competition with the non-social science filmmakers for mass audiences), they should be left to their own devices. It is unnecessary for (in their own view, "real") "filmmakers" to judge social science filmmakers against their own (non-social scientist) conventions. Or, if they are unwilling to do so, then they should also accept that social scientists have the right to judge *their* (non-social science) films against social science standards.

REFERENCES CITED

Brandes, Stanley (1981). Cargos Versus Cost Sharing in Mesoamerican Fiestas, with Special Reference to Tzintzuntzan. Journal of Anthropological Research 37: 209-225.

Brandes, Stanley (1988). Power and Persuasion: Fiestas and Social Control in Rural Mexico. Philadelphia: University of Pennsylvania Press.

Byers, Paul (1977). Cameras Don't Take Pictures. Afterimage, April, 1977, pp. 8-9.

Foster, George M. (1965a). Peasant Society and the Image of Limited Good. American Anthropologist 67: 293-315.

Foster, George M. (1967). Tzintzuntzan: Mexican Peasants in a Changing World. Boston: Little, Brown and Company.

Foster, George M. (1979b). Fieldwork in Tzintzuntzan: The First Thirty Years. IN Long-Term Field Research in Social Anthropology, G.M. Foster, T. Scudder, E. Colson, and R.V. Kemper (eds.). New York: Academic Press, pp. 165-184.

Harris, Marvin (1968). The Rise of Anthropological Theory: A History of Theories of Culture. New York: Thomas Y. Crowell.

Kemper, Robert V. (1977). Migration and Adaptation: Tzintzuntzan Peasants in Mexico City. Beverly Hills: Sage Publications.

Kemper, Robert V. (1981). Obstacles and Opportunities: Household Economics of Tzintzuntzan Migrants in Mexico City. Urban Anthropology 10: 211-229.

Kemper, Robert V. and George M. Foster (1975). Urbanization in Mexico:The View from Tzintzuntzan. IN Urbanization and Inequality: The Political Economy of Urban and Rural Development in Latin America, Wayne A. Cornelius and Felicity M. Trueblood (eds.). Beverly Hills, CA: Sage Publications. (Latin American Urban Research Vol. 5), pp. 53-75.

Kemper, Robert V. and Anya Peterson Royce (1979). Mexican Urbanization Since 1821: A Macro-Historical Approach. Urban Anthropology 8(3-4):267-289.

Mead, Margaret (1975). Visual Anthropology in a Discipline of Words. IN Principles of Visual Anthropology, Paul Hockings (ed.). The Hague: Mouton, pp. 3-12.

Nichols, Bill (1988). The Voice of Documentary. IN New Challenges for Documentary, Alan Rosenthal (ed.). Berkeley: University of California Press, pp. 48-63.

Nichols, Bill (1991). The Ethnographer's Tale. Visual Anthropology Review 7(2): 31-47

Rabiger, Michael (1987). Directing the Documentary. Boston: Focal Press.

Rollwagen, Jack R. (1989). Anthropology and "Contemporary Issues": Anthropology, Political Economy, and the General Education Curriculum. (in "Teaching Anthropology: From the Curricular System to the World System," a special issue.) Urban Anthropology 18(1): 135-151.

Rollwagen, Jack R. (1988). The Role of Anthropological Theory in "Ethnographic" Filmmaking. IN Anthropological Filmmaking, Jack R. Rollwagen (ed.). New York: Harwood Academic Publishers, pp. 287-315.

Rollwagen, Jack R. (1981). Some Implications of the World System Approach for the Anthropological Study of Latin American Urbanization. (In a special issue of URBAN ANTHROPOLOGY entitled "Social Urbanization in Latin America"; Louise Margolies, special issue editor). Urban Anthropology 8(3-4): 249-265.

Rollwagen, Jack R. (1980a). New Directions in Urban Anthropology: Building an Ethnography and an Ethnology of the World System. IN Urban Life: Readings in Urban Ethnography, George Gmelch and Walter Zenner, editors. New York: St. Martin's Press, pp. 370-383 (second edition, pp. 149-160).

Rollwagen, Jack R. (1980b). Cities and the World System: Toward an Evolutionary Perspective in the Study of Urban Anthropology. IN Cities in a Larger Context, Thomas Collins (ed.). Southern Anthropological Society Proceedings No. 14. Athens: University of Georgia Press, pp. 123-140 (first edition); pp. 149-160 (second edition).

FILMS CITED

Tzintzuntzan in the 1990s: A Lakeside Village in Highland Mexico: Videotape #1: An Ethnographic Overview (1993; 126 minutes; color). (Others forthcoming.) Jack R. Rollwagen, executive producer. Available from: The Institute, Inc., 56 Centennial Avenue, Brockport, NY 14420.

The Cows of Dolo Kem Paye: Resolving Conflict Among the Kpelle. (1970; 32 minutes; color) James L. Gibbs (writer, narrator, music), Marvin Silverman (photographer, editor), and Henry Breitrose (educational consultant). Phoenix/BFA Films and Video, distributor.

The Nuer. (1970; 75 minutes; color). A film by Hilary Harris and George Breidenback; produced by Robert Gardner and Hilary Harris for the Film Study Center of the Peabody Museum, Harvard University. CRM Films, distributor.

from ANTHROPOLOGICAL FILM AND VIDEO IN THE 1990s
Jack R. Rollwagen (editor). Brockport, NY: The Institute, Inc.
© 1993, The Institute, Inc. All rights reserved. ISBN 0-9635206-1-X

The Design Of Ethnographic Hypermedia[1]

Peter Biella
Department of Anthropology
Temple University

ABSTRACT: Recent developments in computer hardware and software allow texts, documents and audiovisual materials to be stored as digital information and presented as integrated multimedia on computer screen. This paper considers the instructional opportunities of computer-based hypermedia for students of anthropology and the resources that hypermedia can provide to professional anthropologists. In an essay that appears earlier in this volume, I discuss the potential of hypermedia in ethnographic scholarship. The emphasis of the present essay is more pragmatic. It begins with an overview of the basic elements of hypermedia – databases, navigation tools and expert systems – and presents alternative uses to which they can be put. Despite the proliferation of Skinnerian models in computer-based instruction, a strikingly different educational philosophy may also be expressed (Delany and Landow 1991). This essay considers the benefits and hazards which the emerging "literary turn" in theory offers to the design of ethnographic hypermedia (Scholte 1987).

Specific design features of hypermedia are described through the presentation of one application, the author's work on the Ilparakuyo Maasai of Tanzania. Special emphasis is given to design-features of the program that integrate audiovisual field recordings and texts. *Maasai Interactive* runs on Macintosh computer, is based on *HyperCard* 2.1 software, and will be distributed on CD-ROM.

I. Overview: Components and Problems

Because hypermedia is based on emerging technologies and is unfamiliar in most branches of research and instruction, it must overcome the skepticism of many users.[2] Hypermedia's basic components (i.e., audiovisual and text databases, interactive search-and-navigation tools, and expert-system) have enormous educational potential. The essay first discusses these components. It then presents two alternative strategies of hypermedia-based instruction. Competing philosophies of education and of expertise lead to alternative designs. The essay concludes with a case study, the history, components and design of a particular project in ethnographic hypermedia, the author's CD-ROM based *Maasai Interactive*, currently in production.

Hypermedia's adolescence is precocious but troubled. Although computer applications can no more solve the epistemological problems of anthropology than can the media of which they are composed, they create an easy illusion of exhaustiveness and exactitude. In light of the diversity of anthropology's approaches and the complexity of its subject, caution with closure is advised. Some of the expertise that belongs in expert-system hypermedia should be used to resist over-simplification. Indeed, the resistance should not be difficult since hypermedia's power to annotate and qualify far surpasses that of ethnographic film. The power is sometimes abused, however, through the temptation of hypermedia to overwhelm its users with information-links and endless emendations. *Maasai Interactive* suggests a middle way. It offers a design by which scholarship is integrated into ethnographic film, neither undermining all perspective with a hyper-meteor shower of links and annotations nor promoting false insight with the illusion of closure.

a. Databases

Databases store information, navigation tools allow rapid access to it, and expert systems exemplify uses to which information can be put. Large, easily-searchable databases are therefore among the most important resources that computers offer the social sciences. In their more familiar incarnation as libraries, databases are a major component of anthropological research. Professionals and students must be familiar with a wide variety of library holdings. Like library bookshelves that hold texts, photographs, documents and audiovisuals, computer databases provide access to a variety of materials.

Because databases make a large number of texts available at a single location, the computer screen, they save time spent searching through library shelves. Of particular use in the socials sciences are CD-ROMs with specialized subject matter: these may contain texts that are too rare or arcane to warrant shelf-space in most libraries. CDs conveniently store materials that could otherwise be seen only through the help of inter-library loans or travel to non-circulating collections.

At present (1993), a single CD-ROM has the memory capacity to store about 640 megabytes of information.[3] Although figures vary considerably (see II:d, below), this amount of memory permits one CD to hold more than 140,000 pages of text, or 8,000 6x7 cm. photographs of good resolution, or 15 hours of sound recordings at medium-resolution, or 90 minutes of video-and-sound at poor-resolution.

CD-ROMs and laserdiscs are currently the most popular technologies used in large hypermedia programs. Unlike floppy disks and hard-drives, CDs and laserdiscs can only be "read." That is, consumers cannot enter information onto them. Although this limitation is soon to be removed (Gussin 1993), alternative hypermedia configurations like Brown University's Intermedia already allow users to add to the database by networking with a mainframe computer

(Yankelovich, et al. 1985). The capacity to enlarge a database with new publications and even student papers increases its attractiveness and complexity. In the near future, comparatively inexpensive upgrades to writeable CD-ROMs will allow them to remain current with the disciplines they serve.

Many CD-based hypermedia packages include a floppy disk on which the user can store notes, the results of searches, records of progress through assigned audiovisuals and texts, and even course exams and papers.

b. Interactive Navigation and Search Tools

Among the principal attractions of hypermedia is the fact that it allows users to concentrate on intellectual relationships between multimedia documents by allowing users to study related documents together on one computer screen. A hypermedia document, a "collection of data that is related or linked to another body of information," is called a *node* (Seyer 1991:13). Designers of hypermedia are like the creators of hard-copy reference works, bibliographies and card catalogues: they are experts in the subjects covered by multimedia-nodes in their databases. Designer-experts know that certain relationships between documents will be of importance to many users, and they embody their expertise in the hypermedia program by making such relationships known. Designers create what are called permanent, electronic *links* between the related nodes of information. The existence of a link can be indicated on-screen in many ways, the most common of which is to place icons, called *buttons*, beside linked keywords in the documents. When hypermedia-users activate a link in a first node, by executing a mouse-click or keystroke, they are *navigated to* a second, linked node. The latter appears on screen beside the first or in its place. Hypermedia effortlessly crosses databases and thus make possible the integration of different media.

Electronic buttons were rarely employed in first-generation instructional media because these applications were generally based on Skinnerian models of learning. Students' progress (or *navigation*) through a lesson plan was unalterably linear. Students' mastery of a subject was evaluated through responses to "objective" tests, whether multiple-choice, true-false or single-answer.

The concept of *interactivity* in computer applications developed historically as an alternative to the behaviorist dependence on linear instruction and belief that short answers to predetermined questions were the only viable measure of mastery. Interactivity in a hypermedia application is understood as a measure of the extent to which the application allows users to pursue many alternative, non-linear paths, either to predetermined instructional objectives or to the users' own research goals. The number and variety of links between different nodes in a hypermedia database are important criteria by which interactivity is assessed.

Permanent links between related documents, and the buttons that indicate their existence, are created by designers and are therefore finite in number. Users of *open-system* hypermedia, however, may themselves independently uncover and explore many more relationships. Users may create their own temporary links between the nodes,[4] and cause the linked documents to be presented together on screen. Users can discover new relationships and can temporarily link the related documents through hypermedia search tools. The sophistication and efficacy of these tools are further measures of interactivity in a hypermedia application.

Users' independent searches may begin with author-, title- or subject-queries, single words or phrases sought in the keyword-indices created for each database. When too many nodes are found to contain a keyword, irrelevant items, called *false hits*, may be eliminated through the use of Boolean, multiple-keyword, searches – *and, or, not, nor* and *exclusive-or*. Like a user's search in a card catalogue, Boolean search-tools employ the users' own keywords. Unlike bibliographies and permanent links provided by experts, Boolean searches explore the users' assumptions and guesses of relevance. As such, Boolean searches allow users to make unprecedented discoveries about the relationships between multimedia nodes. Such searches may also be extended through the use of fuzzy-sets which locate the presence of keyword-synonyms and roots.[5]

All links which designers have placed in open-system hypermedia applications may be displayed simultaneously on screen with a graphic image called a *web-view* (Landow and Delany 1991) or *browser* (Seyer 1991:23). Web-views usually emphasize the reason that nodes have been linked (by identifying their shared properties) and web-views provide navigation to all nodes that are displayed. Individual documents are often linked to many others. Web-views therefore are non-hierarchical and can be displayed in many different transformations. Any one keyword or document may be depicted as the center point in a web of nodes to which it is related. Database index searches may also allow users to create their own web-views of found documents.

Another navigational tool, called the *retrace function*, presents users with a record of each information node that they have accessed since entering the hypermedia program. Neophyte users often fear becoming "lost in hyperspace," losing their bearings in vast databases and being unable to remember where they encountered information. The retrace tool provides a small web-view of the user's travels and offers the means to return to any node.

Finally, a few hypermedia applications include *guided tours* with proposed *travel itineraries*. As part of establishing their instructional objectives, tours familiarize users with the application's search-and-navigation options. Tours help users to gain the expertise that will permit them to leave the tour and begin their own independent scholarship.

c. First Generation Expert Systems

Computer programs that duplicate the performance of human experts in solving problems are called *expert systems*. The design of expert-system programs begins with the assumption that humans are successful at achieving particular goals because they have mastery over a spectrum of information and can retrieve necessary parts of it as needed. Databases and search-and-navigation tools are thus important components of the artificial intelligence that goes into expert-system design. These, combined with the computer's capacity to perform high-speed binary calculations, made possible the first generation of expert systems.

In medicine, available funding and the nature of the subject matter stimulated the creation of some of the earliest expert-system applications. Procedures employed by expert diagnosticians were analyzed and modeled, an activity which took thousands of hours to complete. Software and databases were then combined to duplicate expert diagnostic procedures. Expert-system applications of this type progress toward a correct diagnosis by eliminating incorrect binary alternatives or branches. The systems also contain feedback loops which catch misdiagnoses and correct them. Such models can be used as expert consultants to physicians.

Much of the same knowledge-base can also be used in the education of medical students. Very sophisticated expert systems have been designed to represent the reactions of patients, with specific medical problems, to tests and medications (e.g., Actronics 1993, DAROX 1992). The computer simulates a patient, presents his condition to a medical student, and responds as would the patient to whatever questions, tests or medications that the student suggests. If the student acts too slowly or prescribes improper treatment, the simulated-patient can "die."

In the social sciences, too, a number of applications simulate expert consultants who assist in the discovery and application of pertinent data. In one, the user plays the role of a United Nations representative who wishes to win ratification of a pollution-control treaty: this diplomat seeks information from many sources, including experts (Gamble and CBEL 1991). Similar programs insert users in the midst of historical dramas, make available advice, and offer realistic choices: alternate paths open before each decision, on the basis of which the user fares well or ill (True 1992, Collegium... 1992).[6] These applications are fascinating and suggestive, but they leave much unsaid about expertise. To appreciate alternative models of expertise, one must understand the design-limitations of the first generation.

Keller (1987) makes a generalization about first-generation expert systems designs which well applies to the applications described above. The designs must meet three criteria: 1) the problem to be addressed by the simulated-expert requires a limited knowledge-base for its solution; 2) the data required for the solution of the problem contains no ambiguities; and, 3) the correct or best solution to the problem can be agreed upon by all experts. Keller's criteria have a strong behaviorist accent, but expert system applications which are based on them do assist in the mastery of many kinds of expertise, such as the establishment of correct medical diagnoses or the comprehension of international diplomacy. The behaviorist interpretation of expertise that is exemplified in these applications is also valued in a number of contemporary social scientific paradigms. The latter, too, can boast of their own achievements, however reductive their philosophy of knowledge and expertise may be.

Limitations of the behaviorist interpretation of expertise are not difficult to identify. Experts in the social sciences cannot often satisfy Keller's first criterion for a closed knowledge-base. Anthropologists must weigh many theoretical approaches and recognize countless influences on the phenomena they study. Their knowledge-bases must always be open systems. Keller's second criterion, to avoid unquantifiable ambiguities, is also often impossible to meet: the data required in many social scientific analyses is partial, contextual, impressionistic, and ideological. The reality of such data may depend on nothing but belief, but it has profound social consequences. Finally, the third criterion is more wishful than accurate. Few conclusions in the social sciences are considered to be "correct" by all experts. Many paradigms are mutually-hostile. Even within a single paradigm, experts often select conclusions because they are appropriate in a given context, at a given time, rather than because they are correct in an absolute sense. Surprisingly, there is no denial, even from strong proponents, that the behaviorist model of expertise falls short of the human original.[7] Expertise includes such imponderables as style, grace and creativity, behaviors which at least presently defy computer simulation (Bateson 1972).[8]

d. Alternative Expertise

Computer-based hypermedia can reflect many different educational philosophies (Gagné 1987). The open-system design (mentioned in section I:b, above) represents a philosophical break with the behaviorist assumptions of first-generation expert systems. Behaviorist simulations keep the hierarchical logic of their search-and-navigation trees transparent to the user. Open-system hypermedia is anti-hierarchical, specializing in the exhibition of all possible web-views. Open systems lay bare their nodes and webs, emphasize historical and intellectual movements, point out the common problems and competitive approaches of many scholars in one discipline. To those who can comprehend, web-views represent the paradigmatic knowledge-base of disciplinary expertise.

Open-system hypermedia also de-emphasizes the authority of the individual expert (including the designer), and thereby helps to redefine the scholar's task and self-conception. Scholars, offered a textbook without a binding, are urged to conceive of their works as merged with those of others. Hypermedia readers become more "writerly" (Barthes 1978: 4-6). The distinction between author/authority and reader/recipient becomes less tenable (cf. Landow 1992).

Open-system hypermedia does not offer over-simple answers or single-destinations, but it may be accused of proliferating overwhelming opportunities. Open-system designers justify this *embarras de richesse* on the grounds that paradigmatic alternatives are the warp and weft of expertise in the postmodern age: documents exist in anti-sequential, decentered, authorless space. As Landow and Delany (1991:6) quip, "Hypertext creates an almost embarrassingly literal embodiment" of postmodern critical concepts.

Unlike its behaviorist forebears, open-system hypermedia is rarely oriented to lesson plans or problem-solving role play. Its alternate vision of expertise is communicated largely in its designers' selection of database entries and in the links that designers create between them (Rada 1991:145). If an open-system application indiscriminately adds and automatically indexes new documents, the guidance that would otherwise be available from an expert designer will be diminished (cf., Yankelovich, et al. 1985, Yankelovich 1991). Many of Brown University's Intermedia applications (discussed at length, below, in II:e) are acephalous: users are frequently left to their own devices. They must contend unguided with ambiguities, undifferentiated paths and textual contradictions.[9] Yet the dangers of open-system hypermedia also exist in any library, and libraries have been judged worthy of the risk.

Like other technologies, hypermedia leaves unkept modernism's promise of redemption (Angus 1989:96). Paradigms struggle within it. Although the expertise in open systems does not aspire to the false optimism of behaviorism, it may add to the fragmentation of postmodern scholarship.

The second section of this essay proposes a middle way for hypermedia. It suggests that, by providing some guidance, open-system hypermedia need not overwhelm its users. Guided tours and recommended pathways can assist the first-time user through the maze of juxtaposed multimedia. The tour guide proposes optional interpretations, softening blows which sometimes lurk in texts. At the same time, *Maasai Interactive* is left open for independent scholarship. Search-and-navigation tools allow users to quit the tour and begin to emulate the expert tour-guide's method.

e. Difficulties: Financial, Technical, "Spiritual"

No overview of hypermedia for potential designers would be complete without mention of its unique combination of liabilities. From a funding agent's point of view, hypermedia is new and largely untested. It is expensive, requiring a considerable amount of labor to create. The computers that hypermedia needs to function are rather costly and sometimes unavailable. More than this, many hypermedia applications which present themselves as serious interactive learning tools are little more than video games or computerized Skinner Boxes: these multimedia toys give legitimate efforts a bad name, increasing the difficulty of convincing funding agencies that investment in such projects will benefit scholarship. Funding agencies regard hypermedia with suspicion and, with important exceptions,[10] are reluctant to invest funds in its development. Hypermedia's conceptual and technical advancements are thus principally the innovations of commercial vendors.

Hypermedia's usefulness for instruction is also lessened by a number of technical problems related to the computer screen. Rada (1991) lists several. He begins with a discussion of experiments that contrast student work on a small screen with work on a screen that was almost 50% larger. He writes:

> the larger screen consistently supported better reading and writing behavior (Hansen and Haas, 1988), but was not as good as paper. Text on computer screens can take 30 per cent longer to read than text on paper with roughly equal comprehension (Shneiderman and Kearsley, 1989). If the studies include the confusion over page-turning commands and anxieties that some users have in reading from a computer, then the time required to read a text on the computer can double relative to the time required to read the same text on paper [Rada1991: 13].

In addition to these problems, a few people aver that texts reproduced on computer screen are completely impossible to read. Although this is an exaggeration, it is true that computer-borne texts cannot, currently, without great expense, be carried around like a paperback and perused in any convenient location.[11]

Hypermedia also entails what might be called "spiritual" difficulties. Computer searches and electronic media cannot always improve on the services provided by the library. As access to library books becomes increasingly limited, replaced by the CD and electronic text, advantages of browsing in the vicinity of a favorite catalogue number will be lost. Users of electronic media are deprived of a perspective on antiquity and humanity that is preserved in dusty stacks. Users who compose their texts on computer screen also lose perspective: every draft of an electronic text appears perfect, no matter how rough it is. Retyping clean drafts gives time for insight and reflection. Reworking text on paper leaves a trace of history (c.f., Lyman 1984, Garson 1989).

Despite hypermedia's many problems – despite even the fear that it seeks someday to make academic teaching obsolete – hypermedia presents an ideal to anthropology that is difficult to ignore. It promises to integrate, for the first time, all of the teaching tools that anthropologists use to pass their discipline to the future. The thought that this ideal might be reached makes the limitations of earlier media less easy to reconcile.

II. *Maasai Interactive:* A Case Study in Ethnographic Hypermedia

Like any work in hypermedia, *Maasai Interactive* [henceforward, *MI*] was shaped by its financial history, its particular mix of audiovisual recordings, and its platform and authoring system – in this case, Macintosh and *HyperCard*. The project, too, must conform to the memory limitations of its medium, a single CD-ROM. In the following, I describe how these factors influenced the development and shape of *MI*. I then discuss the project's screen design, its databases, navigation tools and expert system.

a. Financial History

The tape recordings and photographs used in *MI* were made as the audiovisual component to a text-based dissertation in cultural anthropology (Biella 1984, 1988). Funding for the 1980 fieldwork, the filmmaking, the processing, and the translations was provided by Temple University and my family. Eleven years later, I approached Apple Computer with a proposal to apply the material to hypermedia. I received one of Apple's grants to individuals, a powerful Macintosh IIci and an image-scanning device. Other efforts to raise hypermedia post-production funds have, thus far, failed.[12]

Figure 1 estimates the man-weeks and cash expenses (past and anticipated) used in the creation of *MI*.[13] I do not translate weeks into dollars because of the common failing of

TIME AND EXPENSE CATEGORIES	Project Director (weeks)	Others (weeks)	Expenses Cash	In-kind
FIELDWORK				
Labor				
Pre-departure	3	1		
Field period	6	12		
Expenses				
Transportation			$ 5,000	
Per diem			1,200	
Film and tape stock			3,000	
Cameras, recorder				$ 2,000
AUDIO-VISUAL PREPARATION				
Labor	8	8		
Darkroom				2,500
TRANSLATION / TRANSCRIPTION	8	6		
HYPERMEDIA				
Labor				
Writing	30			
Programming & design	10	3		
Ethnographic & hyper- media consultations		3		
Digitization & correction of texts, photos, sound	5	17		
Sound-to-translation synchronization		5		
Proof reading		3		
Hard-copy layout		2		
Expenses				
Computer hardware			1,500	4,000
CD pre-mastering and mastering			1,800	
CD publication (1,000 copies)			1,300	
Copyright clearances			3,000	
Hard copy publication			1,200	
Office			2,500	
TOTALS	70 wks.	60 wks.	$ 20,500	$ 8,500.[13]

FIGURE 1. *Labor-time and expenses in production of the* Maasai Interactive CD.

anthropological mediamakers to complete projects even if they are paid poorly, or not at all.

The production of hypermedia is extremely labor-intensive. Assistants can perform many essential functions, but Project Directors can expect to be busier than if they were writing a book. Yet the interpretation of *Figure 1* requires the following caveats, important to those who would use its data to estimate the costs of their own hypermedia productions. First, *Figure 1* cites a total of 70 weeks of my time as Project Director consumed in the creation of *MI*. A full third of that time contributed equally to the creation of my dissertation and several publications. Thus, anthropologists who undertake hypermedia projects need not be so consumed by them that they are prevented from performing other professional activities.[14]

Had labor for this project been funded even at a moderate level, its cost would have exceeded $100,000. Instead, my own work was complemented by the unpaid contributions of many others – colleagues, students and family.[15] The project is still incomplete. Another six months of my time and that of two assistants are still required to fine-tune the programming, enter and synchronize seven hours of Kiswahili and Olmaa recordings to English translations, and complete the writing of what will be about three hundred pages of guided tours, annotations and Help-screens.

An expert would have required much less time to program *MI* than I.[16] In the future, the hardware and software needed for ethnographic hypermedia will be standardized and improved to a point where ethnographers can produce works without having to master a programming language or create their own applications. Most of the technology required is already available on college campuses. To an even greater extent, the expenses in the future will be the makers' own time.

As a consequence of declining costs, the external funds required to produce and distribute a major work in hypermedia will come more closely to resemble those required for the publication of a book (tens of thousands of dollars) than those funds needed for the production and distribution of a major anthropological film or video (hundreds of thousands). Scholars who choose to work in hypermedia will therefore become less dependent on external funding than ethnographic filmmakers, and they will proliferate. Like authors of unsolicited journal-manuscripts, hypermedia-makers will be free to innovate, sometimes faltering, sometimes achieving unexpected and important results. Hypermedia authors will not need to satisfy the understandable expectations of granting agencies that the projects they fund should be quite likely to achieve success, or that they should represent approved theoretical paradigms. If the rate of ethnographic hypermedia failures will be high because of the absence of censure and funding-oversight, so too will the number of unfunded, successful projects increase.

b. Audiovisual Mix

Maasai Interactive's 20 hours of sound recordings and 7,000 still photographs were produced over a period of thirty days in the field. Because the original material was shot in black-and-white and was neither video nor 16mm, its transformation to hypermedia was simple. At present, the computer-memory required for even moderately-long, color motion pictures exceeds the capability of educational-media technology. As shown below, however, thousands of black-and-white still photographs and many hours of sound may be stored on a single CD-ROM. *MI* is thus able to include a high percentage of the original recordings made in the field. This availability is useful for a number of reasons, particularly because it offers visual scholars a larger sample of activities.[17]

In the field, sequences of still photographs from single camera positions were taken along with uninterrupted sound recordings (Biella 1984, 1988). Almost none of the photographs have precise sync-points with the sound track. Lack of sync influences the annotations that I give the audiovisuals. Instead of discussing kinesics and image-sound synchronization, I concentrate on the ethnographic implications of utterances, on relationships discernible from still photographs, and on unfolding group dynamics. In retrospect, I believe that I would not have proceeded in *MI* very differently if I had had moving pictures as a database, since kinesics are not of special interest to me. Nevertheless, the fact that the images do not move and have few sync-points is an important limitation of my data. It will prevent some analyses from being made.

The lack of sync-points between picture and sound also effects the screen design of the audiovisual files. To avoid giving the impression of picture-sound synchronization, I allow two different photographs visible on screen at any given moment. Both were taken at approximately the same time as the sound that is being heard or being read in translation.

c. Platform and Authoring System

A high priority of *MI* was for it to be reasonably easy to use. Before I began working, I compared Macintosh and IBM. I found the former to be more intuitive to use and more attractive stylistically.

I was drawn to Macintosh in part because of *HyperCard*, its omnipresent hypermedia program. The user's control of *HyperCard* is largely dependent on buttons so that little memorization of commands is required. I sought an application that would not soon become obsolete, and Apple Corporation has guaranteed that it will support and upgrade *HyperCard* for many years. I was also attracted to *HyperCard* because I anticipated having difficulty learning computer programming. HyperTalk, *HyperCard*'s programming language, is comparatively easy for the neophyte to master.

Unlike dedicated database applications, *HyperCard* is comparatively slow in database searches; it is comparatively unsophisticated in word-processing. Yet its combination of adequacies makes it versatile and viable.

d. Memory Assignment

USE OF MEMORY	Number / type of units	Per unit (KB)	Memory used (MB)
APPLICATION PROGRAMS			
HyperCard™ *2.1*	1	800	.8
Simple Player™	1	138	.1
TEXT INFORMATION	2,000 pages	3	6.0
Textbook/Guided tour of machine-readable text			
Other works by Biella			
Transcribed translations of field recordings			
Annotations on the translations			
Ethnographic and historical essays by others in the field			
PHOTOGRAPHS (Black and white)			
75-dpi resolution	2,000 pictures	75	150.0
300-dpi resolution	175 pictures	1,350	236.3
SOUND RECORDINGS			
16-bit resolution	450 minutes	478	215.1
22-bit resolution	30 minutes	657	19.7
VIDEOS	3, 20-second movies	3,500	10.5
TOTAL MEMORY REQUIREMENT			638.5 MB

FIGURE 2. *Assignment of CD-ROM memory in the design of* Maasai Interactive. (Numbers reflect 1993 compression-software and technologies as well as qualitative decisions [see text]).

As discussed in section II: a, above, a storage medium commonly used in hypermedia is CD-ROM. A single disk has the capacity to store some 640 megabytes of information, whether audio, text, still photographs or video. The designer of a hypermedia program must assign fractions of this total capacity to the different media.

Figure 2 shows how I plan to share the available memory of the *MI* CD. (The figures given here reflect 1993 compression technologies which will soon be obsolete.)

Authoring systems. HyperCard 2.1 will be included in *MI* by agreement with Software Licensing at Apple Computer. *HyperCard* provides a combination of tools – search functions, simple word processing, linking capabilities, and the ability to display photographs and videos. The *Simple Player* program will also be included by agreement: it plays sync-sound videos on-screen. Having few videos, *MI* uses *Simple Player* primarily for its capacity to reproduce sound: audio recordings are linked, with accuracy of a tenth of a second, to textual translations.

Text information. The computer memory requirement for storage of a single page of text is very low. Some hypermedia projects, like MacFarlane's (1990) on the Naga of the Assam-Burma border, store 10,000 pages of text. *MI*, however, includes only about 2,000 pages. My reason for not including more is not the shortage of memory. Rather, I stop at that point for three practical reasons. First, I own the copyright to only half of the textual material that will be included in *MI*. Acquiring copyright clearance and paying copyright fees for even a thousand pages is daunting. Second, in order to enter journal or other textual materials onto a CD, it is necessary first to scan each page digitally into a computer. The scanned texts are imperfect and must be proof-read, a very time-consuming proposition.[18] Third, a thousand pages of previously-published ethnographic texts, in addition to another thousand of my own writings and the translations of fifteen hours of sound, will provide sufficient

FIGURE 3. Resolution of photographs on computer screen. The upper-left image reflects the average quality of most photographs in Maasai Interactive. The upper-right image is a 400% magnification of the photograph if it is scanned at 75-dpi. The lower-right image is a magnification of the photograph if scanned at 300-dpi.

material to demonstrate possibilities of hypermedia, and will serve the project's needs.

Photographs. All of *MI's* photographs are black-and-white and therefore have only one-third the memory-requirement of color. Photographs may be stored in memory at different degrees of resolution (or dots-per-inch), and at different enlargements. Almost all of the photographs are stored at a fairly low resolution, 75-dpi at an enlargement of 3" by 3.5." At this size, images appear on the computer screen roughly as sharp as the upper-left photograph in *Figure 3* (though they are almost twice as large). Because the memory consumed by photographs at 75-dpi is relatively low, a single CD could store more than 8,000. I have elected to include 2,000.

HyperCard allows users to magnify photographs that are on screen. This is an attractive option, both for the users' pleasure and curiosity as well as for some kinds of research.

Unfortunately, pictures stored at 75-dpi cannot be magnified and retain clarity. The upper-right image of *Figure 3* demonstrates the decrease in sharpness that comes from a 75-dpi photograph when enlarged to 400%. Because I do wish some pictures to be enlarged, I decided to store 175 of the most interesting photographs at 300-dpi. These images can be enlarged significantly while still remaining relatively sharp, as shown in the lower-right image of *Figure 3.*[19] This decision has two drawbacks. First, because the higher-resolution images contain so much more information, they come up on the computer screen much more slowly than do the others. On my system, they need as long as eighteen seconds, eight times longer than the other photographs, to appear. Second, images stored at 300-dpi consume sixteen-times the memory needed for storage at 75-dpi.

The memory-consumption of photographs may be reduced by using Apple's *QuickTime* compression program. I decided against this option, however, because decompression of the photographs takes an unacceptably long period of time.

Sound recordings. The *MI* CD includes eight hours of original sound recordings. (These eight and seven additional hours of the recordings are translated and included as text.) Like photographs, sound may be stored at different levels of resolution, with correspondingly different consumption of memory. For purposes that I envision, sound recordings of conversations will be reproduced with adequate clarity when stored at 16-bit quality. Thirty minutes of songs are stored at the highest quality.

Videos. No video was shot in the fieldwork period, but the project was influenced by several films, portions of which will be stored as *QuickTime* movies and quoted in *MI*. Because the memory consumed by video is so high, only three 20-second clips are included.

e. Screen Design

A goal of *MI* is to provide a prototype and demonstration of ethnographic hypermedia. *MI* is intended to be used as a textbook, with assigned readings and exercises, as well as a resource for scholars and students of scholarship in visual anthropology. As designer, I put into the program as many options as I could imagine for others to build on. The shell of *MI* – its files and navigation tools without data – will, I hope, be licensed and adopted by future hypermedia-makers, including those who work with video, as a platform for their own audiovisual presentations and analyses.

Much of the philosophy of open-system hypermedia scholarship that is embedded in *MI* is expressed by Landow (1991) and Landow and Delany (1991). They are major contributors to Intermedia, the most impressive example of hypermedia that I have seen by far. Despite my extensive agreement with these scholars, the screen design of *MI* and that of Intermedia also clearly reflect our philosophical differences, in very different styles and solutions to shared problems. A contrast of the two designs brings out trenchant features of hypermedia production.

Intermedia presents its users with a multi-layered, multi-windowed screen. Intermedia users can gain access to linked texts in several ways, including the two ways represented in *Figure 4,* a sample screen. Users can call up – make visible on-screen – any document in Intermedia's database by selecting from the complete list of texts in a web-view, shown at the lower-right of *Figure 4.* Alternately, users can take advantage of the arrow-shaped icons, imbedded above keywords in Intermedia texts, which indicate the existence of a link to another, related, text. Users click on the icon in the one to call up the other. The new text-window then appears, outlined in gray, covering all or part of the previous window.

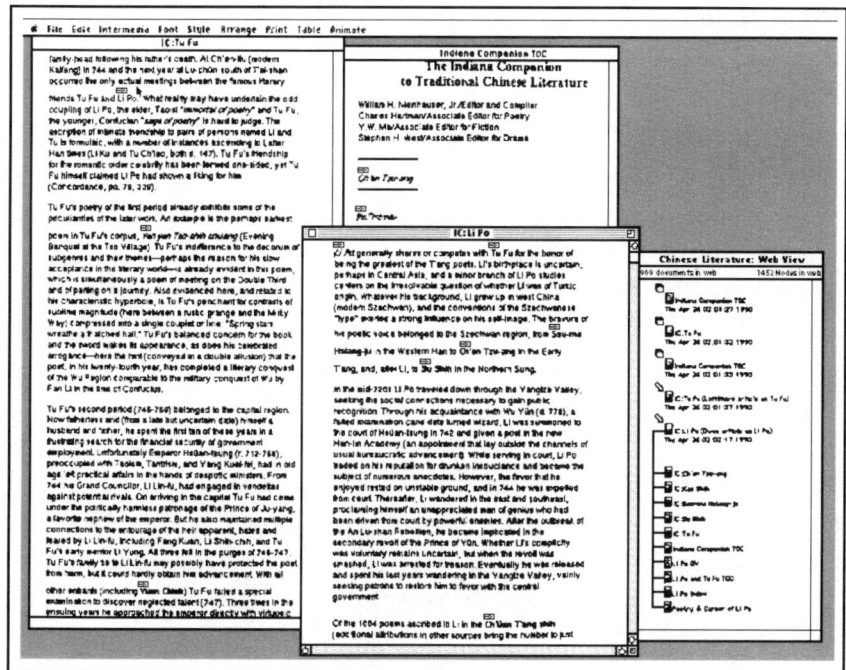

FIGURE 4. *A typical text screen from an Intermedia database.* Texts and web-views may be called up and arranged anywhere on screen at the discretion of the user. (Adapted from Kahn [1991:240]).

Intermedia has one basic screen: metaphorically, it is a single location to which all documents are brought and held in place. Many texts are made simultaneously visible through the image of overlapping, or juxtaposed, text-windows. Often, only one document is completely visible: it lies on top of a three-dimensional pile as the current active text, the center of attention. Any other text that is visible on screen need only be clicked to be brought to the forefront.

The design of *MI* suggests a different metaphor: the computer window is the vehicle for travel to many locations – different files or "screens" – each of which is purposed to feature one particular document. The main text featured in any screen always appears in the upper-left and is flanked by three other quadrants. The latter provide linked Commentaries and

Contrasting Texts about the main text, as well as a space for the user to keep a travel itinerary and take notes.

Figure 5 represents the Document-view of a typical *Scenes* window from *MI's* audiovisual database. (*Scenes* windows also sport alternative Summary-and-links views, not unlike that depicted in *Figure 6,* discussed below.) The Document-view always reserves the upper-left quadrant of the screen for the main text, the English translations of the scene. As the user scrolls through that text field, photographs to the right of the screen, originally taken as the sound recording was being made, shift correspondingly.

The main-text quadrant of *Figure 5* contains the translation of *Scene 5, Rivals' Dispute,* and a *QuickTime* control-bar that plays the scene's original audio recording. As conversations in Kiswahili and Olmaa are reproduced over a speaker or headphones, contiguous phrases of the translation in the main text are successively highlighted, providing a moving subtitle across the totality of the textual translation.

Data-windows which present sync-sound videos instead of still photographs and sounds also employ a control-bar to provide random access to *QuickTime* movies. Movies occupy the same location as the photograph in *Figure 5,* the upper-right quadrant of audiovisual screens. Translations flow as brief subtitles below the movie as well as in the main text.

The audio control-bar at the top of the main text, and the field scroll-bar along the right boundary of the main text, are electronically synchronized: in response to random-access scrolling of either control, sound recordings and their textual translations always remain in sync.

Nominally, the main-text quadrant of a data-screen is the current center of attention, analogous to Intermedia's uppermost document. Attention may wander, however. *Figure 5* represents a moment when the user has stopped playback of the audio with a mouse-click on the asterisk for main-text footnote #56. The mouse-click calls up, in the lower-left quadrant of the

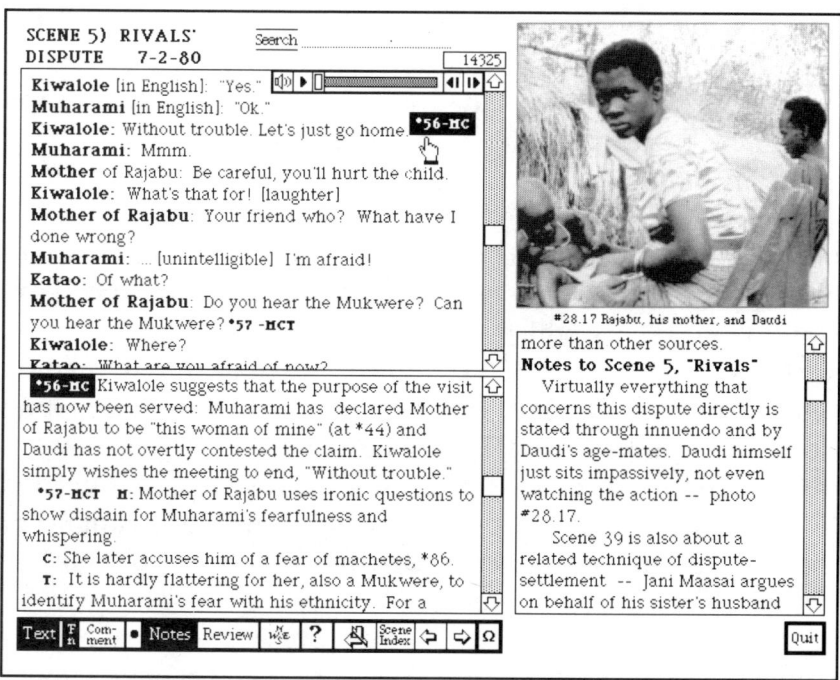

SCENE 5) RIVALS'   Search
DISPUTE   7-2-80   14325
Kiwalole [in English]: "Yes."
Muharami [in English]: "Ok."
Kiwalole: Without trouble. Let's just go home. *56-MC
Muharami: Mmm.
Mother of Rajabu: Be careful, you'll hurt the child.
Kiwalole: What's that for! [laughter]
Mother of Rajabu: Your friend who? What have I
done wrong?
Muharami: ... [unintelligible] I'm afraid!
Katao: Of what?
Mother of Rajabu: Do you hear the Mukwere? Can
you hear the Mukwere? *57 -MCT
Kiwalole: Where?
Katao: What are you afraid of now?

*56-MC Kiwalole suggests that the purpose of the visit
has now been served: Muharami has declared Mother
of Rajabu to be "this woman of mine" (at *44) and
Daudi has not overtly contested the claim. Kiwalole
simply wishes the meeting to end, "Without trouble."
*57-MCT M: Mother of Rajabu uses ironic questions to
show disdain for Muharami's fearfulness and
whispering.
   c: She later accuses him of a fear of machetes, *86.
   T: It is hardly flattering for her, also a Mukwere, to
identify Muharami's fear with his ethnicity. For a

#28.17 Rajabu, his mother, and Daudi

more than other sources.
Notes to Scene 5, "Rivals"
   Virtually everything that
concerns this dispute directly is
stated through innuendo and by
Daudi's age-mates. Daudi himself
just sits impassively, not even
watching the action -- photo
#28.17.
   Scene 39 is also about a
related technique of dispute-
settlement -- Jani Maasai argues
on behalf of his sister's husband

Text F Com- ● Notes Review W/e ? Scene ⇦ ⇨ Ω   Quit
      A ment   Index

FIGURE 5. A Scenes *window from the Audiovisual database* (Document view).
Data placement is not at the user's discretion, although data visibility is.
This view has four permanent quadrants which always contain the same
kinds of information: they are, counter-clockwise from the upper-left: main
text, author's commentaries, user's notes (or photograph, not shown), and
contrasting texts by other authors (or photograph, shown).

screen, an annotation that I, as ethnographer, wrote about the
line of text flagged with the footnote.[20] Annotation-links are
studied at the user's discretion. The lower-left quadrant may
alternately contain the assigned guided tour(s) that appear for
Scene 5 in various chapters of the textbook component of *MI*. As
described more fully in the *Texts database* section (II:f, below),
the user may click on a line of computer code placed in the
guided tour to call up portions of the main text that are being
discussed. At the user's discretion, too, the code may be
ignored and all commentaries may be covered as the main-text
quadrant is enlarged.

Both the upper and lower quadrants on the right of the standard *MI* screen serve multiple, but interrelated, purposes. Both upper and lower quadrants can display photograph sequences that unfold with the progress of the sound recordings and translations.

In the screen depicted in *Figure 5*, a photograph, #28.17, occupies the upper-right quadrant. (A *QuickTime* movie could also appear here.) The same quadrant is available to display Contrasting Texts which pertain to the subject of the scene, such as Beidelman's (1961) study of Ilparakuyo dispute settlement from the late-1950s. I have selected Contrasting Texts to be linked to main texts for many different reasons determined in the course of writing the textbook and guided tours. As will be seen, users themselves can take advantage of the open-system component to discover, create and pursue any number of text-links as well.

The lower-right quadrant also can present one of two fields which list the user's specific travel agenda and research notes. The user's travel itinerary, called the *Review* field, may be created either by the author, as a part of an assigned guided tour in the textbook component of *MI*, or by the user as part of independent research. The second field that can appear in the lower-right quadrant is shown in *Figure 5,* and is reserved for the user's *Notes* field. Notes may be typed by the user, as shown, or may be quotations, copied with a copy-and-paste button, from any text files – main, Commentary or Contrasting. Unlike the content of other text fields, the content of the *Review* field and of *Notes* always travel to each screen with the user, as he or she navigates anywhere. The user therefore cannot become lost in the databases because the itinerary is always at hand. Notes are always available to be added to, used as contrast to main texts, or deleted. As mentioned, in the audiovisual database, the user may elect to allow the lower-right quadrant to be occupied by photographs that are choreographed with the audio and the main text.

To summarize, the design of information screens varies significantly among different hypermedia applications. Alternative styles affect the way that study and independent research are conceived and conducted. Brown University's Intermedia screen creates a metaphor of many over-lapping windows which together offer a wealth of alternative texts. The proliferation of alternatives, however, makes the texts difficult to prioritize and their relationships difficult to grasp. The difficulties are not accidental by-products of design. Rather, they correspond clearly to the vision of text, scholarship and authorship proposed by designers Landow and Delany. As will be seen, it is a vision with which *MI* parts company.

> The notion of an individual, discrete work becomes increasingly undermined and untenable within [hypermedia], as it already has within much contemporary critical theory.... The reader is now faced by a kind of textual randomness. The writer, conversely, loses certain basic controls over his text: the text appears to break down, to fragment and atomize into constituent elements (the lexia or block of text), and these reading units take on a life of their own as they become more self-contained because less dependent on what comes before or after in a linear succession (Landow and Delany 1991:9-10).

In contrast to Intermedia's vision of endless windows, out of which the hapless writerly-reader may sometimes be tempted to leap, the screen design of *MI* presents a rather sedate metaphor. Like Intermedia, *MI* offers powerful tools for undirected sampling and open-system research (described below), but the application is equally committed to non-random, non-broken readings and analyses. The four quadrants of the standard screen formalize this commitment.[21] Every main text is linked to three other kinds of documents, each of which contextualizes and interprets the first. Thus, contrary to Landow and Delany, the consequence of exposure to hypermedia is not *necessarily* a growing conviction of textual "randomness" and incorrigible "fragmentation," words which suggest, to me, bafflement. Hypermedia links in the *MI* design are intended to lend at least a moderate sense of comprehension – by the interpretations they provide of texts' and audiovisuals' constituent elements (or lexia), of texts' intellectual predecessors, contemporaries and descendants, and of their competitors in alternative paratradigms.[22]

f. Databases

MI is composed of four principal databases: Audiovisuals, Texts, Graphics and Glossary. Each database includes indices to its holdings as well as numerous data-screens. The databases serve users of *MI* in two principal ways. First, they are windows of information to which users are guided in the textbook-and-tour components of the program. Databases provide the raw material for examples of, and assigned exercises in, audiovisual scholarship. Second, *MI's* databases make available a moderately large collection of graphic documents, recordings, and texts. Experts and students of visual anthropology alike can use the databases to conduct open-system research that is entirely independent of the guided tours.

Audiovisual database. This database includes, first, a selection of 2,000 still photographs taken from the original 7,000 that were shot in the field; second, 8 hours of sound recordings, and 15 hours of textual translations which were culled from the 20 hours originally recorded; and third, annotations, keyword-lists and summaries that I have prepared for the above materials.

The Audiovisual database has three special indices described in the *Search-and-Navigation Tools* section (II:g, below), and two varieties of data-screen. One variety of screen presents *Scenes*, a view of which has been seen in *Figure 5*. The second presents *People: Figure 6* is an example. It shows the summary, links and index fields for Katao ole Koisenge, a man who figures

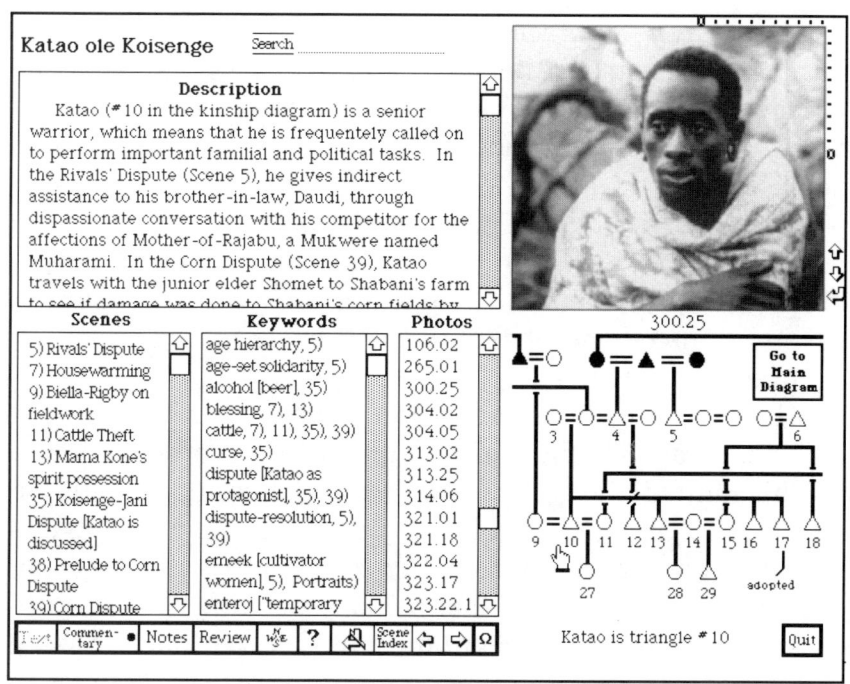

FIGURE 6. *A People window from the Audiovisual database* (Summary-and-link view). Like Document-views, this screen is composed of quadrants which always contain the same types of data: a description of the person, linked scenes in which the person appears, keywords to those scenes, linked photos in which the person appears, a linked kinship diagram, and a photograph quadrant.

prominently in the recordings. In *Figure 6*, as in all *People* screens, the main text in the upper-left quadrant describes the person, with particular emphasis on scenes in which he or she appears.

MI has forty-three scenes. Katao appears or is discussed in the eight which are listed in the lower-left quadrant of *Figure 6*. There, the name of each scene is a link: a mouse-click on any item in the field navigates the user to that scene's window.

The Keywords field, in the center of *Figure 6*, is a compilation of search-terms culled from scenes in which Katao appears. In this field, scene numbers follow each search-term keywords list. Here, the items are not links to scenes (since the field to the left provides that function), but may be copied into the user's notes for later reference and navigation ideas. The Keywords field is important, also, because it is scanned whenever a user performs an Audiovisual-database keyword search.

The next field in *Figure 6*, *Photos*, provides linked access to every photograph in which Katao appears. A mouse-click on any location-code number in the field causes that photograph to appear on the screen.

The lower-left quadrant of Katao's *People* screen is the portion of the database's Main Kinship Index which represents Katao and his immediate family. Numbered circles and triangles in the diagram are links which may be used either to call to this window a photograph of the person represented in the diagram, or to navigate the user to that person's window.[23] A mouse-click in the "Go to Main Diagram" button takes the user to the complete Main Kinship Index. It provides links to all thirty of the Ilparakuyo who were filmed sufficiently often to warrant their own *People* screens.

Finally, the upper-right quadrant of *Figure 6* displays photographs. The photographs may be of Katao, called up by a user from the Photos field, or may be of his kin, called up from the Kinship Diagram. The tiny arrows to the right of the photograph, and the slide-buttons in the upper-right, permit users to change the enlargement and placement of photographs.

The Summary-and-link view depicted in *Figure 6* provides access to the major nodes of information in *MI* that relate directly to Katao, to windows of other scenes, to keywords and to photos. Although a sample screen-view is not included in this essay, *Scenes* windows also have Summary-and-link views that are analogous to that of *Figure 6*. Like it, *Scenes* windows can also display links to related people, keywords and photos. From the Summary-and-link view of a scene, users may either click open the Document-view, shown in *Figure 5*, or may simply browse through the summary.

Texts database. More than thirty essays by other anthropologists and historians of East Africa are contained in the Texts database, along with my own fieldnotes, dissertation and publications about filming the Ilparakuyo. Like the other databases in *MI*, Texts are itinerary stops on the guided tours. In addition, they provide one of several kinds of available data which users may review for their independent research. In both cases, the texts enrich the audiovisuals, giving both a sense of the ethnographic interpretations that informed our field recordings and a background in scholarship for the users' own interpretations.

Figure 7 represents the Document-view for the *Texts* window of Beidelman's (1961) "Beer Drinking and Cattle Theft in Ukaguru." The essay concerns Ilparakuyo-cultivator dispute settlement, and provides pertinent background information to the events that transpire in many scenes. The "Text" button in the lower-left corner of the screen is blackened (or *highlighted)* to indicate that the main text of the window is visible. As before, in *Figure 7* the upper-left quadrant holds the main text. The quadrant would be enlarged, and more main text seen, if the user were to close the *Commentary* field with a click on the "Comment" button at the bottom of the screen.

Figure 7, however, represents a moment in time when the user is studying the Commentary. The user has followed instructions in the *Commentary* field by highlighting what is currently its lowest line. This line, which reads: " <Set the scroll of field 2 to 6752> " is HyperTalk programming code. It is *active text*, which means that when the line of text is clicked, it instructs the computer to perform an action. Here, a click causes a particular paragraph of the main text to be brought into view. When a Commentary refers to *several* quotations in a main text, separate lines of programming code are inserted

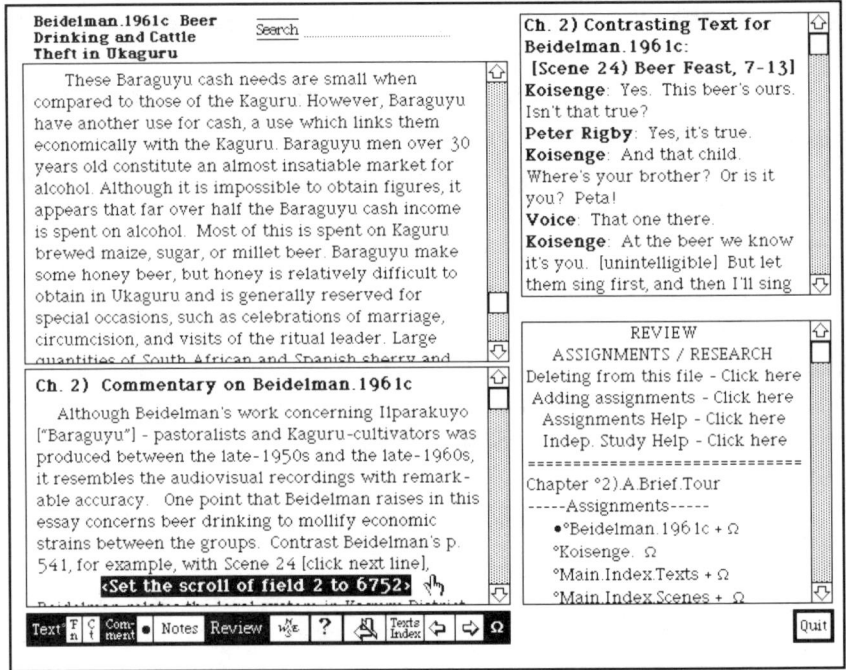

Figure 7. A data window from the Texts database (Document view). The main text quadrant contains a complete essay, from which the guided-tour Commentary has the power to call up particular quotations; the Review field provides an itinerary for the guided tours or independent research; a selection from the *Scenes* transcripts provides contrasting text.

appropriately in the Commentary to permit the user to call up each quotation as it is discussed.

Every chapter in the *MI* textbook constitutes a different guided tour, and more than one tour may have reason to return to a single main text with different Commentaries. Each chapter's Commentaries contain their own code to call up different quotations from the text. Accessing quotations with active-text in the Commentary leaves the entire original essay unchanged: out-of-context quotation is quite impossible.

Commentaries in the Audiovisual database make references to and provide access to specific quotations from *Scenes* in the same way. When the user clicks on the active line of code in an audiovisual Commentary, the English translation of the recording is scrolled to the required location, the *QuickTime* audio track scrolls appropriately forward or back, and photographs shift synchronously. As with Texts, quotations from Audiovisuals are precise, repeatable, and do not require fragmentation of the original.

The *Commentary* field is *MI's* most powerful tool for the scholarly integration of audiovisual data and textual analysis. It has the precision of the film director's hand, calling forth an instant or span of recordings. It also has the reflectivity of the scholar's colloquy – seeking input from informed contrasting texts, returning to the multimedia data when necessary.

It should also be noted that the lower-left quadrant, depicted in *Figure 7*, stores two additional types of information which are not shown. The first, footnotes, has been discussed, for *Figure 5*, with respect to my annotations of audiovisual windows. In Text database windows, the footnotes which appear in this quadrant were written by the author of the main text. They are called up as a result of a click on an asterisk in the main text, or a click on the "Fn" button at the bottom of the screen. Similarly, a mouse-click on a bibliographic citation in the main text, or on the "Ct" button below, will call up citations.

The lower-right quadrant may display either the user's *Notes* field, as shown in *Figure 5*, or the *Review* field, shown in *Figure 7*. A pocket-sized itinerary and navigation tool, the *Review* field leads users to the windows it names and discourages users from becoming lost. The "Review" button is highlighted, in Figure 7, as an indication and result of the fact that field has been made visible. With each arrival to a window named in the *Review* field's itinerary, a black dot appears to the left of the name.

Contrasting Texts are located in the upper-right quadrant of Text and Audiovisual screens. In *Figure 7*, the user juxtaposes data in a main text with that of another source. Beidelman's early ethnographic description of Ilparakuyo is here contrasted

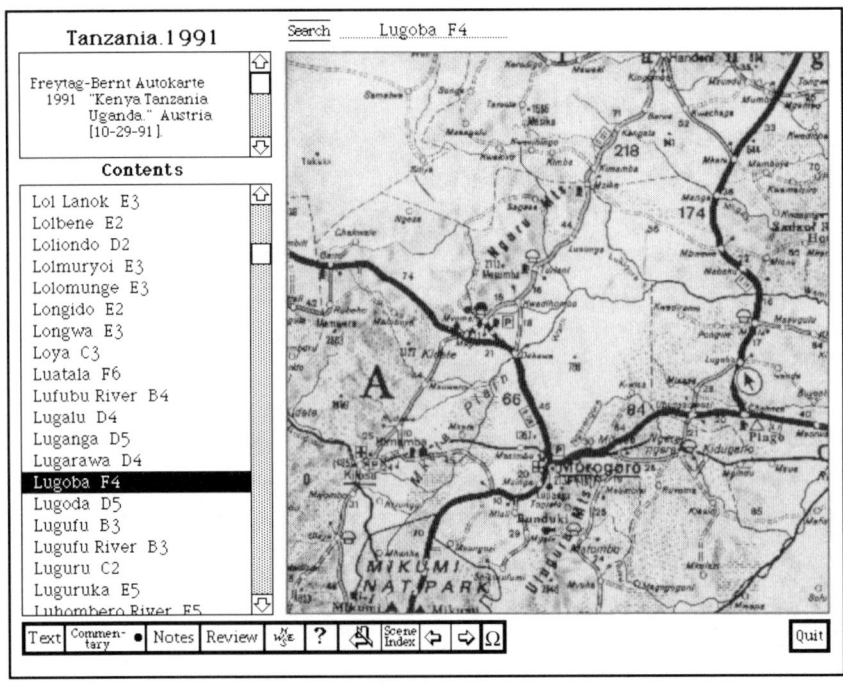

FIGURE 8. A Map data-screen from the Graphics database. Place-names may be browsed in the Index list to the left of the screen; each name there is a link of active-text which, when mouse-clicked, locates the proper region of the map. Place-name queries may also be entered into the open "Search" field at the top of the screen.

with *Scene 24*, a beer feast that was filmed some twenty years later. The omega symbol, "Ω," which appears on the button for Contrasting Texts at the bottom of the screen, is highlighted to indicate the visibility of its field. "Ω" represents resistance in electronics, and seems a fitting icon for the sometimes dissident function served by Contrasting Texts.

Graphics database. *Figure 8* depicts a normal Document-plus-index window from the Graphics database. The map represented here is the most detailed in the *MI* collection. Locations of 1,100 place-names in Tanzania have been identified and logged for it. When the user clicks on a place-name in the index field to the left of the screen, the map scrolls to the proper region and displays the location. A wider view of Tanzania, with fewer visual distinctions, can be called up with a mouse-click on the close-up map in *Figure 8*.

Users may store a link for this map (or for any graphic or photograph) in the *Review* field, and may call it up when prompted to do so by a question raised in a text or audiovisual document. From any screen, the user may also search any of the place-names in the *Glossary* or Maps Index.

Other graphics in the database include early ethnographic photographs of Ilparakuyo and Maasai, *QuickTime* movies, historical and ethnographic maps, and sketches of the region and neighborhood where filming and fieldwork took place. All maps have place-name keywords and provide search-and-navigation tools like those described for *Figure 8*.

Glossary database. The *Glossary* is among the few windows in *MI* that may be brought to hover above main texts like a ghost from Intermedia. Accessed through the "Search" button at the top of every window, the *Glossary* permits users to look up the names of people and places that are mentioned in texts or transcripts, as well find as words in Kiswahili and Olmaa that have been left untranslated. Once a person- or place-name is found in the *Glossary*, the user may select either to return to the main text which initiated the search or follow up by visiting the appropriate *People* or *Map* window from which the *Glossary* entry was derived. Because the *Glossary* floats over the text while it is being used, it does not of require the user to navigate to a entirely different window. The user's concentration is less likely to be broken from the subject that initiated the search.

g. Search-and-Navigation Tools

Users of *MI* navigate through its databases in two capacities, either as students, whose intention is to follow guided tours and the arguments proposed in Commentaries, or as independent scholars, whose agendas require them to follow less-trodden paths, to research the ethnographic data relatively unguided. In both capacities, users are aided by search-and-navigation tools that *MI* provides. This section discusses tools.

The Review Field. On first encounter with *MI*, users are urged to become students, to follow, at least briefly, predetermined paths and links with guided tours created by the designer. The tours introduce students to database-holdings and instruct students in independent search-and-navigation tools. The tours then begin their principal work, to offer audiovisually-integrated course material, the textbook-long introduction to Ilparakuyo ethnography, fieldwork and filmmaking. In these excursions, the student-users' guide-bus is a single navigation tool, the *Review* field: it leads users through assigned explorations and follows them to every stop *en route*. A sample *Review* field may be seen in *Figure 7.*

When a student-user begins a new chapter of *MI*, the travel itinerary and links for the new chapter's guided tour must be loaded as lines of active text into the *Review* field. The tour's Commentaries and Contrasting Texts, as well as the location codes of the data-screen windows in which they are to appear, must also be loaded into the computer's random-access memory for use as needed.

To begin a tour, student-users navigate first to a region of *MI* called *Overview and Assignments* where they can load the desired chapter into memory. Users then mouse-click on the first destination that is named in the newly-formed *Review*-field itinerary. Instantly transported, users see the appropriate data-window open to its Summary-and-links view (as in *Figure 6*). After getting their bearings and perhaps reading the screen-summary, users call up the main text and Commentary which comprise the window's Document-view (as in *Figure 7*). This is done by activating the screen's "Text" and "Commentary" buttons with mouse-clicks. Users then follow the Commentary's various instructions for reading, listening or viewing. They may copy audiovisual links as well as quotations from the several text fields and paste into their notes, and type their comments there as part of the tour's exercises in scholarship. When a Commentary ends, users are asked to navigate to the next window that is indicated on the *Review*-field itinerary.

Keywords, Indices and Boolean Search Tools. In guided tours, users follow well-traveled links between documents. *MI's* independent search-and-navigation tools permit scholars to make their own unprecedented discoveries about documents and to create their own temporary or permanent links. Single-term keyword searches can be conducted from any window of *MI*. The user need only type a search-term into the field located the top of the screen (as in *Figure 8*). Then, with a mouse-click on the Search button, users initiate an electronic search in the current window or in any desired database.

Search-results – the names and location-codes of audiovisuals and data-windows that are discovered by a search – are automatically entered into the *Review* field. There they remain, temporarily or permanently, as links to the discovered documents. The user may scroll through the *Review* field at any time to find the search-results, and may activate links to visit the documents. Photographs or *QuickTime* movies, with location-codes stored in the *Review* field, may be called up in any screen for comparison and contrast with the documents found there.

All of the databases in *MI* also have their own Main Index screens. In such screens, users may gain an overview of the database by scrolling through various summary-fields which itemize holdings. The Main Index screens to the two largest databases, Audiovisuals and Texts, allow users to conduct Boolean, multiple-keyword searches on the holdings. *Figure 9* is a view of the Main Index to the Audiovisual database. Four summary-fields serve this window, *Scenes, Photos, People* and *Keywords*. (Only the first two fields are visible in the current view of *Figure 9*.) *Figure 9* represents the results of a Boolean "not" search that has been conducted in the database's *Scenes*

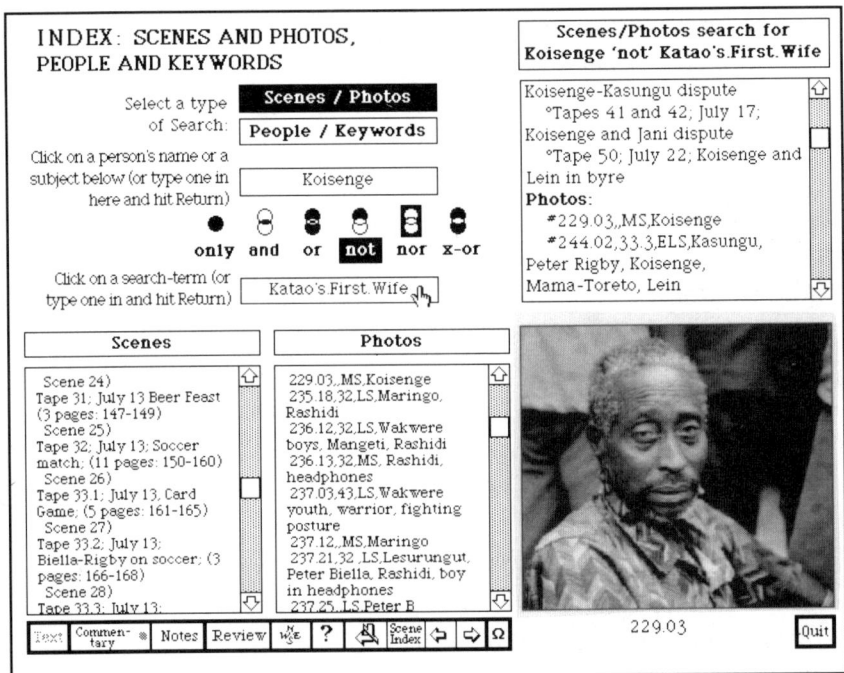

FIGURE 9. *The Main Index of the Audiovisual database.* A Boolean "not" keyword-search through the *Scenes* and *Photos* files renders the search-result displayed in the upper-right quadrant. The photograph in the lower-right is automatically called up because it is the first hit, or search-result, found in *Photos.*

and *Photos* files. The search-results appear in the upper-right quadrant of the screen. At the user's discretion, these results may be placed in the *Review* field as navigation-links.

Browsing Tools. Users may wish to explore *MI's* holdings without benefit of keyword searches. Seeking inspiration in databases at random, users may save what is of interest to them in the *Notes* field. The name and location-code of any data-window may be entered into the *Review* field for later return.

The principal browsing tool is the multi-button *Navigation* palette with added subdirectories. The latter permit almost instantaneous access to any data-screen in the entire program. As seen in *Figure 10,* the palette is made visible with a click on

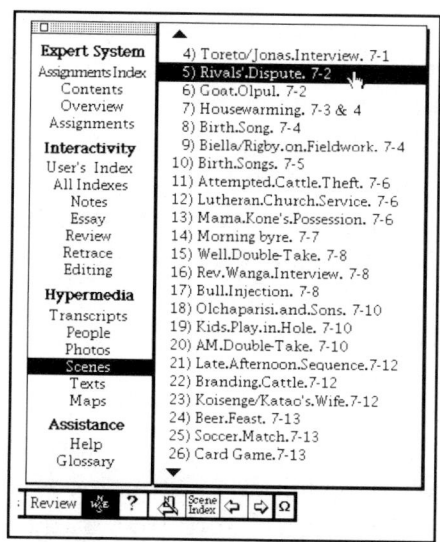

Expert System	▲
Assignments Index	4) Toreto/Jonas.Interview. 7-1
Contents	5) Rivals'.Dispute. 7-2
Overview	6) Goat.Olpul. 7-2
Assignments	7) Housewarming. 7-3 & 4
	8) Birth.Song. 7-4
Interactivity	9) Biella/Rigby.on.Fieldwork. 7-4
User's Index	10) Birth.Songs. 7-5
All Indexes	11) Attempted.Cattle.Theft. 7-6
Notes	12) Lutheran.Church.Service. 7-6
Essay	13) Mama.Kone's.Possession. 7-6
Review	14) Morning byre. 7-7
Retrace	15) Well.Double-Take. 7-8
Editing	16) Rev.Wanga.Interview. 7-8
Hypermedia	17) Bull.Injection. 7-8
Transcripts	18) Olchaparisi.and.Sons. 7-10
People	19) Kids.Play.in.Hole. 7-10
Photos	20) AM.Double-Take. 7-10
Scenes	21) Late.Afternoon.Sequence.7-12
Texts	22) Branding.Cattle.7-12
Maps	23) Koisenge/Katao's.Wife.7-12
Assistance	24) Beer.Feast. 7-13
Help	25) Soccer.Match.7-13
Glossary	26) Card Game.7-13
	▼

Review ? Scene Index ⇦ ⇨ Ω

FIGURE 10. *Partial Screen: Navigation Tool and Subdirectory.* The "Navigation" button has been used to call up the "Navigation Palette." This in turn has opened the *Scenes*-database subdirectory, in which a data-window, Scene 5), is considered.

the "North-East-South-West" button at the bottom of the screen. In the palette, the user clicks on any database name—here, *Scenes* — to call up its respective subdirectory, the complete list of its data-windows. In *Figure 10*, the user is shown considering selection the data-window, *Scene 5, Rivals' Dispute*, from the *Scenes* subdirectory. If the selection is completed, the user will be navigated to the screen shown in *Figure 5*.

Browsers may also wish to explore the Summary-and-link views of *Text, Scene,* and *People* data-windows. (*Figure 6* is an example of the latter.) The summary-fields itemize holdings and give links to related documents. The pursuit of these links provides opportunities to discover new relationships. Similarly, the Kinship Diagram (of which a portion is shown in *Figure 6*) and a similar Age-Set Diagram (not shown) provide different web-views of the *People* database, giving a graphic representation of human relationships as well as navigation to each screen.

A user may realize the importance of a screen only after departing it. To recover the missing name, the user may call up the *Retrace* screen which provides lists of all previous visits to windows in *MI*.

Annotation-links. Lastly, independent scholars may find one more source of navigational inspiration in Annotations to the *Scenes* windows. There, thousands of cross-referenced, active-text footnotes lie dormant. In *Figure 5*, for example, the annotations in the lower-left quadrant make reference to two other moments stored in the Audiovisual database. A click on either of these footnote asterisks will call up its respective, cross-referenced English translation. This, along with its synchronized *QuickTime* audio track, will be placed, next to the main text, in the *Contrasting Text* field for concurrent evaluation.

h. Expert Systems and Expertise

Maasai Interactive is among the first ethnographic hypermedia projects which goes beyond a compilation of databases to the design of an expert system.[24] Existing models of hypermediated-expertise in other disciplines range philosophically from multiple-choice, behaviorist over-simplifications to the postmodern, wide-open "docuverse." *MI's* vision of expertise seeks a middle way between the illusion of analytical closure and the unpleasantness of analytical chaos.

In recognition that beginning scholars require examples and a modicum of tender loving care, *MI's* expert system first adopts the form of a guided tour. It leads users on narrated journeys through the databases – the audiovisuals, texts and graphics – and provides users with combinations of all three for consideration on a single screen. Different aspects of Ilparakuyo culture, political economy and history are brought to the fore in the juxtaposition of recordings, ethnographic texts and Commentaries. Ethnographic knowledge is queried in tours which consider the epistemological status of photographs, audio tracks and translations, and their pertinence to fieldwork in general.

As users become more familiar with the search and navigation capabilities of *MI*, they are assigned exercises in controlled audiovisual research. They are led, through predetermined bibliographic- and keyword-searches, to find ethnographic texts in the database which shed light on specific ethnographic recordings.   Users then become increasingly capable of conducting independent scholarship, and are required to integrate outside theoretical and ethnographic materials.   These exercises are the model for future uses to which *MI* can be put.

Maasai Interactive's expert system design encourages efforts to interpret film and audio from alternative perspectives.   Its text-based *Commentary* field and guided tour calls up precise instants in ethnographic recordings and subjects them to repeated scrutiny.   The tour also introduces contrasting texts and contrasting media into the debate.   These are cued appropriately for use with the main text, but both are also complete and available for scrutiny themselves.

Hypermedia shapes users' philosophical approach to learning and it effects what users learn.   The medium, however, is not the entire message.   Particularly important messages can even transcend the vagaries of alternative expert-system designs.   On rare occasions, messages that people want to send cause the boundaries of existing media to be transformed.   The development of hypermedia closes the era when ethnographic recordings and anthropological analyses could not be integrated intelligibly and repeatably.   The integration is the work of scholarship in hypermedia, the foundation of a new expertise in social science.

NOTES

1   I would like to thank Dr. John Finch, Assistant Director of the ITEC Center at Temple University, for his critical attention to a draft of this essay, and for his good will while revealing to me the mysteries of repeat-loop computer programming.   I also want to thank Apple Computer, Inc. and Karl Kinscherf for the media grant which provided the Macintosh computer and scanner used in production of *Maasai Interactive*.

    Apple, Macintosh, HyperCard, HyperTalk, and *Simple Player* are trademarks of Apple Computer, Inc.   Other registered trademarks mentioned in this essay are *OmniPage*, *MicroSoft Word* and *MacroMind Director*.

2   Computer-based works like *Maasai Interactive* received the name *hypermedia* from Nelson(1981) because their capacity to integrate media goes beyond that which was possible in the pre-computer era. Such works are also called *courseware* because they serve as tutorials in academic courses while containing a software component.

In this essay, I follow current usage by treating the word *hypermedia* as singular. I observe an equally inelegant tradition by referring to the people who work with hypermedia as *users*.

3   A megabyte is a thousand kilobytes, a million bytes. The figure of 640 MB for the memory capacity of a CD-ROM allows room for the additional 10 MB of memory required by the CD for its own purposes – desktop file, volume directory, allocation table and other items important to the orderly functioning of the CD but transparent to the user.

Within a few years, blue-light lasers are anticipated to allow storage of two gigabytes (2,000 MB) of information on a single CD (Gussin 1993).

4   Unlike CD-ROM-dependent hypermedia, applications which are networked to a mainframe computer can be designed to allow users to create *permanent* buttons and links that are available to all future users. As Yankelovich (1991) points out, however, it is naive to expect the average user to take the trouble required for the task. Brown University's Intermedia system therefore introduced a Document Search tool: "Every time a new document is created and saved, the text of the document becomes automatically indexed without any user intervention" (Yankelovich 1991:135).

5   A useful discussion of information-retrieval strategies is presented by Woodhead (1990). He writes that, on one hand, synonym and other generalizing searches locate a high percentage of all relevant items in a database; unfortunately, they also suggest many items that are irrelevant. In such searches, the user is required to weed through the mass of unwanted texts. Strict, term-based searches, on the other hand, rarely turn up items that are irrelevant, but they also miss many items that would be of use. Woodhead adds, "In some cases Boolean combinations can increase recall measure, e.g. by use of alternatives [synonyms], and in other cases they can increase precision, e.g. by use of AND to conjoin restrictive criteria" (1990:44).

6   Unlike the software cited in this essay, most computer-based teaching materials for the social sciences are databases, not expert

systems. The most famous of these is Harvard's *Perseus Project*, about classical Greece.

7   Keller(1987:34) readily admits that the simulations of expertise that are attainable through his model and criteria are not complete. He argues only that simulations can assist, and partially train, experts.

8   Keller(1987:*xx)* suggests that each advancement in artificial intelligence is welcomed by a public that quickly ceases to be impressed. If calculators, word processors and databases once appeared to simulate aspects of phenomenally-capable human beings, the people now no longer seem as capable. Machine replications of other aspects of intelligence will no doubt further cheapen the coin of human expertise.

9   Some Intermedia files, like Landow's Dickens Web (Landow 1992: 96) include graphic concept maps as well as many expert introductions which function as guided tours. The present essay emphasizes the aspect of Intermedia which is more acephalous and chaotic than a guided tour would be.

10   The Annenberg Foundation, for example, contributed more than a million dollars to the development of Brown University's Institute for Research in Information and Scholarship (IRIS), which created Intermedia, the UNIX-based network frequently discussed in the text (George P. Landow, personal communication, February 1993). Another major foundation grant is described in footnote 12.

11   Some scholars prefer to read in bed: others orient themselves to working in the tub! Like the limitations of memory that prevent films from being stored on disk, the difficulty of reading from computer screens and the difficulty of carrying a computer on the bus are understood by the industry to require attention. Such problems are slowly being corrected.

12   Wenner-Gren rejected funding for *Maasai Interactive* and several branches of the National Science Foundation responded negatively to queries because the project, a prototype in educational media, had no research component. The Rockefeller, Ford, Kellogg, MacCarthy and Annenburg Foundations responded to queries by stating that hypermedia production was not within their current funding priorities. The disinterest expressed by funding agencies may be superseded, however, if hypermedia production is linked to one of the foundation's priorities. An example is Rockefeller's recent support for a hypermedia project which received funding because it gave exposure to minority filmmakers (Abrash and Egan 1992).

13   Photographic and sound equipment, as well as a fine darkroom, were loaned by Temple University. Macintosh computer equipment and a scanner were provided by a grant from Apple Computer, Inc.

14   Like anthropologists who become filmmakers, those who turn to hypermedia must dedicate themselves to many activities which have little to do with the normal practices of the discipline. Weeks spent meditating on screen design are not spent teaching, conducting fieldwork, reading journals or publishing. The production of educational software, like the production of ethnographic films, is not part of the normal progress toward tenure. Yet, in the future, hypermedia-making is more likely than filmmaking to be recognized as legitimate, because academic anthropology favors text.

15   Richard Cross, a Pulitzer-nominee since killed on photo-assignment in Honduras, was project photographer. The consulting anthropologist, Peter Rigby, is an member of the Ilparakuyo family on whom the work concentrates. He has published extensively on Maasai, Ilparakuyo and his own adoptive Ilparakuyo family (Rigby 1985, 1992). Fifteen hours of sound recordings were translated by an Olparakuoni sociologist, Melkiori Matwi, who worked with me in the United States for a period of six weeks.

      In the early design of *Maasai Interactive*, I was assisted greatly by the incisive wit of Laura Kunreuther. Scott Kecken also helped enormously by scanning hundreds of photographs and maps and by suggesting many improvements in the graphic layout. Finally, my ever-generous mother, Anne Biella, dedicated a month to scanning and correcting documents in the Texts database.

16   When I began work on the project, I could find no software applications which would serve my purpose. I concluded that I had to create my own shell and became a student of *HyperCard*'s HyperTalk computer language. (I relied primarily on Goodman [1988] and Apple Computer, Inc., ed. [1990] as teachers.) At least two months passed before I had an inkling of what one might be able to accomplish. After six months, I was able to write scripts that functioned much more rapidly than my earlier attempts. After a year, I could identify elegant scripting.

17   I discuss advantages of including uncensored field recordings in my earlier essay in this volume. Howard (1988:308) points out that the cost of incorporating large amounts of text into ethnographic hypermedia will be so low "that we will not have to exclude such a large segment of what we learned in the field to accommodate cost-conscious publishers." Accommodating time-conscious users is a problem that will always remain.

18   CD-ROMs are capable of storing texts simply as bitmap-images of the pages. The acquisition-time for bitmap storage is comparatively brief, but words stored as bitmap-images are not machine-readable. That is, they cannot be copied and pasted, as text, into other texts, and they cannot be searched with Boolean tools. Hypertext-makers are therefore forced to transform hard-copy works in print into machine-readable, machine-searchable, electronic text. To do so, a page of text is first digitized by a machine called an *optical scanner*. Software then evaluates the digitized result: it makes an hypothesis about which alpha-numeric character was signified by every ink-mark that was scanned from the page. Erroneous hypotheses are often made, sometimes resulting in a page of text that contains hundreds of errors. For the most part, however, scanning errors are usually limited to five or ten per page.

Spell-checking computer programs, while helpful in correcting scanning errors, cannot be relied on to catch them all. Such errors sometimes transform one word into another one that is also spelled correctly and which therefore is not flagged by a spell-checking program. Frequently, indigenous names and non-English words, which proliferate in ethnographic texts, are considered by the spell-check program to be spelling errors. Each foreign word must be added to the spell-check dictionary as a correct, properly-spelled word. Proofreaders of electronic texts are therefore forced to work in the traditional clumsy way, comparing original with computer copy to check each unfamiliar word.

Anyone who considers scanning several thousand pages of text should investigate all available programs thoroughly. We use *OmniPage* which scans, hypothesizes alpha-numeric equivalents, and exports the hypothesized characters into *MicroSoft Word* or any other word-processing application. There, spell-checking procedures are conducted as usual. Using this method, I could not scan and correct a 20-page article in less than two hours. Scanning and proof-reading hours are often boring and always exacting.

Scans made from enlarged photocopies of text always give better results than scans from the original smaller pages. In poorly printed texts, occasionally, even enlarged photocopies cannot correct for a major problem, the filling-in of the lower-case letter 'e.' In such texts, so many words with 'e' are rendered incorrectly that retyping the entire article becomes the only viable acquisition technique.

19   A potential confusion lies in the fact that, regardless of the dots-per-inch-of-photograph stored in memory, Macintosh screens cannot reproduce images more sharply than 75 dots-per-inch-of-screen. Thus,

two reproductions of the same photograph, made at a given enlargement but stored in memory at, say, 75-dpi and 300-dpi respectively, would appear identical on-screen when shown at the original enlargement. Only if the two reproductions were magnified *above* that enlargement would the major qualitative differences shown in *Figure 3* become apparent.

20   Hypermedia designers will soon be able to place footnote asterisks within *QuickTime* movies. The asterisks, sometimes called *micons* or moving icons, are presently available for movies created and played back in the MacroMind Director application.

21   The formal arrangement of data in regular quadrants and screens is almost universal in hypermedia applications: *Maasai Interactive* follows the precedent. Intermedia's preference for scattered document-windows is an exception to the rule.

22   One of Landow's "rules" for hypermedia-makers is that links should only be created if they "condition the reader to expect purposeful, important relationships between linked materials" (1991:83). This implies that links contribute to the user's recognition of order, the opposite of randomness. Ramey argues in a related vein: "Computer systems are rhetorical entities.... The communicative aspects of the computer system (the human-computer interface), including all text presented to the user, therefore ought to follow the ordinary rules of rhetoric" (1989:398).

23   Howard (1988) discusses the use of kinship diagrams in hypermedia applications, at length.

24   Search components of Maasai Interactive's expert system resemble the system described by Brown, et al. (1990).

REFERENCES CITED

Abrash, Barbara and Catherine Egan, eds. (1992). Mediating History: The MAP Guide to Independent Video By and About African American, Asian American, Latino, and Native American People. New York: New York University Press.

Actronics (1993). Cardiopulmonary Resuscitation [software]. Actronics, Inc., 810 River Avenue, Pittsburgh, PA 15212 (800)851-3780.

Angus, Ian H. (1989) Circumscribing Postmodern Culture. **IN** Cultural Politics in Contemporary America. Ian Angus and Sut Jhally (eds.). New York: Routledge, pp. 96-107.

Apple Computer, Inc., ed. (1990). HyperCard Script Language Guide: The HyperTalk Language. Reading, MA: Addison-Wesley Publishing.

Barthes, Roland (1978). S/Z. Richard Miller, trans. New York: Farrar, Strauss and Giroux.

Bateson, Gregory (1972). Style, Grace and Information in Primitive Art. IN Steps to an Ecology of Mind. New York: Ballentine, pp. 128-152.

Beidelman, Thomas O. (1961). Beer Drinking and Cattle Theft in Ukaguru: intertribal relations in a Tanzanian chiefdom. American Anthropologist 53:534-49.

Biella, Peter (1984). Theory and Practice in Ethnographic Film: The Ilparakuyo Maasai Film Project. Ph.D. dissertation, Department of Anthropology, Temple University.

Biella, Peter (1988). Against Reductionism and Idealist Self-Reflexivity: The Ilparakuyo Maasai Film Project. IN Anthropological Filmmaking: Anthropological Perspectives on the Production of Film and Video for General Public Audiences. Jack R. Rollwagen (ed.). Chur and London: Harwood Academic Publishers, pp. 47-72.

Brown, D., C. Taylor, R. Baldy, G. Edwards and E. Oppenheimer (1990). Computers and QDA – Can They Help It? A Report on a Qualitative Data Analysis Program. Sociological Review 38(1):134-150.

Collegium for Research in Interactive Technologies, USD (1992). Warsaw 1939 [software]. Chariot Software Group, 3659 India St., Suite 100C; San Diego, CA 92103. (800)242-7468.

DAROX (1992). Diagnostic Decision in a Patient in Shock [software]. DAROX, Inc.; 1103 West Isabel; Burbank, CA 91506; (800)869-9196.

Delany, Paul and George P. Landow, eds. (1991). Hypermedia and Literary Studies. Cambridge, MA: M.I.T. Press

Gagné, Robert M. (1987). Introduction. IN Instructional Technology: Foundations. Robert M. Gagné (ed.). Hillsdale, NJ: Lawrence Erlbaum, Associates, pp. 1-10.

Gamble, John K. and CBEL - Teaching and Learning Technologies at Penn State University (1991). The Political Process Exercise: A Pollution Control Treaty Simulation [software]. Intellimation Library for the Macintosh; 130 Cremona Dr.; P.O. Box 1922; Santa Barbara, CA 93116-1922. (800)346-8355.

Garson, G. David (1989). Computer Assistance of Social Science Writing. Social Science Journal 26(3):335-343.

Goodman, Danny (1988). The Complete HyperCard Handbook (Second ed.) Toronto: Bantam Books.

Gussin, Lawrence (1993). Horsesense and Other Tales: Intermedia '93. CD-ROM World 8(7):54-55.

Hansen, Wilfred J. and Christina Haas (1988). Reading and Writing with Computers: A Framework for Explaining Differences in Performance. Communications of the Association of Computing Machinery 31(9):1080-1089.

Howard, Alan (1988). Hypermedia and the Future of Ethnography. Cultural Anthropology 3(3):387-410.

Kahn, Paul (1991). Linking Together Books: Experiments in Adapting Published Material into Intermedia Documents. IN Paul Delany and George P. Landow (eds.). Hypermedia and Literary Studies. Cambridge, MA: M.I.T. Press, pp. 221-256.

Keller, Robert (1987). Expert System Technology: Development and application. Englewood Cliffs, NJ: Yourdon Press.

Landow, George P. (1991). The Rhetoric of Hypermedia: Some Rules for Authors. IN Paul Delany and George P. Landow (eds.). Hypermedia and Literary Studies. Cambridge, MA: M.I.T. Press.

Landow, George P. (1992). Hypertext: The Convergence of Contemporary Critical Theory and Technology. Baltimore: The Johns Hopkins University Press.

Landow, George P. and Paul Delany (1991). Hypertext, Hypermedia and Literary Studies: The State of the Art. IN Paul Delany and George P. Landow (eds.). Hypermedia and Literary Studies. Cambridge, MA: M.I.T. Press, pp. 81-103.

Lyman, Peter (1984). Reading, Writing and Word Processing: Toward a Phenomenology of the Computer Age. Qualitative Sociology 7:75-89.

MacFarlane, Alan (1990). The Cambridge Experimental Videodisc Project. Anthropology Today 6(1):9-12.

Nelson, Theodor G. (1981). Literary Machines. Swarthmore, PA: Self-published.

Rada, Roy (1991). Hypertext: From Text to Expertext. London: McGraw-Hill Book Company.

Ramey, Judith (1989). Escher Efects in On-Line text. IN Edward Barrett (ed.), Hypertext, Hypermedia, and the Social Construction of Information. Cambridge, MA: The MIT Press, pp. 388-402.

Rigby, Peter (1985). Persistent Pastoralists: Nomadic Societies in Transition. London: Zed Books.

Rigby, Peter (1992). Cattle and Capitalism. Philadelphia. Temple University Press.

Seyer, Philip (1991). Understanding Hypertext: Concepts and Applications. Blue Ridge Summit, PA: Windcrest Books.

Shneiderman, Ben and Greg Kearsley (1989). Hypertext Hands-On! Reading, MA: Addison-Wesley.

Sholte, Bob (1987). The Literary Turn in Contemporary Anthropology. Critique of Anthropology 7(1):33-47,

True, D. C. (1992). Shadow President: The Simulation of Presidential World Power [software]. D.C. True; 1840 Oak Ave.; Evanston, IL 60201. (708)866-1864.

Woodhead, Nigel (1990). Hypertext and Hypermedia: Theory and Applications. Wilmslow, England: Sigma Press, Addison-Wesley Publishing.

Yankelovich, Nicole (1991). From Electronic Books to Electronic Libraries: Revisiting "Reading and Writing the Electronic Book." **IN** Paul Delany and George P. Landow (eds.). Hypermedia and Literary Studies. Cambridge, MA: M.I.T. Press, pp. 133-141.

Yankelovich, Nicole, Norman Meyrowitz, and Andries van Dam (1985). Reading and Writing the Electronic Book. IEEE Computer 18:15-30.

from ANTHROPOLOGICAL FILM AND VIDEO IN THE 1990s
Jack R. Rollwagen (editor). Brockport, NY: The Institute, Inc.

A Teaching Model
For Ethnographic Film[1]

James W. Green
Department of Anthropology
University of Washington

ABSTRACT: A model for using ethnographic film in undergraduate teaching is presented. Its central elements are the film maker's "project," the internal organization of ethnographic films, and image events, the aesthetic component of all films. Each of these features is describe and illustrated using examples from two well-known ethnographic films. The author argues that the model can be used by teachers unfamiliar with film and film history, or who lack training in film production. He also suggests ways it contributes to a more interactive classroom style. The goal of the model is enhanced visual literacy and more effective use of ethnographic films.

Nearly a decade ago, when I decided I would no longer treat ethnographic films as entertaining adjuncts to anthropology texts and lectures, I innocently assumed that my undergraduate audience, wise in the ways of television since infancy, would be more visually literate than audiences of my generation who grew up listening to the radio. Unhappily, that assumption was wrong.

When students were asked to write a paragraph describing the plot of a film they had just seen, they produced brief and inconsequential replies. Class discussions of the film's point of view, character motivations, or ethnographic context were equally thin. The idea that visuals might have a powerful aesthetic component, and that aesthetics could contribute to an educational film's emotional charge seemed of little interest. Yet when we turned to discussion of commercial films, including quasi-ethnographic potboilers such as THE GODS MUST BE CRAZY, student responses were often lucid and insightful. When seeing the GODS film crew shoot a sequence in a phony !Kung village, itself recorded by John Marshall in N!IA, THE STORY OF A !KUNG WOMAN, some students immediately understood the dichotomy between ethnographic realities and ethnographic-like fictions. Why the different response? How could I capitalize on that enthusiasm and encourage students to be more informed in matters of film generally?

Some portion of the blame for our visual illiteracy must lie with the sheer saturation that a media-oriented culture imposes. We all suffer exposure to thousands of visual images daily, mostly from advertising and television, and I suspect we all cultivate habits of intellectual passivity as a defense. Television in particular promotes a distancing of oneself from others, a response that spills over into classroom film viewing. I am also aware that as a teacher I have not always been explicit about what it means to be visually and film literate. Perhaps that is understandable since most anthropologists have little or no training in film production and analysis nor a good sense of the history of anthropological film making. That is changing, thanks in part to the journal VISUAL ANTHROPOLOGY and to newer research on the film traditions and popular culture of societies that used to interest us more for their myths or kinship systems. (For an example see Heider [1991] on Indonesia and how its national culture is reflected in the products of its film industry.) With these new resources, we are less dependent on treatises devoted to abstruse theories of film aesthetics for getting a sense of what film and film making is all about.

Finally, I confess that I have not always used films as creatively as they deserve. My practice at times has been little more than screening a visual illustration of points already made in lectures or books, a virtual invitation for students to relax and wait out the class hour. At least I have resisted the occasional temptation to "show a movie" just to fill class time.

Having experimented with and on undergraduates for some years, I am now convinced that films, like the readings we assign and discuss, are a kind of text and, like any text, they must be "read" using conventions appropriate to their purposes and form. One obstacle to that has been a lack of teaching models that would direct attention to the special features of ethnographic film and suggest how those features can be engaged in classroom activities and in individual study. In this chapter, I will briefly comment on some of the ways ethnographic films typically convey their message and then move to a general teaching model with which I have had some success.

Ethnographic Film as Documentary Text

Ethnographic film can be considered a species of documentary in that the film maker presumes to recreate or represent some historical, social or personal circumstance, not a work of creative fiction or a fictionalized history. Presumably, he or she wants to inform us about some piece of the world "as it really is, or once was." The methods for doing this vary, resulting in differing styles of visual persuasion. This is not the place for an extended discussion of documentary film making but if we look briefly at several documentary styles it will help us understanding something of how these films inform us and what kind of texts they are.

Nichols (1988; 1991) describes some of the distinctive styles in the evolution of documentary film and how, in their different ways, they help create the "real story" of a time and place.

The earliest of these relied on what he calls the "voice-of-god" approach. A voice-over, always male and properly modulated, "explains" the content and the meaning of the visuals. Through intimation and intonation, it tells us that we are witnessing something of consequence. As a device, the "voice-of-god" establishes both the truth and the higher meaning of the presentation. Verbal exposition drives the film, the visuals serving mostly as illustrative props. This "expository mode addresses the viewer directly, with titles or voices that advance an argument about the historical world" (1991: 34). Whose "argument" is being made, and why they advance it, is never stated, nor is it expected to be. Because older style "voice-of-god" documentaries were clearly prone to propagandistic as well as analytic use, they have gone out of favor. The style survives, however, in television journalism with its reliance on short film clips and voice-over newsreaders, and in stereotypic off-screen announcers on daytime game shows extolling the quality of the prizes. It is also common in National Geographic television specials, where the authoritative voices of travelers and naturalists turn the programs into moving images of the magazine.[2]

The presumptiveness and ethnocentrism of earlier "voice-of-god" documentaries prompted several reactions. One, *cinéma verité*, purported to represent some portion of the "real world" by filming it "raw," abandoning voice-over commentary and obvious editorial manipulation and allowing actors to speak and act as they normally would. Viewers were allowed intimate access to what subjects did "naturally," as though the presence of film makers, cameras, and the viewer's gaze were irrelevant to what appeared on the screen. *Cinéma verité* created an apparent honesty and naturalism denied by earlier "voice-of-god" impositions. But the style overlooked and even discounted the importance of context, minimizing background information that would enable the viewer to understand the world of the film's subject in some larger perspective. This deficiency was sometimes corrected by using an on-screen or off-screen interviewer, or by direct address of the film subject to the camera, so that he or she could tell their own story in their own words. One recalls the old Mike Wallace television interviews with their half-lit faces and curling cigarette smoke, effects contributing to an aura of gritty realism, a format that presaged Donahue and Oprah-style public confessionals before a "host," a studio audience, and millions of anonymous consumers of out-of-the-closet secrets. In ethnography, a similar style developed with "informants" telling their own stories, sometimes aided by a co-host ethnographer whose presence authenticated the veracity of the cinematic argument presented. Films such as N!IA, THE STORY OF A !KUNG WOMAN and THE SPIRIT POSSESSION OF ALEJANDRO MAMANI make the lived experience of anthropological respondents central to the film's story. They invite us to look at an exotic world from an emic perspective, the anthropologist "filling-in" with background commentary and directing attention to salient features of the respondent's performance.

A Model for Reading Film

Given these (and other) ways of presenting documentary information, how can teachers encourage students to be more critical, informed viewers of visual texts? I begin where anthropology always has, whether the subject be potsherds or marriage ceremonies. A film can be read by examining its cultural context, specifically, the culture of its shooting, editing, and viewing. For students to develop a sense of visual literacy they must engage a film in each of these areas, recognizing that what finally appears on the screen is the product of an ideology as well as the result of technical skills. To achieve that end, I make use of a model adapted from the work of Sol Worth (1981), a film maker of broad ethnographic, sociological and psychological interests. The model is composed of the following elements:

(1) the film maker's project;
(2) the film's organization;
(3) image events; and
(4) viewer response.

Reading a film requires attention to each of these areas and forces students to address a number of issues including how ethnographic films are made as part of fieldwork, how film creates an ethnographic Other subject to our gaze, and the aesthetics of cinematic images. I will discuss these points briefly, using two well-known films to help illustrate the teaching model. The films are POTLATCH, A STRICT LAW BIDS US DANCE directed by Dennis Wheeler and Napoleon Chagnon's MAGICAL DEATH.

Very briefly, POTLATCH documents the history of the Canadian government's efforts to outlaw the potlatch winter ceremonial, an event for which Northwest Coast Indians are famous. The government's intent was to speed Indian assimilation to the emerging industrial economy of turn-of-the-century British Columbia. In defiance of law, a number of Alert Bay Kwagiutl participated in a large, clandestine potlatch in 1921, after which they were discovered, tried, and many jailed. Masks, ceremonial coppers, blankets, and other potlatching paraphernalia were confiscated, some of it reappearing later in museums and private collections. The story of that trial is narrated by the daughter of the man who gave the potlatch and is told through still photos, old newsreels, docudrama and interviews, combined with scenes of preparation for a modern potlatch in 1974. The legality of potlatching in British Columbia was never settled; it was simply dropped in the 1970s when the national government revised its legal codes affecting Indians. The film concludes with the 1974 potlatch which commemorates the death of the narrator's brother and the return of several ceremonial coppers. The survival and re-emergence of the ritual core of Kwagiutl life is the film's dominant theme.

Chagnon's MAGICAL DEATH is quite different, partly because the Yanomamo he lived among in the 1960s and 1970s had only begun to have contacts with Venezuelans and other outsiders. The film is but one part of the large filmmaking enterprise Chagnon carried out among these people over many years. It shows a group of Yanomamo shamen directing their spiritual energies against the children of a enemy village, hoping to kill the souls of as many as possible. In doing so, they fulfill one of the obligations of a pact among their own recently warring communities. The central character is an elder shaman, Dedeheiwa, a political leader, mediator, and well-known curer. He and the other men prepare an hallucinogenic snuff, *ebene*, blasting it into each other's nostrils with a blow pipe. During their intoxication they are possessed by *hekura* spirits who aid them in their spiritual attack. Over two days of chanting, dancing, and inspired visions, the shamen work at accomplishing their lethal goals, finally collapsing in physical and mental exhaustion. Throughout the ritual, Chagnon's voice-over explains details of the performance, including features of Yanomamo cosmology and the importance of shamen in Yanomamo life.

1. The Film Maker's Project

Shooting film footage on location is not a project; the project in this model is the film maker's agenda: the set of beliefs, attitudes, and expectations that are implicit and explicit in the film. I like the word "project" because it suggests purpose, partly an academic or research purpose but also the film maker's motivations, his or her "feeling concern," as Worth (1981: 40) would describe it, toward the film's subjects and the issues that are to be given cinematic representation.

Purposes, agendas, and ideologies are important to discuss because students often believe that documentaries are about "facts," ethnographic truisms, and that what the film maker produces is objective academic reporting based on travels and discoveries in exotic places. Teachers who use films in classrooms simply to illustrate textbook facts and theories abet this innocent view of the anthropological enterprise. It is critical for students to learn that field research and film making are part of something more than scientific hunting and gathering. They need to know that modern ethnographers continue a very old western tradition of intrusion into other people's lives and societies, along with armies, bureaucrats, traders, missionaries, tourists, diseases, weapons, and alcohol. They also need to know that as anthropologists we have personal motivations along with professional expectations, as well as time and financial constraints when we go into the field. These factors influence what we look for and what we report. Inevitably, films and ethnographies offer a point of view, an argument, about the meaning and sense of what is shown on the screen.

For example, the film maker's overt project in POTLATCH is made explicit at the beginning. A Indian voice-over states: "Every people has a story. This is part of our story — that we went to jail for nothing." POTLATCH is remarkable in part because it is told from an Indian point of view and because Indian people were much involved in its production. Indian respondents face the camera and tell us what happened to them and members of their families when they illegally danced and made speeches at potlatches in the 1920s. The docudrama portions of the film, with sepia toning to recreate the authenticity of old newsreels, presents the Royal Canadian Mounted Police, the court, and bureaucrats as the Indians would have seen them (or imagined them to be) at the time of the trial many years ago. We rapidly come to feel that, here as so often before, the Indians were wronged and indeed they went to jail "for nothing."

While this theme is fairly evident throughout, student viewers are not always aware why the Indian role in this film is important. They perceive an injustice, as the film makers intended, and are usually sensitive to its moral import. But there is something more to know. At this point my standard rhetorical question to a class (borrowed with acknowledgment from the dynamic duo of Baluchi and Ackroyd of BLUES BROTHERS fame) is: Were the POTLATCH film makers on a mission from God? If so, what was it? I want students to think about the historical relationship of Indians and anthropologists, and about the stereotype of Indians they have seen in Hollywood westerns. We discuss some of the difficulties of access to Indian respondents, and why Indians might be suspicious of film makers or anthropologists bearing noble intentions. We consider what bargains the POTLATCH film makers and the Indian subjects might have made concerning control of scripts, editing, and royalties. Might conflicts have arisen during the shooting? I ask students to enter imaginatively into the film maker's role and consider how they would comport themselves during a sacred ceremony while packing around cameras, lights, and microphones. Would they feel intrusive? Defensive? Justified? On the side of the gods? At one point POTLATCH recreates a well-known speech delivered by a Kwagiutl chief to Boas when the latter requested permission to do research in the man's village. That speech, in its liberality of spirit, provides a convenient foil for discussing Indian views of whites, then and now. If in viewing POTLATCH the Indians become an ethnographic Other, can we imagine ourselves as an Other to them? What kind of speech might a contemporary Kwagiutl want to make to us today?

MAGICAL DEATH is more challenging because the relationship of the ethnographer to the Yanomamo is not stated and the events portrayed, supernatural killing and drug-inspired rituals, are more remote from our experience. But this film is intended as ethnography, not docudrama, and we have the advantage not only of Chagnon's well-known book YANOMAMO (1992) and its descriptions of Yanomamo society but the introductory film to the Yanomamo series, A MAN CALLED BEE. A MAN CALLED BEE is in some ways very conventional, belonging to the genre of heroic ethnographic exploration. But along with the text it helps establish the context for sending magical death to the children of a distant village. Together, these films create a strong contrast to an American sensibility. Why should anyone want to kill children anyway? Do the shamen really believe in their hekura spirits and their power to kill? What might Chagnon personally think of the shamen and why does he think it is important to show us this ceremony? What does he want us to feel about them and their culture? Why does he speak for them? Couldn't he have included talking head interviews with simultaneous translation to help us better understand the ritual? What might he have said to Dedeheiwa before and after the filming, and what might he have said to his field assistants or himself, but in English?

In following this line of questioning with a class, my intent is not to put Chagnon's work in doubt. It is to get students to articulate their understanding of Chagnon's project and of ethnography as an academic activity. All anthropological research has its technical requirements (field notes, interviews, etc.) but it also creates heavy personal stresses and these influence the objectivity of both film and ethnography. More than that, filming is part of a long historical tradition of scientific data collection, formal description, and theory testing. In what ways are these activities worthy, and to whom? Can they be important to the Yanomamo? In the current edition his text, Chagnon makes an impassioned plea for the Yanomamo as a test case for our willingness to aid the survival of tribal people everywhere (1992: 239-246). Some students share that concern but some do not, especially when it comes to the ebene and sending spirits to kill children, and they say so. At that point, the project of imaging and imagining an ethnographic Other ceases to be an academic formality; competing visions of what the world is like and how it ought to be are made explicit and the film maker's project has been engaged.

2. The Film's Organization

The second element of the model, film organization, refers to the mechanics of how a visual argument is presented. The simplest way of doing this is to think of a film as having a beginning, a middle, and an end. Beginnings and ending are the easy part. A good opening establishes a mood of tension, suspense, or conflict that anticipates what is to come. In POT-LATCH, the beginning is a recreated rural courtroom in which a group of Indians sit in silence as a voice intones their names, followed by "carried goods to recipients, 6 months in jail" and "made a speech and danced, 2 months in jail." This "establish-ing scene" tells us what kinds of conflicts will be played out in the rest of the film.

The opening for MAGICAL DEATH is equally dramatic but in a very different way. Dedeheiwa and the other shamen have just taken a blast of ebene. In addition to the substance's strong psychoactive effects, it produces in its users prodigious and colorful nasal discharges. Chagnon's camera is slightly above the head of a kneeling shamen who rises with an unfocused stare as he gasps and spits. He is just entering a trance state. The scene grabs the viewer with the implicit message that drama and more of the same lie ahead.

Opening and closing scenes are highly conventional but any film is more than its beginning and end. Organization also includes a story line, the development of characters, subplots, motivations, the rise and fall of action, accumulating tension, and finally resolution. POTLATCH tells much of its story through old photos, newsreels, re-enactments, and personal narratives. We see the drama from both Indian and white points of view but it is clear that the dominant voice is that of the Indians. Their jailing, behind the scenes legal maneuvering, and theft of their ceremonial regalia reveal the bias of the Canadian laws and the racism of local officials. But in the film's final segment, all that is put behind as the scene shifts to preparation for the 1974 potlatch, organized by the children and grandchildren of those who went to jail. The old anti-potlatching laws were never explicitly repealed by Parliament, they were just dropped, and many of the ceremonial masks confiscated in the 1920s remain in museums and private collections. Indian grievances are not fully satisfied, but at least potlatching is no longer illegal. One of the high points of this sequence is the return of a ceremonial copper, its presence announced with great dignity by an old chieftain. The film ends with the dancing and speech making that was once a criminal offense.

The structure of MAGICAL DEATH is much different, alien and seemingly more complicated, and we rely on Chagnon's voice-over to tell us where we are in the sequence. After a brief introduction to Yanomamo shamanism, and the reasons these particular shamen have gathered, the film moves to their ritual performance. Directed by Dedeheiwa, it is punctuated by a set of distinctive events and minidramas: preparing and inhaling the ebene; calling and commanding the hekura spirits; sending spirits off to do their dangerous work; a spiritual counter-attack by a shaman in the enemy village; eating the souls of the dead children and hunting down any that may have escaped; and magically killing a youth through pantomime. Dedeheiwa even produces a bit of string from his mouth as evidence that he was spiritually in the enemy village. In one of the more dramatic scenes, the spiritually charged shamen hug one another as they rock back and forth in a tight circle and Chagnon tells us that in this state they are at once themselves, their hekura, and their victims.

Student responses to the structure of these two films are quite different, and that provides an opportunity for discussion of the implicit influence of culture on perceptions. MAGICAL DEATH is shaped emically; the shamen decide what to do next, not the film maker, and they seem oblivious of the camera. For some students that creates a problem for they do not perceive that there is any order to the ritual, the chanting and dancing seem redundant, and they don't know "where Chagnon is going" with the film. A neat and linear beginning, middle, and end is not evident. By contrast, the structure of POTLATCH is clear and the reason for that is its wholly Euro-American form. Despite its being presented as the Indian's story from an Indian point of view, its structure is that of the fairytale, especially its Americanized, Disney-like variant. In that model, good people (here, harmless Indians) are overwhelmed by a great evil through no fault of their own; they endure repeated indignities with great courage; finally they are restored to a semblance of their former, whole state because of their quiet perseverance and simple dignity. The film has a clear beginning, middle, and end and it closes with the moral triumph that, we want to believe, is earned by those who suffer unjustly. The parallel to a children's fairytale is clear.

One of the most effective ways I have used for introducing students to the idea that films have a shape and that the shape is part of the message is an in-class exercise using small discussion groups of three to five individuals. To introduce it, I explain the function of a story board in film planning and tell the groups that they are to develop a story board that redesigns the first scene of a film they have just seen. Each group is to be a small film company and to get them comfortable with the assignment I ask them to start by naming their company, preferably something whimsical. Then they are to assign themselves roles: script writer, camera operator, music director, credits writer, and director. In their work as a company, they can rename the film, add music to it if they like, redesign titles and credits, script a voice-over or not, plan new camera shots, or highlight different themes. But whatever they do, they must develop the new scene with a complete set of written directions and justify their changes in terms of the remainder of the film as the ethnographer originally made it. They work as a group but individual story boards are turned in and graded for creativity and completeness.

3. The Image Event

The third feature of the model, the image event, is in some ways the most difficult. It is difficult because it challenges the most basic assumption of visual illiteracy, that "seeing is believing." There is a lengthy discussion in the film theory literature as to whether or not film is made up of implicit codes or a visual grammar that the viewer can learn to read. My concern in teaching, however, is with how imaginative students can be in deciphering or interpreting a specific shot, sequence, or visual element. I define an image event as a visual representation, usually a single shot but sometimes a short sequence, that pulls together many of the major themes of the film. An image event is a summarizing as well as dramatizing representation and good ones are aesthetically strong as well. They grab viewers viscerally and pull them into the story. Different viewers will respond to different images so that a student's decision that a certain shot is an image event is a personal one.

In POTLATCH, there are a number of possible image events: shots of partially rotted and listing totem poles; low angle views of potlatch dancers in traditional regalia; an Indian Agent and RCMP officer conferring in the arched doorway of a frontier church; a backlit view of a modern Kwagiutl artist painting a banner for the planned potlatch. I especially like a medium length shot of an old man, the chief referred to earlier, cane in one hand and a copper cradled in the other, slowly walking past the dancers and drummers to a place near the fire. He is to give a speech, in his traditional language, about the return of the copper to his village by a U.S. art collector. Through a translator he tells us, "the coppers are real, and stay." In his age and arthritic slowness, he symbolizes a stolen glory. But he also affirms a future. In his hands the copper becomes an icon for previous potlatch transactions but also for a reclaimed history and the beginnings of cultural reconstruction. As an image event, the old man and his short speech to an ethnically diverse crowd at a modern potlatch gathers up many of the strands of the story line, personalizes them, and offers a judgment on the troubled history of Indians and whites in British Columbia.

MAGICAL DEATH also presents dramatic images: the graphic opening scene of the shamen rising from his ebene blast; the huddled dancers experiencing (according to Chagnon's account) three contradictory roles at once; the men devouring children's souls and licking what they take to be body fat from their fingers; Dedeheiwa resting after two days of dancing and ebene, a band wrapped around his head to calm the throbbing and headaches. The imagery of MAGICAL DEATH is less familiar to most undergraduates and what they initially see is strangeness or, in the literalistic views of some, the handiwork of Lucifer himself. To move them beyond that, I discuss various design elements in a framed scene so they can begin to think of visuals as having a deliberate, aesthetic structure. That structure helps tell the story and contributes to its "feeling tone." Long shots, close shots, freeze frames, low-angles, mise en scene, and other technical devices help create an emotional response in the viewer. I also discuss what anthropologists mean by a signs, symbols, and icons and, in describing an image event as a sign or a symbol linked to an ethnographic context, I am asking them to think like an anthropologist who would work from a detail of daily life up to the larger cultural context where that detail resides.[3] To help with all of this, I use overheads of specific scenes from commercial and art films. But the transfer of these ideas to ethnographic films is easily made and some students get very excited about dissecting visual images not only in ethnographic films but commercial ones as well.[4]

Preparing to Teach a Film

This kind of teaching obviously takes more time and preparation than using films simply to illustrate points from lectures and text. But it can be effective because as a teaching approach it is systematic, it appeals to student interest in the visual, and it can be done without any great knowledge of film making, film aesthetics, or film theory. Best of all, it is intellectually exciting and it brings students alive to the possibilities of both anthropology and visual media.

I am sometimes asked by interested faculty at my university how they might use ethnographic film in their own teaching. The following are some of my recommendations. They are not profound but others have apparently found them useful so I repeat them here.

First, preview the films you want to use so you have time to think about them yourself. That seems obvious but I am always surprised at how some people are willing to show a film they have never seen just because someone else recommended it. I did that once and was embarrassed by what appeared on the screen. But rather than apologize, I made an object lesson of the film's shortcomings. Still, using films without knowing what is in them is a risky strategy.

Second, read published reviews of the films you are using. Ethnographic films are regularly reviewed in the AMERICAN ANTHROPOLOGIST, usually a year or two after their release. Also ask at the campus media center where reviews can be found or if they have promotional fliers that are sent out by many film distributors. I have photocopied film reviews, distributed them to a class, and used them as a basis for discussion. I once passed out copies of a newspaper ad for THE GODS MUST BE CRAZY to better make a point about what is meant by the ethnographic Other.

Third, learn something of the cultural features of the region where the film was made. If the film is about Indian family life, read something about families in India. Two excellent South Asian films I use are DADI'S FAMILY and MODERN BRIDES: ARRANGED MARRIAGES IN SOUTH INDIA. Both require a minimal knowledge of caste relations, women's roles, and family structure. Neither requires a South Asian specialist in order to analyze them using the model I follow.

Fourth, invite someone to class who is a member of the culture represented in the film. Ask guests to critique the film in term of their own background, and how that contrasts with their experience of being in America. International students are often willing to do this if approached beforehand. Some are more insightful than others, and on occasions I have endured grandstanding, but a live speaker who knows the culture adds to the interest of any film. Take notes on what guests say and use them for building a background file on each film you use.

Fifth, as a writing project ask students to prepare a film review for a film shown in class. Most students are intrigued by this kind of assignment although they have little idea of what a film review looks like. Ask them to bring to class newspaper or magazine reviews of commercial films, read some aloud, and generate a format for student papers to follow.

Finally, don't be intimidated if you feel you lack a detailed knowledge of films, film making, or film critique. Start with one or two films you know and like and develop your own teaching style with them.

One effect of using films this way is to make classes, especially large one, more interactive. Film viewing and particularly film analysis breaks up the dreary pattern of daily lectures. It also encourages everyone to be a contributor to the learning enterprise since everyone has seen the same film and has some kind of reaction to it. Even films that are weak in their technical presentation, or which take a view out of political fashion, can generate a lively response. Films covering sensitive racial and ethnic issues sometimes intimidate students, especially in large classes where few are willing to take a risk by speaking up. The model proposed here is a framework for developing and guiding discussion on difficult topics.

Most important, in this model the film becomes the focus for discussion and learning; it is no longer an appendage to lectures and books. Students in my classes quickly learn that film viewing is not a pleasant break from critical thinking. It is the time when thinking must begin.

NOTES

1   An earlier version of this paper was presented at the 1992 American Anthropological Association meeting at a session on teaching with film. I thank the participants on the panel and those in the audience for their suggestions.

2   The old MovieTone News features are good examples of the technique, as is the explicitly racist CANNIBALS ONCE, part of the "Ports of Call Series" shown in movie houses in the 1930s. Important early network television examples were VICTORY AT SEA and HARVEST OF SHAME.

3   In lectures I briefly discuss the differences between signs, symbols, and icons to advance student's understanding of visual representations. My definitions are rough but usable for undergraduate purposes. A *sign* is anything we can use to infer something else, as skid marks suggest a tire. A *symbol* is any representation to which an arbitrary and shared meaning has been assigned, such as a flag. *Icons* are a subclass of symbols which are taken to be isomorphic with the thing they symbolize, such as some Christian statuary.

4   The opening "ape sequence" of Kubrick's massive 2001, A SPACE ODYSSEY is rich in a very Westernized symbolic imagery and serves as an interesting example of a mythologized view of human evolution in a film that celebrates twenty-first century machinery. Indeed, the

mythic is what makes it work so well, from the quasi-Cain and Abel fratricide to the mysterious monolith that impels us, *deus ex machina*, to the next stage of our evolution. I sometimes use the sequence as an introduction to physical anthropology, using the model outlined here.

REFERENCES CITED

Chagnon, Napoleon A. (1992). Yanomamo. Fort Worth: Harcourt Brace Jovanovich. Fourth edition.

Heider, Karl G. (1991). Indonesian Cinema, National Culture on Screen. Honolulu: University of Hawaii Press.

Nichols, Bill (1988). The Voice of Documentary. Challenges for Documentary, Alan Rosenthal (ed.). Berkeley: University of California Press, pp. 48-63.

Nichols, Bill (1991). Representing Reality. Bloomington: Indiana University Press.

Worth, Sol (1981). Studying Visual Communication. Philadelphia: University of Pennsylvania Press.

FILMS CITED

Magical Death. 1973. A film by Napoleon A. Chagnon. 28 minutes, color. Available from Documentary Educational Resources, 101 Morse Street, Watertown, MA 02172 (617/926-0491).

Potlatch, A Strict Law Bids Us Dance. 1975. A film by Dennis Wheeler. 53 minutes, color. Available from Canadian Filmmaker's Distribution West, 1131 Howe St., Suite 100, Vancouver, B.C. V6Z 2L7, Canada (604/684-3014).

from ANTHROPOLOGICAL FILM AND VIDEO IN THE 1990s
Jack R. Rollwagen (editor). Brockport, NY: The Institute, Inc.

Integrating Film Into Teaching About Ethnicity and Multiculturalism

Ellen C. K. Johnson
Social and Behavioral Sciences
College of DuPage

ABSTRACT: Ethnicity and multiculturalism are major concepts of our time and relate to significant issues in the United States as well as in other countries. Ethnicity refers to people's identification with others who are similar in some culturally significant ways. Some ethnic groups have aspects of corporate structure. Having diverse cultural units in some larger entity, like a nation, or even a community, is termed "cultural pluralism. " Multiculturalism (many cultures) is characteristic of culturally diverse and culturally plural societies. Many people today hope that recognition and acceptance of cultural diversity will lead to greater understanding and tolerance between people, as between people of different ethnicities. Others fear that emphasis on differences obscures commonalities between people and can lead to prejudice and discrimination. Recognition of multiculturalism in our world has led to increased interest in understanding it and teaching about it, which is the basic purpose of this paper/curriculum unit.

This paper demonstrates how films/videos and readings can be integrated in teaching a unit about ethnicity and multiculturalism. The unit focuses on ethnic and cultural diversity in the United States and deals with the immigrant experience, core and boundary maintenance, and on implications of relations between ethnic units for the wider society and for individuals. The unit also contrasts static versus processual paradigms for understanding and dealing with ethnicity and multiculturalism and includes illustrations of how individuals and groups dialogue or negotiate identities. Cultures are thus reference systems and part of a "culturing" process. The paper demonstrates how videos provide basic data for understanding concepts and paradigms as well as personalizing them by presenting individuals living and negotiating their lives.

Introduction

Multiculturalism has emerged as one of the most significant issues of our times, as people with differing cultural backgrounds are increasingly coming into contact with each other. Demographics in the United States are also shifting, with minorities increasing rapidly in the population, making cultural pluralism and ethnic differences in the U. S. more apparent.

Films and videos, integrated into teaching along with readings, lectures, and discussions, can effectively enhance learning and understanding about ethnicity and multiculturalism. In the curriculum unit which I shall describe here, videos are used in essentially three ways: (1) to present and/or clarify concepts; (2) to illustrate, support, enrich, or personalize crucial understandings in conjunction with readings; and (3) to broaden the base of diversity (e. g. provide examples). The unit, Teaching About Ethnicity and Multiculturalism, could be used in a variety of courses, but especially in the social sciences or humanities. Portions of the unit have been taught in an Introduction to Education course, and the unit will be used as a preface to an Americans and Their Cultures (Anthropology) course.

The goals of the unit are the following: (1) Students will understand and be able to use effectively such terms as "ethnicity" and "multiculturalism" and other related concepts; (2) Students will discover the logic in others' lives and become more aware of, sensitive to, and tolerant and appreciative of cultural diversity; and (3) Students will be willing to explore the nature of American society and culture and examine their stereotypes and judgments as well as their conceptions of "culture."

Crucial Understandings and Concepts in the Unit

Basically, *multiculturalism* refers to the recognition of the essential validity of different ways of being and living and co-existing in plural society. Many hope that recognition of such *cultural pluralism* in the United States, *i. e.* that the U. S. is made up of many defined categories or groups of people identifying themselves as somehow culturally similar to each other but different from other categories or groups, will enable us to deal more effectively or kindly with each other. It will also, hopefully, foster more *tolerance* or respect for others, as in "us" vs. "them" situations, and lead to less *prejudice* and *discrimination*, especially the discrimination based on *racism* or involving *stereotypes* and *labelling* which can lead to issues of power and control (or empowerment) and the sometimes violent jockeying of *majorities* and *minorities,* with someone "losing out. " Using stereotypes and perpetuating racism can be quite emotionally charged, and power relations can perpetuate inequity and groupness.

Multiculturalism also implies that the American myth of *assimilation* or complete *acculturation* is just that — a myth. We are not a melting pot; rather, we are more like an ethnic stew, where ingredients may blend in the gravy but a carrot remains identifiably a carrot.

Thus, *cultural diversity* rather than *cultural uniformity* is celebrated by multicultural approaches. There are even diverse groups delineated within diverse groups. The *culture* concept here is a relatively static notion, though it is recognized that, despite their being holistic and integrated, cultures do change. *Ethnic groups* are viewed as relatively static, also, having *core values*, ethos or patterning, definable *boundaries*, and recognizable identities (*cultural identity* or *ethnic identity*) to which people can belong, whether they are loyal or disloyal, or which they can use as reference units.

Ethnicity is seen as being a product of history and experience, as the immigrant experience, and as characteristic of oneself or "one's people" or homeland. *Nationality* thus is one aspect of ethnicity, along with race, language, religion, food, festivals, etc. *Ethnocentrism*, characteristic of most of us, is thinking our culture, our way of life, is the best. On the other hand, *cultural relativism* implies that we should examine each culture and each *value* or custom in its own *context*.

Thus, deconstructing the term "multiculturalism" as it has been generally used makes apparent our basic assumptions about what the world is like and how we think about it, including how we categorize and how we relate to those categories (e. g. *a* culture, or *an* ethnic group). We have tended to perceive the world as a congeries of ethnic groups, each maintaining its culture and boundaries and teaching its young to do so, also. This delimitation of people, this "groupness" view of the world, can lead to appreciation of difference, but it can also lead to stereotyping and discrimination. Variation in the real world is more continuous and our (Americans, anthropologists, others) need to classify can blind us to more processual and dialogic paradigms of culture.

Usually what has been taught to students in the guise of multiculturalism has emphasized one of three approaches: (1) Diversity between different cultures, a separatist or centrist approach, based on core and boundary ideas and "us" vs. "them"; (2) Uses made of notions of diversity, where an ethnic group is a social unit in a larger system and where emphasis may be placed on power relations and what prejudice and discrimination can wreak or have wreaked; and (3) Stories of individuals' lives. I suggest that it is this latter humanizing approach which may prove the most fruitful ultimately for developing appreciation and tolerance in students, as they can come to "know" people as people and not only as representatives of groups. Films are a very useful tool here. All of the films incorporated within this unit present aspects of individuals' lives.

Dealing with people's stories also brings us into reformulations in the culture concept which have been taking place in anthropology. Culture is increasingly being viewed as processual and dialogic rather than as static or structural and passed on into descendants' heads "as is. " "Slippage" occurs over time, too, and some things never get passed on; some things may get passed on but rejected, as by teenagers dealing with a different world from that of their parents. "A culture," then, becomes a *reference system*, to be called upon as needed; we may choose different cultural scripts or different identities for different occasions and others may let us use them or may "call us on them. " We reinterpret, shift emphases, and recreate history and customs. We put on performances both for ourselves and others. Thus, we create our cultures, our ethnicities, and our identities as we live our lives. We construct our *cultural cores* and boundaries in particular situations or contexts. Seen this way, multiculturalism is even more complex than congeries of cultures in plural society and ethnicity is basically a reference system that is situational and relational.

Culture as a reference system or *dialogue* is also intimately related to processes of self and group identity formation and maintenance. Culture and ethnicity viewed in this way can also be used or called upon in various ways in various contexts of power and politics, such as in deliberations over whether schools should use a multicultural curriculum and of what such a curriculum should consist. Too much focus on the separation of categories and the boundaries can both obscure the working out of individuals' lives and hamper people crossing boundaries to fully interact with others. This is not to say that a sense of one's own identity is not important, just that too much "groupness" emphasis can lead to problems relating to others. And at stake is the identity and unity of the nation.

Readings, Films and Procedures

Diversity and Multiculturalism
Student Readings::

> Riche. "We're All Minorities Now"
> Gray. "Whose America?"
> Schlesinger. "The Cult of Ethnicity, Good and Bad"
> Time magazine: "What Do We Have in Common?"

Film:

BLUE COLLAR AND BUDDHA

These articles introduce students to the ethnic and cultural diversity in the United States and our demographic transition to a plural, multicultural society. They also deal with immigration, Riche's article especially. Riche notes the diversity within groups and remarks that people take pieces from various identities and integrate them into lives. Gray raises the question of what should be taught in educational curricula, shared values (whatever they may be) or ethnic agendas? History has needed reinterpretation to include more diversity of people and cultures, but an ethnic diversity emphasis may make it difficult for individuals to create new identities. Schlesinger notes that we in the U. S. have always been multiethnic but we have survived by creating an American national identity. This identity has historically *been* Eurocentric.

Concepts emphasized in this section include multiculturalism, cultural pluralism, cultural diversity, ethnic group, majority and minority, prejudice, stereotypes, acculturation, assimilation, and nationality.

Students should consider, individually or in groups, the following questions:

1. What changes are taking place in demographic patterns in the United States?
2. What implications do these changes have for our society?
3. What should school curricula, especially in social studies or humanities, be like? What topics should be covered, with what emphases?
4. Where does "American culture" come from and what do you think characterizes it? What has been the role of immigrants?
5. Do you think individuals have less chance or more chance to develop unique identities in a world emphasizing ethnic agendas? Explain.
6. What can result when people emphasize their own groups, "us" as opposed to "them"? Give examples.

After discussion of the articles, show the film BLUE COLLAR AND BUDDHA. The film focuses on the Laotian experience in Rockford, Illinois and includes the bombing of their temple, stereotypes and prejudices of others toward them, the immigrant experience of Rockford, Laotian culture, and commentary by a variety of Laotians and a variety of Rockford citizens. Several Laotians discuss their identities as refugees and their adapting to American ways.

Before students view the film tell them to watch for information on immigration, diversity of opinions regarding Laotians and their culture, and evidence of prejudice and stereotypes or tolerance.

After they have viewed the film, have them consider these questions:

1. How do the Laotians fit into the culturally plural history of Rockford? What other ethnic groups came to Rockford? Have they all become assimilated or acculturated?

2. What other viewpoints did people exhibit regarding the Laotians? How do you explain this diversity?

3. Who was prejudiced against the Laotians? What evidence was there of discrimination? Why do you think the Laotians were objects of discrimination?

4. What are important features of the emerging Laotian-American identity? Give examples of people creating their identities.

5. Can you say that some beliefs or customs or values are Laotian and others American? Explain.

Facets of Multiculturalism
Student Readings:

DeVoe. (ed. by Selig) "Refugee Children in School: Understanding Cultural Diversity in the Classroom"

QEM Network. (ed. by Selig) "Multicultural Education"

Breitborde. "Multiculturalism and Cultural Relativism after the Commemoration"

Perry. "Why Do Multiculturalists Ignore Anthropologists?"

Weiner. "Anthropology's Lessons for Cultural Diversity"

All of these articles discuss aspects of multiculturalism as a concept and/or its implications for society. DeVoe's article deals with how understanding students' backgrounds well can help educators design effective teaching strategies, but understanding only a little can lead to further stereotyping. The QEM article notes that multicultural curricula have been organized in one of two ways, as separate courses on each group or as infusions into a variety of courses and levels. Breitborde shows how celebration of an event, *e. g.* the Quincentennial of Columbus' coming to America, can focus the struggles between groups with different interpretations of the event. He discusses ethnocentrism and cultural relativism and how cultural relativism can strengthen our commitment to our values and lead to respect for others when we understand contexts. Crossing cultural boundaries to understand others need not mean we have to give up our own culture. The Perry and Weiner articles deal with the history of the culture concept, cultural relativism, and cultural diversity. Weiner also discusses political implications of conceptions of race and culture and our earlier crusade to produce "100 percent Americans. "

Concepts emphasized in this section include multiculturalism, of course, as well as stereotyping, racism, ethnocentrism, cultural relativism, cultural diversity, and culture.

Students should consider, individually or in groups, the following questions:

1. Do you think knowing more about Laotian culture or the Laotian refugee experience (e. g. as portrayed in BLUE COLLAR AND BUDDHA) would be helpful for teachers in Rockford? Why? How would it be helpful (or not helpful)?

2. How are stereotypes created and maintained? What furthers stereotypic thinking? What "breaks" it? What role does racism play in stereotyping? Students might present and discuss some stereotypes.

3. What are the pros and cons of having separate courses focusing on different ethnic groups' cultures? Would a separatist multicultural approach advance equal opportunity for all and promote alternative life choices? Why or why not? What about a bilingual curriculum with many courses taught in a minority language?

4. Have students consider cultural relativism. What are its implications? Students could discuss (or take roles to play and then discuss) different groups' possible perspectives on some local or national event or impending decision.

The Culture Concept
Student Reading:

Wax. "How Culture Misdirects Multiculturalism"

Films:

JERUSALEM: WITHIN THESE WALLS
HEART BROKEN IN HALF

The article, to be read after the films have been viewed, distinguishes between culture and the process of culturing as well as on the history of the culture concept and cultural relativism. Wax views the legacy of "static cultures" as misleading, and states that cultures are, in reality, processual, being continually reinterpreted. Wax also deals with some problems of multiculturalism as it gets played out in schools and school curricula.

Concepts emphasized in this section include culture, values, cultural uniformity, boundaries, ethnicity, and cultural relativism.

First, have students express their views of what a culture is. What implications do these views have for interactions between people? If a culture is "a way of life," then who has it? An individual or only a group?

Next, have students, individually or in groups, consider American culture. What characteristics does it possess? Does every American have to possess all these characteristics? What makes someone an American, or a representative of American culture? What he says or does? What others say? Note that American-born children of immigrants *are* Americans.

My students began by saying that a "typical American" is a WASP. We "took that apart:" White (What percent of what would make one non-white?), Anglo-Saxon descent ("primarily" from certain parts of Britain), Protestant. Students were surprised that only two persons of the thirty in the room were WASPS! (Many students at the College of DuPage, located in suburbs west of Chicago, are grandchildren of residents of the city's ethnic neighborhoods, many of which are Catholic.) Yet, the students all considered themselves to be "100 percent American"!

Show the film JERUSALEM: WITHIN THESE WALLS. The film portrays very clearly the ethnic quarters within the old city, each having its own territory bounded by walls, its own sacred site, its own language, history, religion, etc. , in short, its own culture. The city is portrayed as a mosaic, not a melting pot. Have students watch for and note the characteristics of these quarters as the film progresses.

After the film is shown, have students consider these questions:

1. Define "ethnic group," based on the film. What are the elements here of ethnicity, e.g. religion, and how are people expressing and representing and continuing their ethnic identities?
2. Do you think these cultures in Jerusalem are uniform within, with core values shared? Explain. Is this conception of ethnic group cultures, each in its own place and maintaining its own boundaries, characteristic of the U. S. ?
3. The film also introduces particular individuals representing the various ethnic cultures. How are they contextualized? Is it clear "where they stand" in their society? Are they sufficiently defined to avoid further stereotyping?

Next, show the film HEART BROKEN IN HALF about gangs in Chicago. Interestingly, the gangs are territory-based as well as ethnicity-based. One Latin Kings hero killed was not even Latin but Southeast Asian! The film is especially good at showing symbolic aspects of gang culture, or subculture, and processual aspects of culture, such as how boundaries are negotiated and maintained. Gangs are engaged in dialogues both with members and with others.

The following questions may be used to direct student perusal and/or discussion of the film:

1. What are key Latin Kings, or people and folks, symbols? What do the symbols mean to members? To others? How are the symbols manipulated (like a language) to communicate or dialogue with members or others?

2. How do the Latin Kings memorialize dead members and carry this into future gang experience? How do they pass on their traditions?

3. Does a gang like the Latin Kings have a culture? Explain. Are they thus like an ethnic group? Why or why not?

4. Compare the images of static or processual "groupness" in Jerusalem and in Chicago gangs. Are Chicago gangs like Jerusalem's ethnic quarters? Explain. Do you think it is the peoples' lives that explains your response or the different conception (paradigm) of culture presented in the two films?

Now have students read Wax's article. Have them consider the following questions:

1. Which conception (paradigm) of culture do you think explains more? Which are you more comfortable with? Why?

2. Can the conceptions of culture as created from dialogue or culture used as a reference system explain individuals' dealings with each other, like communications between two people forming a couple? In other words, do you think that the same processes operate at different levels? What about between nations? Explain. Do processual conceptions of culture explain how individuals form identities (e. g. picking and choosing who they are from various cultures) better than static concepts of culture? Explain.

Culture and Identity
Film:

MADE IN CHINA

The film, made by Lisa Hsia, portrays her growing up in Evanston, Illinois as the American daughter of parents of Chinese descent and intersperses scenes of her childhood with her experiences in China as a young adult. She is Chinese and yet not Chinese. She is in the process of finding out who she is and constructing her identity.

Concepts focused on here are ethnicity, ethnic or cultural identity, and nationality.

Have students consider the situations and experiences which have gone into Lisa's creation of her identity. What is she viewing as "Chineseness" or "Americanness" in herself? In what situations? Are these selves so easily separable? Explain.

Have students consider their own ethnic and/or cultural identity(-ies) and how their values and perceptions have come through their own situations and experiences. To what groupings or cultures could they refer, if they chose to? With whom do they dialogue? And, looking beyond their differences, what do they have in common? What might they have in common with the Laotians, with Chicago gang members, with others? Who is an American, anyway, and what is "American culture?" (There will be dialogue over that for some time to come!)

As a concluding activity, have students write papers, imagining that they are writing a manual on understanding ethnicity and multiculturalism for persons (in any field - business, education, social service, etc.) who will be interacting with a variety of people from diverse ethnic and cultural backgrounds. What is it important to understand, or to know, in order to interact appropriately and well? Have them include illustrative examples to support the points they make.

Alternatively, have students select a concept or a topic covered in the unit and write a paper clarifying or discussing it, using examples.

Finish the unit by reading Maya Angelou's poem "On the Pulse of Morning" read at William Clinton's inauguration in January 1993.

Conclusion

Even though the United States contains people from many diverse cultural backgrounds, who have had different experiences, we are all individuals, individuals with needs and dreams. We are all just trying to do as well as we can in a country which proclaims opportunity, liberty, and justice for all. Perhaps we will allow ourselves to tolerate and even appreciate our differences, to dialogue with each other, and to be enriched by each others' culture.

Yes, we are different, but we are much the same, too. Cultural pluralism and ethnic diversity needn't tear us apart as a nation. After all, identities and cultures are processual, not static. We can create who we will be.

And, films and videos can be an essential part of this creation process, here being used in teaching and learning about ethnicity and multiculturalism. Videos are not merely "add-ons" to the "real" classroom stuff. Videos can be used to present and clarify concepts, such as "culture"; to personalize understandings and ideas, such as when we met Lisa Hsiu "dialoguing out" her identity; and to provide examples to support readings, e. g. the diversity in America as represented even in Rockford, Illinois. Readings relate to films and films relate to readings and all tie in with discussion topics.

REFERENCES CITED

Angelou, Maya (1993). On the Pulse of Morning. Chicago Tribune Jan. 21. News Section:14.

Breitborde, Lawrence B. (1993). Multiculturalism and Cultural Relativism after the Commemoration. Social Education 57(3): 104-108.

DeVoe, Pamela A. (1991). Refugee Children in School: Understanding Cultural Diversity in the Classroom. Anthro Notes 13 (2):1-4, 10, 11.

Gray, Paul (1991). Whose America? Time 138 (1): :12-17.

Perry, Richard J. (1992). Why Do Multiculturalists Ignore Anthropologists? The Chronicle of Higher Education 38(26): A 52.

QEM Network (Quality Education for Minorities) (1991). Multicultural Education. Anthro Notes 13(2): 5,6.

Riche, Martha Farnsworth (1991). We're All Minorities Now, American Demographics 13(10): 26-34.

Schlesinger, Arthur, Jr. (1991). The Cult of Ethnicity, Good and Bad, Time 138(1): 21.

Time (1991). What Do We Have In Common? Time 138(1): 19-20.

Wax, Murray (1993). How Culture Misdirects Multiculturalism, Anthropology and Education Quarterly 24(2): 99-115.

Weiner, Annette B. (1992). Anthropology's Lessons for Cultural Diversity. The Chronicle of Higher Education 38(46): B1,2.

FILMS CITED

BLUE COLLAR AND BUDDHA. 1987. (VHS, 57 min, color). A film by Taggart Siegel and Kati Johnston. Siegel Productions, 5345 N. Wintrop, Chicago, Il 60640.

HEART BROKEN IN HALF. 1990. (VHS, 56 min, color) A film by Taggart Siegel. Siegel Productions, 5345 N. Wintrop, Chicago, Il 60640.

JERUSALEM - WITHIN THESE WALLS. 1986. (VHS, 59 min, color). A film by National Geographic Society. National Geographic Society, Educational Services, P. O. Box 98019, Washington D. C. 20090-8019.

MADE IN CHINA. 1985. (VHS, 28 min, color). A film by Lisa Hsia. Filmmakers Library, 124 East 40th St. New York, NY 10016.

ADDITIONAL RESOURCES
Articles:

Keefe, Susan Emily (1992). Ethnic Identity: The Domain of Perceptions of and Attachment to Ethnic Groups and Cultures, Human Organization 51(1): 35-43. [Delineates three dimensions of ethnicity: ethnic culture, ethnic group membership, and ethnic identity.]

Nash, Manning (1989). Ethnicity: Meanings and Vicissitudes. IN The Cauldron of Ethnicity in the Modern World, Manning Nash, (ed). Chicago: U. of Chicago Press, pp. 1-20. [Mentions nation-state building blocks and markers of ethnicity and deals with idea of ethnicity through time.]

Nelson-Barber, Sharon and Terry Meier (1990). Multicultural Context a Key Factor in Teaching. Academic Connections (Spring): 1-11. [Focuses on teachers in multicultural classrooms.]

O'Connor, Terence (1989). Cultural Voice and Strategies for Multicultural Education. Journal of Education 171(2): 57-73. [Dialogic politics in schools related to multicultural education in plural society (majority and minorities).]

Sleeter, Christine E. (1989). Multicultural Education as a Form of Resistance to Oppression. Journal of Education 171(3): 51-71. [Relates multicultural education to questions of racism, minority/majority relations, and oppression.]

Films

[There are numerous films dealing with ethnic or multicultural topics. These are some I have used.]

BECOMING AMERICAN. 1981. (VHS, 58 min, color). New Day Films, 12 West 27th St. Suite 902, New York, NY 10001. [Hmong refugee family settle in Seattle.]

BILL COSBY ON PREJUDICE, 1972, (VHS, 24 min, color). A film by Bill Cosby. Pyramid Film and Video, Box 1048, Santa Monica, CA 90406. [Stereotyping, ethnic labelling, bigotry.]

FIGHTING BACK (EYES ON THE PRIZE, SERIES I). 1965. A film by PBS. PBS, 1320 Braddock Pl. , Alexandria, Va 22314-1698. [Integrating Little Rock and the U. of Mississippi.]

GATHERING UP AGAIN: FIESTA IN SANTA FE. 1992. (VHS, 46 min, color). A film by Jeanette DeBouzek. Quotidian Independent Documentary Research, P. O. Box 2623, Santa Fe, New Mexico 87504. [Ethnic identities and performances.]

THE PRIMAL MIND. 1984. (VHS, 58 min, color). A film by Jamake Highwater. Cinema Guild, 1697 Broadway, New York, NY 10019. [Contrasts native American concepts with European ones.]

WINDS OF CHANGE: A MATTER OF CHOICE. 1990. (VHS, 60 min, color). A film by PBS. PBS, 1320 Braddock Pl. , Alexandria, Va 22314-1698. [Native Americans on and off the reservation.]

Further Articles, Books Reference Information

ANTHROPOLOGY AND EDUCATION QUARTERLY. [Source for many articles pertaining to diversity of cultures and education.]

Kromkowski, John A. (ed.) (1993). Race and Ethnic Relations. 93/94. Guilford, CT: The Dushkin Publishing Group, Inc. [Articles on ethnicity and race, updated each year.]

Schlesinger, Arthur M. (1992). The Disuniting of America: Reflections on a Multicultural Society. New York: W. W. Norton and Co. [Describes how interpretations of history come to the fore in ethnic battles in America's plural society. The cult of ethnicity can be divisive and we need to re-emphasize an *American* identity. A good book for student reading and discussion.]

Social Education (1992). Vol. 56, No. 5 (September 1992). [Contains articles on multiculturalism, including the NCSS Curriculum Guidelines for Multicultural Education.]

Spindler, George, and Louise (1990). The American Cultural Dialogue and its Transmission. New York: The Falmer Press. [Describes values in American mainstream and minority cultures.]

Spindler, George, and Louise (eds. (1987). Interpretive Ethnography of Education: At Home and Abroad. Hillsdale, N. J. : Lawrence Erlbaum Associates, Publishers. [Contains a section of articles dealing with cultures and education.]

Thernstrom, Stephan, Ann Orlov, and Oscar Handlin (eds.) (1980). Harvard Encyclopedia of American Ethnic Groups. Cambridge, MA: Harvard U. Press. [Contains information about the various ethnic groups in the U. S.]

Waters, Mary C. (1990). Ethnic Options: Choosing Identities in America. Berkeley: U. of California Press, 1990. [Discusses how suburban Americans are choosing which ethnic identities they want to relate to.]

Williams, Brackette F. (1989). A Class Act: Anthropology and the Race to Nation across Ethnic Terrain. Annual Review of Anthropology, Bernard J. Siegel, Alan R. Beals, and Stephen A. Tyler (eds.). Palo Alto, CA: Annual Reviews, Inc. pp. 401-444. [A bibliographic review article on ethnicity, ethnic groups, boundaries, and cultural systems in nation-states.]

from ANTHROPOLOGICAL FILM AND VIDEO IN THE 1990s
Jack R. Rollwagen (editor). Brockport, NY: The Institute, Inc.
© 1993, The Institute, Inc. All rights reserved. ISBN 0-9635206-1-X

Ethnographic Cinema: Sources For Teaching Regional Courses

Peter S. Allen
Department of Anthropology and Geography
Rhode Island College

ABSTRACT: This essay contains an extensive review of the ethnographic cinema and the literature on ethnographic film for nine world areas: North America, Latin America and the Caribbean, Europe, the Middle East and North Africa, Africa, India and South Asia, Southeast Asia, the Far East, and Oceania. It is designed as an aid for educators using films and videotapes in their teaching of anthropology courses, especially courses with a geographical focus. For each region, major (and sometimes minor) ethnographic films and videos are listed and described. References to specialized film guides and general works on ethnographic film are also included. Although there is relatively little evaluative material in the text, most of the films and videos mentioned are substantial and well known productions. Moreover, review references are provided for the majority of the films and videos listed, thus enabling the reader to seek out critical opinions. Individual filmmakers who have produced significant corpi of ethnographic films are also mentioned with references to their work in particular areas.

Author's Note:

This account does not pretend to be definitive nor comprehensive. It reflects the personal tastes and biases of the author
and is undoubtedly deficient in many areas. For example, it
does not contain references to archaeological films, an important and substantial sub-category of anthropological film, but
interested readers can find information on archaeological films
in ARCHAEOLOGY ON FILM compiled by Peter Allen and
Carole Lazio (1983). Moreover, reviews of archaeological films
are published in each issue of ARCHAEOLOGY magazine and
most productions of any merit released since the publication of
ARCHAEOLOGY ON FILM have been reviewed there.

With very few exceptions, the films cited here are documentaries and little mention is made of the myriad commercial
feature films with valuable ethnographic content. Thus, the
excellent works of Satyajit Ray on India, Ousmane Semb'ene on
Senegal, and many others have been entirely ignored.

All films referred to in this article which have been reviewed in the AMERICAN ANTHROPOLOGIST are followed
with a review reference containing the volume number and
page number(s). For written works I have followed the
AMERICAN ANTHROPOLOGIST endnote style, but have
also included references to reviews in the AMERICAN AN-
THROPOLOGIST for those works reviewed there. In addition
I have listed several books in the bibliography which are not
cited in the text, but which will be of use to individuals
interested in ethnographic film and video.

This article aims to provide some basic sources for those
using films to teach regional courses in anthropology. It is by no
means comprehensive and readers are strongly advised to
monitor the film reviews that appear on a regular basis in the
AMERICAN ANTHROPOLOGIST, VISUAL ANTHROPOL-

OGY, VISUAL ANTHROPOLOGY REVIEW, and ANTHRO-
POLOGY TODAY, the newsletter of the Royal Anthropological Institute. The main source for any user would be the
published guides cited below. However, since they are all out
of date to one degree or another, there is an attempt here to
bring the reader up to date in various world areas by citing
some of the more significant recent works that have been
released since the publication of these guides.

In choosing films for the teaching of anthropology, there are
a number of useful guides. The best general guide is Karl
Heider's FILMS FOR ANTHROPOLOGICAL TEACHING
(1983) (86: 501-502) which contains an extensive listing of
anthropological films and videos dealing with all geographical
areas. It has a lot of good production and distribution information, but it is more than a decade out of date. Nevertheless, it is
the place to begin. Particularly valuable are the review references
it contains because most of the film descriptions are lifted
verbatim from distributors' promotional materials and are not
very objective. The reviews provide much more critical ap-
praisals. The brand new A BIBLIOGRAPHY OF ETHNO-
GRAPHIC FILM (Husmann et al, 1992) is the best source for
written materials on ethnographic film. In addition to a bibliography of books and articles, it contains a listing of conferences
and festivals, lists of catalogues and filmographies, review
references, a list of relevant journals, and valuable indexes.

Another important resource are the catalogues of film
distributors either specializing in anthropological film or having large holdings in the genre. Many are published annually
and thus provide regular updatings of holdings. Documentary
Educational Resources in Watertown, Massachusetts is perhaps the best known distributor dealing exclusively in anthropological films. Their publication, FILMS FROM D.E.R
(Volkman, 1982) should be consulted by anyone using their
films or looking for first quality films on virtually all world
areas. They have the rights to most of John Marshall's and

Timothy Asch's films and they also distribute written accompaniments to these and several other productions. The Pennsylvania State University has a very large collection of anthropological films and videos and periodically publishes a special catalogue of its holdings entitled, FILMS AND VIDEO: THE VISUALIZATION OF ANTHROPOLOGY. The University of California Extension Center for Media and Independent Learning also publishes a regular supplement to its main catalogue, WORLD CULTURES ON FILM AND VIDEO , in which are listed productions from their excellent collection. Other institutions with good collections include Indiana University and Syracuse University. Of the commercial distributors, Filmakers Library, First Run/Icarus, and Cinema Guild stand out for the depth and breadth of their offerings in anthropology while Films for the Humanities and Sciences, New Day Films, Karol Media (distributor of the National Geographic Society's productions), Films Incorporated (which distributes the Disappearing World series), the International Film Bureau, PBS Video, Coronet Films, Encyclopedia Britannica Films, the National Film Board of Canada, and Landmark Films all have good collections in anthropology. Third World Newsreel distributes some excellent films on the peoples of underdeveloped countries as well as films on the underclasses of more developed nations including the United States. Women Make Movies specializes in films with feminist themes of which many are of anthropological interest.

For the serious anthropological educator, the best resource is the AMERICAN ANTHROPOLOGIST where film reviews have been a regular feature since 1966. Most films of real anthropological significance from the past four decades have been reviewed there by competent professionals. Moreover, in the late 1970s the Film Review Editor of the AMERICAN ANTHROPOLOGIST, John Adams, embarked on a campaign to review important productions that had been released before films were reviewed in the journal. Thanks to this policy we have good reviews of NANOOK OF THE NORTH (78: 725-726); THE HUNTERS (82: 228-229); the films of Margaret Mead and Gregory Bateson (78: 726-726) and other classics that were not reviewed at the time they were made. In recent years, however, mainly as a result of the proliferation of video technology, far more ethnographic productions have become available and the quantity has far outstripped the review capacity of the journal. Other journals reviewing anthropological films include the AMERICAN JOURNAL OF PHYSICAL ANTHROPOLOGY, ARCHAEOLOGY, JOURNAL OF AMERICAN FOLKLORE, and the MIDDLE EAST STUDIES ASSOCIATION BULLETIN, although these tend to be specialized to the disciplines indicated in the titles.

There are also the various festivals featuring anthropological films. Chief among these are the annual Margaret Mead Film Festival sponsored by the American Museum of Natural History in New York City and the Film and Video Festival of the American Anthropological Association. Each September several dozen new films of anthropological interest are screened at the Margaret Mead Festival. Many are premiers and most are introduced by the filmmaker himself/herself or someone who worked on the production. It is very competitive (only one in 20 or 30 entries is selected) and the quality of the films shown here tends to be very high although the anthropological content of some is minimal. The quality is also high at the American Anthropological Association Film Festival, a regular feature of the association's annual meeting for the past five or six years. The American Film Festival, the most comprehensive screening of documentary films in the world, has an ethnographic film category and several other categories in which films of anthropological interest are included. A number of film and video festivals focus on particular subjects or areas that are also of anthropological interest. The most important of these is the Museum of the American Indian's annual Native American Film and Video Festival where two or three dozen new productions on Native Americans are showcased and the American Indian Film Festival in San Francisco, a regular event for almost 20 years. And at the annual meeting of the Middle East Studies Association new titles relating to the Middle East are regularly screened, largely through the tireless efforts of Ellen-Fairbanks Bodman, and although not all are anthropological, most are of interest to anthropologists working in this area.

Before proceeding with a discussion of the major world regions, mention should be made of several film series that have been produced in cooperation with professional anthropologists. Chief among these is the Grenada Television series, "Disappearing World," a collection of approximately 50 films from most of the major world areas. They are notable in part because they have all been produced in close collaboration with respected anthropologists and the quality of both the content and technology is high. Africa is the best represented area accounting for almost a third of the titles and includes films on three of the four sectors of the continent; only South Africa is not represented. Almost all focus on tribal peoples and the majority (11 of 14) are on East Africa; two are on North Africa, and there is a single title for West Africa. There are six programs each from East and South Asia, five on Europe, three on Oceania, two on Southeast Asia, and one on North America. Films Incorporated is the American distributor of the "Disappearing World "series.

The British Broadcasting Corporation has produced a large number of high quality films in its "Worlds Apart" series under the direction of such capable filmmakers as Melissa Llewelyn-Davies and Chris Curling. Productions like the comprehensive DIARY OF A MAASAI VILLAGE (88. 1037-1040) are a testament to the high quality and anthropological sensitivity of the films in this series.

In the United States several good series have been produced at various times. One of the most ambitious (and at the time successful) is the "Faces of Change" series, 27 films on five different areas (Kenya, Afghanistan, the China Coast [Hong Kong], Taiwan, and Bolivia) organized by the American Universities Field Staff in the early 1970s. First rate filmmakers were enlisted and all of the films were made with the cooperation and collaboration of knowledgeable anthropologists. A textbook, FACES OF CHANGE: FIVE RURAL SOCIETIES IN TRANSITION (Wheelock Educational Resources, 1975) was published to accompany the films. They are still available, but not very extensively utilized which is unfortunate considering their quality and the wide range of topics covered. They were reviewed in the AMERICAN ANTHROPOLOGIST by Beatrice Whiting (79: 751-758).

In the late 1970s Michael Ambrosino , the originator of the acclaimed "Nova" science series, put together two series of films entitled, "Odyssey," all of which are anthropological or archaeological. He enlisted well known professionals and the end products are generally of very high quality. Fifteen of the approximately twenty original titles are available from Documentary Educational Resources. Another ambitious project was the "Faces of Culture" series, a 26-program television course in cultural anthropology designed to accompany William Haviland's introductory text, CULTURAL ANTHROPOLOGY (1984). This program was created with the cooperation of good professional anthropologists and it remains a valuable educational tool. It was reviewed by Karen L. Field in the AMERICAN ANTHROPOLOGIST (87: 216-218).

Multi-Cultural Films

Very few films deal with more than one culture. It is not unusual for a series, such as those mentioned above, to include films on different cultures, but rarely is more than one culture or society featured in a single film. Margaret Mead and Gregory Bateson pioneered in this approach with several films in their series, "Character Formation in Different Cultures." Although most of the films in this series focus on individual cultures, two titles combine material from more than one culture: BATHING BABIES IN THREE CULTURES (78: 725-726) and CHILDHOOD RIVALRY IN BALI AND NEW GUINEA. Later Mead helped make FOUR FAMILIES (83: 743-744) with the National Film Board of Canada. In this production she appears on camera discussing child-rearing practices in India, Japan, France and North America (Canada), the four cultures of the title. Although her commentary has not withstood the test of time very well, the images are still compelling and informative and the whole idea of doing cultural comparisons on film is demonstrated in such a way as to recommend imitation. It is unfortunate that others have not attempted similar film projects.

Native North Americans

There are far too many good films and videos on Native North Americans to single out even a vaguely representative selection. Readers are strongly advised to consult the two volumes produced by the Museum of the American Indian, NATIVE AMERICANS ON FILM AND VIDEO, Volumes I and II (Weatherford, 1981 and Weatherford and Seibert, 1988). These guides have the dual advantages of having fine summaries as well as being relatively up to date, and although they are not comprehensive, there are more than enough titles in these two volumes to satisfy the wants and needs of most educators. Another source for Native Americans is Gretchen Bataille's and Charles Silet's IMAGES OF AMERICAN INDIANS ON FILM: AN ANNOTATED BIBLIOGRAPHY 1985 (89:775). This and its predecessor, THE PRETEND INDIANS: IMAGES OF NATIVE AMERICANS IN THE MOVIES (Bataille and Silet,

1980), deal almost exclusively with Native Americans in feature films, but are still of use to educators looking for critical materials on filmed resources. For an up date on productions released since the publication of the guides listed above, the review sources noted in the first part of this essay should be consulted as well as the programs of the annual Native American Film and Video Festival and the American Indian Film Festival.

Native Americans of the far north have generally been well represented in anthropological film. The Iñuit are ennobled in the peerless NANOOK OF THE NORTH (80: 196-197), perhaps the greatest ethnographic film of all time and well depicted in the important Netsilik Eskimo Films series (68: 1327-1328; 72: 722-724; 79: 510) which forms the basis of the MACOS (Man: A Course of Study) project, an integrated text and film program designed to introduce other cultures to students at the secondary and college level. In particular, the longer film from this series, ESKIMO FIGHT FOR LIFE, is outstanding. There are also numerous other productions available from the National Film Board of Canada on the Iñuit as well as some newer films from other sources: INUGHUIT: THE PEOPLE AT THE NAVEL OF THE EARTH (92: 551-553) and IN IRIGU'S TIME (92: 551-553). At the western end of the continent Sarah Elder and Leonard Kammerling have produced a rich corpus of films on various Alaskan natives including UKSUUM CAYUAII: THE DRUMS OF WINTER (92: 551-553). Unlike NANOOK and the Netsilik films which are re-creations of traditional life styles, their films focus on contemporary native peoples and their problems. A view of traditional activities among Aleuts can be found in AMIQ: THE ALEUT PEOPLE OF THE PRIBILOF ISLANDS: A CULTURE IN TRANSITION (88: 257-258) and PETER PICKED A SEAL STICK: THE FUR SEAL HARVEST OF THE PRIBILOF ISLANDS (88: 257-258).

For Native Americans further south, one should begin with the "American Indian" series (69: 271-272; 76: 728-730), a collection of more than a dozen strictly ethnographic films. Beyond this, there are literally hundreds of films and videos, many of good quality and value, that can be used. The bulk of new productions on Native Americans tend to chronicle their struggles to win title to tribal lands and other properties, the revival of traditional culture, and the continuing quest for Indian identity. A few productions still explore more traditional native practices and among the best of these are HOPI SONGS OF THE FOURTH WORLD (87: 223-225); and WEAVE OF TIME: THE STORY OF A NAVAHO FAMILY 1938-1986 (90: 486-487).

Among those films which examine the contemporary situation of Native Americans, the following are just a few titles from the many worthy productions that are available: Sarah Elder's iDANCE OF THE YUKON DELTA and A RIVER OF STRUGGLE: ALCOHOL AND AN ALASKAN TOWN; VILLAGE OF NO RIVER (85: 233-234); WHITE JUSTICE (92: 551-553); BROKEN RAINBOW (89: 1014-1015); ABNAKI: THE NATIVE PEOPLE OF MAINE (90: 774-778); OUR SACRED LAND (90: 774-778); .INCIDENT AT RESTIGOUCHE (90: 774-778); NATIONS WITHIN A NATION: SOVEREIGNTY AND NATIVE AMERICAN COMMUNITIES (90: 774-778); HOME OF THE BRAVE (90: 774-778); CONTRARY WARRIORS - A FILM OF THE CROW TRIBE (90: 774-778); and HUNTERS AND BOMBERS (94: 526-527).

Finally, serious students of the Navaho should be aware of the "Navaho Film Themselves" project where Navaho Indians were trained to use movie cameras and then encouraged to make films about their cultures. The seven resulting productions are not very dramatic, but they are very revealing of Navaho culture, especially the enigmatic INTREPID SHADOWS, the most complex of the seven. Distribution rights were acquired by the Museum of Modern Art which usually limits its interests to films of high artistic merit. The project was organized by John Adair and Sol Worth and was reviewed by

John Collier in the AMERICAN ANTHROPOLOGIST (76: 481-486). A valuable book, THROUGH NAVAHO EYES by Worth and Adair (1972) (76: 890) accompanies the series.

Other North Americans

Relatively few strictly ethnographic films have been shot on the non-Indian populations of North America, but most documentaries have some ethnographic content and are of interest to anthropologists. It would be impossible to list even a moderately representative sample of such films, but it is worth mentioning a few important sources. Guides to such films are a bit hard to come by and there is no comprehensive list, but Judith Trojan's AMERICAN FAMILY LIFE FILMS (1981) (86: 500-501) is useful for aspects of family life, but is by no means comprehensive, even in that category. AMERICAN FOLKLORE FILMS AND VIDEOTAPES, A CATALOGUE, volumes I and II (Ferris and Peiser 1976; Slack 1982) have excellent listings for many films that might be considered more anthropological than folkloric and should be consulted by anyone searching for films on American culture.

Latin America and the Caribbean

Latin America is well documented on film, but the record is very uneven with some people having been subjected to considerable filming and others entirely undocumented. Mesoamerica is far better covered than most of South America on the whole, although there are several exceptions, most notably the highlands of Peru and Bolivia which have attracted many filmmakers and the Yanomamo of the Orinoco River basin who have been extensively documented by Timothy Asch and Napoleon Chagnon. Those interested in the region can choose from a wide variety of films on a broad range of subjects. There are excellent films on the ancient cultures of Mesoamerica and South America as well as outstanding productions on the modern inhabitants. Bridging the gap between ancient and modern cultures is the fine production,THE ONA PEOPLE: LIFE AND DEATH IN TIERRA DEL FUEGO (88: 267-269), by Anne Chapman and Ana Montes de Gonzolez.

Hunters and gatherers are represented in NOMADS OF THE RAIN FOREST (88: 782-783), and THE PANARE: SCENES FROM THE FRONTIER (88: 782-783), two films that shed light on a rapidly disappearing way of life. Two other productions show a sort of transitional people who have settled in to cultivate gardens but are still foraging for much of their food: THE KAYAPO (93: 514-516) and THE KAYAPO: OUT OF THE RAIN FOREST (93: 514-516). Tribal peoples are also the subject of THE TURTLE PEOPLE (76: 489), a first rate film on the coastal Mosquito Indians of Nicaragua and WE ARE MEHINAKU (84: 980-982) on a group of Arawakan speakers in the Xingu River headwaters of Central Brazil. The Yanomamo of Venezuela and Columbia are perhaps the most thoroughly documented of any Latin American peoples thanks to the collaboration of filmmaker/anthropologist Timothy Asch and ethnographer Napoleon Chagnon. Together they produced more than two dozen films on these complex horticulturalists and an almost equal number of workprints available for classroom use. Among the most outstanding of the films are THE FEAST (73: 500-502); MAGICAL DEATH (77: 179); A MAN CALLED BEE (78: 950); and THE AXE FIGHT (79: 747). Others have also made films about the Yanomamo, notably Geoffrey O'Conner and Bruce Albert whose CONTACT: THE YANOMAMI INDIANS OF BRAZIL (93: 252-254) is among the better productions.

Viktor Fuks' epic efforts have paid off with his capture of the Waipi Indians of northern Brazil on film (91: 1091-1092). These important films are a bit rough and could use some editing, but they are particularly useful for specialists. Another filmmaker of note specializing in Latin America is Hubert Smith of the "Yucatan Maya Film Project" who has been systematically documenting aspects of peasant life among modern Maya peoples for the past 15 or so years. His "Living Maya" series (85: 233-235) had some success on television in the early 1980s and remains a valuable pedagogical tool.

Any discussion of film in South America would be incomplete without mention of Jorge Preloran, the doyen of ethnographic cinema in Latin America. Most of his films chronicle the cultures of his native Argentina, but he has also shot in Venezuela and Ecuador and even in North America (LUTHER METKE AT 94). His particular interest is in the native peoples of his own country as represented in ARAUCANIANS OF RUCA CHOROY (75: 594), CHUCALEZNA, and ZERDA'S CHILDREN, but his best known production is the splendid IMAGINERO (73: 1473-1475), a cinematic portrait of a colorful folk artist from the northern part of Argentina. Also of interest is his film, THE WARAO on an Indian group in Venezuela.

Mention should also be made of John Cohen who has produced half a dozen or so exquisite films on various cultures of Latin America, mostly highland Peru. His titles include PERUVIAN WEAVING: A CONTINUOUS WARP FOR 5000 YEARS (87: 488-489); MOUNTAIN MUSIC OF PERU (88: 267); CHOQUELA: ONLY INTERPRETATION (90: 487); and CARNIVAL IN Q'EROS: WHERE THE MOUNTAINS MEET THE JUNGLE (94: 522-523).

Robert Gardner has only one film from Latin America, IKA HANDS (92: 1105-1106), which deals with craftsmen from a tribal group in Columbia, although he collaborated on the English version of Preloran's IMAGINERO. Many other titles from Latin America deserve mention here and they include I SPENT MY LIFE IN THE MINES (87: 484-485); GUAMBIANOS (87: 963-964); ALPACA BREEDERS OF CHIMBOYA (87: 963-964); TODOS SANCHOS CUCHUMATAN: REPORT FROM

A GUATEMALAN VILLAGE (87: 229-230); TEPOZTLAN (73: 982-983); TEPOZTLAN IN TRANSITION (73: 982-983); THE TREE OF KINSHIP (86: 235); THE MAGIC WINDOWS (86: 796); THE LACANDON MAYA BALCHE RITUAL (91: 831); CAYAGUA (92: 842-843); ICEMAN OF CHIMBORAZO (92: 1105-1106); OUR GOD THE CONDOR (92: 1105-1106); MARTIN CHAMBI AND THE HEIRS OF THE INCAS (92: 1105-1106); TODOS SANTOS: THE SURVIVORS (94: 528-530); and LA OFRENDA: DAY OF THE DEAD (93: 772-773). There are also a number of good productions which examine aspects of folk Catholicism and religious syncretism: VISIONS OF JUAZEIRO (91: 832-834); CHICHICASTENAGO (91: 832-834); GOMALAPA: TRADITIONS AND TEXTURES (91: 832-834); HOLY WEEK IN ANTIGUA GUATEMALA (91: 832-834); SACRED GAMES: RITUAL WARFARE IN A MAYA VILLAGE (91: 832-834); PERUS - WHEN THE WORLD TURNED DARK (91: 832-834); MAYA FIESTA (93: 255-256); and APPEALS TO SANTIAGO (70: 1050-1051). Also worthy of mention here are three films from Brazil: MACUMBA, TRANCE AND SPRIT HEALING (90: 229-230); HAIL UMBANDA (91: 529-530); and BAHAI: AFRICA IN THE AMERICAS (91: 530-531).

Religion has also been a major focus of films on the Caribbean for which most of our noteworthy films are on Haiti. One exception to both these trends is LAST OF THE KARAPHUNA (87: 987-988), a useful film on cultural extinction. Filmmaker Karen Kramer has many good films on this region as well as some on displaced Caribbeans. Her titles include HAITIAN SONG (84: 978-979); TO SERVE THE GODS (84: 976-978); LEGACY OF THE SPIRITS (89: 257-258); and SONG FOR THE PEOPLE OF HAITI (84: 979-980). Other notable films on the area include DIVINE HORSEMEN; THE LIVING GODS OF HAITI (84: 979-980); DIVINE MADNESS: TRANCE, DANCE AND HEALING IN GUYANA (87: 480-481); CARNIVAL T. N.

T. (87: 979-980); VOODOO AND THE CHURCH IN HAITI (93: 261-262); and THE SPIRIT OF KUNA YALA (94: 260-261).

In recent years there have been a large number of films released which focus on the various conflicts that have plagued Latin America and its peoples. Among the more noteworthy are: THE RAGGED REVOLUTION (86: 238-239); LOS HIJOS SANDINO (86: 237-238); FROM THE ASHES: NICARAGUA TODAY (86: 237-238); WOMEN IN ARMS (86: 793-796); THANK GOD AND THE REVOLUTION (86: 793-796); SANDINO, TODAY AND FOREVER (86: 793-796); WHEN THE MOUNTAINS TREMBLE (87: 992-994); EL NORTE (87: 992-994); GRENADA: PORTRAIT OF A REVOLUTION (88: 263-264); GRENADA: THE FUTURE COMING TOWARDS US (88: 263-264); GRENADA: THE LAND OF SPICE (88: 263-264); and OF LIVES UPROOTED (93: 256-257). Finally, there are numerous good films that examine the ecology of Latin America and yet have enough cultural content to be labelled ethnographic. Some of the best are A DECADE OF DESTRUCTION (87: 735-739); RAONI (90: 487-489) RECLAIMING THE RAIN FOREST (90: 487-489); RUNA: GUARDIAN OF THE RAIN FOREST (93: 1035-1036); and BLACK WATER (94: 253).

Europe

To date there are no good written guides to anthropological film on European subjects, but the Society for the Anthropology of Europe has compiled one which is scheduled for publication in early 1994. There is also an article surveying the state of ethnographic film on Europe due to appear in a forthcoming issue of the French journal, MERIALES (Allen). Like the written ethnography of Europe, ethnographic film on the region has been marginalized and minimalized until quite recently. Although some of the best known names in film have produced true classics on European peoples, their subjects, for the most part, have been marginal peoples. These classics include LAND WITHOUT BREAD (TERRE SANS PAIN) by Luis Buñuel; AN OF ARAN (79: 749-751) by Robert Flaherty ; FARREBIQUE (80: 200) by Georges Rouquier; and Jean Rouch's CHRONICLE OF A SUMMER (80: 1020-1022). Given the pedigrees of these films, it can hardly be argued that ethnographic film in Europe has been impoverished, but it has been marginalized. In fact, most anthropological film shot in Europe has focussed on such peripheral peoples.

Some countries are better represented than others. For example, there are a number of good titles on Spain thanks in large part to the efforts of Jerome Mintz who has produced several good films on people in the province of Cadiz in the southern part of the country. His titles include: THE SHOE-MAKER (82: 226-227); PEPE'S FAMILY (82: 226-227); ROMERIA: DAY OF THE VIRGIN (90: 781-782); CARNAVAL DE PUEBLO (TOWN CARNIVAL) (90: 781-782); THE SHEPHERD'S FAMILY; and PERICO THE BOWLMAKER. An older and rather simple film is VILLAGE OF SPAIN (77: 710) which documents life in preindustrial rural Spain. EL PUEBLO (88: 524-525) is more impressionistic, but also good on traditional rural life.

There are also a number of good titles from Greece among which is KYPSELI: WOMEN AND MEN APART - A DIVIDED REALITY (79: 194), a film that has had a mixed reception but is still immensely popular. Several films examine exotic rituals and/or activities: ANASTENARIA (74: 1581-1584); KALOGEROS (74: 1581-1584); and AEGEAN SPONGE DIVERS (74: 1581-1584), just to name a few. More recently French anthropologist/filmmaker Colette Piault has produced a series of excellent films on the people of a single mountain village in the northern province of Epirus. Titles include: EVERY DAY IS NOT A FEAST DAY (84: 754-756); THE THREAD OF THE NEEDLE (86: 510-511); MY FAMILY AND ME (90: 491-492);

THE CHARCOAL MAKERS   (94: 523-524); LETS'S GET MARRIED ; and "A HARD LIFE..."
    Although there are many films on France available in France, few have English soundtracks/subtitles and thus do not circulate in this country. Among the few that do are BIQUEFARRE   (89: 1013-1014), Rouquier's sequel to FARREBIQUE; THE BASQUES OF SANTAZI (90: 1045-1046); and A FRENCH VILLAGE. Italy is likewise poorly represented in the English language, but we do have the excellent THE HOUSE THAT GIACOMO BUILT (86: 1063) which has the advantage of an accompanying text (Pitkin: 1985). There is also the fictional film, BANDITS OF ORGOSOLO (74: 1574-1575), a true classic on sheep rustling in the bleak mountain highlands of Sardinia.
    East and Central Europe have produced many good films on the peoples of this region, but few have been distributed in the United States. The same is true for Scandinavia which is virtually entirely unrepresented except for a few films on the Lapps like SAMI HERDERS (88: 783-784). For most other European countries it is the same. A brand new film on an unusual political procedure in Switzerland, MEN IN THE RING is perhaps the only anthropological film on that country available in the United States.
    Ireland has been the subject of several good films in addition to MAN OF ARAN, notably THE VILLAGE (74: 1577-1581); A CONNEMARA FAMILY (88: 518-519); and THE MCPEAKE FAMILY OF IRELAND. The rest of the British Isles have largely been ignored by ethnographic filmmakers although there is the very fine film, THE SHEPHERDS OF BERNERAY (85: 225-226) on a family of Scottish island pastoralists.

The Middle East and North Africa

For the Middle East and North Africa there are several sources, principal among which is THE MIDDLE EAST AND NORTH AFRICA ON FILM: AN ANNOTATED FILMOGRAPHY (1982) (86: 227) by Marsha Hamilton Mc Clintock, a massive and comprehensive listing. It is about 10 years out of date, but it is well organized and full of valuable information. Ellen-Fairbanks Bodman's THE WORLD OF IS-LAM IMAGES AND ECHOES: A CRITICAL GUIDE TO FILMS AND RECORDINGS (1980) (84: 974-975) is also good, but far more limited, and it also contains listings of films outside the Middle East. A BIBLIOGRAPHY OF DOCUMENTARY AND EDUCATIONAL FILMS ON SUDAN (1982) (88: 516) by Osman Hassan Ahmed is useful for educators and scholars interested in the Arab/Islamic population of this country. Among distributors who specialize in the Middle East are the Middle East Institute Film Library which as a small but excellent and diverse collection and the University of Texas at Austin whose film library publishes a separate listing for its modest holdings in the Middle East. First Run/Icarus has a good inventory of titles, not all of which are listed regularly in their promotional material and Landmark Films, distributes several major series on the area along with a number of individual titles.

Merion Cooper; and Ernest B. Schoedsack;'s GRASS (82: 229-230) is one of the real classics from this part of the world. It documents the dramatic annual migration of the Bakhtiari herdsmen and their flocks over the steep Zagros Mountains of Iran. It is far more appealing than a subsequent film on the same subject, BAKHTIARI MIGRATION (82: 229-230), although the latter contains more ethnographic information. SHAHSAVAN NOMADS (89: 783-784) also deals with pastoral nomads in Iran, but their migrations are far less dramatic than those of the Bakhtiari; nonetheless, it is a good film.

There are many good series on the Middle East including "The Arabs: A Living History" (10 titles from Landmark Films); " In the Footsteps of Abraham" (13 titles from Landmark Films); " Jerusalem of Heaven and Earth" (8 titles from Landmark Films); " Understanding the Middle East" (5 titles from PBS Video); " The Middle East and North Africa" (5 titles from Films Incorporated); " The Middle East" (14 titles from Encyclopedia Britannica Films); " The Middle East Series" (4 titles from Coronet Films); "Cities of Islam" (5 titles from Films for the Humanities and Sciences); "The World of Islam" (6 titles from Films for the Humanities and Sciences); "Testament" (7 titles from Films for the Humanities and Sciences); "Ancient Lives" (8 titles from Films for the Humanities and Sciences); and "The Traditional World of Islam" (5 titles from the Middle East Institute Film Library). However, there is no one filmmaker who has produced a significant corpus of films on any part of the area with the exception of Peter Loizos who has made several films on Greek Cypriots, two of which are available in the United States: LIFE CHANCES: FOUR FAMILIES IN A CHANGING CYPRIOT VILLAGE (78: 955-956) and SOPHIA'S PEOPLE — EVENTFUL LIVES (90: 782).

RAMPARTS OF CLAY is a fine low key semi-fictional epic on village life in Tunisia (filmed in Algeria) and there are any number of reasonably good films on the Bedouin and other "tribal" peoples of the region, especially those of North Africa. BERBER VILLAGES OF SOUTHERN TUNISIA: A STUDY IN ENVIRONMENT (80: 208); A DAY AMONG THE BERBERS (80: 208); DESERT NOMADS (80: 208-209); KABYLIA (80: 209); MOULAY IDRISS (80: 209); NEW WAYS FOR OLD MOROCCO (80: 209-210); SUITE OF BERBER DANCES (80: 210); and THE BERBERS OF NORTH AFRICA: A BACKWARD CIVILIZATION (despite its title) are all fine older productions in black and white. Also good is THE TUAREGS (85: 496), not to be confused with the "Disappearing World" series film, THE TUAREGS (75: 212) which is also worthwhile. Another older title, THE NOMADS OF BADAKHSHAN deserves mention although it is about a group in Afghanistan, and thus not technically in this area.

One truly exceptional film is Melissa Llewelyn-Davies' and Elizabeth Fernea's SOME WOMEN OF MARAKESH (87: 237-238), an extraordinary production about women and sex roles in Morocco which was originally made for Grenada Television in England and later featured in the "Odyssey" series. A SENSE OF HONOR (89: 782-783) is a more recent film on sex roles which has merit. There are a large number of films focusing on the Israeli-Arab situation that have appeared in recent years, some of which are better than others. Not all are ethnographic, by any means, but they have often proved of use to anthropologists teaching about this conflict. Some of the better ones are: GAZA GHETTO: PORTRAIT OF A PALESTINIAN FAMILY (89: 1018-1022); THE PALESTINIAN PEOPLE DO HAVE RIGHTS (89: 1018-1022); ISRAEL AND THE PALESTINIANS: THE CONTINUING CONFLICT (89: 1018-1022); THE HUNDRED YEARS' WAR: PERSONAL NOTES (89: 1018-1022); ON OUR OWN LAND (89: 1018-1022); TALKING TO THE ENEMY: VOICES OF SORROW AND RAGE (92: 843-844); SHOOT AND CRY (92: 743-744); DAUGHTERS OF ABRAHAM: A FIGHT TO SURVIVE? (92: 743-744); VOICES FROM GAZA: CHILDREN OF FIRE (93: 1040-1042); A WIFE FROM MY ENEMIES; RAB ISRAELI DIALOGUE; HRINE UNDER SEIGE; THE KEY; .PALESTINIAN REFUGEES IN LEBANON; .WAR GENERATION: BEIRUT; .ABRAHAM AND ISAAC; .SHELTERED DREAMS; and JERUSALEM: PROPHETS AND PARATROOPERS.

Finally, some mention should be made of the two fine productions on Egyptian rituals by Fadwa El Guindi. EL SEBOU': EGYPTIAN BIRTH RITUAL (90: 242-243) and EL MOULID: EGYPTIAN RELIGIOUS FESTIVAL.

Africa

Hundreds of titles are contained in AFRICA ON FILM AND VIDEOTAPE 1960-1981: A COMPENDIUM OF REVIEWS (1982) (85: 489) compiled by David S. Wiley. It is the sort of guide needed for every major world area, but like so many other such resources listed here, it is a decade out of date, although more current than two other important sources: Warren D. Stevens ' AFRICAN FILM BIBLIOGRAPHY (n.d.) and the UNESCO publication, PREMIER CATALOGUE SELECTIF INTERNATIONAL DE FILMS ETHNO-GRAPHIQUES SUR L'AFRIQUE NOIRE (1967).

Africa is well represented in the "Disappearing World" series, especially East Africa. Among the classics for sub-Saharan Africa are the many films of Jean Rouch from West Africa: Ghana, Mali, Niger, Ivory Coast, and Upper Volta. Unfortunately, fewer than half a dozen of the more than 100 films he has made are available in the United States although they include three of his most impressive pieces: LES MAITRES FOUS (73: 1471); THE LION HUNTERS (74: 1567-1568); and JAGUAR (76: 697-698). Another outstanding film on West Africa is THE COWS OF DOLO KEM PAYE (73: 983-984) which looks at dispute management and other issues in tribal Liberia. Robert Gardner's DEEP HEARTS (82: 224-225) is a somewhat neglected film on the Bororo Fulani of Nigeria that deserves more attention than it usually gets. From Mali there is SOGOW BAMBARA MASKS (86: 1066), a rather specialized piece and THE WAYS OF NYA ARE MANY (86: 1064-1065) where aspects of ritual and symbolism are explored. Sabina Jell-Bahlsen has two films on peoples of Nigeria, EZE NWATA: THE SMALL KING (86: 801-802) and MAMMY WATER: IN SEARCH OF THE WATER SPIRITS IN NIGERIA (93: 254-255), both of which have been well received by Africanists. Other notable titles dealing with West Africa include BONO MEDICINE (86: 802-803); SONS OF THE MOON (88: 527-528); LIVING AFRICA: A

VILLAGE EXPERIENCE (88: 779-780); and VILLAGE THE-
ATRE - SENEGAL: QUEEN NDATE AND THE FRENCH
CONQUEST (88: 779-780).

For East Africa there is THE NUER (74: 1028), a true classic
on the Ethiopian cattle herders made famous by Evans-
Pritchard. Robert Gardner's RIVERS OF SAND (79: 197; 80:
945-946) on the Hama of southwest Ethiopia, although controversial and possibly flawed, is still a valuable film. The Mursi,
Nilotic cattle herders in southwest Ethiopia, are the subject of
Philip Singer's trilogy, "In Search of Cool Ground" series. Titles
include THE MURSI (89: 780-781), THE KWEGU (86: 512-513,
89: 780-781), and THE MIGRANTS (89: 780-781). An important
corpus of work on East Africa is represented by the work of
David and Judith MacDougall on the Turkana and Boran of
Kenya and the Jie of Uganda. In particular, their trilogy,
"Turkana Conversations" which includes LORANG'S WAY
(86: 803-806), THE WEDDING CAMELS (86:803-806), and A
WIFE AMONG WIVES (86: 803-806), is noteworthy as are
David MacDougall's four films on the nomadic Boran herds-
men of Kenya for the "Faces of Change" series (79: 753-754) and
three films on the Jie: TO LIVE WITH HERDS (75: 597-598),
UNDER THE MEN'S TREE, and NAWI. Taken together these
films represent important ethnographic statements about these
tribal peoples. Chris Curling and Melissa Llewelyn-Davies
have also made some important films on East Africa including
MASAI MANHOOD (78: 958); MASAI WOMEN (78: 958); and
DIARY OF A MAASAI VILLAGE (88: 1037-1040), five hours of
Maasai ethnography. On her own, Llewelyn-Davies is responsible for THE WOMEN'S OLAMAL: THE
ORGANISATION OF A MAASAI FERTILITY CEREMONY
(88: 1037-1040) and THE SOUTH EAST NUDA (88: 528-529) for
which NUBA WRESTLING (94: 1028-1029) is a good companion piece. Finally, an older but still good production on foraging
peoples of Tanzania is THE HADZA (74: 1024-1025).

Central Africa is the part of the continent least well represented in ethnographic film. However, special note should be made of a minor classic from Zambia, LIEBALALA (77: 701-703), a film shot by Margaret Carson Hubbard in 1935. Although it is an acted film, it nevertheless accurately depicts marriage rituals of the Lozi people. It was re-released in 1975 and remains important. Two other titles of importance from Central Africa are CHILDREN OF THE FOREST (88: 743-744) on the Mbuti and SPIRITS OF DEFIANCE: THE MAGETU PEOPLE OF ZAIRE (93: 520-521).

The non-white populations of South Africa have been well documented in ethnographic film, particularly so the !Kung (San) Bushmen of the Kalahari Desert in Namibia (Southwest Africa) thanks to the work of John Marshall. His THE HUNTERS (82: 228-229) is still the definitive film on hunting and gathering and a true classic of the ethnographic genre. It chronicles a giraffe hunt by a small group of !Kung living in the heart of the Kalahari. Marshall has also produced more than two dozen additional titles on the !Kung, some of which document aspects of traditional hunter and gatherer life while others focus on the changes affecting the world of these fragile peoples. Notable among the latter are AN ARGUMENT ABOUT A MARRIAGE (76: 689-691) and N!AI: THE STORY OF A !KUNG WOMAN (88: 527). All of Marshall's films are a valuable antidote to the dangerous silliness of THE GODS MUST BE CRAZY (87: 582-584) and its equally fatuous sequel. NGOMA THERAPY IN AN URBAN SOUTH AFRICAN SETTING (90: 489-490) is a good film on urban South Africans, but of the many films on the plight of the non-white population in South Africa, THE LAST GRAVE AT DIMBAZA is still the best and most compelling. Finally, mention should be made of Gai Zantzinger's excellent little film, SONGS OF THE ADVENTURERS (90: 1048-1049), an upbeat film about non-whites in South Africa and a nice companion to his earlier work on Cape Verdeans, SONGS OF THE BADEUS (90: 242).

Although a number of the above mentioned films examine sex roles in Africa, they are likely to do so as part of a broader agenda. The following films have as their main focus aspects of women's statuses and roles: FROM SUNUP (92: 271-272), THE RIBBON (92: 557-558), WITH THESE HANDS (92: 557-558), and THE STRUGGLING PEOPLE (92: 557-558).

India and South Asia

There are, to my knowledge, no comprehensive guides to films on India or South Asia despite the fact that there are dozens if not hundreds of ethnographic films on the region. There is a fine collection of films at the South Asia Area Studies Distribution Office of the University of Wisconsin at Madison and Asia House in New York City also has a film library, but there are no good guides. One classic film from this area is SONG OF CEYLON, a beautiful epic on the Buddhist culture of Sri Lanka filmed in 1934. A standard for more mundane aspects of life on the subcontinent is NORTH INDIAN VILLAGE, a straight-forward exposition on village life and the operation of the caste system in rural India.

Tribal life in India is the subject of RAJ GONDS (88: 271-273) and THE MURIA (88: 271-273) from the BBC "Worlds Apart" series . Three films by John and Pat Hitchcock also deal with tribal peoples although they are set in Nepal: HIMALAYAN SHAMAN OF NORTHERN NEPAL, HIMALAYAN SHA-MAN OF SOUTHERN NEPAL, and GHURKA COUNTRY. These can usefully be used with SHAMANS OF THE BLIND COUNTRY (90: 1049-1050). Tibet has also been the focus of many films, most of which deal with religion. Among these are THE FRAGILE MOUNTAIN (86: 1072-1073); TIBETAN BUD-DHISM: PRESERVING THE MONASTIC TRADITION (86: 1073-1075); TIBETAN BUDDHISM: CYCLES OF INTERDE-PENDENCE (86: 1073-1075); SHERPA (89: 264-265);   THE

LION'S ROAR (89: 264-265); BETWEEN TIME: A TIBETAN VILLAGE IN NEPAL (88: 517-518); and LORD OF THE DANCE, DESTROYER OF ILLUSION (90: 782-784). A religious ritual is also the subject of Barry Machin's IRAMUNDUN (90: 493-494) from Sri Lanka. Other films from outside of India proper include AMRA DEIJON (TOGETHER) (89: 520) on marriage in Bangladesh and two pieces on Afghanistan: THE LOST TRIBES (88: 780-781) and AFGHAN EXODUS (88: 780-781). Five other films on Afghanistan (79: 755-756) comprise a part of the "Faces of Change" series and are well worth viewing. There are several good films on family life and sex roles in India. DADI'S FAMILY (85: 228-229) from the "Odyssey" series is excellent in just about every way. KHETURNI BAYA (86: 240-241) is another good film on family life and A ZENNANA: SCENES AND REFLECTIONS (86: 807-809) by Australian filmmaker Roger Sandall and his Indian colleague, Jayasinhji Jhala, is an interesting piece on sex roles. More recently, Sandall and Jhala teamed up to produce THE BHARVAD PREDICAMENT.

The spirituality of India and its inhabitants has long captivated the imagination of Westerners and anthropological filmmakers are no exception. An extraordinary proportion of films on India and its subcontinent neighbors focus on religion and / or other aspects of spiritual life. In recent years Robert Gardner and a couple of associates, Ákos Östör and Allan Moore tackled India and produced a trilogy of films, "Pleasing God" which includes LOVING KRISHNA (89: 259-262), SERPENT MOTHER (89: 259-262), and SONS OF SHIVA (89: 259-262), along with FOREST OF BLISS (91: 273-274), all of which examine aspects of Indian religion. FOREST OF BLISS is a very complex and somewhat controversial film which aims to evoke a reaction rather than explain things. Gardner had already worked in India ten years earlier, producing ALTAR OF FIRE (80: 197-199), a film on a rare Vedic ritual, but it never received the attention it deserved. Other films on religion in India include: MANIFESTATIONS OF SHIVA (84: 988-989) and THE

WAGES OF ACTION: RELIGION IN A HINDU VILLAGE (86: 807-809). There are also two interesting films by Philip Singer, HINDU LOAVES AND FISHES (88: 1042-1043) and "PSYCHIC SURGERY": A CASE HISTORY OF SHAMANISTIC SLEIGHT OF HAND (92: 847-848), both of which deal with shamanism.

Several filmmakers have produced a number of films on India, often focusing on different aspects. Ron Hess has many credits to his name of which some of the best are: MUNNI ("LITTLE GIRL"): CHILDHOOD AND ART IN MITHLA (86: 807-809); COURTS AND COUNCILS (86: 1071-1072); GIVEN TO DANCE (88: 1040-1042); and INDIA'S ODDISI TEMPLE. And before she abandoned the documentary genre for feature films, Mira Nair also made some excellent non-fiction films on India among which are SO FAR FROM INDIA (86: 807-809) and INDIA CABARET (90: 493).

India's cities have also attracted the attention of filmmakers and there are many good productions. Louis Malle's CALCUTTA (73: 503) is a true classic, but also of value are AHMEDABAD: LIFE IN A CITY IN INDIA and BENARES: STEPS TO HEAVEN. Finally, there are a number of good productions that defy easy classification, but should be of use to anthropologists with specialized interests: MAHARESHI MAHESH (76: 707); TRAGATA BHAVRI: A RURAL THEATRE TROUPE OF GUJARAT (87: 532-533); FREAK STREET TO GOA: IMMIGRANTS ON THE RAJPATH (91: 273); AHIMSA, NON-VIOLENCE (91: 1094-1095); and PHOTO WALLAHS (94: 1029-1030).

Southeast Asia

There is no single guide to films on Southeast Asia, but Toby Volkman's FILM ON INDONESIA 1985) (88: 1036) is an excellent resource for Indonesia and especially Bali. It is only a few years out of date and has informative annotations. Overall the cultures of Southeast Asia are reasonably well represented in anthropological film. Two minor classics are NOMADS OF THE JUNGLE , an older film on Malayan foragers , and LAND DAYAKS OF BORNEO (69: 127) which focuses on a river village of tribal horticulturalists.

Bali is particularly well represented with the majority of productions focusing on music, dance, and trance, the three (often related) features of Balinese culture that have captured the imagination and interest of the West. Bali has long attracted anthropological filmmakers, beginning with Margaret Mead and Gregory Bateson whose TRANCE AND DANCE IN BALI (78: 725-726) is still the standard by which other such films are measured. It retains its vitality and drama more than a half century after it was shot, which is not necessarily true of Mead and Bateson's other films on Bali. Many good films have been made about Bali since including THE THREE WORLDS OF BALI (85: 750); LEARNING TO DANCE IN BALI (85: 267); KETUT DE BALI (85: 227-228); LEMPAD OF BALI (89: 532); LIGHT OF MANY MASKS (87: 740-741); THE ELEVEN POWERS (85: 1012-1013); and BALI BEYOND THE POST-CARD, just to name a few. Special mention should be made of the excellent films on Bali by Tim Asch, Patsy Asch and Linda Connor: A BALINESE TRANCE SEANCE (86: 809-811); JERO ON JERO: A BALINESE TRANCE OBSERVED(86: 809-811); and JERO TAPAKAN: STORIES IN THE LIFE OF A BALINESE HEALER (86: 809-811), all of which are further informed by JERO TAPAKAN: BALINESE HEALER: AN ETHNO-GRAPHIC FILM MONOGRAPH (Connor, Asch, and Asch 1986).

Timothy Asch teamed up with James Fox to shoot two fine films on Roti, a small island in eastern Indonesia: THE WATER OF WORDS: A CULTURAL ECOLOGY OF A SMALL IS-LAND IN EASTERN INDONESIA (89: 260-261) and THE SPEAR AND THE SWORD (93: 775-776). Other notable films

on Indonesia include SANCTUARY OF THE EARTH GOD-
DESS (90:244-245); JOURNEY OF THE LAND OF THE EARTH
GODDESS (90: 244-245); and TOBELA MARRIAGE 94: 261-
262). Finally, mention should be made of THE BAJAO: SEA-
GOING NOMADS OF THE PHILIPPINES (89: 254-255), a fine
production on a tribal peoples of the Philippines.

The Hmong (also known as the Meo or Miao) of Cambodia
(Kampuchea) are well represented by the high quality productions, THE MEO and MIAO YEAR (71:800). These highlanders
are not only colorful, but of considerable ethnographic interest
as well. Large numbers have settled in the United states where
they have been the subject of numerous ethnographic films:
NO MORE MOUNTAINS: STORY OF THE HMONG (86: 513-
514); BECOMING AMERICAN (86:514-515); THE BEST PLACE
TO LIVE (86:515); FAREWELL TO FREEDOM (86:515); GREAT
BRANCHES, THE NEW ROOTS: THE HMONG FAMILY (86:
515-516); and PEACE HAS NOT BEEN MADE: A CASE
HISTORY OF A HMONG FAMILY'S ENCOUNTER WITH A
HOSPITAL (88: 776-778).

The Far East

Before 1975 most ethnographic films on China were shot in
Taiwan or Hong Kong and there are few distinguished films
from this period. As China opened up, so did opportunities for
shooting film there and as a result we have a whole set of films
on China from the 1970s and 1980s, some of which are truly
outstanding. One of the first films to come from mainland
China was THE BAREFOOT DOCTORS OF RURAL CHINA,
an interesting film about medicine in rural areas. Among the
most notable films on China are those of Carma Hinton and
Richard Gordon (and other collaborators). All their productions were shot in "Long Bow" a village well known to Hinton,
the daughter of sinologist William Hinton. Taken together

these half dozen films present a good cross section of village activities and attitudes in post-Mao rural China. SMALL HAPPINESS: WOMEN OF A CHINESE VILLAGE (87: 739-741) is the most dramatic and compelling with its emphasis on changing sex roles and abuses of the past. Other titles include STILT DANCERS OF LONG BOW (86: 576-577); ALL UNDER HEAVEN 89: 253-254); GENERATIONS (89: 255-256); TO TASTE ONE HUNDRED HERBS: GODS, ANCESTORS AND MEDICINE IN A CHINESE VILLAGE (90: 1050); and FIRST MOON: CELEBRATION OF A CHINESE NEW YEAR (90: 1050).

Another excellent film on life in a Chinese communal village is WUXING PEOPLES' COMMUNE (87: 739-741), a 1978 production which documents rural life in China before the impact of the opening to the West. ZENGBOU AFTER MAO (92: 272073) is a first rate ethnographic film on life in a prosperous village in China's "capitalist" zone and makes a nice companion to WUXING PEOPLES' COMMUNE. GUI DAO - ON THE WAY: A STATION ON THE YANGZI (87: 739-741) is another useful film as are WOMEN IN CHINA and WOMEN IN CHINA TODAY (87: 739-741) although the latter is not available in the United States. BUDDHISM IN CHINA (86: 1074) is one of the few films that treats religion in China and is valuable for that reason alone.

There are several good films on China in the "Disappearing World" series including two on tribal groups, two on the Chinese Revolution, and two on Mongolians. Of less general use are the two series, "A Taste of China" (88: 1049-1050) with four titles and "Cities of China" (85: 491-492) which considers Xian, Suzhou and Beijing.

Good ethnographic films are made in Japan but they rarely come to this country. Two older black and white films are VILLAGE POTTERS OF ONDA and the classic, JYOMONDE: THE AINU BEAR FESTIVAL. Although THE PATH (77: 463-466) was shot in a tea house in California, it documents a highly authentic Japanese tea ceremony and is about Japanese culture, not American or Japanese-American culture. More recently we have the excellent JAPANESE FIGHTING FESTIVAL (88: 778-779), a colorful documentary of a religious festival involving intracommunal competition.

Oceania

Two guides to films on Oceania are available for consultation by anyone using films on cultures from the area: PREMIER CATALOGU SELECTIF INTERNATIONAL DE FILMS ETHNOGRAPHIQUES SUR LA REGION DU PACIFIQUE (UNESCO, 1970) and A GUIDE TO FILMS ABOUT THE PACIFIC ISLANDS (1986) (89: 1012-1013). They are useful particularly for older productions.

For some reason, the majority of good anthropological films from Oceania are on the peoples and cultures of New Guinea. Other parts of the region have received attention, but, with the exception of Australia, surprisingly little. Sam Low's THE NAVIGATORS (86: 518-519) is a fine film on seafaring in Polynesia , but there are few other films of real quality on Polynesia and equally few on Micronesia, MOKIL (76: 715-717) and ULITHI being two notable exceptions.

Except for the execrable commercial film, THE SKY ABOVE AND THE MUD BELOW, New Guinea was practically virgin territory when Robert Gardner shot DEAD BIRDS (67: 1358-1359) in the early 1960s, a film that caused quite a sensation among anthropologists and film buffs alike when it was released in 1963. It has become somewhat more controversial of late as critics subject it to more scrutiny, often unfairly considering that it dates from a time when the genre of ethnographic film was still in its infancy. However, it endures and is widely regarded as one of the most significant anthropological films of all time. Moreover, it contains the best and most extensive film coverage of pre-pacification native warfare from the New Guinea highlands. Margaret Mead and Gregory Bateson shot some of the earliest ethnographic film footage in New Guinea as part of their "Character Formation in Different Cultures" series (78: 725-726). These films focus on child rearing practices among peoples of the Sepik River area and many will find them useful still.

Ian Dunlop's and Maurice Godelier's epic TOWARDS BARUYA MANHOOD (77: 706-709) has more value for specialists than educators, but portions still find their way into classrooms on occasion. More useful for the Baruya are the films of the Jablonkos: TO FIND BARUYA'S STORY: MAURICE GODELIER'S WORK WITH A NEW GUINEA TRIBE (85: 751-753) and HER NAME CAME ON ARROWS: A KINSHIP INTERVIEW WITH THE BARUYA OF PAPUA NEW GUINEA (85: 751-753). These shed additional light on the culture of the highland Baruya. New Guinea is also the province of the outstanding films of Chris Owen among which are numbered GOGODALA (A CULTURAL REVIVAL?) (84: 989-990); MALAGAN LAMBADAMAN (A TRIBUTE TO BUK BUK) (85: 223-2224); TIGHTEN THE DRUMS (SELF DECORATION AMONG THE ENGA) (85: 224-225); THE RED BOWMEN (85: 498-499); and A MAN WITHOUT PIGS (94: 256-257). Dennis O'Rourke's YUMI YET: INDEPENDENCE FOR PAPUA NEW GUINEA and SHARKCALLERS OF KONTU also deserve mention here as does NEMEKAS: MUSIC IN LAKE CHAMBI . For specialists, Karl Heider's four films on the highland new Guinea Dani peoples should also be considered: DANI HOUSES; DANI RECESS; DANI SWEET POTATOES; and DANI TECHNOLOGY .

In 1985 two Australian filmmakers, Bob Connolly and Robin Anderson stunned the anthropological world with FIRST CONTACT (86: 1076-1077), a riveting film incorporating footage from an early expedition into the unexplored highlands of New Guinea. Here, perhaps for the first time, is recorded on film the actual encounter of individuals from an industrialized Western society and tribal horticultural peoples who had never before been contacted. It is now widely used in courses on culture change, Oceania, modernization and development, race and racism, and applied anthropology, just to name a few. It has been succeeded by two films which follow up on the fortunes of one of the offspring of the expedition leader and a native woman: JOE LEAHY'S NEIGHBORS (92: 846-847) and BLACK HARVEST (94: 1026-1027), both of which have been enthusiastically received by the anthropological community though neither is as compelling as FIRST CONTACT. The success of FIRST CONTACT is probably responsible for a number of other films that examine the contact situation in New Guinea including MY FATHER, MY COUNTRY and SENSO DAUGHTER. ANGELS OF WAR (86: 517-518) released shortly before FIRST CONTACT, examines the contact situation during World War II and uses some dramatic archival footage. The recent production, CANNIBAL TOURS (91: 274-275), follows a group of European tourists on their highly programmed visit to New Guinea showing how the natives and their culture have been commodified for the benefit of these fatuous and insensitive tourists who have no understanding of nor any true interest in the real lives of the people they are seeing.

TROBRIAND CRICKET (79: 506) is an exquisite film on how the islanders made famous by Malinowski adapted and transformed the English game of cricket according to their own cultural strictures. TROBRIAND ISLANDER is a fine accompaniment as well as a good general introduction to these people who have figured so prominently in the history of anthropology. KAMA WOSI: MUSIC IN THE TROBRIAND ISLANDS (88: 521-522) is also a nice complement to these films as is a companion piece, NAMEKAS: MUSIC IN LAKE CHAMBRI (88: 521-522).

In the past most films on Australian Aborigines documented aspects of their traditional hunting and gathering
lifestyle. Such films are epitomized by Ian Dunlop's "People of
the Australian Western Desert" series (70: 437-438) and subsequent films by the prolific Dunlop and Kim McKenzie along
with others for the Australian Institute of Aboriginal Studies
whose titles are distributed in the United states by the University
of California Extension Center for Media and Independent
Learning. A good listing of older titles can be found in FILMS
FOR ANTHROPOLOGICAL TEACHING. Particularly notable is Dunlop's MADARRPA FUNERAL AT BURKA' WAY
which is a visual accompaniment to Howard Morphy's book,
JOURNEY TO THE CROCODILE'S NEST (1984). Roger Sandall
has also made a number of good films for the Institute which
focus on traditional Aboriginal lifestyles. They include CAMELS
AND THE APITJANTJARA (73: 477-478); CONISTON MUS-
TER; AKING A BARK CANOE; .PINTUBI REVISIT YARU
YARU; INTUBI REVISIT YUMARI; ALBIRI RITUAL AT
GUNADJARI (72: 202-203); EMU RITUAL AT RUGURI (62:
1201-1202); WALBIRI RITUAL AT NGAMA (72: 1202); and
WALBIRI FIRE CEREMONY: NGATJAKULA .
    Lately, films on natives of Australia have shifted from a
focus on traditional cultures to a consideration of their current
situation. Most paint a rather negative picture of their lives
today as they try to fit into a new kind of society while trying
at the same time to retain something of their former culture.
WAITING FOR HARRY (86: 813-814) is a good example as are
the myriad films of David MacDougall and colleagues on this
subject: FAMILIAR PLACES; .GOODBYE OLD MAN; .THREE
HORSEMEN ; STOCKMAN'S STRATEGY; LINK-UP DIARY;
and TAKEOVER. Also notable are TWO LAWS by the
Borroloola Aboriginal Community, Carolyn Strachan and
Alessandro Cavadini and Tracey Moffatt's NIGHT CRIES: A
RURAL TRAGEDY (94: 257-258).

Finally, no summary of films on Australia would be complete without mention of CANE TOADS (92: 1110-1111), a wonderfully whimsical tongue-in-cheek look at the consequences of introducing a toxic species of toad into Australia in the 1930s to combat an insect devastating the sugar cane crop. Although it is ostensibly about amphibians, this production is really about the Australian people and is truly anthropological rather than zoological as the title might suggest.

REFERENCES CITED

Ahmed, Osman Hassan (ed.) (1982). Bibliography of Documentary and Educational Films on Sudan. Washington: Office of the Cultural Counsellor, Embassy of the Sudan.

Allen, Peter S. (n.d.). Europe on Film. Meriales. (forthcoming).

Allen, Peter S., and Carole Lazio (1983). Archaeology on Film. Boston: Archaeological Institute of America.

Bataille, Gretchen M., and Charles L. P. Silet (1980). The Pretend Indians: Images of Native Americans in the Movies. Ames: Iowa State University Press.

Bataille, Gretchen M., and Charles L. P. Silet (1985). Images of American Indians on Film: An Annotated Bibliography. New York: Garland Publishing.

Bodman, Ellen-Fairbanks (1980). The World of Islam, Images and Echoes: A Critical Guide to Films and Recordings. New York: American Council of Learned Societies.

Collier, John, Jr., and Malcolm Collier (1986). Visual Anthropology. (Revised and Expanded Edition). Albuquerque: University of New Mexico Press.

Connor, Linda, Tim Asch, and Patsy Asch (1986). Jero Tapakan: A Balinese Healer, An Ethnographic Film Monograph. Cambridge: Cambridge University Press

Crawford, Peter Ian, and Jan Kestil Simonsen (eds.) (1992). Ethnographic Film Aesthetics and Narrative Tradition: Proceedings from NAFA 2. Aarhus: Intervention Press.

Crawford, Peter Ian, and David Turton (eds.) (1992). Film as Ethnography. Manchester: University of Manchester Press and New York: St. Martin's Press.

Ferris, Bill, and Judy Peiser (1976). American Folklore Film and Videotape: An Index. Memphis: Center for Southern Folklore.

Hammett, Judith D. (1986a). Guide to Films About The Pacific Islands. Honolulu: Center for Asian and Pacific Studies, University of Hawaii at Manoa.

Haviland, William (1984). Cultural Anthropology. New York: Holt, Rinehart and Winston.

Heider, Karl G. (1983). Films for Anthropological Teaching. Washington: American Anthropological Association.

Hockings, Paul (ed.) (1975). Principles of Visual Anthropology. Chicago: Aldine.

Husmann, Rolf, Ingrid Wellinger, Johannes Rühl, and Martin Taureg (1992). A Bibliography of Ethnographic Film. Hamburg and Münster: Lit Verlag (Göttinger Kulturwissenschaftliche Schriften, 1).

McClintock, Marsha Hamilton (1982). The Middle East and North Africa on Film: An Annotated Filmography. New York: Garland Publishing.

Morphy, Howard (1984). Journey to the Crocodile's Nest. Canberra: Australian Institute of Aboriginal Studies (New York: Humanities Press).

Morris, Rosalind C. (1993). New Worlds from Fragments: Film, Ethnography and the Representation of Northwest Coast Cultures. Boulder, CO: Westview Press.

Pitkin, Donald (1985). The House that Giacomo Built. Cambridge: Harvard University Press.

Rollwagen, Jack R. (ed.) (1988). Anthropological Filmmaking. New York: Harwood.

Ruby, Jay (1993). The Cinema of John Marshall. New York: Harwood.

Ruby, Jay (ed.) (1992). The Cinema of Jean Rouch. New York: Harwood.

Slack, Ellen (ed.) (1982). American folklore Film and Videotape: A Catalogue, Vol. II. London and New York: Bowker for the Center for Southern Folklore.

Stevens, Warren (n.d.). African Films Bibliography. Bloomington: Indiana University Audio Visual Center.

Stoller, Paul (1992). The Cinematic Griot: The Ethnography of Jean Rouch. Chicago: University of Chicago Press.

Trojan, Judith (1981). American Family Life Films. Metuchen, N.J.: Scarecrow Press.

UNESCO (1967). Premier Catalogue Selectif International de Film Ethnographique sur l'Afrique Noire. Paris: Unesco.

UNESCO (1970). Premier Catalogue Selectif International de Film Ethnographique sur La Region du Pacifique. Paris: Unesco.

UNESCO (1970). Catalogue de Film d'Interet Archaeologique, Ethnographique, ou Historique. Paris: Unesco.

Volkman, Toby Alice (1982). Films from D.E.R. Watertown, MA: Documentary Educational Resources.

Volkman, Toby Alice (1985). Films on Indonesia. New Haven: Yale University Southeast Asian Studies Center.

Weatherford, Elizabeth (1981). Native Americans on Film and Video, Vol. I. New York: Museum of the American Indian/Heye Foundation.

Weatherford, Elizabeth, and E. Seubert (1988). Native Americans on Film and Video, Vol. II. New York: Museum of the American Indian/Heye Foundation.

Wheelock Educational Resources (1973). Faces of Change: Five Rural Societies in Transition. Hanover, NH: Wheelock Educational Resources.

Wiley, David S. (1982). Africa on Film and Videotape, 1960-1981 (A Comprehensive Review). East Lansing: African Studies Center, Michigan State University.

Worth, Sol, and John Adair (1972). Through Navajo Eyes. Bloomington: Indiana University Press.

CONTRIBUTORS

Peter Allen is Professor of Anthropology at Rhode Island College where he has taught since 1972. His undergraduate degree is from Middlebury College and his Master's and Doctorate from Brown University. He has conducted research in Greece and Cyprus and published extensively on social change, kinship, and urbanization. Dr. Allen regularly teaches a course on ethnographic film and has served as a consultant for several ethnographic and archaeological films. From 1982 until 1990 he served as Film Reviews Editor of the AMERICAN ANTHROPOLOGIST, and since 1978 has been the Film Review Editor of ARCHAEOLOGY magazine. With Carole Lazio, Dr. Allen is co-author of ARCHAEOLOGY ON FILM: A COMPREHENSIVE GUIDE TO AUDIO-VISUAL MATERIALS.

Robert Ascher is Professor of Anthropology and a member of the Graduate Field, Theatre Arts/Film, at Cornell University. He has done field work in North and South America, the Middle East and Europe. His early research was in experimental and interpretive archaeology and in problems related to the origins of humankind. In collaboration with his wife, Marcia, a mathematician, he developed the relatively new field of ethnomathematics. His main current work is anthropological filmmaking. At Cornell, he teaches courses in visual anthropology and anthropological film. His films have received awards in several festivals and have been screened in Europe, Australia, and the Middle East as well as in the United States. In the fall of 1992, he presented his films thus far at the Museum of Modern Art in New York City.

Peter Biella received a Master's in Film Production, studying with John Collier, Jr., at San Francisco State University. He went on to Temple University where he earned a Ph.D. in Cultural Anthropology in 1984. His dissertation is based on experimental ethnographic films, made in collaboration with Peter Rigby, among Ilparakuyo Maasai of Central Tanzania. Biella continued to shoot and/or direct many videos and films — some collaborative and ethnographic (in Egypt ,with Elizabeth Wickett; in Costa Rica, with Iván Drufovka-Restrepo; and in Central New York State, with Karen Taussig-Lux), strictly documentary (in El Salvador, with Laura Jackson), and applied (on mainland-Puerto Rican AIDS prevention, with David Haas, executive producer). Biella has published on theories of visual communication and ideology, and on problems of collaboration between anthropologists and filmmakers. Recently, he became a hypermedia maker, and is currently studying the scholarly integration of film and ethnographic texts on computer screen. This recent work is the subject of his essays in the present volume.

Allan Burns is professor of Anthropology and Latin American Studies at the University of Florida where he regularly teaches courses in visual anthropology and ethnographic film. He has carried out anthropological studies among the Maya of Yucatan, Guatemala, and the U.S. with special attention to the inter-ethnic relations. He is the author of three books, over fifty articles and book chapters, and is presently completing a book on visual anthropology. He has produced documentaries on the Maya and cultural preservation in Micronesia. He has developed a videotape archive on the history of anthropology with the Smithsonian Institution and the Wenner-Gren Foundation for Anthropological Research, and has used film and video in a variety of projects including research on aphasia, African American culture, and mental health. He was an exchange professor at the Universidad Complutense of Madrid in 1985-86 and held a Fulbright Senior Lectureship at the Institute of Anthropology, University of Copenhagen, 1991-92. In both places he developed courses and working groups in visual anthropology.

Fadwa El Guindi is Research Anthropologist at El Nil Research, Los Angeles. She received her Ph.D. from the University of Texas, Austin in 1972, and teaches anthropology at the University of California, Los Angeles, at the University of Southern California, and at the Foreign Service Institute at the Department of State. She has conducted intensive fieldwork in Nubia, in Egypt, and among the Zapotec of Oaxaca, Mexico. She was Senior Fulbright Fellow in Islamic Civilization in 1981-1982, conducting fieldwork on the emergent Islamic movement in Egypt. Dr. El Guindi's research publications include *Religion in Culture, Life-Crisis Rituals Among the Kenuz, Myth in Ritual*, "Veiling Infitah with Muslim Ethic," among numerous others. Her areas of expertise include ritual, religion, gender, Arab culture, Arab-Americans, Islam. Her filmography consists of two 16mm films: EL SEBOU': EGYPTIAN BIRTH RITUAL (27 minutes) and EL MOULID: EGYPTIAN RELIGIOUS FESTIVAL (38 minutes).

Jay Courtney Fikes, President of the Institute for Investigation of Inter-Cultural Issues, is currently organizing educational tours to Native American reservations and archaeological sites. He is also finishing his first documentary film, GLIMPSES OF THE HUICHOL RITUAL CYCLE SEEN THROUGH THE ARCHIVAL LOOKING GLASS, the culmination of post-doctoral research sponsored in 1991-93 by the Smithsonian Institution.

After completing his doctorate in anthropology at the University of Michigan in 1984, Dr. Fikes taught courses in cultural anthropology, policy research, and social science research methods at the United States International University, Marmara University in Istanbul, and New México Highlands University. He did fieldwork and policy research on Navajo Indian housing production in 1983. In 1990, employed as a "lobbyist" by the Friends Committee on National Legislation, he advocated passage of national legislation beneficial to Native Americans. He is the author of numerous scholarly essays, and the book, CARLOS CASTANEDA, ACA DEMIC OPPORTUNISM AND THE PSYCHEDELIC SIXTIES.

James W. Green teaches at the University of Washington and recently received a two year National Science Foundation grant to create a model curriculum for teaching introductory anthropology in large classes. His interest in film began in 1975 when he created a series of training videos on child abuse for physicians and protective service workers. Since then he has published a textbook on multicultural health and social services entitled CULTURAL AWARENESS IN THE HUMAN SERVICES (Prentice-Hall, 1972). A second edition will soon appear. His field research has been in the Caribbean with inter-island labor migrants and, more recently, in Pakistan where he trained Pakistani anthropology students in community development research. His teaching interests include Islam, South Asia, cross-cultural aging, and comparative religion.

Sidney M. Greenfield is Professor and Chair of the Department of Anthropology at the University of Wisconsin-Milwaukee. He has conducted field research on the family and kinship in the West Indies and has done a study of West Indians who went to the Brazilian Amazon to build a railroad and settled there. He has studied economic development, social organization and systems of patronage and clientage in Latin America, with fieldwork primarily in Brazil. He has done research on entrepreneurship in Brazil and ethnicity and on ethnic identity among Cape Verdeans in New England. He as also studied the history of sugar cane, slavery and slave plantations in Portugal and the Atlantic Islands. His most recent research has been on Brazilian religions, including "popular" Catholicism, Spiritism, and several Afro-Brazilian syncretic cults. For the past decade he has been studying Spiritist healing and surgeries in Brazil and other religious based systems of healing.

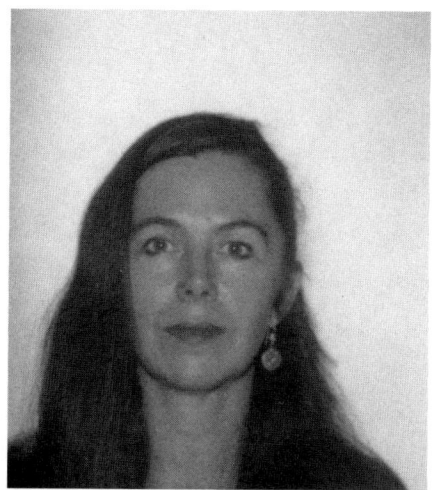

Janet Hoskins is Associate Professor of Anthropology at the University of Southern California, Los Angeles, and has previously held positions at the Research School of Pacific Studies, Australian National University, The Institute for Advanced Study, and the University of Oslo, Norway. Since 1979 she has conducted ethnographic fieldwork among the Kodi people of Sumba, and has published extensively on gender, exchange, notions of time and history, and ritual communication. With filmmaker Laura Scheerer Whitney, she has written and researched two 16 mm films (FEAST IN DREAM VILLAGE and HORSES OF LIFE AND DEATH), and a number of more specialized videos. Her most important work, containing detailed analysis of the events filmed, is THE PLAY OF TIME: KODI PERSPECTIVES ON CALENDARS, HISTORY AND EXCHANGE (University of California Press, 1993).

Ellen C.K. Johnson is Associate Professor of Anthropology and Education at the College of DuPage in Glen Ellyn, Illinois. She taught social studies and wrote curriculum materials for fourteen years at University High School, Urbana, Illinois, a Curriculum Laboratory for academically gifted students, and has also taught in public schools. She is one of the authors of the Macmillan/McGraw-Hill textbook GLOBAL INSIGHTS and has written college-level curriculum materials pertaining to gender and culture, women and development, and multiculturalism and American education. She has been an active participant in the Teaching Anthropology Committee of the Council on Anthropology and Education of the American Anthropological Association and in the Committee on Teaching about Asia of the Association for Asian Studies. Her graduate studies in Anthropology were at the University of Illinois, Urbana-Champaign, and her graduate studies in Education primarily at Northern Illinois University.

Jack R. Rollwagen is professor of Anthropology at the State University of New York (SUNY) College at Brockport, New York. He has been editor and publisher of the internationally distributed journal URBAN ANTHRO-POLOGY and STUDIES OF CULTURAL SYSTEMS AND WORLD ECO-NOMIC DEVELOPMENT for 23 years. In recent years, he has embarked on the production of a set of "visual resources" for university classrooms as executive producer of VISUAL RESOURCES FOR UNIVERSITY CLASS-ROOMS AND ADULT EDUCATION. The first of these videotapes, TZINTZUNTZAN IN THE 1990s: A LAKESIDE VILLAGE IN HIGHLAND MEXICO: TAPE #1: An Ethnographic Overview" was released in March, 1993. The first in a second series on China, FENGJIA: A MODEL VILLAGE IN SHANDONG PROVINCE, PEOPLES REPUBLIC OF CHINA will be available in late 1993 or early 1994. He is also editor of the book AN-THROPOLOGICAL FILMMAKING, which is now in its third printing.

Karen Orr Vered is a Doctoral student and Teaching Assistant at the University of Southern California in Critical Studies of Cinema and Television. Her contribution to this volume is excerpted from her MA thesis, "Feminism And Ethnographic Filmmaking As Political Praxis," Department of Anthropology, Temple University. Her doctoral research is an extension of this work through reception studies and audience ethnography. Ms. Vered has taught Mass Media courses and is presently teaching Education courses in video production for K-12 classroom teachers. Prior to her academic career she worked as a photojournalist and videotape editor.

INDEX

INDEX

NOTE: Items in capital letters are film titles or book titles.

G